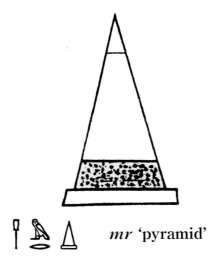

mr 'pyramid'

*'Any gods who shall cause this pyramid and
this construction of the King to be good and
sturdy, it is they who will be vital, it is they who
will be respected, it is they who will be
impressive, it is they who will be in control…it
is they who will take possession of the crown.'*
Pyramid Texts 1650

The Complete
Pyramids

MARK LEHNER

556 illustrations, 83 in colour

Thames and Hudson

To Bruce Ludwig, for his steadfast support

Half-title: *Old Kingdom hieroglyph for 'pyramid' from the Tomb of Ptahhotep I at Saqqara.* Title-pages: *The pyramids of Menkaure, Khafre and Khufu at Giza.* Contents page: *The pyramids of Khafre and Khufu at Giza.*

© 1997 Thames and Hudson Ltd, London

Reprinted 1998

British Library Cataloguing-in-Publication Data
A catalogue record for this book is available from the British Library

ISBN 0-500-05084-8

Printed and bound in Slovenia by Mladinska Knjiga

CONTENTS

I
TOMB AND TEMPLE

II
EXPLORERS AND SCIENTISTS

Pyramids, Land and People

The Egyptian pyramids are very human monuments, although their builders may have tried not to emphasize that fact. At dawn, as the sun rose over the eastern cliffs, its rays caught the pyramids, energizing their sacred precincts with heat and light well before the morning mists had lifted from the cool, sleeping valley floor. At high noon forty-five centuries ago, when the pyramids were complete with their freshly smoothed white limestone casings, their brilliance must have been blinding. Only in this light can we appreciate the intensity with which the pyramids symbolized the sun god.

First to be lit in the morning and catching the last of the sunlight in the afternoon, the brilliance of the Giza pyramids has been dimmed by the removal of their casing and a patina of age.

This powerful special effect was extinguished when the outer casing of most pyramids was robbed long ago. Where it remains, for example at the top of Khafre's pyramid at Giza, the weathering of the ages has coated it with a tan patina. And so what we mostly see today are the stripped core bodies of the pyramids, composed of substantially rougher masonry than the outer casing. Even the Great Pyramid of Khufu, the finest of all, has a core formed of cruder blocks, set with gypsum mortar, and sometimes a fill of broken stone. Other pyramids have cores of smaller stones set in desert clay, or a debris fill that slumped into low mounds when the casing was removed, or dark bricks of mud and straw. In places on their exposed cores we can find evidence left by workers who practically lived on the gradually rising pyramids during the years, even decades, that it took to build them.

In 1984 I directed a project with Robert Wenke, of the University of Washington, to collect samples of organic material embedded in the fabric of pyramids for radiocarbon dating. It was an amazing

sensation, climbing over the Great Pyramid looking for minute flecks of charcoal left in the gypsum mortar. Such close encounters with pyramids reveal not the 'footprints of the gods', but rather the 'fingerprints of the people': straw and reed, wood, fragments of rope and stone tools, flecks of copper and sherds of pottery.

The geography of the pyramids

Since their lives were governed by rhythmic movements along two cosmic axes, the ancient Egyptians were immediately aware of the cardinal directions. The sun rose and set over the beige desert and bronze cliffs framing them on east and west. The north–south axis was defined by the linearity of the Nile, which channelled the flow of goods, services and the administration of the land. Even in the Delta, travel was easiest up and down the Nile as opposed to straight across.

Approximately 4,000 years before the founding of the modern capital of Cairo, Egypt's first 'capital', Memphis, began as a fortified settlement close

to the apex of the Delta. From here to the entrance to the Fayum was a long, narrow section of the Nile Valley which throughout Egyptian history would be the 'capital zone' and also the pyramid zone. West was the traditional direction of the dead and the high western desert along the northern capital zone became the burial ground for royalty, courtiers, officials and sacred animals. In the Old Kingdom the seat of administration may have been the chief royal residence in the valley below the clusters of pyramids.

Karl Butzer has estimated that the two areas of greatest population density in dynastic times were between Luxor (ancient Thebes) and Aswan (Elephantine) at the 1st cataract, and from Meidum at the Fayum entrance northwards to the apex of the Delta. In between was Middle Egypt, a geographic buffer zone with a lower population density. It is worth bearing in mind that the total population of Egypt at the time the Giza pyramids were built is estimated to have been 1.6 million, compared with 58 million in AD 1995.

Produce from the lands and people of Egypt was delivered to the pyramids from estates in Middle Egypt and the Delta. This is a drawing of an offering bearer from a relief in the pyramid temple of Senwosret I at Lisht.

Chronology of the Pyramid Builders

Egyptian chronology and the dates of dynasties and pharaohs are still the subject of scholarly debate, with different systems proposed. The dates used here are based on the chronology developed by Professor John Baines and Dr Jaromir Malek and set out in their Atlas of Ancient Egypt. *Details of those pharaohs who built pyramids or are featured in the text are given in full, where known.*

Late Predynastic	*c.* 3000 BC

Early Dynastic Period

1st dynasty	**2920–2770**
Menes (Hor-Aha); Djer, Wadj; Den, Adjib, Semerkhet; Qa'a	
2nd dynasty	**2770–2649**
Hetepsekhemwy; Raneb; Ninetjer; Peribsen; Khasekhem(wy)	
3rd dynasty	**2649–2575**
Nebka	2649–2630
Djoser (Netjerykhet)	2630–2611
Sekhemkhet	2611–2603
Khaba	2603–2599
Huni	2599–2575

Old Kingdom

4th dynasty	**2575–2465**
Sneferu	2575–2551
Khufu (Cheops)	2551–2528
Djedefre	2528–2520
Khafre (Chephren)	2520–2494
Menkaure (Mycerinus)	2490–2472
Shepseskaf	2472–2467
5th dynasty	**2465–2323**
Userkaf	2465–2458
Sahure	2458–2446
Neferirkare	2446–2426
Shepseskare	2426–2419
Raneferef	2419–2416
Niuserre	2416–2388
Djedkare-Isesi	2388–2356
Unas	2356–2323

6th dynasty	**2323–2150**
Teti	2323–2291
Pepi I	2289–2255
Merenre	2255–2246
Pepi II	2246–2152
7th/8th dynasties	**2150–2134**
including Ibi	dates uncertain

First Intermediate Period

9th/10th dynasties	**2134–2040**
11th dynasty *(Theban)*	**2134–2040**
Intef I	2134–2118
Intef II	2118–2069
Intef III	2069–2061
Mentuhotep	2061–2010

Middle Kingdom

11th dynasty	**2040–1991**
Mentuhotep I	2061–2010
Mentuhotep II	2010–1998
Mentuhotep III	1998–1991
12th dynasty	**1991–1783**
Amenemhet I	1991–1962
Senwosret I (Sesostris I)	1971–1926
Amenemhet II	1929–1892
Senwosret II (Sesostris II)	1897–1878
Senwosret III (Sesostris III)	1878–1841?
Amenemhet III	1844–1797
Amenemhet IV	1799–1787
Sobekneferu	1787–1783
13th dynasty	**1783–1640**
including	
Ameny-Qemau	*c.* 1750
Khendjer	*c.* 1745
14th dynasty	contemporary with 13th or 15th

Second Intermediate Period	
15th–17th dynasties	**1640–1532**
New Kingdom	
18th–20th dynasties	**1550–1070**
including	
Ahmose (Amosis)	1550–1525
Third Intermediate Period	
21st–25th dynasties	**1070–712**
25th dynasty	**770–712**
(Nubian and Theban Area)	
Kashta	770–750
Piye	750–712
Late Period	
25th dynasty	**712–657**
Shabako	712–698
Shabatko	698–690
Taharqa	690–664
Tantutamun	664–657
26th dynasty	**664–525**
including	
Necho I	672–664
Psamtik I	664–610
(Psammetichus I)	
27th dynasty	**525–404**
28th dynasty	**404–399**
29th dynasty	**399–380**
30th dynasty	**380–343**
2nd Persian Period	**343–332**
Graeco-Roman Period	**332 BC–AD 395**
Meroitic kingdom	**300 BC–AD 350**

The pyramid as temple

It is true that the pyramids are pharaonic tombs, but the tomb of a pharaoh of ancient Egypt was far more than just the grave of a king. One of the hallmarks of the Egyptian state from its very beginning in the 1st dynasty was the tradition centred on the king as an incarnation of the god Horus, whose totem was the falcon. In the world of the ancient Egyptians the falcon soared above all other living creatures. When an incarnation of Horus died, the god passed to the next reigning king. Physically entombed within the pyramid, the dead king became identified with Osiris, the divine father of Horus. The pyramid complex was, in one sense, a temple complex to the Horus-Osiris divinity, merged with the sun god in the central icon of the pyramid.

As a temple complex, the pyramid was also the largest of what have been called 'pious foundations', that is, enormous endowments of people, lands and produce, for the sustenance, upkeep and service of a tomb, temple or pyramid. When the Egyptians built the pyramids, they also founded new farms, ranches and whole new towns in the provinces. The livestock and produce from these estates flowed into the area of the pyramid complex where they would be redistributed to the workforce and to the priests and special classes of people who served the temple complex. So the pyramid was also an economic engine, and, especially during the Old Kingdom, a major catalyst for internal colonization and the development of Egypt as one of the world's first true states.

The complete pyramid played many roles: massive labour project; baker and brewer for hundreds of consumers; colonizer of the Egyptian provinces; employer of farmers, herdsmen and craftsmen of all kinds; temple and ritual centre at the core of the Egyptian state; reliquary of a king; embodiment of light and shadow; and the union of heaven and earth, encapsulating the mystery of death and rebirth.

Products of the land and people of Egypt's oldest kingdoms, in their pristine form the pyramids were the closest mankind has ever come in architecture to creating an illusion of transcending the human condition. Their aura of otherworldliness still inspires the popular imagination to seek their origin anywhere other than the people who inhabited the lower Nile Valley between five and three thousand years ago.

Two of the lesser pyramid builders: the 4th-dynasty pharaoh Djedefre (top), who began a pyramid at Abu Roash, north of Giza; and the 5th-dynasty ruler Userkaf (above), who built a pyramid adjacent to Djoser's Step Pyramid at Saqqara and was also the first pharaoh to construct a sun temple in addition to his pyramid, at Abusir.

(Left) The great pyramid builders of the Old Kingdom: Djoser (far left), here depicted in a life-size painted statue, built the world's first stone pyramid, the Step Pyramid at Saqqara. Khufu (second left) oversaw the construction of the most magnificent pyramid, the Great Pyramid at Giza, but is preserved only in this tiny ivory figurine, about 5 cm (2 in) high. Khafre (third left) is depicted in this life-size statue, merged in identity with the Horus falcon. Menkaure (near left) is shown standing next to his queen, Khamerernebty.

9

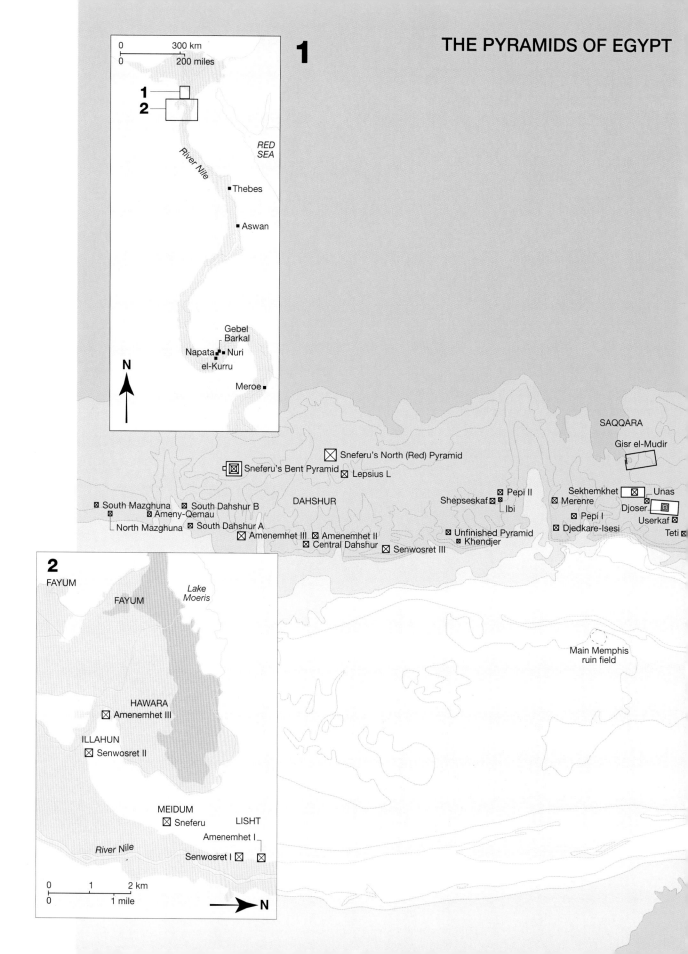

THE PYRAMIDS OF EGYPT

1

0   300 km
0   200 miles

1
2

River Nile

RED SEA

■ Thebes

■ Aswan

Gebel Barkal
Napata ■ ■ Nuri
el-Kurru

Meroe ■

N

SAQQARA

Gisr el-Mudir

⊠ Sneferu's North (Red) Pyramid

⊡⊠ Sneferu's Bent Pyramid
⊡ ⊠ Lepsius L

DAHSHUR

⊠ Pepi II
Shepseskaf ⊠ ⊠
⊡ Ibi

Sekhemkhet ⊠ ⊠ Unas
⊠ Merenre
Djoser ⊡ ⊠

⊠ South Mazghuna   ⊠ South Dahshur B
⊠   ⊠ Ameny-Qemau
⊡ North Mazghuna   ⊠ South Dahshur A

⊠ Amenemhet III ⊠ Amenemhet II
⊠ Central Dahshur ⊠ Senwosret III

⊠ Pepi I
Djedkare-Isesi ⊠

Userkaf ⊠

Teti ⊠

⊠ Unfinished Pyramid
⊠ Khendjer

2

FAYUM

FAYUM   *Lake Moeris*

Main Memphis ruin field

HAWARA
⊠ Amenemhet III

ILLAHUN
⊠ Senwosret II

MEIDUM
⊠ Sneferu   LISHT

Amenemhet I

Senwosret I ⊠   ⊠

River Nile

0   1   2 km
0   1 mile
N

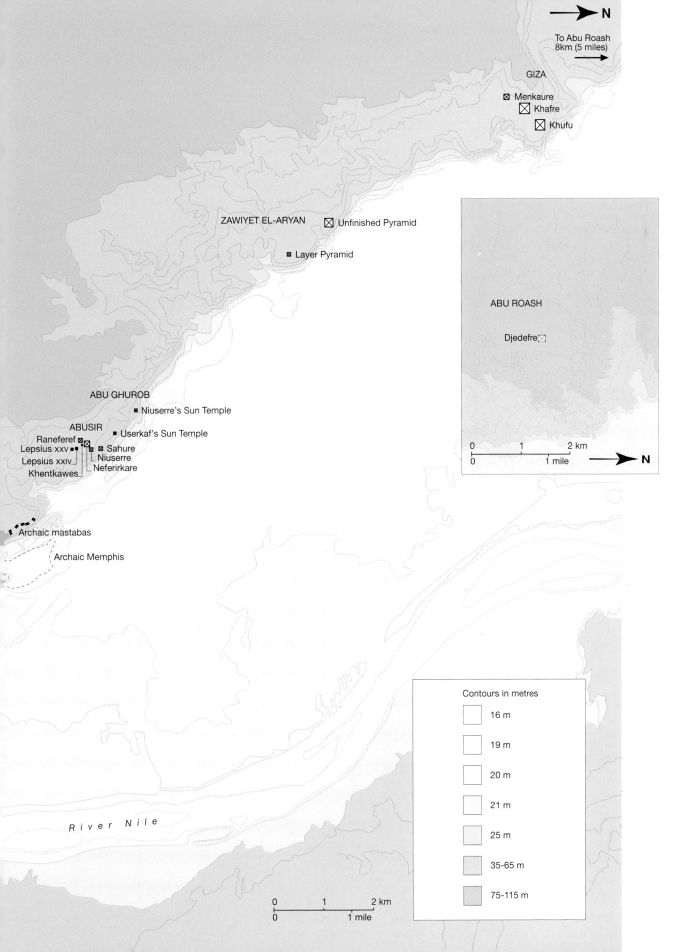

N

To Abu Roash
8km (5 miles)

GIZA

⊠ Menkaure
⊠ Khafre
⊠ Khufu

ZAWIYET EL-ARYAN   ⊠ Unfinished Pyramid

⊠ Layer Pyramid

ABU ROASH

Djedefre ⊠

0   1   2 km
0   1 mile   N

ABU GHUROB
◼ Niuserre's Sun Temple

ABUSIR
Raneferef ⊠ ⊠
Lepsius xxv ◼ ◼   ◼ Userkaf's Sun Temple
Lepsius xxiv   ⊠ Sahure
Khentkawes   Niuserre
                    Neferirkare

⬧ Archaic mastabas

Archaic Memphis

River Nile

Contours in metres

16 m

19 m

20 m

21 m

25 m

35-65 m

75-115 m

0   1   2 km
0   1 mile

Pyramids in the Landscape

Egypt was a cradle of civilization that allowed the same basic language and culture to flourish for nearly 3,000 years. For most of this long history, pharaoh was 'Lord of the Two Lands', a reflection of the natural division of the country into two inhabitable parts: the Nile Valley and the broad Delta. Each pharaoh wore the double crown, combining the Red Crown of Lower (northern) Egypt and the White Crown of Upper (southern) Egypt.

In shape, the Nile and its Y-shaped Delta can be compared to three of the plants that flourish in the valley and which the pyramid builders petrified in stone in carvings and columns: the palm tree, the lotus and the papyrus. Upper Egypt is the trunk or stem; and the Delta is the palm frond, the lotus flower or the head of the papyrus. If the Delta is the lotus blossom, the Fayum is its bud. The Fayum is a large fertile basin, at various times filled by a lake whose remains today are the brackish waters of Lake Qarun. The lake was fed by the only major tributary of the Nile in Egypt, the Bahr Youssef ('River Joseph'), which enters the Fayum by way of the ancient Hawara Channel.

Stone for Pyramids

The ancient Egyptians favoured various stones for their pyramids and carvings. Over millions of years (primarily the Eocene, 65–35 million years ago) the sea covered much of Egypt, depositing sediments that became the limestone of Egypt's tableland. Limestone was quarried for the cores of pyramids in block sizes often corresponding to the thickness of successive natural layers or beds. Finer limestone for outer pyramid casings came from eastern quarries across the Nile. Farther south, and formed in older geological periods, sandstone was used for the last pyramids in the Nile Valley – at Napata and Meroe.

Granite was important as the second stone for pyramid casings, and often the primary material for sarcophagi and burial chambers. Diorite and grey-wacke were highly prized for statues. Basalt was long preferred for the pavements of temples. To obtain these materials the Egyptians mounted quarry expeditions to the places where these harder and geologically older igneous rocks lay exposed – the Fayum, the Red Sea Mountains and Aswan and its desert quarries. They also contained the copper needed for tools, as well as gold, silver and iron, the last mostly used only in later periods.

Key
- ■ diorite
- ▭ granite
- ▢ quartzite
- ▨ sandstone
- ▦ basalt
- ▢ limestone
- ◊ alabaster
- ✕ copper
- ▲ lead

0   100 km
0   60 miles

Nomes and basins

Through processes of erosion and deposition, the Nile created a convex floodplain. That is, the highest land is nearest the river and, perhaps contrary to what we might expect, the lowest land is closer to the desert. In between were natural basins, terraced downstream from south to north. The basins were one of the largest and most basic landscape features of the yearly cycle, forming an immense natural irrigation system that was wiped out by the modern dams at Aswan. Surrounded by dykes and carefully managed, the great cell-like basins held water for six to eight weeks each year during the annual flood. In the last century, from Elephantine to just north of the Fayum there were 136 principal basins.

How did the ancient Egyptians organize this landscape and its peasant farmers to provide the food and labour that supported pyramid building? During the last century such control involved independent systems of basins, consisting of (rarely) one or (usually) several basins watered by a single feeder canal. The head of this canal was a breach in the Nile bank. Beginning in the 18th dynasty, the canals that seasonally channelled flood waters to the basins were named with the hieroglyph of the human arm – they were 'armatures of water'. Each basin system also had a tail-end escape to allow the waters to flow back into the Nile after they had deposited their fertile silty slime. This was breached first, followed by successive openings in each transverse dyke back to the head basin.

Field beds appeared at the bottom of the basins from south to north. The Egyptians planted by broadcast sowing – simply scattering the seed by hand – and this was best done soon after the basin was drained when the beds were still wet. Draining and sowing therefore needed to be closely co-ordinated and the basin administrators must have rapidly surveyed and identified field boundaries.

The southernmost Upper Egyptian basins were usually dry by 5 October, and the northernmost by 30 November. Sowing and growing took place in the season of *peret*, 'coming forth', followed by *shemu*, 'harvest', and, beginning in late summer, *akhet*, 'inundation'. The three seasons each consisted of four months, for a 12-month year.

It was usual for a temple or large household to own, rent or manage an assemblage of fields that may not have been contiguous and were not necessarily near the house. In ancient Egypt as other societies based on flood recession agriculture, an archipelago of land holdings of different quality spread throughout the country may have been an insurance against floods that were too high or too low. The Old Kingdom pyramids were among the earliest developers and owners of such land portfolios. One of the most frequent scenes in the pyramid temples is a long train of offering bearers, each personifying a village, estate or nome (p. 228).

For administrative purposes, the ancient Egyptians divided Upper Egypt into districts called nomes, with Nome 1 at Elephantine on the 1st cataract and Nome 22 just north of the Fayum entrance. These nomes, each with a main settlement that developed into a 'capital', were established by the 5th dynasty. The complete set of 20 northern nomes, beginning with Lower Egyptian Nome 1 of Memphis, and taking in the Delta, was established only in late antiquity.

It is tempting to think that the nomes, and the first proto-kingdoms that amalgamated in the late predynastic to become the Egyptian 'state', originated in these basins. Certainly the communication required for the sequential filling and discharge would have been easier across the smaller basin systems such as those of the Qena Bend, from where rulers of Egypt emerged more than once.

Basins and pyramids

Research on the flood basins and the geography of the Memphite region is now clearing up some old misconceptions. The average depth of the Nile flood waters was not sufficient to float huge limestone casing blocks or granite beams to the foot of the pyramid plateau. Yet there is no evidence that the Old Kingdom Egyptians cut perennially flooded canals transversely across the flood plain.

In the northern pyramid zone, from Dahshur to Giza and particularly in the area of Memphis, the Nile flowed closer to the west bank during the early periods of Egypt's history. At intervals along the edge of the desert were lakes that held water after the flood receded. These probably existed in front of pyramid sites such as Abusir, Saqqara, Dahshur

and possibly Giza. Where perennial lakes did not occur, the pyramid builders could have created them by widening and deepening the natural flood basins that would then have served as the harbours that every standard pyramid complex required. It is possible that older canals that still survive near the escarpment at Saqqara and Abusir, particularly the Bahr el-Libeini, are vestiges of ancient channels.

There is a high place on the Mokkatam Hills southeast of Cairo where one can look across the valley and see, silhouetted in the desert haze, the pyramids of Giza, Abusir, Saqqara and Dahshur. In the valley below, the Nile no longer floods the basins. The nome centres and royal communities – with their bakeries, granaries, breweries and multitudinous workshops – have been replaced by the sprawl of Africa's largest city. The pyramids no longer connect with living Egypt and so we have lost sight of their original role in ancient Egyptian lives. But from the Mokkatam Hills, there is still the sense of the pyramid field as one vast Memphite necropolis, the pyramids standing as giant tombstones of distant god-kings.

Lake Dahshur, the last surviving of the pyramid lakes on the desert edge, gives a haunting impression of pyramid ecology. Sneferu's Bent Pyramid rises to the west.

A simplified cross-section of the Nile Valley between Sohag and Asyut, where the river runs next to the east escarpment today, based on Karl Butzer's work. A convex flood plain leaves high land along Nile levees, and low basin land towards the desert. The Nile has migrated eastwards through time.

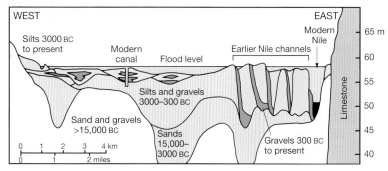

The Giant Pyramids: Their Rise and Fall

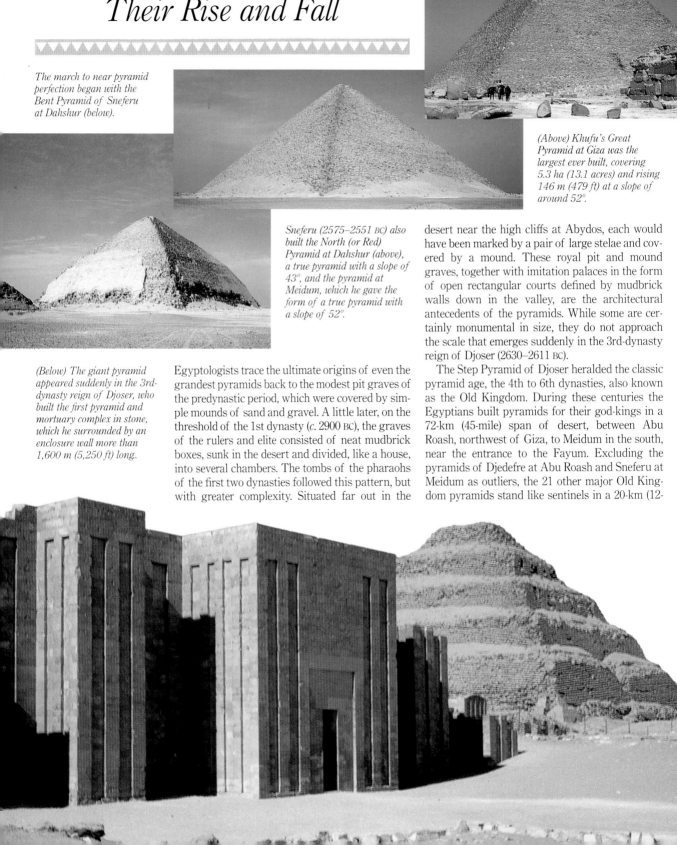

The march to near pyramid perfection began with the Bent Pyramid of Sneferu at Dahshur (below).

(Above) Khufu's Great Pyramid at Giza was the largest ever built, covering 5.3 ha (13.1 acres) and rising 146 m (479 ft) at a slope of around 52°.

Sneferu (2575–2551 BC) also built the North (or Red) Pyramid at Dahshur (above), a true pyramid with a slope of 43°, and the pyramid at Meidum, which he gave the form of a true pyramid with a slope of 52°.

(Below) The giant pyramid appeared suddenly in the 3rd-dynasty reign of Djoser, who built the first pyramid and mortuary complex in stone, which he surrounded by an enclosure wall more than 1,600 m (5,250 ft) long.

Egyptologists trace the ultimate origins of even the grandest pyramids back to the modest pit graves of the predynastic period, which were covered by simple mounds of sand and gravel. A little later, on the threshold of the 1st dynasty (c. 2900 BC), the graves of the rulers and elite consisted of neat mudbrick boxes, sunk in the desert and divided, like a house, into several chambers. The tombs of the pharaohs of the first two dynasties followed this pattern, but with greater complexity. Situated far out in the desert near the high cliffs at Abydos, each would have been marked by a pair of large stelae and covered by a mound. These royal pit and mound graves, together with imitation palaces in the form of open rectangular courts defined by mudbrick walls down in the valley, are the architectural antecedents of the pyramids. While some are certainly monumental in size, they do not approach the scale that emerges suddenly in the 3rd-dynasty reign of Djoser (2630–2611 BC).

The Step Pyramid of Djoser heralded the classic pyramid age, the 4th to 6th dynasties, also known as the Old Kingdom. During these centuries the Egyptians built pyramids for their god-kings in a 72-km (45-mile) span of desert, between Abu Roash, northwest of Giza, to Meidum in the south, near the entrance to the Fayum. Excluding the pyramids of Djedefre at Abu Roash and Sneferu at Meidum as outliers, the 21 other major Old Kingdom pyramids stand like sentinels in a 20-km (12-

mile) stretch west of the capital the 'White Wall', later known as Memphis, clustering at Giza, Zawiyet el-Aryan, Abusir, Saqqara and Dahshur.

The truly gigantic stone pyramids were built over the course of only three generations: Sneferu, Khufu and Khafre. If Sneferu did indeed build the Meidum pyramid as well as his two stone pyramids at Dahshur, his pyramids alone contain more than 3.5 million cu. m (124 million cu. ft) of stone. All the other pyramids of Egyptian kings combined (excluding queens' and other satellite pyramids) contain only 41 per cent of the total mass of the pyramids of Sneferu, his son Khufu and grandson Khafre. Menkaure still used multi-tonned stone blocks for the third pyramid of Giza, but the total mass was less than that of Djoser.

In the 5th and 6th dynasties each king still built a pyramid, but on a much smaller scale and with smaller stones and a core of stone rubble fill. In one sense this is inferior construction; however, the Egyptians accomplished the same pyramidal form with fine casing and less expense. At the same time the pyramid temples increased in size, complexity and craftsmanship in comparison with those of the early 4th-dynasty pyramids. True standardization was reached in the pyramids of the late 5th dynasty, and particularly those of the 6th. In spite of the difference in length of reigns, the pyramids of Merenre (9 years) and Pepi II (over 90 years) were nearly identical in their outer dimensions.

Pyramid building almost ceased during the First Intermediate Period when unified rule gave way to rival principalities. It was resumed in the Middle Kingdom, when the first pyramids were built with a core of small and broken stone in casemate or retaining walls, and later pyramids were built with a mudbrick core. Sizes were not as standardized as the later Old Kingdom. Entrances no longer opened consistently from the north side of the pyramid, and passages followed a circuitous off-axis route to the burial chamber. The geographic range of pyra-

mids was still in the north near the apex of the Delta, but the margins had shifted southwards, from Dahshur in the north, to Illahun and Hawara at the Fayum entrance to the south.

New Kingdom pharaohs built their tombs in a communal royal burial ground, the Valley of the Kings, at Thebes (modern Luxor). Above the valley towers a mountain peak that takes the form of a natural pyramid for the multiple corridors and royal burial chambers cut into the crevasses of its lower slopes. Manmade pyramids were reduced to small superstructures above the rock-cut tombs of the scribes, artisans, craftsmen and officials who served the king and were employed on the construction of the royal tombs.

Throughout ancient times, Nubia (in modern northern Sudan) mirrored many facets of Egyptian culture, including building pyramids as royal tombs. More than 800 years after the last royal pyramid was completed in Egypt, pyramids on a smaller scale began to be built for rulers of the Kingdom of Napata, beginning about 720 BC, and the Kingdom of Meroe, ending about AD 350. In the course of 1,000 years, about 180 royal pyramids were built in Nubia, twice the number in Egypt.

The Middle Kingdom mudbrick pyramid of Amenemhet III and the Old Kingdom stone North Pyramid of Sneferu, seen across the Dahshur lake, the last remaining pyramid harbour lake.

Three generations in the 4th dynasty accomplished the bulk of pyramid building. Later, more standardized smaller pyramids reflect a less centralized society.

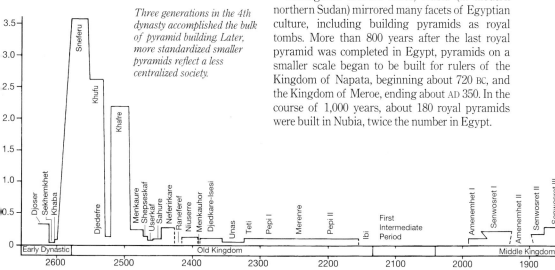

The Shape of Pyramid History

Profiles of the major pyramids, drawn to the same scale, from the earliest stepped mound of the 1st dynasty, through the stepped pyramids of the 3rd dynasty and the massive 4th-dynasty pyramids, to the much smaller monuments of later Egyptian history. According to one chronology only 60 years passed between the completion of the Step Pyramid of Djoser and the beginning of the Great Pyramid of Khufu. If so, someone could have been a small child when Djoser's pyramid was new, and lived to see, in old age, the building of the Great Pyramid, when 'Egyptian masonry rose to a peak of excellence'. The giant pyramids represent an accelerated cultural development, comparable to our modern space programme or computer revolution.

After the end of the 5th dynasty, pyramid entrances are no longer consistently on the north, and the passages and chambers follow circuitous routes, so that the profiles do not show the interiors.

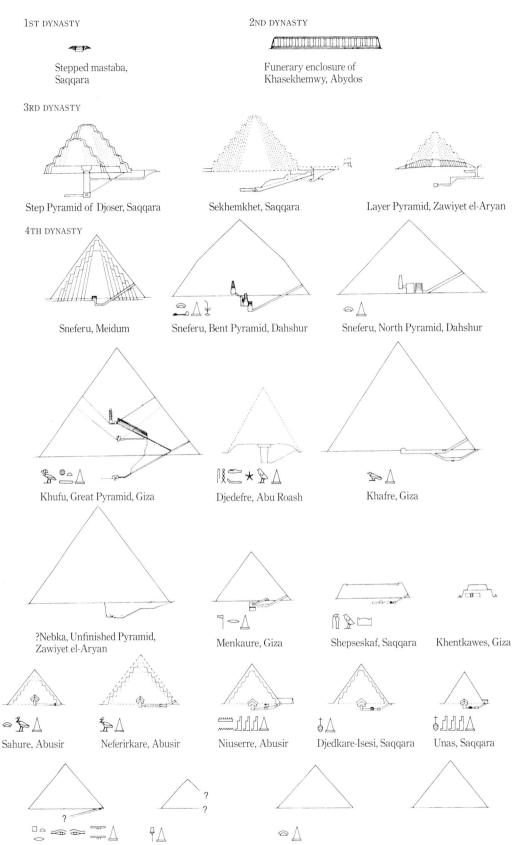

1ST DYNASTY

Stepped mastaba, Saqqara

2ND DYNASTY

Funerary enclosure of Khasekhemwy, Abydos

3RD DYNASTY

Step Pyramid of Djoser, Saqqara

Sekhemkhet, Saqqara

Layer Pyramid, Zawiyet el-Aryan

4TH DYNASTY

Sneferu, Meidum

Sneferu, Bent Pyramid, Dahshur

Sneferu, North Pyramid, Dahshur

Khufu, Great Pyramid, Giza

Djedefre, Abu Roash

Khafre, Giza

?Nebka, Unfinished Pyramid, Zawiyet el-Aryan

Menkaure, Giza

Shepseskaf, Saqqara

Khentkawes, Giza

5TH DYNASTY

Userkaf, Saqqara

Sahure, Abusir

Neferirkare, Abusir

Niuserre, Abusir

Djedkare-Isesi, Saqqara

Unas, Saqqara

12TH DYNASTY

Amenemhet I, Lisht

Senwosret I, Lisht

Amenemhet II, Dahshur

Senwosret II, Illahun

Senwosret III, Dahshur

Major Pyramid Statistics

Pharaoh	Location	Dyn.	Base (m)	Height (m)	Volume (cu. m)	Slope	Satellite	Queens'	Ancient Name
Djoser	Saqqara	3	121x109	60	330,400				
Sekhemkhet	Saqqara	3	120	7 (unfinished)	33,600				
Khaba (?)	Zawiyet el-Aryan	3	84	20 (unfinished)	47,040				
Sneferu (?)	Meidum	4	144	92	638,733	51°50'35"	√		Sneferu Endures
Sneferu	Dahshur	4	188	105	1,237,040	54°27'44"/ 43°22	√		The Southern Shining Pyramid
Sneferu	Dahshur	4	220	105	1,694,000	43°22'			The Shining Pyramid
Khufu	Giza	4	230.33	146.59	2,583,283	51°50'40"	√	3	*Akhet* Khufu
Djedefre	Abu Roash	4	106	67	131,043	52°	√		Djedefre is a *Sehed*-Star
Khafre	Giza	4	215	143.5	2,211,096	53°10'	√		Great is Khafre
?Nebka	Z. el-Aryan	4	200	(unfinished)					
Menkaure	Giza	4	102.2x104.6	65	235,183	51°20'25"		3	Menkaure is Divine
Shepseskaf	S. Saqqara	4	99.6x74.4	18	148,271	70°			The Purified Pyramid
Khentkawes	Giza	4	45.5x45.8	17.5	6,372 (upper)	*c.* 74°			
Userkaf	Saqqara	5	73.3	49	87,906	53°7'48"	√		Pure are the Places of Userkaf
Sahure	Abusir	5	78.75	47	96,542	50°11'40"	√		The Rishing of the *Ba* Spirit
Neferirkare	Abusir	5	105	*c.* 72	257,250	53°7'48"			Pyramid of the *Ba* of Neferirkare
Raneferef	Abusir	5	65	(unfinished)					The Pyramid which is Divine of the *Ba* Spirits
Niuserre	Abusir	5	78.9	51.68	112,632	51°50'35"	√	2?	The Places of Niuserre Endure
Djedkare-Isesi	S.Saqqara	5	78.75	*c.* 52.5	*c.* 107,835	52°	√	1	Beautiful is Isesi
Unas	Saqqara	5	57.75	43	47,390	56°18'35"	√		Perfect are the Places of Unas
Teti	Saqqara	6	78.75	52.5	107,835	53°7'48"	√	2	The Places of Teti Endure
Pepi I	S.Saqqara	6	*c.*78.75	*c.* 52.5	*c.* 107,835	53°7'48"	√	5	The Perfection of Pepi is Established
Merenre	S.Saqqara	6	*c.*78.75	*c.* 52.5	*c.* 107,835	53°7'48"			The Perfection of Merenre Appears
Pepi II	S.Saqqara	6	78.75	52.5	*c.* 107,835	52°7'48"	√	3	Pepi is Established and Living
Ibi	S.Saqqara	8	31.5	21?	6,994?				
Khui	Dara	FIP	130						
Amenemhet I	Lisht	12	84	55	129,360	54°27'44"			The Places of the Apearances of Amenemhet
Senwosret I	Lisht	12	105	61.25	225,093	49°23'55"	√	9	Senwosret Beholds the Two Lands
Amenemhet II	Dahshur	12	*c.* 50						Amenemhet is Provided
Senwosret II	Illahun	12	106	48.6	185,665	42°35'	√? or	1?	Senwosret Appears
Senwosret III	Dahshur	12	105	78	288,488	56°18'35"		7	
Amenemhet III	Dahshur	12	105	75	274,625	57°15'50"			Amenemhet is Beautiful
Amenemhet III	Hawara	12	105	*c.* 58	200,158	48°45'			Amenemhet Lives
Amenemhet IV or Sobekneferu	S.Mazghuna	13	52.5	(unfinished)	30,316				
Ameny-Qemau Khendjer	S.Saqqara	13	52.5	*c.* 37.35	44,096	55°			

Teti, Saqqara

Pepi I, S. Saqqara

Merenre, S. Saqqara

Pepi II, S. Saqqara

Ibi, S. Saqqara

13TH DYNASTY

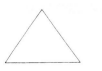

Amenemhet III, Dahshur

Amenemhet III, Hawara

Amenemhet IV or Sobekneferu, S. Mazghuna

Khendjer, S. Saqqara

Unfinished, S. Saqqara

The Standard Pyramid Complex

The pyramids covered the tombs of divine kings and, late in their history, they marked graves of the aristocracy and high officials. They satisfy a principle that the great Giza excavator George Reisner stated: 'Every substructure [grave] implies a super-structure which marks the site of the grave and provides a place where the offerings to the dead may be presented'. As the tomb superstructure, the pyramid was the central element in an assembly that makes up the 'standard pyramid complex'.

We see the most basic elements in two extreme cases. Tombs in Lower Nubia (A-group), contemporary with the late predynastic in Upper Egypt, consisted of pits sunk into the ground, covered by a ceiling of sandstone slabs, on which was constructed a mound of debris encased in drystone masonry. Pottery was left at the base of the mounds, some of which had specially constructed offering places on the west and south sides. We then turn to the pyramids at Giza, as more complex versions of the same basic scheme – on a gigantic scale. The grave pit is now carved out of bedrock at the end of a long corridor which points the king's soul to the northern circumpolar stars, or, uniquely for Khufu, is moved up into the very body of the masonry. The pyramid is simply the mound transformed to sublime geometry and expanded into a man-made mountain.

The offering place is now a mortuary (or pyramid) temple on the eastern side, with a colonnaded court with black basalt pavement, granite pillars and walls with painted relief carving. By the 5th dynasty a front or outer part of the mortuary temple was separated from an inner temple by a transverse hall. Beyond were magazines, and, lastly, an inner sanctuary – the whole route ending in a false door, the symbolic portal of the pyramid complex.

It was long thought that the pharaoh's funeral took place in the mortuary temple, but there are problems with this (p. 25). We are certain at least that it functioned symbolically as a kind of eternal palace for the deceased king, for whom daily rituals were carried out, including processions out and around the pyramid, perpetuating his worship as a god-king. From the mortuary temple a causeway, with walls and usually a roof, ran down to the valley temple, the entrance to the whole complex. The classic complex required that the pyramid be near the valley floor, where it could be reached by a canal, or a channel that held water after the annual Nile flood receded. At the same time the pyramid had to be far enough out in the desert on the plateau to have a dramatic approach. Its base was enclosed by one or two courtyards, defined by walls of stone or mudbrick. Within the inner or outer enclosure was a small satellite pyramid, a miniature double that may have been associated with the king's *ka* or 'spirit' (p. 22). Many complexes include smaller pyramids for queens and several are flanked by pits for the burial of boats, either real or imitation.

These standard elements – pyramid, satellite pyramid, queens' pyramids, mortuary temple, causeway and valley temple – are clear from a survey of the remains of complexes along a stretch of the Nile Valley from Abu Roash to Meidum. For the Egyptians of the pyramid age, other elements on the valley floor might have been equally standard. These structures, concerned with the society and economy of the living pyramid, were mostly built in mudbrick, and have therefore been lost due to the wetter conditions of the floodplain and modern urban expansion. But we read of them in ancient papyri and tomb texts that relate to the functioning of pyramids. Recently, researchers have recovered some remains of these missing elements.

In the standard pyramid complex access via a harbour or canal was necessary. The valley temple, in essence nothing more than an elaborate portico, formed the entrance to the entire complex. From here the causeway ran up to the mortuary temple and pyramid.

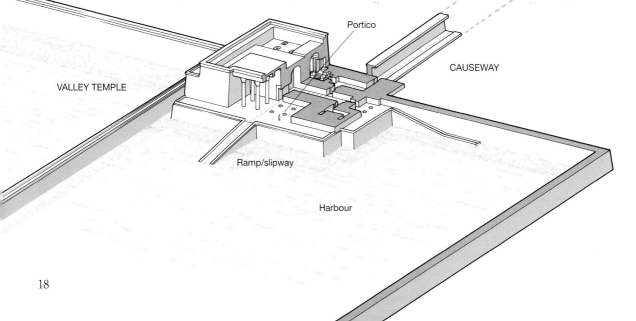

VALLEY TEMPLE

Portico

CAUSEWAY

Ramp/slipway

Harbour

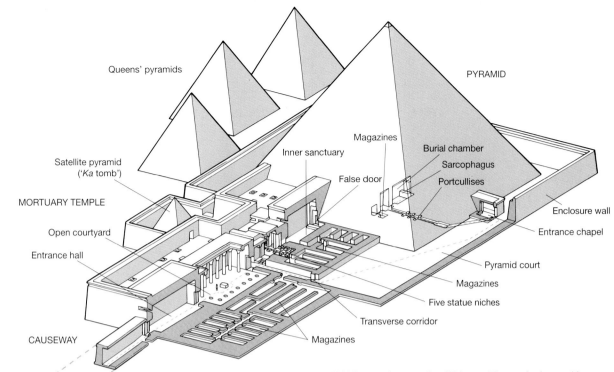

Queens' pyramids

PYRAMID

Satellite pyramid ('Ka tomb')

MORTUARY TEMPLE

Open courtyard

Entrance hall

Inner sanctuary

False door

Magazines

Burial chamber

Sarcophagus

Portcullises

Enclosure wall

Entrance chapel

Pyramid court

Magazines

Five statue niches

Transverse corridor

Magazines

CAUSEWAY

The standard arrangement, with its east–west axial alignment, of the classic Old Kingdom pyramid complex first appeared in simple form with the Meidum pyramid (p. 97). It was almost immediately and astonishingly amplified and expanded by Khufu's Giza complex (p. 108), and it remained essentially unchanged throughout the Old Kingdom. But the first pyramid of Djoser at Saqqara had a different arrangement (p. 84). A long north–south rectangular enclosure was defined by a niche-decorated wall with a single entrance at the far south end of the east side. The sudden explosion of stone building represented by Djoser's complex had a profound influence on later pyramid builders. In the Middle Kingdom, when the earliest Meidum-type pyramid complexes were already fading into ruin, pyramid builders returned, in a time of experiment and renewal, to some of the basic elements of Djoser's complex.

So it is proper to speak of two basic types of pyramid complex that were separate in conception, but mixed in later monuments. Dieter Arnold has documented the curious switching between the ideal 'Djoser type' and the 'Meidum type'. Already in the 5th dynasty Userkaf returned to elements of the Djoser type. Then in the 12th dynasty Senwos-

ret III adapted it, as did his son, Amenemhet III for his second pyramid at Hawara. Although one or the other layout is favoured, these later arrangements always include influences from both early types.

At the end of 1,000 years of pyramid history in Egypt, the non-royal 'private' pyramid complexes returned to the basic features of the simple mounded tombs: the pyramid as the symbol of both grave mound and resurrection, the chapel as a place to commune with the dead and leave offerings, and the grave chamber below the hallowed space.

The standard pyramid complex, based on the pyramid of Unas, but with the addition of three queens pyramids as found at Pepi I's pyramid.

The Two Main Pyramid Complex Types

	Djoser Type	Post–Meidum Type
Orientation	North–South	East–West
Entrance	South end of east side	Centre east side
Parts	N–S sequence	E–W axial symmetry
Enclosure wall	Niched, no inner wall	Smooth outer wall, occasionally niched inner wall
'Ka Tomb'	South tomb, no satellite pyramid	Satellite pyramid
Temple	North or south temple, simple or no east chapel	East temple, only north 'entrance chapel'

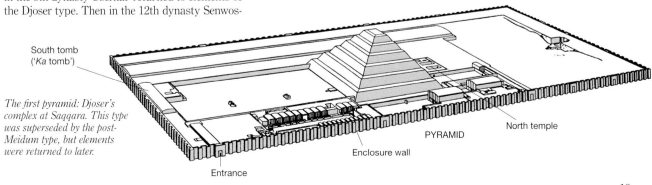

South tomb ('Ka tomb')

The first pyramid: Djoser's complex at Saqqara. This type was superseded by the post-Meidum type, but elements were returned to later.

North temple

PYRAMID

Enclosure wall

Entrance

E ach major pyramid was a tomb for a king of Egypt. Since the king was a god, each pyramid was also the focus of a temple complex maintained by a priest-hood long after the pharaoh had been laid to rest. The pyramid complex was an economic engine, too, deploying people and redistributing goods. This was possible only because the pyramid was designed to be a cosmic engine as well; in fact, each pyramid ensured the rule of universal order, the turning of the days and seasons, and the flooding of the Nile. The mechanics of the pyramid as cosmic engine depended on the Egyptian concept of a person and the distinct phases of life and death, called *kheperu*. These 'transformations' continued when the *ka*, the *ba* and the body, which had become separated at death, interacted in the final transformation – becoming an *akh*, a glorified being of light, effective in the Afterlife. The pyramid was an instrument that enabled this alchemy to take place for the pharaoh, who had ruled as the god incarnate, and allowed that incarnation to pass from father to son, from Osiris to Horus. Encapsulating the dangerous interface between cosmic order and the terrible formlessness of time before the beginning, the pyramid is better understood as the meeting point of life and light with death and darkness. Our earliest insight into such ideas comes from the Pyramid Texts, written on the walls of pyramid chambers beginning with Unas in the 5th dynasty. These texts speak to us of what the pyramid meant as icon and offer glimpses of the burial ceremonies for the god-king and the rituals that were carried out once his mortal remains had been mummified and entombed, setting the cosmic engine in motion.

The 'opening of the mouth' ceremony from a New Kingdom Book of the Dead.

I TOMB AND TEMPLE

The Ka, the Ba and the Body Embalmed

(Above) A simple predynastic grave, the body buried in a pit beneath a mound. The body was naturally desiccated by the hot, dry desert sands.

(Above right) Early evidence of mummification: a human arm from the tomb of King Djer at Abydos, with linen wrappings and four bracelets.

'This Unas has come…His two wings having grown as those of a falcon, feathered as those of a hawk, his *ba* having brought him, his magic having equipped him. You shall open your place among the stars in the sky.'

Pyramid Texts, 245, 250–51

When we visit the pyramids we walk on ancient graveyards. The pyramids and their temples, and the burials of kings, nobles and commoners, express the unique ancient Egyptian idea of death. Death is a ritual process for the living and the Egyptians marked their passage into the hereafter perhaps more than other ancient societies. For them death was not the end, but just one of the transformations in life's natural cycle. The final change in status depended on the first duty in the housekeeping of death – the treatment of the corpse.

During life the body was called *khet* or *iru* – 'form', 'appearance'; the corpse was *khat*. Transformed into a mummy, it was *sah*, a word whose root is also used for 'to be noble'. Mummification was not so much the preservation of the body as it had been during life, but the transfiguration of the corpse into a new body 'filled with magic', a simulacrum or statue in wrappings and resin.

The origins of mummification

It is often stated that mummification was inspired by simple predynastic pit burials in which the body was naturally desiccated by contact with the desert sands. As time went on graves became more elaborate, separating the body from the sand. Ironically, these measures promoted decay instead of preservation. The first steps towards mummification – wrapping the body in linen – coincide with the development of tomb superstructures, just after the rise of the Egyptian state. An arm with bandages and wearing four bracelets, dating to the 1st dynasty, was found in the tomb of Djer at Abydos.

In fact, mummification may have stemmed from a practice diametrically opposite to preventing the body's decay. Petrie found evidence which suggested to him that as early as predynastic times certain people were prepared for death's passage by allowing the body to decompose, with the skeletal parts

Canopic Vessels

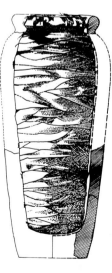

(Left) Alabaster canopic chest of Queen Hetepheres I, from her secret tomb at Giza.

(Right) In Pepi I's pyramid, fragments of canopic jars were found, and one tightly wrapped package of viscera, still retaining the shape of its jar.

In the process of mummification the Egyptians removed the viscera – particularly the liver, lungs, intestines and stomach – from the body in order, as is usually thought, to prevent decay. They were then wrapped up and stored in the tomb separately. At Meidum, the tomb of Rahotep and Ranefer contained small square recesses for the canopic packages in the south wall of the burial chamber. Ranefer's canopic recess still retained his linen-wrapped organs. The Giza tomb of Hetepheres contained the oldest known canopic chest, carved of alabaster and divided into four compartments. When it was opened it still contained packages, presumed to be the queen's viscera, in a natron solution.

By the time of Meresankh III, Khufu's granddaughter and wife of Khafre, the viscera were placed in four separate jars. Later canopic jars were fitted into the chests. One of Pepi I's canopic bundles was found in his pyramid, mixed with the fragments of alabaster jars that had once contained it and the others.

Canopic is a word derived from a Greek myth about Canopus, a sailor who died and was subsequently worshipped in Egypt in the form of a jar, and associated with Osiris.

then reassembled. Before preparing the mummy, the objective was to remove all body parts that would putrefy. By early dynastic times the skeleton was re-incorporated in a linen-wrapped effigy. Discoveries in elite tombs at Meidum, on the threshold of the pyramid age, show how dismemberment and recomposition of corpses was practised on the bodies of the most important people in the land. Well into the Middle Kingdom, human remains inside mummies are often little more than skeletons.

This observation is all the more intriguing when we realize that dismemberment and decay in death were among the primary fears of the Egyptians. Certain funerary texts from all periods contain, along with such fears, positive allusions to the recomposition of the body. In the Pyramid Texts (p. 31) spells call for the recomposition of the royal body, implying a prior state of dismemberment. All this relates to Egypt's central myth about Osiris who was killed and dismembered by his brother Seth, reconstituted by his sister-wife Isis as the archetypal mummy and avenged by his son Horus, the god incarnate in every king.

Dismemberment renders something dysfunctional. In the tomb precinct, a liminal zone between this world and the Netherworld, the Egyptians seem to have been anxious to dismember things that might be highly charged by contact with the dead. Structures associated with death and burial were sometimes ritually disassembled and carefully buried separate from the body. The southern ships of Khufu are particularly large and wonderfully complete examples (p. 118). Another is the canopy found under Khafre's satellite pyramid. Probably used for transporting a funerary statue, it had been chopped up and the pieces packed in a box, buried in a blind passage under the pyramid (p. 126).

If one goal of mummification was to put away and to incapacitate the dead, the point was also to reassemble the body to gain release in another plane of existence. The paradox of the bound mummy was that it also allowed liberation and continued life – not so the dead could haunt the living, but so they could be reborn in the Afterlife. The two realms did, however, interact. In fact they were mutually dependent. For this reason the Egyptians wanted the spirits of their departed to be bound to the mortal remains – but confined to the other side of the tomb. The reassembled body served as an anchor for a spiritual reassembly on the other side of the false door, a mysterious alchemy of a person's separate parts, the *ka* and the *ba*.

The *ka*

The *ka* is one of the most important dimensions of the human being in Egyptian thought, yet there is no easy translation. It is written with the sign of upraised arms, bent perpendicular at the elbows. Perhaps the most succinct translation is 'life force'. The *ka* is associated with 'food sustenance', *kau*,

and therefore with the food offerings in the tomb. 'For your *ka*' was an Egyptian toast with food and drink offerings similar to our salute 'to your health'.

While residing discretely in each person the *ka* was characterized by its transferability and commonality. In Egyptian artistic convention the upraised arms of the *ka* hieroglyph represent an embrace. For the Egyptians an embrace transferred vital force between two people, or between gods and king. The *ka* was transferred through the family lineage – it was generic and, in our terms, genetic. For everyone, this life force extended back through countless generations to the creator god who transferred his *ka* to the gods, who, in turn, transferred theirs to the king. The king is the life force, the *ka*, of his people – 'the *ka* of the living'.

At death one's *ka* went to rest, subsumed back into its generic folds. This return to commonality took place while the body was prepared and transformed into the mummy. The *ka* then needed to be reactivated so that the spiritual transformation of rebirth could take place and so that the link to the land of the living, through the tomb, could be established and maintained. For this to happen the deceased had to travel to join their *ka*, but not as the body, bound up in its wrappings. It is the *ba* that makes the journey.

The *ba*

If the *ka* is the generic life force, the *ba* is a person's individual renown or distinctive manifestation – the impression made on others. The *ba* has often been translated as 'soul' and considered a part of the total human being along with the *ka* and *akh*. But detailed studies indicate that the *ba* and *akh* are entities in their own right. The *ba* seems to have been a fully corporeal mode of existence with the ability, for instance, to eat, drink, travel and copulate. It is represented by the hieroglyph of the ibis; from the 18th dynasty it had a human head.

The *ba*s of gods were their manifestation in nature – stars, inanimate objects, even other gods. A *ba* of Shu, god of the air, is wind. Likewise the *ba*s of the king are the manifestations of his power – an armed expedition, for example. Cities had *ba*s. Even inanimate objects like temple pylons, threshing floors, doors and sacred books had *ba*s. During life this power was revealed primarily through the body. With death the body becomes inanimate and so the former personality and status of a person were distilled into a being that could travel to the realms of the Afterlife and then return to the tomb.

In the Afterlife the *ba* could not function if the corpse was decaying and putrefying – it was for this reason that all potential for decay had to be stripped from the body. The Coffin Texts tell the deceased 'thy *ba* awakest upon thy corpse', but for this to happen the corpse had to be made 'firm', 'established', 'stable', 'enduring', 'whole', 'sound'.

This wonderfully complete, life-sized wooden ka-*statue of the 13th-dynasty king Auibre-Hor was found in his tomb at Dahshur, within the precinct of Amenemhet III's pyramid.*

The ba *hovering over a
mummy, from a New
Kingdom Book of the Dead.*

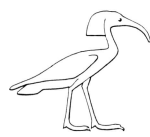

The akh *was represented as
the crested ibis. This was the
final transformation of the
deceased.*

As in rituals around the world, Egyptian rites of death and passage to a higher status involved a stage where the distinguishing features of life were stripped and dissolved. As a collection of excarnated bones, desiccated flesh and hair, the naked body of a king looked like that of anyone else. The burial ritual re-established social status and personality, now realized as the *ba*. The Pyramid Texts speak of the royal insignia, the uraeus and the Eye of Horus, being given to the king. For passing through the doors of heaven, the king puts on a *ba*-garment, the leopard pelt of princely and priestly power.

As miraculous as this new mode of existence may have been, it was still only part of the final transformation. A journey followed to the sky, to sunlight, to the stars. In the celestial realms the deceased hoped to attain higher status, second only to becoming a god – resurrection as an *akh*.

The *akh*

The Pyramid Texts speak of the king ascending to Nut, the sky goddess, leaving 'a Horus', a new living king, behind him. Joining the stars, the king becomes an *akh*. *Akh* is often translated as 'spirit' or 'spirit state'. It derives from the term for 'radiant light', written with the crested ibis, as though the crest transforms the ordinary ibis bird of the *ba*. The *akh* is the fully resurrected, glorified form of the deceased in the Afterlife. *Akh* is also a word for 'effective', 'profitable', 'useful'. The reunion of the *ba* with the *ka* is effected by the burial ritual, creating the final transformation of the deceased as an *akh*. As a member of the starry sky, called *akh-akh* in the Pyramid Texts and the New Kingdom Book of the Dead, the king is free to move on and over the earth. Like the *ba*, the *akh* was thought of as a com-

plete entity, co-existing with the *ka* and the *ba*. An 'effective, equipped *akh*' comes close to our concept of a ghost, for it could reach across the liminal zone of the tomb to have positive or negative effects on the realm of earthly life. Being an *akh* had its practical responsibilities in the world of the living.

Pyramid as place of transformation

The success of an ancient Egyptian in the Afterlife depended on the burial rites and later offering rituals in the tomb. For the king, the pyramid was the place of ascension and transformation. His independent modes of being – particularly his *ka* – stood at the head of all his living and dead subjects. This was particularly true in the Old Kingdom, when only the king's pyramid was inscribed with funerary texts. No wonder, then, that it was so important to take care of his *ka*, for in a sense it contained the life force of all his living subjects.

The names of pyramids show that they were perceived as places of ascension and transformation. Khufu's was *Akhet*, the 'Horizon', of Khufu. Built on the word *akh*, the name signified not just the horizon but the 'radiant place' of glorification. A series of 5th-dynasty pyramid names contain a reference to the *ba*. Six of the 26 known pyramid names refer to the rising of the king, while five refer to his perfection. Five others affirm that the king is 'established' and 'endures', while eight pyramids are named for the king's 'places' or 'thrones' which 'rise', 'flourish' and are 'established', 'pure', 'divine' and 'perfect'. As the kings ascended and re-established their courts in the Afterlife, generations of Egyptians moved as cohorts across death's threshold to live again as a 'community of *ka*s', focused on the pyramid and its surrounding necropolis.

'Horus takes him to his fingers, that he may cleanse
this Unas in the Jackal [Anubis] Basin;
He will release the *ka* of this Unas in the Morning
Basin;
He will wipe off the flesh of the *ka* of his body;
He conducts the *ka* of this Unas and of his body to the
Great House.'

Pyramid Texts 268

Burial Rituals
and the Pyramid Complex

Burial rituals enacted at the pyramid ensured the transfer of kingship from the dead pharaoh to the living one. These rituals might therefore help us in understanding the function of parts of the pyramid complex. Much of our information for Egyptian funerals comes from scenes in tombs of high officials, since the king's funeral is never shown in any of the pictorial fragments recovered from pyramid temples. On the basis of such scenes the funeral ceremony has been divided into 4, 5 or as many as 16 episodes. In typical Egyptian fashion there were rituals embedded within rituals, for embalming, purification, burial and offering. This sacred theatre was probably seldom complete in all its acts – except, perhaps, for the king.

The voyage of the dead

Our first glimpse of the opening scenes of the funeral pageant is in reliefs in 6th-dynasty tombs. Women shriek and wail, people fall to the ground, rend their clothing and throw dirt on their heads as the coffin is carried on a bier. Already we see a cast of characters who will remain the principals throughout the funeral. The Old Kingdom procession includes a woman labelled 'the Kite', either a professional mourner or the widow. Later there were two Kites, identified with Isis and Nephthys, mourners of Osiris. They are mentioned in the Pyramid Texts, where the dead king is identified with Osiris. Also present was the 'Embalmer',

whose name, *Wet*, means 'the Wrapper', who was in charge of those who changed the cadaver into the mummy. The 'Lector Priest', 'one who carries the ritual', possessed knowledge which was key to the transformation of the deceased into an *akh*.

Flanked by the two Kites and accompanied by the others, the coffin was loaded on to a boat. Those who had lived some distance from the necropolis probably reached it by old river channels, canals or a harbour-lake for the pyramid complex. For those who had lived in towns at the base of the pyramid plateau, there could have been a voyage on a token canal, perhaps indicated by scenes of the boat towed by rows of men on the banks. The disassembled boats ritually buried in pits outside Khufu's pyramid enclosure (p. 118) may have been used to carry the king's body on this voyage. Docking at the pyramid harbour, the deceased was unloaded before the 'Doors of Heaven', described in the Pyramid Texts as part of the watery celestial world. In tomb scenes of the funeral, the doors were associated with the *Ibu*, the 'Tent of Purification.'

The *Ibu* and the *Wabet*

So far, the corpse had probably not received any elaborate treatment. But before it could enter the sacred necropolis it had to be purified. As we have seen, the 'cleansing' at some point involved the

Mourners, dressed in white, precede the coffin hauled along on a long-poled bier in this scene from the New Kingdom Book of the Dead of Ani.

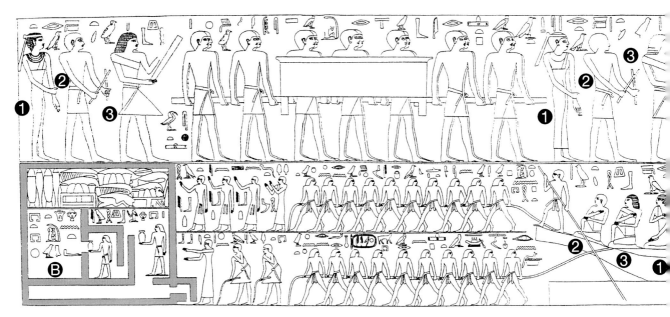

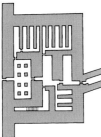

The plan of Pepi II's valley temple reflects the main features of Qar's wabet, highlighted above: two vestibules or antechambers, a blind corridor or stairway (below), main hall and side magazines (top of plan).

removal of most of the soft tissue. Where did this take place? Tomb scenes give the impression that almost immediately after arriving at the necropolis, the body was taken to the *Ibu*, or the *Ibu en Waab*, the 'Tent of Purification'.

In tomb scenes the *Ibu* is a light construction of wood poles and reed mats shielding a rectangular space, on or near the edge of a waterway, with pathways and doors at either end. Comparisons can be made to known pyramid valley temples, particularly those of Khafre at Giza and Pepi II at South Saqqara. Along the front of Pepi II's temple, ramps ascended from the harbour to a platform, with doorways through small kiosks at each end. Khafre's valley temple is also approached by two stone ramps up to a low terrace along the temple front. In 1996 Zahi Hawass found tunnels in the bedrock beneath the ramps, with mudbrick walls forming a corridor, perhaps a token canal. After crossing this symbolic waterway, ramps lead to the north and south doors of the valley temple. The *Ibu* could therefore have been a temporary wood-frame and reed-mat structure on platforms in front of the valley temple, if not part of the valley temple itself.

From the *Ibu* the body was taken to the *Wabet* – from a word meaning 'pure'. In the tomb of Pepi-ankh this is called the 'Pure Place of Wrapping'. *Wabet* is usually translated 'mortuary workshop' and said to be the place of embalming. It has been suggested that the royal *Wabet* could have been in the mortuary temple. However, texts and pictorial representations hint that the *Wabet* was in the valley – perhaps the valley temple – and near the *Ibu*.

If the process of desiccation and partial dismemberment lasted 70 days, or a major part of 272 days as noted in the tomb of Queen Meresankh, the *Ibu* may not have been secure enough. Perhaps ritual lustration and removal of the viscera and brain

were performed in the *Ibu*, while the long period of desiccation followed in the *Wabet*. Relief scenes in the Giza tomb of Qar show his *Wabet* which is labelled '*Wabet* of a period of time' and which has similarities with the valley temple of Pepi II. Both have three main central rooms, a long narrow blind corridor and one side taken over by magazines.

Such individual correspondences between the valley temples of Khafre and Pepi II and features of 6th-dynasty scenes of funeral rituals – the edge of a canal or basin, two pathways, two entrances, a portico, the form of the 'Divine Booth' – have prompted suggestions that the valley temples functioned as the *Ibu*, or the *Ibu* and *Wabet* combined. B. Grdseloff thought that the purification was carried out on the roof of the valley temple and embalming in the vestibule. Herbert Ricke believed the whole process would have taken place in mudbrick buildings elsewhere, then ritually re-enacted in the valley temple. None of the eight excavated valley temples – of 28 that probably existed – contain an obvious place for the processes of mummification.

Journey to the tomb

The mummified body in its coffin was now pulled by oxen on a sledge to the necropolis. At this stage the coffin procession still involved the Kites and priests. The procession to the tomb also included furnishing for setting up house in the Afterlife: linen, tools, weapons, pottery and metal vessels, ointments, oils and symbols of social status. Unfortunately, no pyramid has been found archaeologically with its burial assemblage intact, so we can only guess at the riches it would have comprised.

An important ritual at the tomb was an invocation called 'coming forth at the voice'. The deceased was summoned to come and partake of the offerings. As time went on, offerings became lengthier

The funeral procession to the
Ibu *and the* Wabet, *shown in
great detail in the 6th-dynasty
tomb of Qar at Giza.*
A Ibu
B Wabet
1 *'Kite'*
2 *Embalmer*
3 *Lector Priest*

and more complex. Hermann Junker counted 17 different ritual presentations in Old Kingdom tombs which he could relate to those for the king mentioned in the Pyramid Texts, including censings, libations, gifts of cloth, cattle and fowl. With the addition of a second set of utterances and rites for glorifying the dead, or making them effective (*akh*), the ritual grew so complex that a specialist, the Lector Priest, appears in 5th-dynasty scenes. The 'opening of the mouth' was performed to allow the deceased to breathe, eat and speak in the Afterlife. Texts of the 6th dynasty speak of 80 men who helped set the lid on to the stone sarcophagus. This may have been the full complement of workers but they could not all have fitted into the burial chamber. The final rite was 'bringing the foot' – erasing the footprints of the officiants by dragging a brush, along with more censing and libations.

The focus of any tomb, including the king's, was the offering place and false door – the entrance to the Netherworld. In both large tombs and pyramid complexes, pictorial programmes included scenes of hunting, fowling, fishing and the delivery of offerings. Both pharaoh and nobleman had statues representing the continued existence of the head of the household. In élite tombs the arrival at the sepulchre is labelled 'landing at the *Tjephet* ('Cavern') of the Great Palace' and in the Abusir Papyri the five statue chambers in the mortuary temple are called *Tjephet*. It seems evident that the pyramid complex embodied, at a higher order of magnitude and elaboration, a ritual similar to that depicted in the funeral scenes of late Old Kingdom nobility. The king 'moved' through the pyramid complex in the cycle of rebirth and transformation that the funeral ritual effected, even if the housekeeping of death and burial required real but temporary structures, and side routes or ramps over the enclosure.

A Stage for the Funeral?

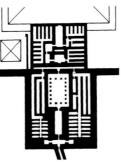

Pepi II's mortuary temple

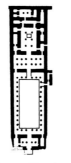

Merenptah's palace

While there are debates as to the role of pyramid mortuary temples in burial ritual, they do reflect the principal features of royal palaces, like Merenptah's at Memphis, from the New Kingdom.

Dieter Arnold, among others, doubts whether the pyramid temples and causeway were in fact used in the royal funeral ceremony. One argument is architectural: rooms and doorways seem too small for the passage of the funeral. From the mortuary temple the body and grave goods had to be taken into the pyramid court and round to the north side of the pyramid to be carried into the burial chamber. In the standard pyramid temples of the 5th and 6th dynasties the exit to the pyramid court was at one end of the transverse hall separating the front from the inner temple. Its doorways seem too narrow to allow the funeral to pass through. In Djoser's Step Pyramid complex, the route from the entrance hall through the mortuary temple and down to the burial vault is just as narrow. Arnold therefore thinks that the funeral rituals would have been conducted outside the pyramid complex in light structures, and the royal body conveyed into the pyramid court by means of a side entrance.

If the mortuary temple was not the stage for the royal funeral, what did it represent? At least one of its aspects was as the deceased king's eternal residence, its parts corresponding broadly to the palace of his lifetime. Indeed, it has the same basic elements as large houses known from the archaeological record: enclosure wall; vestibule; a central meeting place in the form of a pillared hall or open court; a platform for the head of the house to receive visitors; private rooms. The innermost room, the offering hall, corresponded generally to the royal dining room. Behind the false door where offerings were placed, lay the magazines, antechamber and burial chamber under the pyramid, corresponding to the inner foyer and bedroom. The Pyramid Texts identify the burial chamber as the *Per Duat*, an allusion to the Netherworld but also to the *Per Duat*, 'House of Morning' or 'Toilet House' of the palace, where the pharaoh was bathed, anointed and dressed.

This World and the Netherworld

'I come forth by day to any place where I may wish to be. I have gained power over my heart, I have gained power over my breast, I have gained power over my hands, I have gained power over my feet, I have gained power over my mouth, I have gained power over all limbs of mine … I sit down, I stand up.'

The Egyptians did not imagine the Afterlife as an ethereal existence. Each person's hope and expectation was to be reborn fully corporeal, as expressed in Chapter 68 of the New Kingdom Book of the Dead (quotation above). Released from the bondage of the bandages, the deceased had control over all physical and psychic abilities. But the mummy did not return bodily to this world, or walk through the tomb's false door, carved in solid rock. It was plain that offerings left at the base of the door were not eaten. The resurrection of the dead happened in another, parallel world. Food offerings were a token meal shared with the dead, providing sustenance just as stone simulacra of shrines, bodies (statues) and boats gave the dead protection, corporeality and mobility in that world. In the same chapter of the Book of the Dead the deceased control more than their own limbs, they now also control air, water, rivers, floods, shores. The spell begins:

'Opened for me are the double doors of the sky, open for me are the double doors of the earth. Open for me are the bolts of Geb; exposed for me are the roof…And the twin peep-holes…'

On the north side of his Saqqara Step Pyramid, Djoser emerges from his tomb, in statue form, into a statue-box, or *serdab*, which has just such a pair of peep-holes to allow him to see out (p. 90).

Celestial world and underworld

The oldest literature about the Afterlife, the Pyramid Texts (p. 31), emphasizes the celestial world of the sky more than the earthly underworld. The principal elements of the topography of the Afterlife were the sky, the abyss, the *Duat* ('Netherworld') and the *Akhet* ('horizon'). It was the king's destiny to 'go forth to the sky among the Imperishable Ones' and to 'go around the sky like the sun'.

The sky (*pet*) was inhabited by the *ka*s, *ba*s, *akh*s and birds as well as gods. The Pyramid Texts mention the sun, the sky-goddess Nut, Osiris, Horus and even Geb, the earth god, as being there. The 'Imperishable Ones' are the circumpolar stars, about 26° to 30° above the northern horizon in the

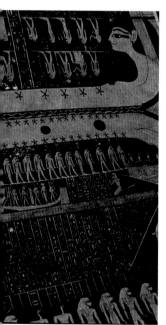

Nut, 'she of a thousand bas' – the stars and sun as her manifestations – from the 19th-dynasty royal tomb of Ramesses VI in the Valley of the Kings.

pyramid zone. Since these stars revolve around the celestial north pole and neither rise nor set, the long, narrow passages sloping up from the burial chamber in the northern sides of many pyramids were aimed like a telescope in their direction.

Doorways that opened on each side of the sky allowed gods and kings to pass through but barred commoners and foreigners. Such exclusivity may reflect that of the doors of pyramid temples which may have kept out all but the priests. The expanse of the sky was conceived as the surface of a large body of 'fresh water' that the king and gods crossed on reed floats. Numerous canals and lakes or basins in this image imply the presence of land – indeed, the sky had banks or levees on the west and on the east. The Milky Way was the 'beaten path of stars', although it was also a watery way. Two fields were prominent in the sky, the Field of Reeds, a rather marshy area on the eastern edge, and the Field of Offerings further north, near the Imperishable Ones. In fact, the vision is that of the Nile Valley at inundation.

Nut was the personification of the sky. She was imagined as bending over the earth with her head in the west, where she swallows the setting sun and stars, and her loins in the east, where she gives birth to the rising sun and stars. This image works for sunset if Nut bends under the earth, suggesting that she was conceived as a sky for the Underworld. In the New Kingdom an image of Nut was carved on the bottom of royal sarcophagi, with her

The most dramatic representation of resurrection from the Duat through the primeval mound was conceived at the end of the 19th dynasty as an embellishment the Book of Caverns, a scene painted in the tombs of the pharaoh Merenptah and the queen Tawosret. Although it is not labelled 'pyramid', the mound has the form of a regular triangle split in half, with the two sides slid apart like a gigantic doorway. The pyramid has a black apex and a blue watery middle band to symbolize the path of the sun through the black darkness and blue waters of the Netherworld. Inside each half a god bends over a black mound enclosing a face, representing the god buried within the Duat. The texts label this, 'the Great God, the Secret of the Duat'. Other texts refer to this motif as 'the Secret Mound, in which there is the interior of the great mystery'. Below the opened pyramid, with wings outstretched for the impending glory of dawn's flight, is the night-form of the sun god with a ram's head. The rising of the sun god takes place in the opening of the pyramid-gate. Other participants total 24, probably representing the 24 hours of the day and night. The birth itself is assisted by gigantic arms that reach down from above to lift out the upside-down figure of a child, a scarab and a sun disk.

Although this scene was composed well over a thousand years after the Pyramid Texts, the same theme of renewal of creation – rebirth – in the depths of the earth is expressed in pictures as it was in stone in the massive pyramids of the Old Kingdom.

arms in the *ka*-like embrace on the sides. The king's tomb was also a cosmic womb, an idea articulated in the Pyramid Texts (616 d–f):

'You are given to your mother, Nut, in her identity of the coffin,
She has gathered you up, in her identity of the sarcophagus,
You are ascended to her, in her identity of the tomb.'

This suggests that the sloping pyramid passages descending to the burial chambers were seen in fact as 'ascending' to Nut in the Netherworld. The word for 'Netherworld' was *Duat*, often written with a star in a circle, a reference to Orion, the stellar expression of Osiris, in the Underworld. Osiris was the Lord of the *Duat*, which, like the celestial world (and the real Nile Valley) was both a water world and an earthly realm. In the Pyramid Texts the *Duat* is connected to the earth or to a darker region lying primarily beneath. Aker, the earth god in the form of a double Sphinx, was the entrance – already the Sphinx is a guardian of gateways.

Akhet is usually translated as 'horizon', where land and the skies touch, but it meant much more in the Egyptian world concept. Written with the same root as the word *akh*, the *Akhet* was where the dead were transformed into effective inhabitants of the world beyond death. As part of the sky, it was also the place into which the sun, and therefore the king, was reborn from within the *Duat*. It is not hard to imagine the early Egyptians being inspired by the pre-dawn glow in the eastern horizon, and by the sunset flaming in the west, to see the area just below the horizon as the place of glorification. Khufu's pyramid was *Akhet Khufu*. Here, and in the Pyramid Texts, *Akhet* is written with the crested ibis and elliptical land-sign, not with the hieroglyph of the sun disk between two mountains that was used later to write 'horizon'. As the place where the deceased becomes an *akh*, a suggested translation is 'Spirit' or 'Light Land'.

The living and the dead

All the cosmic skies and seas, and all the arcane imagery, stem from the uncertainty about the voyage between this world and the Netherworld. At the end of the journey, the Netherworld was a vague reflection of this world – Netherworld celestial geography was similar to the Nile Valley at inundation; Netherworld society lived on in 'That City', where the deceased could be influential if she/he became 'effective' – an *akh*.

To continue an effective life beyond the grave, the dead required living household members to attend to the services of the tomb. In return for this, the living requested that their dead relatives use their influence to maintain the household, of which the tomb was a part. They made their petitions in 'letters to the dead' written on bowls, linen, stelae or even jar stands and deposited in the tomb. Once established in the Netherworld, the deceased was just beyond the veil of the false door. Maintenance of the household and transfer of the estate were the real motives behind the burial rituals, the tomb and all the weird imagery of the Netherworld. The one who buried the deceased head of the household inherited the estate; the prince who buried the dead king in his pyramid inherited the kingship. The most immense tombs – the pyramids – made the

head of the entire Egyptian household supremely effective (*akh*) in the Netherworld. With the surrounding tombs of members of the court and royal family, the pyramid necropolis was a stone simulacrum of 'That City'. Its role was to carry the king as head of the living *ka*s, and therefore the entire community with him, to the new life after death.

The Netherworld in the New Kingdom

In the New Kingdom, just as the pyramid as the royal burial place was replaced by a natural pyramidal mountain above the subterranean tombs of the Valley of the Kings, new funerary texts emphasized a Netherworld in and under the earth. As opposed to the dead flying up to the celestial light, the sun god comes to the dead with his entourage, journeying down the Nile of the night in his barque. Within this imagined realm are underworld pyramids that elaborate themes hinted at in the Pyramid Texts.

This new genre of funerary composition, at first exclusive to the king's tomb like the older Pyramid Texts, decorated the walls of the royal tombs in the Valley of the Kings. For convenience the texts are called 'Books': the Book of Caverns, Book of Gates, Book of Aker. As with the Pyramid Texts of a thousand years earlier, they contain variations on the creation theme, now played out as a journey systematized into 7 gates, 21 doors, 7 heavenly cows, 14 mounds and 12 caverns. These are illustrated map-guides to the Netherworld. The oldest is *Amduat*, the 'Book of What is in the Underworld', which first appears in the reign of Thutmose I (1504–1492 BC).

The journey of the sun god in his night form of a ram-headed man is depicted in the central register of the walls of descending corridors of tombs. Above

and below, registers show the architecture and denizens of the *Duat* which is divided into 12 hours. In the 5th hour a pyramid-like mound rises to interrupt the three registers. Above the pyramid is a small mound of sand – a stylized grave. Both grave and pyramidal mound are subterranean, as indicated by a stippled band to represent sand.

From the apex of the pyramid a head emerges, in some versions identified as 'the flesh of Isis, who is over the Land of Sokar'. Sokar, the most mysterious form of the god Osiris, Lord of the Netherworld, is the core of the scene, awakening inside his ellipse or 'egg' within the pyramidal mound. The texts state that not even the sun god can penetrate Sokar's chamber, but his passage and his words to Sokar in the sealed chamber set off a reaction within the 'egg'.

The exchange between light – the sun god – and darkness – the cavern of Sokar – allows resurrection to take place at the end of the night journey, when the scarab beetle Khepri pushes the ball of the sun through the gates of the horizon, as the mummiform Osiris slips back into the *Duat*. The renewal of creation in the depths of the earth allows the king's soul to ascend from the tomb just as it allows the sun to rise again.

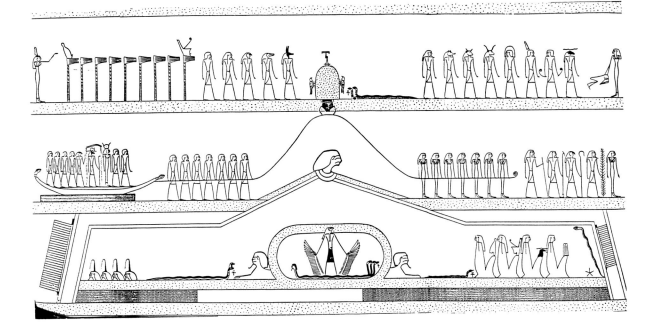

The route through a pyramid complex leads finally to the great stone false door at the back of the offering chapel. On the 'other side', behind solid masonry, deep under the pyramid, lay the most intimate rooms of this house of eternity: the burial chamber and antechamber. Beginning with the pyramid of Unas at the end of the 5th dynasty, the walls of these chambers were inscribed with vertical columns of texts from Egypt's – indeed the world's – oldest religious literature. The Pyramid Texts are a tantalizing, yet confusing, literary window on to the meaning of a pyramid complex.

The Brugsch brothers, Emile and Heinrich, made the initial discovery of Pyramid Texts in 1881 in the pyramids of Unas, Teti, Pepi I, Merenre and Pepi II. Kurt Sethe prepared the first definitive edition of the texts, numbering 714 individual sayings or spells. New texts found in 1925 in the pyramids of Pepi II and his queens, Neith, Iput and Wedjebten extended the number to 759. French excavations in South Saqqara, under Jean Leclant, have continued to find new texts in the last two decades.

In spite of great repetition of the spells and their sequences, the 'editions' of Pyramid Texts differ from one pyramid to another. The oldest edition, that of Unas, contains only 283 of the known texts and includes ones not found in later editions. The

The Pyramid Texts

most recent royal edition, in the small pyramid of Ibi, includes spells unknown in older ones. This suggests a fair degree of fluidity and individual choice of repertoire for each king. On the basis of both archaeological and historical evidence, scholars recognize references to the Old Kingdom state, and therefore date their earliest composition to the period after the unification.

During the First Intermediate Period and Middle Kingdom, Pyramid Texts were also inscribed in the tombs of high officials. They were then subsumed into the Coffin Texts, found inside the coffins of important people. Pyramid Texts were still included in the tombs of officials in the New Kingdom, in the Book of the Dead and in Late Period funerary papyri. The can also be recognized, after radical reworking, in New Kingdom temple ritual. Copies of Pyramid Texts have been found in Late Period tombs and sarcophagi. The fact that such copies, carefully executed in Old Kingdom style, include spells both known and unknown in Old Kingdom editions, hints that the known Old Kingdom texts are a selection from a larger body of texts.

Pyramid texts inscribed before the portcullises in Pepi I's pyramid, translated in the opening quote.

Categories of Pyramid Texts

Scholars have recognized five major categories of spells:

1 Dramatic Texts include spells of lament, spells of the offering ritual, and spells relating to the provision of the king's crowns, to the introduction of equipment to the grave, and to the opening of the mouth and other statue rituals. The Dramatic Texts take the form of recited speech and prescribed action: 'raise up before him' (the deceased), 'lay on the ground in front of him'. Some of the texts suggest that the speaker and the recipient take on the roles of gods in the prescribed ritual action. The formulation of the Dramatic Texts may date to the 2nd and 3rd dynasties.

2 Hymns with Name Formulae set the cult symbols, actions and ritual objects of the Dramatic Texts in the context of mythical stories or allusions, sometimes by adding, 'in this thy name of' or simply 'as'.

3 Litanies are structured as verse and consist of enumerations and sequences of names and name formulae pertaining to particular divine things and

beings. For example, Spell 220 hails the crown as the king takes possession of it: 'He comes to you, O Crown! He comes to you, O Flame; He comes to you, O Great One; He comes to you, O Rich in Magic.' The Hymns and Litanies may have been composed during the 4th dynasty.

4 The Glorifications – the *Sakhu*, literally, 'that which makes one into an *Akh*', form the largest part of the Pyramid Texts. The oldest glorification spells, probably carried out at the tomb during the funeral, mention the sand tomb (PT 1877–78) and the mudbrick mastaba (PT 572c–e). Many of the Glorification Texts are, however, among the youngest Pyramid Texts, composed during the 5th and even as late as the 6th dynasty.

5 The Magical Texts consist of short protection spells for charming snakes and other dangerous beings. From their form of speech, they are judged to be the oldest texts, dating to the early Archaic Period.

Like the programmes of statues and reliefs in the pyramid temples, the overall theme of the Pyramid Texts was the eternal existence of the king in the Afterlife. However, it has not been easy to recognize a completely coherent treatment. The texts do, however, have a decided emphasis on the sky realm of the sun god, an emphasis which makes scholars suspect Heliopolis as the place where much of the corpus was conceived and formulated. The king joins the extended family of the gods; in fact, his death and resurrection is a homecoming. He boards the ship of the sun god and voyages through the sky and the various fields of the Netherworld. Alternatively, the king flies to the sky as a falcon, kite or goose, or leaps upward as a grasshopper. Or he is assisted in his ascent by the natural forces like wind and hail storms. His destiny is both the day and the night sky, for he joins the northern Imperishable Stars. As they identify the dead king with Osiris, the Pyramid Texts also present a chthonic Underworld dimension of the Afterlife.

Fragmented myth and ritual

The Pyramid Texts make allusions to myths, particularly the central pageant of Osiris and the conflict between Horus and Seth over the inheritance of the kingdom, but never provide a coherent narration of the stories. Instead there are, scattered throughout, fragments of myths, as though the story as a whole is too potent for outright telling.

Opinions differ as to the purpose of this poetic discourse, draped like a curtain of ritual and magic around the innermost chambers of the pyramid. For the Egyptians, word and its effect were perceived as one and the same. Kurt Sethe considered the texts a free-form amalgamation of spells that, inscribed permanently on the walls around the king's body, allowed him to be transformed and resurrected, a view which many agree with. Others, while not disagreeing, also see them as the script of the funeral rituals. The idea that parts of the Pyramid Texts were recited in particular contexts is made compelling by directions like 'words to be

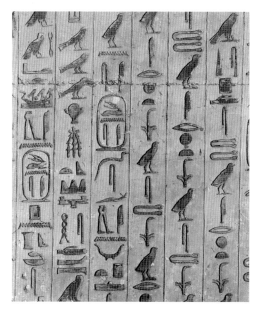

spoken', by the dramatic form of spells comprising the opening of the mouth, by instructions for ritual actions and by the texts which have as their object purifications, censings, presentation of clothes and ointments, and the consecration of the pyramid. It would be perverse to think that the offering ritual would not have been performed in the offering hall of the mortuary temple.

Text, architecture and cosmos

In James Allen's recent 'reading' he looked at the pyramid of Unas – the oldest and most complete rendition. He examined the placement of the spells on the walls, the direction of their narration and the groups of spells. Two ordering principles emerged. First, the narrative flows away from the direction that birds and animal and human hieroglyphs face – the texts progress from right to left except on the north walls of the burial chamber and antechamber where they are read left to right. This is in order to follow the second rule: the texts move from inside the tomb outwards. Thematically, the texts fall into two broad sets: one for the burial chamber and another for the antechamber.

On the western gable of the burial chamber are spells to protect the dead king against snakes, scorpions and other threats. Similar protective spells are found on the east gable of the antechamber. The king's private apartments are thus framed by apotropaic texts, just as outside the pyramid, the causeway and small vestibule contained scenes that protected the passage through the pyramid complex. Parallels between interior text and exterior sign and symbol are evident in the opening spell of the offering ritual on the north wall of the burial chamber, which talks of seizing enemies. The scenes at the lower end of the causeway showed the gods holding ropes binding the enemies of the king. The rest of the offering ritual speaks of the king being dressed, anointed and fed, as he was in the private rooms of the royal residence during life.

On the east gable of the antechamber is also the famous 'Cannibal Hymn' in which the king flies to heaven through a stormy sky: '…impressive as a god who lives on his fathers and feeds on his mothers…' We should understand this 'cannibalism' in the light of the *ka* as the communicative life force that is passed down from Creator to the gods to the king and from parent to child. We should also not forget that the eastern wall of the antechamber faces the 'virtual' exit from the underground apartments of the pyramid – the false door embedded in the east flank of the pyramid at the culmination of the mortuary temple. Beyond the antechamber are the standard three niches, sometimes referred to as *serdab*s as if for statues. However, they could also have been magazines for storing provisions, symbolically transferred into the pyramid chambers from the offerings presented before the false door.

Altogether, the arrangement of Unas's Pyramid Texts reflects the order in which Unas would read them after rising from the sarcophagus, moving through the burial chamber, antechamber and along the corridor. Although Unas's body remains in the burial chamber, just as Osiris remains in the *Duat*, his *ba* awakens, releases itself from the body and proceeds through the *Duat* towards sunrise. The antechamber, east of the burial chamber, the '*Duat*', serves as the *Akhet*, that region between the *Duat* and the day sky, just below the horizon. In the pyramids of Teti, Pepi I and Pepi II, the corridor between the burial chamber and antechamber is inscribed with texts about passing through the marshes at the edge of the *Akhet*, the place of transformation where the king becomes an 'effective spirit' (*akh*) who is able to rise at dawn and to function in the Afterlife.

The flow of Pyramid Texts in the chambers under Unas's pyramid. In the entrance corridor the emphasis is on a rising from the Akhet. The three east recessed magazines are opposite the false door in the offering hall of the pyramid mortuary temple. The goddess Nut was carved into sarcophagi from the New Kingdom onwards.

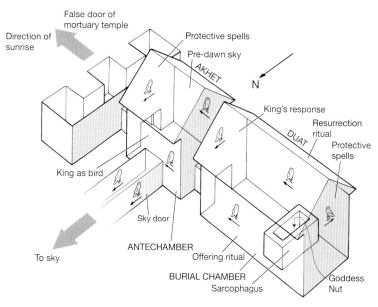

The Pyramid as Icon

The full hieroglyphic determinative for 'pyramid'. Could the red band at the base signify that pyramids were thus painted, as some have thought? Or is it a vestige of the red granite casing at the base of some pyramids, such as Khafre's, Menkaure's and Neferirkare's?

'Atum Scarab!
When you became high, as the high ground,
when you rose as the *ben-ben*, in the Phoenix Enclosure,
in Heliopolis,
you sneezed Shu,
you spat Tefnut, and you put your arms around them, as
the arms of *ka*, that your *ka* might be in them.'

Pyramid Texts

The pyramid was above all an icon, a towering symbol. It has been said that the Egyptians did not distinguish sharply between hieroglyphic writing, two-dimensional art and relief carving, sculpture and monumental architecture. In a sense, the pyramids are gigantic hieroglyphs. But why a pyramid? And how should we read the pyramid glyph?

Pyramid and pyramidion

The word for pyramid in ancient Egyptian is *mer*. There seems to be no cosmic significance in the term itself. I.E.S. Edwards, the great pyramid authority, attempted to find a derivation from *m*, 'instrument' or 'place', plus *ar*, 'ascension', as 'place of ascension'. Although he himself doubted this derivation, the pyramid was indeed a place or instrument of ascension for the king after death.

Our word 'pyramid' comes from the Greek, *pyramis* (pl. *pyramides*), 'wheaten cake'. The Egyptians had a conical bread loaf called *ben-ben*, which was also the word for the capstone of a pyramid or the tip of an obelisk – *ben-benet*, named after the *ben-ben* stone, the sacred icon in the temple of Heliopolis, the oldest centre of the sun cult.

The capstone or pyramidion is the complete pyramid in miniature, bringing the structure to a point at the same angle and with the same proportions as the main body. Stadelmann found the earliest pyramidion at Sneferu's North Pyramid at Dahshur (p. 104), made of the same limestone as the casing and uninscribed. A number of pyramidions also survive from Middle Kingdom royal pyramids and from the small pyramids of non-royal tombs of New Kingdom and later times (p. 186). Amenemhet III's pyramidion, of hard black stone, from his pyramid at Dahshur, is the most complete royal capstone. On one of

The pyramidion of Amenemhet III's pyramid at Dahshur (p. 179). The eyes are the pharaoh's, gazing up from within his pyramid to the beauty of the sun.

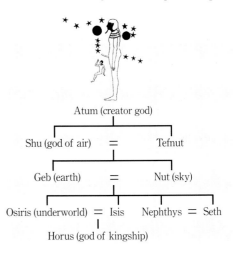

its faces is a winged sun disk in relief. Below are two *wedjat*, sacred eyes, and below them are three *nefer* ('beauty' or 'perfection') signs; below these again we find the hieroglyph for the sun disk, flanked by the name and titles of Amenemhet III. The whole composition can be read as: 'Amenemhet beholds the perfection of Re.' The sacred eyes are those of the king himself. Like the names of the pyramids – 'Sneferu Gleams', 'Great is Khafre' – the eyes tell us that the pyramids were personifications of the dead kings who were buried and revivified within them.

Pyramid and *ben-ben*

The phrase 'beholds the perfection of Re' is one of many indications that the true pyramids were seen as symbols of the sun. The identification of the pyramid with the sacred *ben-ben* stone in the temple of Heliopolis is another sign that the pyramids were sun symbols. To understand the *ben-ben* we must begin with Atum, probably the earliest god worshipped at Heliopolis. An aspect of the sun god, he is the 'old' sun of the evening as opposed to Ra at noon and Khepri – the scarab beetle – the morning sun. Atum was also the oldest creator god; in his most primeval form he was the singularity within the primeval waters of the Abyss. The root, *tm*, in Atum's name means 'complete', 'finish', yet also 'not-be'. In later texts Atum is 'Lord of Totality' and 'the Completed One', and in the Pyramid Texts he is 'self-developing' or 'self-evolving'. Atum is a chthonic god – virtually everything that exists is part of his 'flesh', having evolved as his 'millions of *ka*s'. How did this evolution begin? According to Pyramid Text 527,

'Atum is the one who developed, getting an erection in Heliopolis.
He put his penis in his grasp that he might make orgasm with it,
and the two siblings were born, Shu and Tefnut.'

Shu, the god of air and atmosphere, and his sister Tefnut are the next generation of primeval gods.

Atum (creator god)

Shu (god of air) = Tefnut

Geb (earth) = Nut (sky)

Osiris (underworld) = Isis   Nephthys = Seth

Horus (god of kingship)

The genealogy leads to Geb (earth) and Nut (sky) who beget Osiris, his sister and wife, Isis, his brother and adversary, Seth, and Seth's counterpart Nephthys. Osiris and Isis beget Horus, the god of kingship. Thus kingship goes back to the Creator. Other texts relate Atum's erection and ejaculation to the *ben-ben* pyramidion through a cosmic pun on the root, *bn*, which is associated with procreation and could mean 'become erect' or 'ejaculate'.

Bn could connote the idea of swelling in general. The concept of Atum's masturbation was that he expanded as a mound (*bnnt*) in the abysmal waters of Nun. The Egyptians must have envisaged this as the Nile Valley land emerging from the receding waters of the annual inundation. Within a few lines of this text that speaks of Atum's primeval mound, the theologians are mixing metaphors with impunity, associating Creation with the image of the scarab beetle and the *ben-ben* at Heliopolis. In the same breath, Shu and Tefnut are said to come forth, by onomatopoeia, from Atum's sneezing (*ishesh*) and spitting (*tff*).

As an image of the primeval mound, the pyramid is, therefore, a place of creation and rebirth in the Abyss. The Phoenix, Benu in Egyptian, appears in the tapestry of the Heliopolitan creation myth both by virtue of its sound-similarity with *ben-ben*, and because it returns after long periods to its natural habitat, which the Egyptians pictured as a pyramidal perch of sticks.

Sunlight and the pyramid

Both *ben-ben* and pyramid may have symbolized the rays of the sun, particularly as they appear shining through a break in clouds – the pyramid is thus the immaterial made material. The Pyramid Texts speak of the sun's rays as a ramp by which the king mounts up to the sun, just as the older step pyramids may have been seen as giant stairs. But the pyramid was much more than a magical device for the king to mount to heaven. It was a place of physical and spiritual transformation that tied the king's ascent to the creation of the world and to the daily rebirth of the sun.

There is evidence that the *ben-ben* stone was actually cone-shaped and the pyramid is the easiest way to mimic this in monumental architecture. Here we have to keep in mind the original appearance of the pyramid when most of its surface was newly covered with smoothed white limestone. The reflected light must have been so brilliant as to be almost blinding.

There is a kind of 'picture-window' principle to much of Egyptian art and architecture that might apply to the pyramid as a stone model of immaterial sunlight. In one sense the pyramid may have been a gigantic reflector, a stone simulacrum of sunlight and a window to the sky, as though we were inside the mass of stone looking out at the sunlight, exactly as the eyes of Amenemhet III are

doing on his pyramidion. If we could look through the 'picture-window' of the pyramid, its temples and its underground apartments, we would better appreciate the pyramid complex as a royal house, with its gate house (valley temple), entrance corridor (causeway), vestibule, courtyard, portico and reception room (court and statue chamber), antechamber to the private quarter, dining (offering) hall, and, furthest back, the most intimate apartment where the king sleeps in death only to be reawakened, bathed, and clothed before reappearing in the celestial court.

What makes the arrangement unlike any house is the pyramid itself, towering above the most intimate rooms. It is the pyramid that merges this eternal house with that of the gods – the cosmos. The pyramid is a simulacrum of both the mound of primeval earth and the weightless rays of sunlight, a union of heaven and earth that glorifies and transforms the divine king and ensures the divine rule of the Egyptian household.

The pyramids magically combined the darkest and most dense primeval earth and the rays of celestial light.

Pyramidal icons (from left to right): 2nd-dynasty depiction of the benu *(phoenix) bird on the solar disc at the apex of the* ben-ben; *a New Kingdom* benu *bird from the tomb of Ramesses VI; an obelisk named as the embodiment of Osiris – this, like the late funerary image of Osiris inside a dark step pyramid, reflects the chthonic aspect of the pyramid as primeval mound.*

Long after they were abandoned, pyramids, or the stumps of pyramids, protruded above the debris of their own collapse and the drifting sands of the ages. At first they defied enterprising explorers who dared to try to penetrate their secrets – these early attempts were frontal assaults to find a way inside. As the pyramids were entered one after another, their chambers, shafts and passages were cleared and later mapped. Attention also turned to the ground around the towering ruins. By the turn of the 20th century, it became clear that the pyramids had temples attached, and that the upper temples were connected by long causeways to the lower, valley temples. And so scholars came to see the unity of the pyramid complex. The excavation, mapping and theoretical reconstruction of temples and other features of pyramid ensembles continues to this day at most of the pyramid sites: Abu Roash, Giza, Abusir, Saqqara and Dahshur.

Recently, pyramid exploration has moved in a fresh direction. In addition to recovering the art and architecture of the pyramids, archaeologists now excavate to retrieve evidence of the elementary structures of everyday life of the society that built these great monuments. As their ancient builders intended they should, the pyramids appear mysterious and otherworldly deprived of their social and economic context. Questions that now guide the excavator are: how were the builders housed and fed? What was the economic role and significance of the pyramids as labour projects and functioning ritual centres? What did pyramids contribute to the evolution of Egyptian civilization and, ultimately, to human development? Addressing such questions requires a team of scientists – specialists in bone and plant remains and in radiocarbon dating, in addition to those who still probe the pyramids themselves with remote-controlled robots and cosmic rays, always with the suspicion that the pyramids might hold more secrets.

The pyramids of Giza as depicted by one of Napoleon's artists, from the Description de l'Égypte.

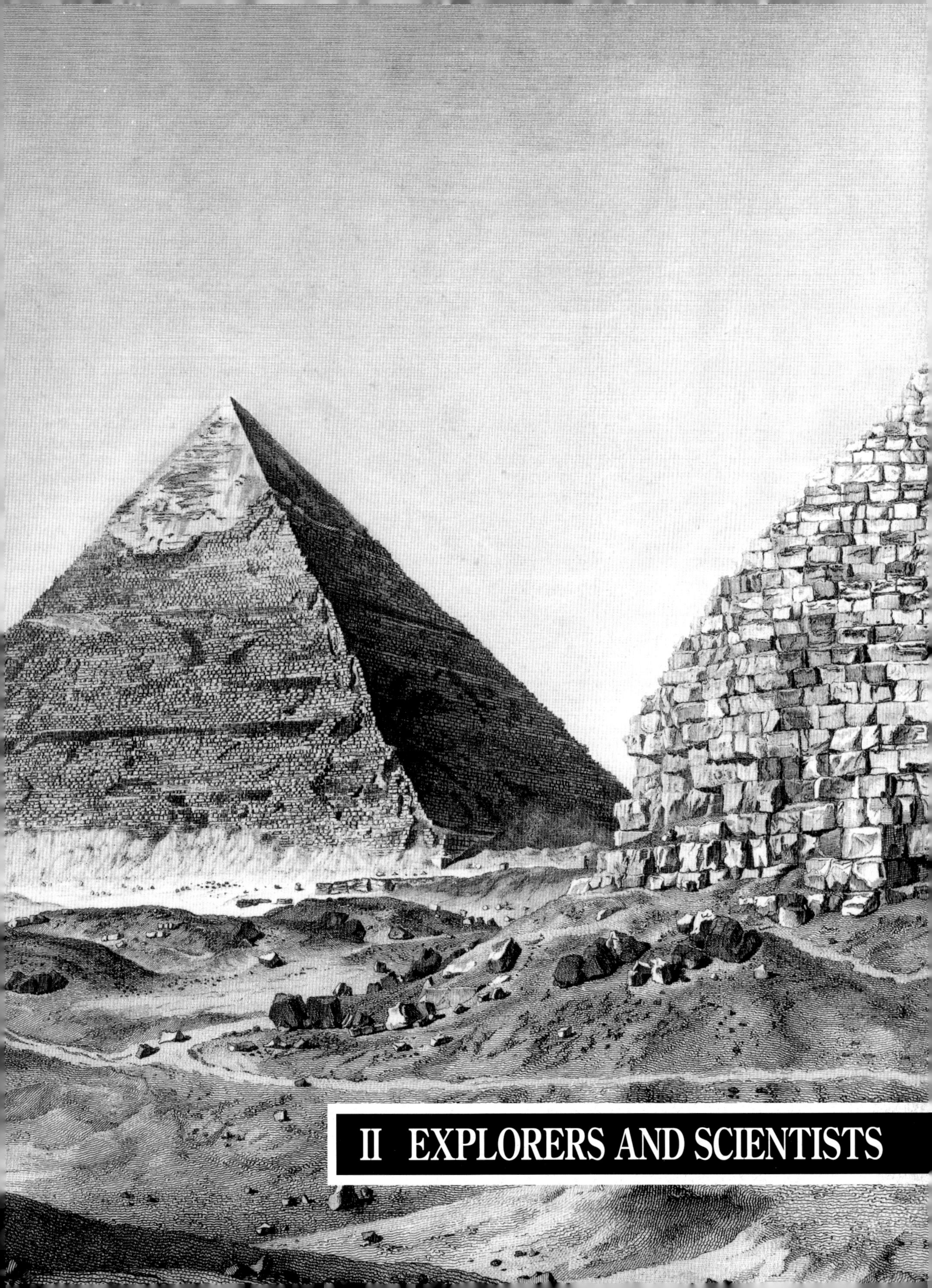

II EXPLORERS AND SCIENTISTS

Early Legends

Abandoned in antiquity

By Middle Kingdom times (11th to 13th dynasties), the early Old Kingdom pyramid builders, such as Khufu (Cheops) and Khafre (Chephren), were already characters of legend rather than history. Some 550 years after Khufu, his pyramid temple and those of his successors seem to have been stripped of their reliefs, since blocks and pieces were reused in the core of the 12th-dynasty pyramid of Amenemhet I at Lisht (p. 168). Amenemhet's pyramid was itself abandoned well before the New Kingdom era of Moses and the Exodus.

The pyramids were thus relics of a bygone era, their stone quarried for other buildings and their temples in ruins. But the names and sequence of their builders were known from king lists and there were occasional attempts to restore the revered monuments of the ancestors. In his stela set up at the Sphinx, Amenhotep II (*c.* 1427 BC) acknowledges both Khufu and Khafre. Khaemwaset (*c.* 1250 BC), son of Ramesses II and High Priest of Memphis, appears to have done some restoration work on 5th- and 6th-dynasty pyramids at Saqqara and Abusir, and other Old Kingdom tombs, including Shepseskaf's Mastabat el-Fara'un.

The New Kingdom rulers did not, however, restore the names of the builders of monuments at Giza. In fact, there is evidence that they removed the fine limestone, alabaster and granite of Khafre's pyramid temples at the same time that they restored the Sphinx in the form of the god Horemakhet. In the Ramessid Turin Canon of kingship, there are hints that the 4th dynasty was undergoing some folkloristic rewriting. For instance, the suspiciously uniform lengths of reign – Huni 24 years, Sneferu 24, Khufu 23 and so on – might well be simple estimates of a generation on the throne.

The 26th dynasty saw an attempt to resurrect the glory of the Old Kingdom. At Giza there was an active priesthood of the Sphinx as Horemakhet and there were also people calling themselves priests of Khufu, Khafre and Menkaure. Ironically, the worship of the powerful kings who built the largest structures in Egypt was now carried out in the tiny Temple of Isis, built against the southernmost of the pyramids of Khufu's queens (GI-c) in the 21st dynasty. A small stela there related another story about Khufu, namely that having found the Isis Temple in ruins he restored the images of the gods, and repaired the headdress of the Sphinx. The style of the text and the deities mentioned all point to its having been written in the 26th dynasty; the story was no doubt told to give greater antiquity and authenticity to the fledgling cult. But its erroneous implication that the Sphinx and Isis Temple predate Khufu shows just how far the perceived history of the site was slipping from fact.

Greek and Roman travellers

In the writings of the Greek historian Herodotus we do indeed find a mixture of fact and folktale about the pyramids. When he came to Egypt between 449 and 430 BC the hieroglyphic script was still read and pharaonic religion still practised, but his report makes us wonder whether the cult of Khufu and his sons in the Isis Temple had been abandoned. The priests who informed the curious Greek gave a decidedly negative account of Khufu:

'[he] brought the country into all sorts of misery. He closed all the temples, then, not content with excluding his subjects from the practice of their religion, compelled them without exception to labour as slaves for his own advantage'

Khufu had already appeared in a slightly bad light in the legends of the Westcar Papyrus (probably dating from the Second Intermediate period, but

By the time of Ramesses II (1290–1224 BC), the Sphinx at Giza had become an object of pilgrimage. Officials, scribes, military leaders, builders and sculptors all made their way there and left behind small commemorative stelae. The scribe Montuher left the oldest depiction of the Giza pyramids on his unique stela.

copying an older document), but it was Herodotus who established the erroneous and now virtually ineradicable association between pyramid building and slave labour. Khufu's pyramid undoubtedly required massive toil, but Herodotus's credibility is strained when he goes on to report that:

'no crime was too great for Cheops: when he was short of money, he sent his daughter to a bawdy-house with instructions to charge a certain sum – they did not tell me how much. This she actually did, adding to it a further transaction of her own; for with the intention of leaving something to be remembered after her death, she asked each of her customers to give her a block of stone, and of these stones [the story goes] was built the middle pyramid of the three which stand in front of the Great Pyramid.'

When Herodotus visited the pyramids Khufu's causeway was intact, with 'polished stone blocks decorated with carvings of animals … a work … of hardly less magnitude than the pyramid itself.' It had taken, he was told, 10 years of 'oppressive slave labour' to build; the pyramid took 20 years,

'including the underground sepulchral chambers on the hill where the pyramids stand; a cut was made from the Nile, so that the water turned the site of these into an island.'

Two centuries after Herodotus, the Egyptian priest Manetho compiled his *Aegyptiaca* – possibly to correct the chronology of Herodotus – which we know only through the edited and abridged versions of Josephus (*c.* AD 70), Africanus (3rd century AD) and Eusebius (4th century AD). Our framework for ancient Egyptian history is still based on Manetho's king list, grouped into 30 dynasties, and he is the first source to organize the kings from Menes to Unas into five dynasties. (The New Kingdom Turin Canon gives the 39 names of this period as a single lineage.) Manetho must have based his grouping on popular tradition and the sequence of the pyramids. He credits Khufu, written 'Suphis', with building the Great Pyramid, and, far from being wicked, with writing the 'Sacred Book'.

Alexander the Great conquered Egypt in 332 BC. For the next 300 years, down to Cleopatra VII, the land was ruled by the Ptolemies, descendants of Ptolemy (I) Soter, the great general who hijacked Alexander's body and took it to Egypt, where he had gained control. In 30 BC Egypt became a Roman province – and a major tourist attraction. On every traveller's itinerary, just as today, were the Giza Pyramids and the Sphinx, Memphis and the Apis house, and – up the Nile Valley at Thebes – the Colossi of Memnon, the Temple of Karnak and the Valley of the Kings. Off the modern tourist trail was the Labyrinth – the temple of Amenemhet III's Hawara pyramid, now levelled.

The Greek author, Diodorus Siculus, in Egypt around 60 BC, reported the Great Pyramid casing as intact, though possibly missing its capstone. In the 1st century AD, Pliny the Elder mentioned the village of Busiris (Abusir) at the foot of the pyramid plateau, whose inhabitants would climb the pyramids for tourists – just like their modern counterparts in the village of Nazlet es-Samman (though it would have been altogether more difficult when the pyramid casing was still largely intact).

Another myth became attached to the pyramids when, towards the end of the 1st century AD, the Jewish historian Josephus included pyramid building among the hardships that the Hebrews had had to endure during their years of labour in Egypt:

'for [the Egyptians] enjoined them to cut a great number of channels for the river, and to build walls for their cities and ramparts, that they might restrain the river, and hinder its waters from stagnating, upon its running over its own banks: they set them also to build pyramids, and by this wore them out…'

This idea persists in the popular imagination, although we now know that the largest pyramids were constructed over a millennium before the era of the Hebrews.

By the Roman period the Egyptian language was written using the Greek script. From the 3rd century AD onwards, the Egyptian language was Coptic. Once Constantine converted to Christianity in AD 312, 3,000 years of pharaonic culture came to an end. The Copts began to destroy the pagan monuments of their ancestors and the last person to read the hieroglyphic script died sometime in the 4th century AD. When the ancient inscriptions became cryptic, real knowledge of the pyramid builders drowned in a sea of myths and legends, and the pyramids fell silent.

About 25 BC, the Roman geographer Strabo reported a movable stone, high up and in the middle of one of the faces of Khufu's pyramid, that allowed access to the Descending Passage. Since any 'trap door' in the original building would have compromised the pyramid's security, this could only have been provided later – perhaps for tourists to reach the subterranean chamber. On the right is a hypothetical reconstruction by the British Egyptologist W.M. Flinders Petrie, based on pivot holes he found at the entrance to the Bent Pyramid at Dahshur.

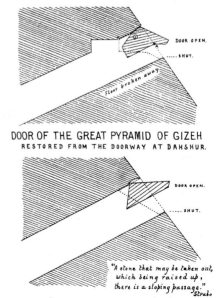

DOOR OF THE SOUTH PYRAMID OF DAHSHUR.
AS SHEWN BY THE EXISTING DOORWAY.

DOOR OPEN.
SHUT.
floor broken away

DOOR OF THE GREAT PYRAMID OF GIZEH
RESTORED FROM THE DOORWAY AT DAHSHUR.

DOOR OPEN.
SHUT.

"A stone that may be taken out, which being raised up, there is a sloping passage."
Strabo

Mythic History of the Copts and Arabs

Books such as The Thousand and One Nights *carry tales of hidden treasure in the Great Pyramid. One such legend tells of the Caliph al-Mamun breaking through the north face. Some stories say he found a vase with limitless water, a golden casket with the ruby-studded body of a man and an animated cockerel of precious stone.*

The Thousand and One Nights,

COMMONLY CALLED, IN ENGLAND,

THE ARABIAN NIGHTS'
ENTERTAINMENTS.

A NEW TRANSLATION FROM THE ARABIC WITH COPIOUS NOTES.

BY EDWARD WILLIAM LANE,

AUTHOR OF "THE MODERN EGYPTIANS."

ILLUSTRATED BY MANY HUNDRED ENGRAVINGS ON WOOD,
FROM ORIGINAL DESIGNS BY WILLIAM HARVEY.

VOLUMES.

'Then Surid ordered the building of the pyramids, had the sciences recorded in them, and had the treasures and pieces of sculpture put into them. Finally, he set an idol to guard each of the three pyramids … After his death, Surid was buried in the "Eastern" [Khufu's] Pyramid, his brother Hujib in the "Western" [Khafre's] one, and Hujib's son, Karuras in the "Pied" [Menkaure's] Pyramid.'

Coptic legend

In AD 395, the Roman empire split in two – east and west – with Egypt under Byzantine control. Two-and-a-half centuries later, in AD 642, Egypt was conquered by the Arabs. The pyramids, being of such obvious antiquity, became linked with legendary and fabulous events.

The pyramids and the Flood

A Coptic legend tells of King Surid who lived three centuries before the flood. His dreams foretold future chaos and only those who joined the Lord of the Boat would escape. The tale is a blend of both the Judaeo-Christian story of the flood and ancient Egyptian themes. Surid may be a corruption of Suphis, a late form of Khufu; his city, Amsus, is Memphis; and the Lord of the Boat is an amalgam of Noah's ark and the barque of the sun god.

One popular Arab legend maintained that the Great Pyramid was the tomb of Hermes – the Greek counterpart of the Egyptian Thoth – who, like Surid, built pyramids to hide literature and science from the uninitiated and preserve them through the flood. The Yemeni Arabs believed the two large pyramids to be the tombs of their ancient kings, one of whom defeated the Egyptians – perhaps a distant memory of the Hyksos invasion in the 2nd millennium BC.

Embellishments of the Arab legends abounded, including of the Surid story. The 15th-century historian al-Maqrizi reported that the king decorated the walls and ceilings of his pyramid chambers with representations of the stars and planets and all the sciences, and placed treasures within such as

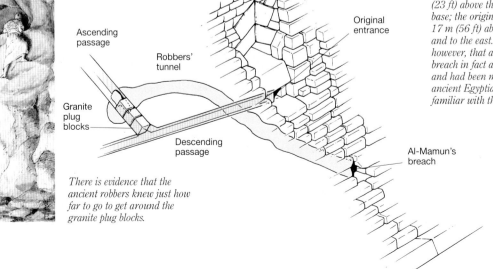

Ascending passage

Robbers' tunnel

Granite plug blocks

Descending passage

Original entrance

Al-Mamun's breach

There is evidence that the ancient robbers knew just how far to go to get around the granite plug blocks.

'Al-Mamun's breach' is 7 m (23 ft) above the pyramid's base; the original entrance is 17 m (56 ft) above the base and to the east. It is possible, however, that al-Mamun's breach in fact already existed and had been made by the ancient Egyptians, who were familiar with the interior.

iron weapons that did not rust and glass that bent without breaking. Maqrizi also says that, according to the Copts, Surid was buried in the pyramid surrounded by all his possessions. If Surid is a memory of Khufu, this may not be so far from the truth.

The breach of al-Mamun

Legends of treasures hidden within Khufu's pyramid persisted. They found their way into the tale of *The Thousand and One Nights*, along with a story that Caliph al-Mamun, son of Haroun al-Rashid, was the first to break into it, around AD 820. With great effort, he forced a passage with iron picks and crowbars, and by pouring cold vinegar on to fire-heated stones. There is indeed a breach – now the tourist entrance – below and to one side of the original entrance. But just when the pyramid was violated remains a puzzle, though it is possible that it was in ancient times. It seems that whoever carried out the operation aimed straight for a point opposite the juncture of the descending and ascending passages before turning east to break through beyond the granite plugs. Saite Period (26th dynasty) priests perhaps made repairs, since at this time there was an attempt to restore Old Kingdom monuments. If the passage was forced in pharaonic times, however, it must have been gaping open in AD 820 – and presumably any repairs would have been detectable. Mamun's men may have enlarged the passage made by ancient robbers.

These confusions do not inspire confidence in the historicity of the story of al-Mamun. Accounts of wild events and fabulous discoveries inside the pyramid increase our doubts. A more sober, and perhaps more trustworthy, version is that of Abu Szalt of Spain. He tells of Mamun's men uncovering an ascending passage. At its end was a quadrangular chamber containing a sarcophagus. 'The lid was forced open, but nothing was discovered excepting some bones completely decayed by time.' But doubt is cast again by Denys of Telmahre, the Jacobite Patriarch of Antioch. He accompanied Mamun's party and states that the Great Pyramid was already opened at the time of their visit.

Quarrying the pyramids

The 12th-century scholar, Abd al-Latif, describes the pyramids as covered with indecipherable writing – probably the graffiti of visitors, some perhaps from pharaonic times. His observation implies that much of the casing at Giza was still intact when he visited. By that time, nevertheless, the pyramids were being systematically quarried for building stone. Abd al-Latif reports the destruction of a number of small pyramids by the Emir Karakoush during Saladin's reign (AD 1138–93). It must have been Karakoush who removed the satellite pyramid south of Khafre's pyramid, and who began dismantling Khufu's subsidiary pyramids. Other stones, probably from the two larger pyra-

Although it is not known when or by whom the Sphinx's nose was broken away, careful examination of the face shows clear evidence of how it was done. Someone hammered long rods or chisels into the nose, one down from the bridge and the other under the nostril. Once in place, the implements were used to pry the nose off to the right (south).

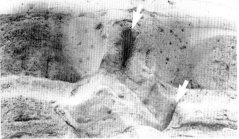

mids, were used for walls in the growing city of Cairo. The plunder of casing stone from the Great Pyramid continued during succeeding generations until the outer mantle was finally stripped bare.

Abd al-Latif also enthused about the Sphinx, already known by its modern Arabic name, *Abu Hol*, 'Father of Terror'. He described its handsome face, 'covered with a reddish tint, and a red varnish as bright as if freshly painted'. He specifically mentions the nose, which leads us to think that it was still intact, contrary to indications that it may have been missing as early as the 10th century. It is certain that someone removed it before the early 15th century when another Arab historian, al-Maqrizi, wrote about it. The nose was long gone, at any rate, by the time Napoleon visited Giza in 1798, although he is often blamed for its removal.

(Below) In AD 1196, Malek Abd al-Aziz Othman ben Yusuf, son of Saladin, mounted a concerted attack on the pyramid of Menkaure to dismantle it and remove its stone. Eight months' work merely damaged the pyramid's northern face. Such enormous – and unsuccessful – efforts increase our admiration for the skill of the ancient builders in creating such durable monuments.

The First European Discovery

(Above) For those who had never been to Egypt, imagination was the only means by which they could picture the Sphinx and pyramids. The renowned 17th-century Jesuit scholar and polymath Athanasius Kircher, for instance, drew the pyramids in 1674 with huge double-door entrances, no doubt since he saw the pyramid as a mausoleum. Kircher had read that the Sphinx was a large bust projecting from the sands, so he illustrated it as a classical bust, with the rounded breasts of the female Sphinx of the Oedipus legend.

(Above right) The pyramids depicted as granaries in a mosaic in St Mark's cathedral, Venice.

'And some men say that they be sepultures of great lords, that were sometime, but that is not true, for all the common rumour and speech is of all the people there, both far and near, that they be the garners of Joseph.'

Voiage and Travaile of Sir John Maundevile

Around the time that Abd al-Latif recorded his experiences, the Crusaders were returning to Europe with intriguing tales of what they had seen in the Near East. A trickle of pilgrims soon became a stream of travellers who wished to amaze and astound when writing their travel memoirs.

Telling tales

One of the domes of St Mark's in Venice has a 12th-century mosaic of the pyramids as Joseph's granaries, an idea first suggested by the 5th-century AD Latin writers Julius Honorius and Rufinus. This image was repeated by many early visitors, even though direct observation should have convinced them otherwise. Likewise, Mandeville's *Voiage* (quoted above), supposedly an informed guide, was concocted in the 14th century by a certain Jean d'Outremeuse, who had never made the journey.

The Renaissance saw renewed interest in the pagan past. It was known that behind the great-ness of Rome was that of Greece. With the travel reports came the realization that behind the great-ness of Greece lay that of the Near Eastern civiliza-tions, including Egypt. Travel became safer when Egypt came under Turkish rule in 1517 and Sultan Selim I confirmed protection for French traders and pilgrims. The invention of the printing press in the mid-15th century allowed the details and images of such travellers' voyages to the pyramids to be more widely disseminated.

Travellers eventually became 'antiquaries' who, in the 16th century, began to retrieve artifacts and ancient manuscripts for the growing number of European collectors and for libraries and muse-ums. A thriving trade in antiquities grew, which included mummies, the embalmed bodies of ancient Egyptians. These had already been a mar-keted commodity for 400 years; the 'mummy pits' of Saqqara were a major attraction.

Seeing and imagining

Those who could not visit Egypt themselves had to depend on their imaginations. A case in point is Athanasius Kircher (1602–80), considered by some 'the Father of Egyptology'. The drawings of the pyramids and Sphinx in his *Turris Babel*, pub-lished in 1674, reflect his ability to conceptualize rather than to depict accurately.

We also have to wonder about the illustrations of some of the 15th- and 16th-century voyagers who did make their way to Egypt. It is clear that many of these illustrations could not have been based on sketches made at the site. Having covered a great deal of ground and seen many things, these writers must have had to rely on memory when they recorded their travels, and their vision of the monu-ments would have been conditioned as much by what was familiar to them as by the exotic struc-tures they had all too briefly beheld. So when they drew the pyramids, they based their images on more familiar steeply angled classical monuments.

Kircher promoted the idea, still potent today, that the pyramids contain some mystic significance.

Europeans tended to represent the pyramids in ways that reflected their own attitudes and cultural values, rather than as they actually appeared. The angles of the sides were often inaccurate and impossibly steep.

While such fanciful notions about the pyramids were still current, some of the early visitors, such as George Sandys who visited the pyramids in 1610, accepted the idea that the pyramids were the tombs of kings.

Early travelogues also contain ambiguous hints about when the pyramids were stripped of their outer casing. In 1546, Pierre Belon observed that the third Giza pyramid was in perfect condition, as if it had just been built. But what about the attack of Othman in 1196, as reported by al-Latif (p. 41)?

Jean Chesneau mentioned that the other two pyramids at Giza were not 'made in degrees'. Did this mean that their inner, stepped cores were not exposed? Prosper Alpinus, one of the first Europeans to attempt an accurate measurement of the pyramids, wrote in 1591 that the viceroy of Egypt, Ibrahim Pasha, enlarged the entrance to the Great Pyramid 'so that a man could stand upright in it'. This must indicate a widening of the passage of al-Mamun. Those who entered next brought a new approach to the study of the pyramids.

This woodcut (above) is from Relation of a Journey Begun in 1610 and shows the poet and traveller George Sandys and his party visiting the Giza pyramids. Sandys agreed with the classical authors that the pyramids were not built by Hebrew slaves, nor were they the granaries of Joseph, but were in fact the tombs of Egyptian kings.

1556
Thevet

1579
Helferich

1647
de Monconys

1650
Boullaye-le-Gouz

1743
Pococke

1755
Norden

The Image of the Sphinx through the Centuries

It took Europeans some time to focus accurately on the image of the Sphinx. In André Thevet's *Cosmographie de Levant*, published in 1556, seven years after visiting Giza, the author related that the Sphinx was 'the head of a colossus, caused to be made by Isis, daughter of Inachus, then so beloved of Jupiter'. He pictures it as a very European curly-haired monster with a grassy dog collar. Johannes Helferich, another much-quoted visitor to Giza, tells in his travelogue of a secret passage by which the ancient priests could enter the Sphinx and pretend to be its voice. Helferich's Sphinx is a pinched-face, round-breasted woman with straight hair. The only edge his rendering has over Thevet's is that the hair suggests the flaring lappets of the headdress.

George Sandys stated flatly that the Egyptians represented the Sphinx as a harlot. Balthasar de Monconys interprets the headdress of the Sphinx as a kind of hairnet, while Boullaye-le-Gouz's Sphinx is

once again a European with rounded hairdo and bulky collar (perhaps the way travellers remembered the protruding and weathered layers of the neck). All these authors render the Sphinx with its nose complete, though it had been missing for centuries.

Richard Pococke's illustration in his *Travels* is closer to the Sphinx's actual appearance than anything previously published, except the illustration, 'Bau der Pyramide', by Cornelius de Bruyn. Indeed, it seems as if Pococke extracted his Sphinx bust from de Bruyn's drawing, down to the gentleman gesturing with his left arm under the Sphinx's headdress. Again, both drawings render the nose more or less complete. Frederick Norden's depiction is more accurate and includes the broken nose. The Sphinx of Casas, though painted slightly later, shows the nose once more complete. It was with artists of Napoleon's Expedition, such as Dutertre, that the Sphinx began to be faithfully rendered.

1799
Casas

1822
Dutertre

In the midst of the quirky illustrations and odd ideas of the 17th century came the first scientific reports about the Great Pyramid of Giza.

The scholars enter

John Greaves (1602–52), Professor of Astronomy at the University of Oxford, first reviewed the existing literature and then went to Egypt to study the pyramids for himself. He dismissed all the accounts of the Giza pyramids having been built by biblical figures or legendary kings. From the classical sources, he concluded that these monuments were erected by Cheops (Khufu), Chephren (Khafre) and Mycerinus (Menkaure), as tombs for the security of the body because of an ancient Egyptian conviction that this would ensure the endurance of the soul. Greaves set out to produce detailed measurements of Khufu's pyramid with the best available instruments and a rigorously scientific approach. He calculated that the Great Pyramid had a perpendicular height of 499 ft (152 m, it is in fact 146.5 m tall), a slope height of 693 ft (211 m) and a base of 480,249 sq. ft (44,615 sq. m). Greaves counted the steps (207 or 208) as he climbed the pyramid. He described climbing a mound of rubbish to the original entrance, in the 16th course of masonry, open since the pyramid had been stripped of its outer casing. Following the Descending Passage, he worked out its slope as 26 degrees. He marvelled at the Antechamber with its portcullis slab and the smooth granite walls of the King's Chamber, giving the dimensions and position of the sarcophagus. This early scholar even noted the basalt pavement east of the pyramid that hinted at the existence of the mortuary temple.

Another clue in the murky history of pyramid destruction was added when Greaves wrote that, while the stones of Khafre's pyramid were not as large or as regularly laid as in the Great Pyramid, the surface was smooth and even and free of inequalities or breaches, except on the south. Today casing remains only on the upper third of the second pyramid.

Benoît de Maillet was the French Consul-General in Egypt from 1692 until 1708, during which period he visited Khufu's pyramid over forty times. His plan and section of the superstructure are not as good as those of Greaves, but his drawing of the passages and chambers is more accurate. The lengths and proportions of the Ascending Passage and Grand Gallery are nearly correct, as are the different parts of the well shaft. The Descending Passage was still unknown beyond its juncture with the Ascending Passage.

Between 1639, when Greaves was at Giza, and 1692, the second pyramid must have been stripped to its present condition, because de Maillet mentions that the casing stones remained only at the top. He also called for a survey to produce an accurate map and documentation of all the ancient Egyptian sites – a plan to be executed a century later by the Napoleonic Expedition (p. 46).

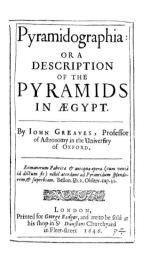

Pyramidographia:

OR A

DESCRIPTION
OF THE

PYRAMIDS
IN ÆGYPT.

By IOHN GREAVES, Professor of Astronomy in the University of OXFORD.

Romanorum Fabrica & antiqua opera (cum veniâ id dictum sit) nihil accedunt ad Pyramidum splendorem, & superbiam. Bellon. lib. 2. Observ. cap. 42.

LONDON,
Printed for *George Badger*, and are to be sold at his shop in S. *Dunstans* Churchyard in Fleet-street 1646.

Greaves's Pyramidographia *of 1646 included the first measured cross-section of the pyramid and its internal passages (left). The Ascending Passage is not in correct proportion and the Descending Passage ends abruptly at the pyramid base, for it had yet to be cleared to the Subterranean Chamber. He also gave the dimensions of all known passages and chambers. De Maillet's 1735 publication includes a cross-section with details more accurate than Greaves's (centre), although the proportions of his pyramid are too tall and steep.*

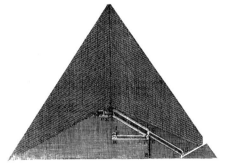

The full plan and precise dimensions of the interior of Khufu's pyramid were only revealed over time (seen here in Borchardt's profile of 1922). In 1765, Davison entered the lowest of the five stress-relieving chambers built directly over the King's Chamber. The four chambers above were then still to be discovered.

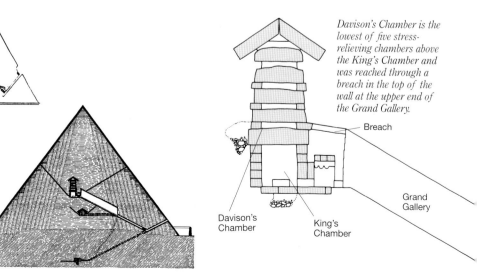

Davison's Chamber is the lowest of five stress-relieving chambers above the King's Chamber and was reached through a breach in the top of the wall at the upper end of the Grand Gallery.

Breach

Davison's Chamber

King's Chamber

Grand Gallery

Pococke's 'pyramids of Dahshur' (below) seem to reflect the Bent Pyramid of Sneferu and the mudbrick tower that remains of the pyramid of Amenemhet III, both at Dahshur.

Norden's drawing of 'The Sphinx and pyramids of Giza' from his Travels *published in 1755. Norden produced the first good map of the Giza pyramids, showing the ruins of the mortuary temples of Khafre and Menkaure, as well as the causeways of Khufu and Menkaure. Unlike most other illustrators of the time, Norden's profile and full-face drawings of the Sphinx show the break of the nose and weathered outlines that are essentially correct.*

From travellers to antiquaries

Throughout the 18th century travellers took up the call, and came to Egypt not only to describe what they saw but also to make accurate records. Travelogues evolved into geographical catalogues, and included the ancient sites and monuments. One antiquary was the Jesuit Claude Sicard, who travelled in Egypt between 1707 and 1726. He documented 20 of the major pyramids, 24 complete temples and over 50 decorated tombs.

Foremost among the 18th-century antiquaries are the Englishman Richard Pococke and the Dane Friderik Norden, both in Egypt in 1737. Pococke's map of Giza is extremely schematic and his profile of the Great Pyramid is borrowed from de Maillet. His report is curious in other ways and includes a description supposedly of Khufu's causeway. He describes it as being 20 ft (7 m) wide, 1,000 yds (914 m) long, built of stone, and reinforced by 61 circular buttresses, 14 ft (4.3 m) in diameter and spaced at 30 ft (9 m). This in no way fits the causeway foundation that runs to the east from the pyramid. The enigma clears, however, when we realize that Pococke was describing the arches in the floodplain north of Khufu's pyramid. Built under Saladin from blocks taken from the Giza pyramid, the arches ran westward and then south towards the pyramid plateau.

Pococke's idea that the pyramids were made by encasing natural mounds of rock calls to mind the assertion of another 18th-century traveller, the Scot James Bruce: 'anyone who will take the pains to remove the sand will find the solid rock there hewn into steps'. Bruce must have noticed that at the northeast corner of Khufu's and the northwest corner of Khafre's pyramids the bedrock is left in the cores of the pyramids, and fashioned into steps.

Norden's *Travels*, published in 1755, marks a great advance in documentation, no doubt owing to his profession as an artist and naval marine architect. Sent by King Christian VI of Denmark to explore Egypt, Norden travelled all the way to Derr in Nubia.

The English diplomat and traveller Nathaniel Davison (d. 1808) is credited with being the first to enter the lowest of five stress-relieving chambers above the King's Chamber in Khufu's pyramid. The German orientalist Karsten Niebuhr had searched for it in vain, apparently after hearing about it from a French merchant named Meynard. Since Niebuhr describes the chamber as being directly above the King's Chamber, albeit of a lower height, it seems that someone must have entered before Davison. Davison was accompanied by Meynard when he entered the pyramid on 8 July 1765, although Davison alone crawled through dirt and bat dung to enter the chamber that would henceforth carry his name. Its floor consisted of the same nine granite blocks that roofed the King's Chamber below, although in Davison's Chamber the surfaces were unfinished. The chamber was roofed by eight large granite beams smoothed on the undersides.

When Davison entered the pyramid, recent rains had washed away some of the sand and debris choking the Descending Passage. He saw that the passage sloped away into the bedrock beneath the pyramid, and followed it into the darkness for 130 ft (39.6 m), where he encountered debris that sealed it off. Davison also investigated the well shaft. He descended from the bottom of the Grand Gallery to a depth of 155 ft (47.2 m) where the well, too, was closed off with rubble. It was to take more than 50 years to discover a link between the two choked passages (p. 48).

Napoleon's Wise Men

French enlightenment, of an ancient seat of knowledge. The military campaign would ultimately fail, but the reconnaissance of an ancient civilization stands as the real achievement of the expedition.

Bringing Egypt to Europe

Napoleon ordered leading French scholars to assemble a team of savants and surveyors for the survey of all Egypt that de Maillet had proposed, and which Norden began. Over 150 non-military personnel were assembled as the Commission on Arts and Sciences. One could not have hoped for a better team to document the sites and monuments of ancient Egypt – just before the major onslaught of plunder and destruction that would begin on the heels of the Expedition. There were surveyors, civil and mining engineers; mathematicians, chemists, botanists and astronomers; archaeologists, architects, artists and printers. There were also students from the military engineering school and recent graduates of the civil engineering school. Most only learned of their final intended destination after the fleet had passed Malta.

Opposing Bonaparte, after he marched across the desert to seize Cairo, were the ruling Mamelukes, descended from Georgian and Armenian slaves who were trained as a military elite. Five hundred years earlier they had taken Egypt for themselves, heavily taxing the native Egyptians with whom they had little affinity. When Napoleon met the Mameluke army at Imbaba, west of Cairo, he is reputed to have pointed to the distant pyramids of Giza, proclaiming, 'Soldiers, forty centuries look down upon you from these pyramids'.

The Mamelukes were easily defeated in this 'Battle of the Pyramids', and scattered into Upper Egypt, where Napoleon's General Desaix pursued them for ten months. The French took over Cairo, but shortly thereafter, in early August, the English destroyed their fleet in Abukir Bay. The stranded expedition gave birth to the Institut d'Égypte, composed of the savants of the Commission on Arts and Sciences and military and administrative officials. Over the three years that the French remained in Egypt, commission members spread throughout Egypt, collecting artifacts and specimens, mapping the entire country, documenting archaeological sites, and recording individual monuments, irrigation systems, and the flora, fauna and culture of contemporary Egypt.

Depicted by the draughtsmen of the Napoleonic expedition, the pyramid of Meidum seemingly rises from the mound of rubble that surrounds it. This rubble includes the remains of the casing, possibly destroyed as long ago as the New Kingdom.

A panoramic and picturesque view of the pyramid field of Saqqara, from the Description de l'Égypte.

'On approaching these colossal monuments, their angular and inclined form diminishes the appearance of their height and deceives the eye…but as soon as he begins to measure by a known scale these gigantic productions of art, they recover all their immensity…'

Vivant Denon, *Travels in Upper and Lower Egypt*

A major threshold in the study of ancient Egypt was crossed with the great expedition led by Napoleon Bonaparte to Egypt in 1798. France's revolutionary government wanted to strike a blow at their foremost enemy, England. Rather than attempt a full-scale invasion across the channel, however, Napoleon decided to take control of Egypt, dredge the canal linking the Red Sea and the Mediterranean, and thereby short-circuit England's trade with India. Napoleon had in mind the precedents of Alexander's and Caesar's Egyptian enterprises. This was not to be just a military and political conquest, however, but a revival, through

The French scholars had to forfeit much of their material, including the famed Rosetta Stone, during the complications of the commission's departure from Egypt along with the French retreat in 1801. They managed to keep hold of a good deal of their material and carry it to France, however, by threatening to throw it in the sea or burn it rather than turn it over to the British.

The fruits of labour

Back in Paris, the material was gathered together in the series of volumes named the *Description de l'Égypte*, itself a veritable monument. The principal books covered antiquities, modern Egypt, natural history and a topographical map. Those on antiquities appeared between 1809 and 1818 (the final volume of antiquities plates in 1822). The complete *Description* required 837 copper engravings for 3,000 illustrations. An engraving machine was developed by Nicolas Jacques Conté which resulted in reproductions of an exceptionally high standard. It was estimated that the machine could complete in three days work that would have taken an artist six months by hand – no small consideration with a work of this magnitude.

The *Description* was a window for Europe into 3,000 years of ancient Egyptian civilization. Nevertheless, it was hardly something that every family could afford – a complete custom-designed cabinet was required to hold the entire set. Instead, a reduced popular account of the Expedition and the monuments of Egypt was out by 1802. Entitled *Voyage dans la Basse et la Haute Égypte*, it was the work of Vivant Denon.

Napoleon's men at the pyramids

The artists of the commission created precise views of many of the pyramids. Colonel Coutelle and the architect J.M. Lepère undertook a detailed study of the interior of Khufu's pyramid while the surveyor E.F Jomard and engineer and artist Cécile re-measured the superstructure, including the height of each course of stones. The views of the Sphinx and pyramids they produced are impressionistic but accurate. The next step in scientific graphic imaging – large true-to-scale contoured maps of the Giza Plateau and Sphinx – was only achieved in the late 1970s. In 1801, Coutelle and Lepère began to dismantle Pyramid GIII-c, the westernmost queen's pyramid of Menkaure, in the hope of finding an undisturbed burial. They abandoned their efforts after removing the upper north quarter of the pyramid.

It is ironic that with the massive French effort at accurate documentation began the era of plunder and destructive, non-systematic excavation that was a hallmark of Egyptian archaeology and pyramid exploration in the 19th century.

Louis François Lejeune's 1806 painting of The Battle of the Pyramids. *In this decisive encounter of 21 July 1798, French troops under the command of Napoleon, defeated the Mameluke rulers of Egypt and drove them from their Cairo power base. The three Giza Pyramids can be seen in the background; Napoleon himself is on horseback at the far right of the picture.*

'Soldiers, forty centuries look down upon you from these pyramids'. The message on this bronze medal.

Belzoni and Caviglia

Belzoni's main contribution to pyramid studies was his opening of the unknown upper entrance of Khafre's pyramid (below) at Giza in 1818. When he reached the burial chamber, he found an Arabic inscription: 'the master Mohammed Ahmed, quarryman, has opened them, and the Master Othman attended this opening, and the King Alij Mohammed'. This suggests that the pyramid may have been entered six to eight centuries earlier. Bones found in the sarcophagus later proved to be those of a bull.

'I reached the door at the centre of a large chamber. I walked slowly two or three paces, and then stood still to contemplate the place where I was. Whatever it might be, I certainly considered myself in the centre of that pyramid, which from time immemorial had been the subject of the obscure conjectures of many hundred travellers, both ancient and modern.'

Giovanni Belzoni, *Narrative*

Even after the departure of Napoleon's fleet, Egypt remained a battleground for Anglo-French rivalry. But the 'campaign' now took the form of a bitter competition to see who could obtain the best antiquities. French efforts were led by Bernardino Drovetti (1776–1852), an Italian-born diplomat who had fought with Napoleon's forces. He was French Consul-General in Egypt from 1802 to 1814, regaining the post in 1820. In 1816 Henry Salt was appointed Consul-General representing British interests. He had been trained as an artist and travelled extensively in the East and Egypt. Both men financed excavations and amassed collections, which they then sold, obtaining funds for further work in Egypt. Drovetti's treasures include the collection that forms the foundation of the Egyptian Museum in Turin. One of Salt's best-known finds is the colossal head of Ramesses II, now in the British Museum. The rivalry between Drovetti and Salt found fertile ground at Giza, the setting also for some of Egyptology's most remarkable characters.

The sailor and the strongman

In the late 18th century Italy produced two unlikely heroes of Egyptology. They shared first names and a passion for the antiquities of the Nile; and both were also possessed of adventurous, fearless spirits. Giovanni Battista Caviglia (1770–1845), born in Genoa, spent his early life sailing a merchant ship around the Mediterranean. But this uneducated, temperamental seaman's real vocation turned out to be Egyptology. Caviglia was employed by several European collectors to find objects. His own obsessive interest in religion led to a conviction that chambers within the Great Pyramid held mystic secrets. From 1816 to 1819 he therefore explored the pyramids and tombs of Giza and he was the first to carry out major excavation on the Giza Plateau.

Caviglia explored Davison's Chamber in the Great Pyramid (p. 45) hoping to find a secret room, but found instead solid rock. In 1817, he descended into the vertical shaft known as the 'well'. Breathing difficulties halted him, in spite of attempts to clear the air by burning sulphur. Caviglia then decided to work down through the Descending Passage. After clearance allowed him to pass about 60 m (200 ft), he smelled sulphur and realized he had found an opening to the 'well'. Thus Caviglia was able to demonstrate that the well was probably a shaft linked to the Descending Passage for the

(Below right) A lithograph of a drawing by M. Gauci shows Belzoni in Turkish dress, and appeared as the frontispiece to his Narrative. *This important book appeared in December 1820 and was the record of Belzoni's work at the pyramids, temples, tombs, other excavations in Egypt and Nubia, and elsewhere. The book appeared in two volumes, one a quarto and the other a folio with 44 colour plates.*

G. BELZONI.

ancient workmen to escape after the Ascending Passage had been sealed. Caviglia also found the unfinished Subterranean Chamber.

Henry Salt later paid Caviglia to excavate the Sphinx. In the course of this work, the Italian found a small open-air chapel between the monument's forepaws, with the famous Stela of Thutmose IV. Caviglia also found fragments of the beard of the Sphinx; one piece is now in the British Museum.

The promising career of this dedicated, hard-working amateur ended after a brief collaboration with Colonel Howard Vyse who came to Egypt in 1835 (p. 50). Vyse had employed Caviglia to assist him in his explorations of the pyramids and was vexed when the Italian spent all his time looking for 'mummy pits' instead. In 1837, Caviglia settled in Paris where he became a protégé of Lord Elgin.

The second Italian was Giovanni Battista Belzoni (1778–1823), born in Padua. Half-facts abound about the life and exploits of this ambitious and eccentric man. Some say he planned to become a monk, and it seems that he studied hydraulics. In any event he spent several years travelling, eventually becoming a circus strongman in London – a calling eminently suited to the great strength of this giant of a man, 2 m (6 ft 6 in) tall. Belzoni's restless nature soon saw him on his travels again, this time accompanied by his Irish wife, Sarah. In 1814, a contact in Malta directed him to the Egyptian court of Mohammed Ali, in an ill-starred attempt to capitalize on his knowledge of hydraulics. Fate brought him into the circle of Europeans interested in antiquities. In 1816 Belzoni began collecting objects for Salt. The consul suggested that he work with Caviglia, but collaboration with a rival did not appeal – in fact, he even took offence when Caviglia's clearance of the Sphinx was mistakenly credited to him in an 1818 British publication.

Belzoni and Giza

After his arrival in Egypt, Belzoni went to Giza and explored the Great Pyramid – at one point having to be extricated from a passage in which he became wedged. He also visited the pyramids of Saqqara and Dahshur, but his greatest contribution to the study of the Giza pyramids was opening the previously unknown upper entrance of Khafre's pyramid. Meticulous observation led him, after one false start, to the true entrance. Belzoni was anxious to enter before Drovetti, who was rumoured to be about to blast the pyramid open using dynamite. He hired local villagers to clear the rubble blocking the opening. He then made his way through the upper passage to the horizontal passage, where with great effort he raised a portcullis slab, and finally, after almost a month, he reached the burial chamber itself. Any hopes of finding an intact burial chamber were soon dashed by the sight of the half-open sarcophagus. Its fine granite lid lay in two pieces. An Arabic inscription on the wall revealed that the chamber had already been entered, probably in the 13th century.

While exploring Khafre's monument, Belzoni had a team working at the third Giza pyramid. But a disagreement with Salt put an end to this work. Although Belzoni's instincts were leading him in the direction of the entrance, it was Howard Vyse who would use gunpowder to blast his way into Menkaure's pyramid 19 years later.

The first major excavation on the Giza Plateau was by Caviglia, whose commission allowed him to roam the monuments at will with his excavation workers. In his major exterior project, he cleared the front of the Great Sphinx, and found an open-air chapel between the forepaws, where rulers from New Kingdom to Roman times worshipped the colossal bedrock statue. The altar at the outer gateway of the chapel still had the ashes of the last sacrificial fire burned to the Sphinx, probably in late Roman times.

Digging by Dynamite

When the cavity created in the back of the Sphinx by Vyse's gunpowder was cleared in 1978 under the direction of Zahi Hawass, it was found to contain not only Vyse's drill hole but also a large chunk of the Sphinx's headdress with its relief-carved pleating.

All in a Day's Work...

24 February 1837

Reis, 7.   Men, 99.   Children, 66.

Great Pyramid.
    Excavation on southern front.
    King's Chamber.
    Davison's Chamber.
    Northern Air-channel.

Second Pyramid.
    Lower Entrance.
    Excavation for base at north-western angle.
    Quarries.

Third Pyramid.
    Interior.
    Excavation for base at north-eastern angle.

Bridge in the southern dyke.

Sphinx.   Boring.

One day's work from Howard Vyse's *Operations Carried on at the Pyramids of Gizeh in 1837*. Vyse (*left*) records that on this day the clearing of the Northern Air-channel proved impossible and that the boring of the Sphinx had reached a depth so far of 9 ft 8 in (2.95 m). He notes that the Maltese, Turks and Arabs were afraid to go out at night – unlike his English assistant who spent every night for five months in Menkaure's pyramid.

'Towards the end of this work gunpowder was used with great effect…'

R. Howard Vyse and J. Perring, *Operations…*

Richard William Howard Vyse (1784–1853) was an English army officer who first visited Egypt in 1835. Like many of his time, his interest in the pyramids stemmed from strongly held religious beliefs. He met Caviglia in Alexandria in 1836 and began excavating with him at Giza the same year. Vyse soon found the Genoese mariner unproductive, however, and in 1837, the year Vyse was promoted to Colonel, he began a collaboration with the engineer John Shae Perring (1813–69) with the aim of exploring and documenting the pyramids. Together they established a camp in the tombs of the eastern cliff at Giza. Work went on night and day, with shifts of workers on several sites at once. Confident in Perring's ability and trustworthiness, Vyse returned to England later in 1837, leaving his new assistant to carry on the work with his financial backing. Perring drew maps, plans and profiles of many of the pyramids – from Abu Roash to Giza, Abusir, Saqqara and Dahshur – that he published in three folio volumes, *The Pyramids of Gizeh*. Vyse reproduced Perring's drawings at a smaller scale in his own three-part *Operations Carried on at the Pyramids of Gizeh in 1837*.

Another contributor to Vyse's publication was the Sinologist and Egyptologist Samuel Birch of the British Museum. Vyse investigated the pyramids a mere 15 years after the brilliant decipherment of Egyptian hieroglyphs by Jean François Champollion, but Birch was able to supply notes to the text and give a rough translation of the inscriptions that the team was finding in and on the mastaba tombs that surround the Giza pyramids. Birch's crude transcriptions of the glyphic words include their Coptic equivalents. Written largely with the Greek alphabet, Coptic had been readable long before Egyptian hieroglyphs; indeed an understanding of Coptic was invaluable in Champollion's decipherment of hieroglyphs.

Excavation by force

At Giza, Vyse cleared the lower entrance of the pyramid of Khafre by blasting apart the granite plugs that blocked it. Belzoni had entered the pyramid from the upper entrance and suspected the existence of the lower entrance when he saw the descending passage, closed with debris, from inside the pyramid.

Although Perring and Vyse carried out valuable documentation of the pyramids, Vyse, despite his evident admiration for the monuments, had no qualms about dismantling parts of the pyramids, using boring rods in the search for hidden chambers or blasting his way through obstacles with dynamite. Opposite his view of Menkaure's queens' pyramids, Vyse wrote of the middle pyramid (GIII-b) that it 'was prepared for boring by removing the stones from the top of it, as I expected to find the sepulchral chamber by penetrating through it.' Vyse ploughed straight through the centre of the superstructure without finding an addition to the passage to the subterranean burial chamber, which contained a granite sarcophagus holding a young female skeleton. Written in red on the roof of the burial chamber is the name of Menkaure, confirming the ancient sources that the third Giza pyramid was the tomb of that king.

Wondering if a chamber existed in the body of the Sphinx, Vyse ordered his men to drill straight down from the top of the back. When his boring rods became stuck at a depth of 8.2 m (27 ft), Vyse ordered the use of gunpowder to free the rod, but,

he said, rather contradictorily, 'being unwilling to disfigure this venerable monument, the excavation was given up and several feet of boring rods were left in it.'

The pyramid of Menkaure

Vyse also burrowed straight into the core of the pyramid of Menkaure, beginning from the chasm that Saladin's son had made in AD 1196. Just off the central axis of the pyramid Vyse turned his tunnel downwards and forced it to the base of the pyramid, requiring his workers to come up out of the pyramid every time a new blast took place. But he found no new passages or chambers in the superstructure. Eventually Vyse located the entrance, instructed his men to clear it and, having paid

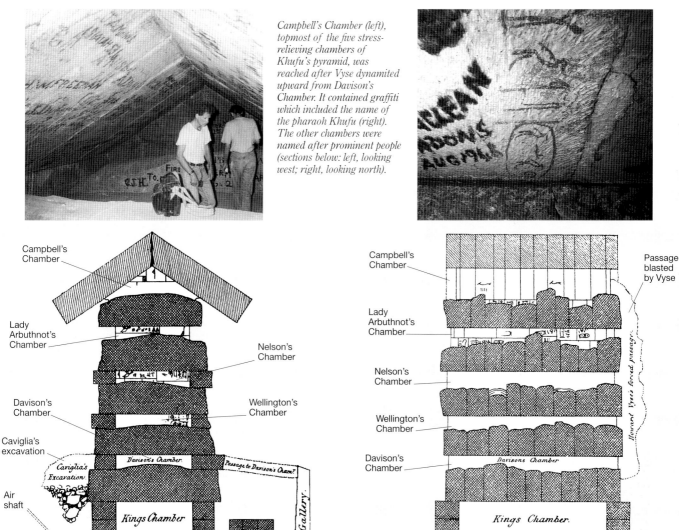

Campbell's Chamber (left), topmost of the five stress-relieving chambers of Khufu's pyramid, was reached after Vyse dynamited upward from Davison's Chamber. It contained graffiti which included the name of the pharaoh Khufu (right). The other chambers were named after prominent people (sections below: left, looking west; right, looking north).

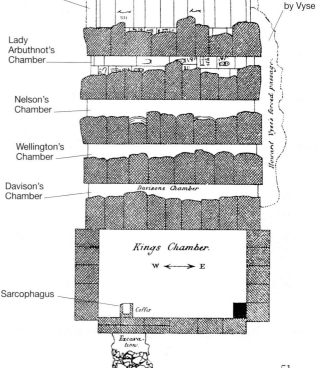

Menkaure's pyramid, with its three queens' pyramids in the foreground. The middle pyramid (GIII-b) was built of limestone, but like the westernmost of the three pyramids it appears not to have been cased.

Perring's detailed plan and profile of the middle queen's pyramid. Vyse removed stones from the top of the middle pyramid and forced his way down through the centre of it without reaching the burial chamber as he expected. The fact that Perring so accurately mapped his intrusion through the 4,600- year-old monument indicates that Vyse saw no harm in what he called 'excavations in the pyramids'. We should at least acknowledge that this may be the beginning of documenting archaeological excavation in Egypt.

them, made his way into the interior and the burial chamber with the artist Edward Andrews who prepared many of the plans and sections illustrating the works of Vyse and Perring. As with Belzoni in Khafre's pyramid, the Arabic graffiti on the walls immediately declared that they had been preceded. In the granite-lined burial chamber they found the original stone sarcophagus but the lid was missing and the sarcophagus lay empty. Pieces of the lid were found in the bedrock-hewn 'Upper Apartment' above the burial chamber, from which Perring and Vyse were able to reconstruct it. With great difficulty Vyse's men removed the sarcophagus for transport to England, but it sank to the bottom of the Mediterranean during a storm, along with the ship transporting it, the *Beatrice*.

With the fragments of the sarcophagus lid, the excavators also found human bones, linen wrappings, and parts of a wooden coffin. An inscription on the front of the coffin identifies its occupant as the 'Osiris [deceased] Menkaure, given life for ever, born of the sky, the sky goddess Nut above you....' Curiously, the style of the coffin shows that it is of Saite (26th-dynasty) date, and radiocarbon analysis of the bones points to the Christian period. Both coffin and bones are now in the British Museum.

This apparent 'burial' of Menkaure some 2,000 years after he lived and died must, in fact, be a reburial and may relate to an inscription on the granite casing just below the entrance to the pyramid. Diodorus Siculus had noted this inscription but it was only found in 1968 when debris was cleared from the pyramid's base. It gives the year (unfortunately damaged), month and day that Menkaure was buried in the pyramid, and states that the king was given a rich burial. One theory is that the inscription may date to the time of Khaemwaset, son of Ramesses II, who carried out a lot of restoration work at Giza. These mysterious facts, like the bones of a bull found in the sarcophagus of Khafre, hint that the history of the pyramids is not always as straightforward as Egyptologists may think.

The pyramid of Khufu

Vyse initially directed his dynamite operations at the pyramid of Khufu to its south side, where he thought he might blast open a second entrance at about the same level as the northern entrance. He

52

Perring's cross-section of Menkaure's pyramid (left) is a meticulous record of his excavation of the site. He found the true entrance and reached the vaulted burial chamber. Within its red granite walls was the royal sarcophagus, made of basalt and in typical Old Kingdom palace façade style. When clearing the chamber before the burial chamber (below), he discovered human remains and a fragment of coffin lid, with Menkaure's name, but in a style not in use until many centuries after his death.

gave up only after creating a large hole in the core masonry. Excavating down to the bedrock, Vyse did, however, uncover some of the original polished casing blocks of the pyramid, together with a pavement that extended out from the base.

Vyse's gunpowder-blasting archaeology did make one highly notable discovery in the Great Pyramid. Caviglia had begun to dynamite his way along the south side of the stress-relieving chamber that Davison found in 1765, hoping to find a communication with the southern air channel that would lead him to a secret room. After falling out with Caviglia, Vyse came to suspect that there was another chamber directly above Davison's since he could thrust a yard-long reed through a crack and up into a cavity at its northeastern corner. He therefore directed his dynamiting straight upward, whereupon he found, over three and a half months, the four additional stress-relieving chambers, all roofed, floored and walled with granite except for the topmost, which was gabled with limestone blocks so that the weight of the pyramid did not press down on the chambers below. Vyse named these chambers after important friends and colleagues: the Duke of Wellington, under whom he had served; Admiral Nelson, hero of Trafalgar; Lady Ann Arbuthnot, wife of Lieutenant-General Sir Robert Arbuthnot, who visited the pyramid just after the discovery of the chamber on 9 May 1837; and Colonel Campbell, the British Consul in Cairo.

Just as significant as the amazing architecture of the Relieving Chambers was Vyse's discovery of numerous graffiti in red paint dating from the time the pyramid was being constructed. Along with levelling lines, axis markers and directional notations were the names of the workgangs compounded with one form of Khufu's name, such as 'Khnum-Khuf' ('the creator god Khnum protects

him'). One of the gangs might have been called something like, 'how powerful is the great White Crown of Khnum-Khuf!' In spite of the extreme difficulty of getting up into the Relieving Chambers, a fair number of visitors have followed Vyse since the 1837 opening. They have, unfortunately, freely added their graffiti to that left by the workgangs 4,600 years ago.

The single instance of the king's name as simply 'Khufu', again as part of a workgang name, is found on the south ceiling towards the west end of the topmost chamber (Campbell's Chamber). Since nobody had entered this from the time Khufu's workmen sealed it until Vyse blasted his way in, the gang names clinch the attribution of this pyramid to the 4th-dynasty pharaoh, Khufu. Workers' graffiti in red paint have since been found in other Old Kingdom pyramids, temples and mastabas.

Lepsius and Mariette

Karl Richard Lepsius (above) recorded and documented many of Egypt's pyramids in his massive work, the Denkmäler. *Most of the plates were based on the drawings of Ernst Weidenbach, such as the one of Meidum shown above. Lepsius's map of the pyramid field of Saqqara (detail right) was a model of detail.*

'From the Labyrinth these lines come to you…We have also made excavations on the north side of the pyramid, because we may expect to discover the entrance there; that is, however, not yet done.'

Karl Richard Lepsius, *Discoveries in Egypt*

Fortunately, disciplined scholarship and the recognition of the importance of preserving and recording the legacy of ancient Egypt gradually took precedence over the more brutal excavation methods of the early 19th century.

Karl Richard Lepsius (1810–84) was a formidable scholar and is widely held to be the greatest Egyptologist after Champollion. Having first studied classical archaeology in Germany, he went on to study Egyptology in Paris. In the 1830s he published several papers on hieroglyphs, including a famous letter to Professor Ippolito Rosellini at the University of Pisa that transformed the study of the subject. Lepsius's contributions to Egyptology are numerous, but undoubtedly his greatest is the 12-volume *Denkmäler*, the massive work on the monuments of Egypt, containing 894 folio plates and published after his death. Five volumes of text were prepared from his notes and appeared between 1897 and 1913.

The expedition of Lepsius

Lepsius's massive work was the result of a survey of Egypt and Nubia ordered by King Frederick William IV of Prussia. As leader he appointed Lepsius, then lecturer in philology and comparative languages at Berlin. In preparation, Lepsius spent four years touring the collections of Europe, recording details of artifacts and copying inscriptions; he not only studied the Egyptian language, but also the practical skills of lithography and copperplate engraving. In 1842, Lepsius and his team set out for Egypt. Their three highly productive years were characterized by careful, methodical

analysis, meticulous recording of detail and outstanding finds. As well as the *Denkmäler*, Lepsius also published a personal account, *Discoveries in Egypt*. The 15,000 casts and antiquities Lepsius brought back form the core of the Berlin Museum collection.

Among the many pyramids Lepsius investigated was the Step Pyramid at Saqqara. He removed from the southeast part of the substructure a door lintel and frame inscribed with the name of the king, together with some of the blue faience tiles from the wall. In 1843, the team excavated at Hawara in the Fayum, at the so-called Labyrinth. The site had been described by Herodotus and Strabo; the former regarded it as a wonder of the world even greater than the Giza pyramids. This vast complex was, in fact, the mortuary temple of the 12th-dynasty ruler Amenemhet III – the largest of all mortuary temples – which lay adjacent to his pyramid. Much of the structure of the Labyrinth had been destroyed over the centuries as it was quarried for its lime. Lepsius also began excavations on the north face of the pyramid but failed to find an entrance.

While studying the pyramids, Lepsius formulated his 'accretion theory', which held that the size of a pyramid was dictated by the length of reign of its builder. Others have since questioned this and the theory is now discredited. Subsequent research has shown that some pyramids, such as those of Djoser and Sneferu at Meidum, were indeed enlarged over the course of successive building stages. It seems the sizes of most were predetermined, and a large pyramid like Khufu's may signify that it was begun by a king in the prime of youth, as opposed to one

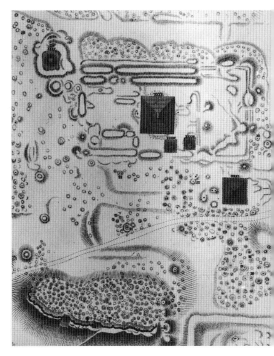

who came to the throne in his later years, and who possessed the confidence, and longevity, to take such a colossal enterprise to its summit.

The birth of the Antiquities Service

Auguste Mariette (1821–81) was a bright young man with varied interests and an inquiring mind. In 1842, he read the papers of one of his relations, Nestor l'Hôte, who had been a draughtsman on the Egyptian expedition of Champollion and Ippolito Rosellini. Mariette's fate was sealed. He studied ancient Egyptian language, art and history, and Coptic; he wrote articles and papers and finally secured a post with the Louvre. In 1850, that institution sent him to Egypt to buy Coptic manuscripts, but he began excavating instead. At Saqqara he found and excavated the Serapeum where the sacred Apis bulls had been buried in a great catacomb.

Then, in 1858, Ferdinand de Lesseps, in charge of the Suez Canal project, pressured the ruler Said Pasha to place Mariette in charge of all Egyptian antiquities. This he did, naming Mariette *mamûr* of a new national Antiquities Service, a position that would be held by a Frenchman until 1952. With the founding of the Egyptian Museum at Boulaq (later moved to Giza, and finally to Qasr el-Nil), to gather and display ancient works of art, the 'reign of Mariette' began. For the next two decades he carried out field archaeology at 35 sites throughout the country. His work practices and methods were criticized by some of the next generation of Egyptologists, but they were advanced for his time and his output has never been equalled.

Also at Saqqara Mariette dug huge trenches, revealing tombs of all periods in what had been a national cemetery of pharaonic Egypt (pp. 62–3), including many dating to the pyramid age. Unfortunately, however, he never produced a proper map of the tombs, and many were covered by the shifting sands and lost again.

Mariette's second major discovery, after the Serapeum, was Khafre's valley temple which was visible above the debris of the ages only as a series of pits and stones. He partially excavated the interior of the valley temple in 1853 and completed its clearance in 1858 by removing a shallow layer of sand that still covered the floor. In the course of this work Mariette blew apart some collapsed structural elements and other major pieces to remove them from the temple. Frustratingly, he published almost nothing about what he found inside the temple. However, one of the finest masterpieces of ancient Egyptian art was found by Mariette in the valley temple – the diorite statue of Khafre himself.

During 1880, the last year of Mariette's life, the foreman of the Antiquities Service, Mohammed Chahin, opened the pyramid of Pepi I at Saqqara. This was the first in which Pyramid Texts were

The Step Pyramid at Saqqara from Lepsius's Denkmäler. *The artist of this particular plate was J. Frey.*

found, which were rapidly copied by Emile Brugsch and, unofficially, by Flinders Petrie. The pyramid of Merenre was entered just before Mariette's death, and more were penetrated by his successor, Gaston Maspero. As Maspero explained:

'The discovery of the Pyramids of Pepi I and of Merenre at the place where the theory affirmed that they would be found, decided me to direct the attack on the entire front of the Memphite Necropolis, from Abu Roash to Lisht. Rapid success followed. Unas was opened on the 28th February, Pepi II, Neferirkera [Neferirkare] on April 13th, and that of Teti on the 29th May. In less than a year, five of the so-called "dumb" pyramids of Saqqara had spoken…'

This rare photograph (below) was taken before Mariette finished clearing the valley temple. It shows a granite beam fallen between the pillars. This and other pieces in the temple were blown apart to remove them.

Petrie at the Pyramids

This photograph taken in 1880 shows Petrie outside the rock tomb in which he lived during the two winter seasons of his pyramid survey. These quarters were three small tombs broken into one room. Petrie managed a comfortable co-existence with the dogs who inhabited the area, controlled the rats and mice with traps, and coped with the heat and the tourists by working in his underwear: 'if pink, they kept the tourist at bay, as the creature seemed to him too queer for inspection.'

William Matthew Flinders Petrie (1853–1942), the 'Father of Egyptian archaeology', was a bright child. When not yet six, he learned the hieroglyphic alphabet and, encouraged by his father, he later combined interests in mathematics and measurement with archaeology. Between 1875 and 1880 he surveyed a number of British sites, including Stonehenge. Then, in 1866, Petrie read Charles Piazzi Smyth's *Our Inheritance in the Great Pyramid* and became excited by the possibility of reconciling science with religion. Although he did not believe in Smyth's extreme religious notions and the concept of Britain as a lost tribe of Israel, he fully adhered to the idea of the pyramid as a gigantic scale model of the Earth's circumference.

In 1880, having become convinced of the need for another survey of the Great Pyramid, young Petrie arrived in Egypt. Petrie's meticulous survey of the pyramid in fact proved the death knell for Piazzi

Smyth's so-called pyramid inch (see box). The theories of pyramidologists like Piazzi Smyth rested on measurements that claimed to be accurate to a matter of fractions of inches. But all this was argued at a time when massive mounds of debris still covered the base of the pyramid.

With the debris banked against the sides of the Great Pyramid, Petrie measured its exterior through an elaborate set of triangulations that encompassed all three Giza pyramids. He resolved the positions of the corners and the lengths of the sides trigonometrically. By this method he also established the positions of many other points, including on the pyramids of Khafre and Menkaure. Unfortunately, Petrie's triangulated map was never published on a scale larger than the page of a paperback.

Some continued to believe in Piazzi Smyth, regardless of Petrie's measurements. Earlier this century, the structural engineer David Davidson actually used Petrie's figures in creative ways to 'prove' the theories of Piazzi Smyth, and even far more ambitious claims.

Petrie after Giza

During 1888 and 1889, Petrie followed up Lepsius's work of 1843 by investigating the site of Hawara. He excavated what remained of Labyrinth and the adjacent pyramid of Amenemhet III, where he

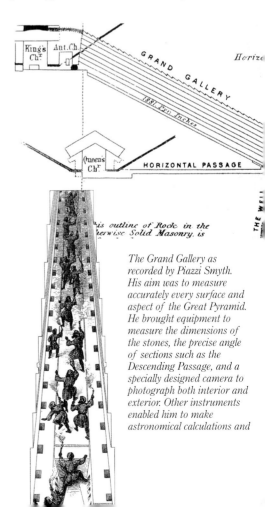

The Grand Gallery as recorded by Piazzi Smyth. His aim was to measure accurately every surface and aspect of the Great Pyramid. He brought equipment to measure the dimensions of the stones, the precise angle of sections such as the Descending Passage, and a specially designed camera to photograph both interior and exterior. Other instruments enabled him to make astronomical calculations and

entered the flooded burial chamber and found two sarcophagi and burnt human remains.

Petrie excavated the pyramid of Senwosret II at Illahun in 1887–8, but failed to find the entrance and passage to the burial chamber, with its red granite sarcophagus, until the following year. In one of the shaft tombs just outside the pyramid, he, together with Guy Brunton, found the exquisite jewellery of Princess Sit-Hathor-Iunet, now in the Cairo Museum and New York's Metropolitan Museum of Art. He also searched unsuccessfully for a passage or chamber underneath the subsidiary 'Queen's Pyramid' of Senwosret II, even though he carved out two criss-crossing tunnel systems, and a deep vertical shaft, directly under the pyramid. It is strange that there are apparently no passages or chambers under this small pyramid considering that Petrie did find the remains of a chapel at its north side, where someone must have been worshipped.

Petrie continued his pyramid investigations at Meidum, where he uncovered the small limestone temple next to the pyramid of Sneferu, with its two uninscribed stelae. He also examined the two anonymous pyramids of Mazghuna, south of Dahshur. They date to the 13th dynasty and closely resemble a number of other pyramids of that period discovered at South Saqqara and Dahshur by Gustave Jéquier and Sami Farag respectively.

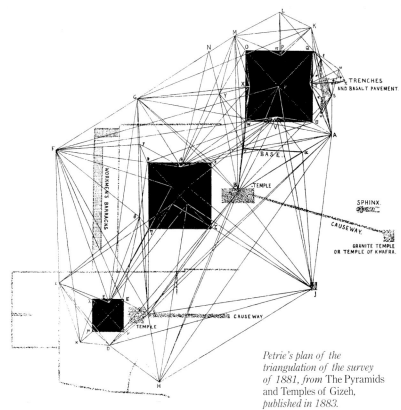

Petrie's plan of the triangulation of the survey of 1881, from The Pyramids and Temples of Gizeh, *published in 1883.*

Piazzi Smyth and the Pyramid Inch

determine the pyramid's latitude. He produced drawings of the pyramid, such as that shown above, using his 'pyramid inch'. In recognition of his work the Royal Society of Edinburgh awarded Piazzi Smyth a gold medal. He was not the only 'pyramidiot', however, as many others were also producing theories and drawings linking the pyramids with the stars or the Bible, among other things.

Charles Piazzi Smyth (1819–1900) was Astronomer Royal of Scotland and Professor of Astronomy at Edinburgh University. He surveyed Khufu's pyramid in 1865, armed with the theories of John Taylor, author of *The Great Pyramid: Why Was It Built? & Who Built It?*, published in 1859. Taylor, who based his ideas on the records of travellers, took a number of mathematical coincidences and declared that the Great Pyramid was built 'to make a record of the measure of the Earth' – similar assertions are still being made today by alternative pyramid theorists such as Robert Bauval and Graham Hancock. One of Taylor's claims was that the Egyptians knew the value of π and that they used an inch close to the British inch to form their cubit of 25 inches. Taylor presented a paper on the subject to the Royal Academy, but it was rejected.

Heavily influenced by Taylor, with whom he corresponded, and by his own religious views, Piazzi Smyth set out for Egypt – having been refused a grant to defray his expenses. He too had come to believe that the Great Pyramid of Khufu was built with just enough 'pyramid inches' to make it a scale model of the circumference of the Earth, and that its perimeter measurement corresponded exactly to the number of days in the solar year. These ideas were tied to his belief that the British inch was derived from an ancient 'pyramid inch', and that the cubit used to build both Noah's Ark and the tabernacle of

Moses was also based on this inch. Piazzi Smyth further believed that the British were descended from the lost tribe of Israel, and that the chambers and passages of the pyramid were a God-inspired record, a prophecy in stone of the great events in world history, made by scientifically advanced ancestors of the British. His theories are contained in *Our Inheritance in the Great Pyramid* (1864), and the three-volume *Life and Work at the Great Pyramid* (1867). In 1874 the Royal Society rejected his paper on the design of Khufu's pyramid, as they had Taylor's, and Piazzi Smyth resigned in protest.

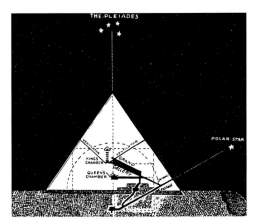

Postcards, Pyramids and

the Rise of Tourism

The sight of tourists travelling by camel to the pyramids (above) was a common one in the 19th-century. The road to the plateau was flanked by a canal and, eventually, by a trolley line that could transport the ever-increasing numbers of tourists.

For about six to eight weeks, when the flood waters were calm (top and below), the ancient Egyptians could see the inverse of the pyramid reflected in the inundation waters. It is interesting to speculate whether they saw in this image the union of the sky and Duat (Netherworld).

The first pyramid postcards began to appear around the end of the 19th century. Perhaps surprisingly they are a valuable source of information from a period when there was a lack of documentation of important excavations by Mariette and Maspero at the Sphinx, and just before the massive clearing operations of the Great Expeditions.

Some of the postcards show the pyramids during full flood of the Nile, a sight lost since modern control of the river level, but a potent, annually recurring image in ancient times. Postcards showing partial inundation reveal the catchment patterns of the valley floor at the base of the pyramid plateau, possible clues for ancient canals, harbours and settlements.

A year before the opening of the Suez canal in 1869 an elevated road was built from Giza to the pyramid plateau to facilitate visits by attending royalty, most notably the Empress Eugenie. At the same time, the Mena House Hotel was built at the base of the plateau, below Khufu's pyramid. A roadway led from the hotel to the foot of the pyramid, just below its entrance. Modern tourism was now in full swing.

‘ A laborious walk in the flaming sun brought us to the foot of the great Pyramid of Cheops. It was a fairy vision no longer. It was a corrugated, unsightly mountain of stone. Each of its monstrous sides was a wide stairway which rose upward, step above step, narrowing as it went, till it tapered to a point far aloft in the air. Insect men and women…were creeping about its dizzy perches…we were besieged by a rabble of muscular Egyptians and Arabs who wanted the contract of dragging us to the top…Each step being full as high as a dinner-table; there being very, very many of the steps; an Arab having hold of each of our arms and springing upward from step to step and snatching us with them…till we were ready to faint, who shall say it is not a lively, exhilarating, lacerating, muscle-straining, bone-wrenching and perfectly excruciating and exhausting pastime, climbing the Pyramids? …Twice, for one minute, they let me rest…and then continued their manic flight up the Pyramid. ’

'The excavator is a destroyer; and the object which he destroys is a part of the record of man's history which can *never be replaced or made good*. He must approach field work with a full consciousness of that fact. The only possible justification for his proceeding is that he endeavour to obtain from the ancient site which he destroys *all* the historical evidence which it contains.'

George Reisner

The Great Expeditions

Most of what we know about the sites of Egyptian and Nubian pyramids – some 300 monuments spanning three millennia – was excavated in little more than three decades near the turn of this century by great expeditions. Our experiences of the pyramids are far different from those of the late 19th- and early 20th-century excavators, who were the first to peel back the protective soil and expose the evidence. But when we visit the sites today we often still see them under the influence of the maps and reconstructions of these pioneers. Their records, often a mixture of documentation and personal interpretation, have become standard templates of Egyptology.

This explosion of large excavations (not just at pyramid sites but throughout Egypt and Nubia) was partly the outcome of Mariette's tight control of archaeology from 1858 until his death in 1881. Sometimes called 'Mariette's Monopoly', his position allowed him, like the pharaohs of old, to conscript masses of corvée labour from local villages.

After 23 years of Mariette uncovering tombs, temples and pyramids, Egyptologists from Egypt, Germany, France, Britain and the United States were eager to dig for themselves. When Gaston Maspero took over as Director of Antiquities he began granting concessions to scholars who directed large clearing operations funded by foreign institutions and benefactors, while others worked in the employ of the Antiquities Service.

Maspero took an interest in the young Flinders Petrie, an 'insistent exponent of controlled method' and of the importance of digging for information. Petrie respected all the details of ancient material culture – not just fabulous architecture and art objects. None the less, the great expeditions used huge numbers of diggers and basket carriers, as well as miniature railways, to move the enormous accumulations of sand and debris from the pyramid complexes and their cemeteries. The quality of

George Reisner (above), Director of the Harvard-Boston Expedition at the pyramids, in his early fifties. Below is his 1917 camp at the Nuri pyramids in the Sudan. Here 1,070 shabtis of King Taharqa are being numbered.

From 1902 to 1908 a German expedition, directed by Ludwig Borchardt, excavated the 5th-dynasty pyramids at Abusir. The pyramid of Niuserre in the background, is to the left of the pyramid of Neferirkare. The inner stepped structure of the latter, the largest of the group, is clearly visible. Here the excavators are working on the remains of the elaborate mortuary temple of Sahure, whose pyramid is the northernmost of the group. The temple's pavement was black basalt, its central court had 16 red granite columns, and the limestone walls above a granite dado were filled with coloured reliefs.

this large-scale archaeology varied. As evidence poured forth, much was destroyed for ever, but much was retrieved. Under Ludwig Borchardt, the Germans pioneered architectural documentation and interpretation. The American George Reisner showed an interest in stratigraphy and site formation as he made advances in archaeological photography and comprehensive systems of site and artifact documentation. Reisner and Petrie trained many young archaeologists, most of whom went on to direct their own excavations, becoming familiar names to future generations.

These were exciting times for pyramid archaeology. At Giza, Reisner was clearing the complete profile of Menkaure's pyramid – from the royal statuary and temples to the town. Together with Hermann Junker he was also clearing the great mastaba fields on the east, west and south of Khufu's pyramid. The Germans uncovered the temples of Khafre's pyramid in 1909–10. In 1926 Emile Baraize began to clear the Sphinx and most of its temple for the Antiquities Service (still under French direction). Meanwhile, Selim Hassan, on behalf of Cairo University, mounted an Egyptian expedition, equal in scale to those of his foreign colleagues, that cleared the mastabas and rock-cut tombs of the Central Field between the Sphinx and Khafre's pyramid. At Saqqara, C.M. Firth and J.-P. Lauer were revealing the multifarious elements of Djoser's Step Pyramid complex. At Abusir, the Germans under Borchardt were clearing the great 5th-

dynasty pyramid complexes and the sun temple of Niuserre, while the Americans were uncovering the 12th-dynasty pyramid temples and cemeteries at Lisht. Between 1916 and 1918 Reisner also excavated at Meroe, Napata and Nuri, capitals of the Nubian rulers of the 25th dynasty and subsequent local rulers down to the 4th century AD.

Then, in the late 1930s, the great expeditions began to wane. At Giza, Reisner was losing his sight as early as 1932, but he continued on at Harvard Camp, dictating his books and directing minor clearing operations necessary for his reports on the mastaba field. In 1924–8 Borchardt carried out small-scale investigations at Saqqara, Abu Ghurob (Abusir) and Meidum, and at Giza he participated in J.R. Cole's survey of Khufu's pyramid. In addition to the old age and infirmities of their leaders, the decline of the great expeditions has been ascribed to the new attitude of the Antiquities Service towards foreign institutions. Growing nationalism was combined with a feeling on the part of the Egyptians that the ancient monuments were their cultural property, in addition to the world's heritage, particularly after tensions with Howard Carter over Tutankhamun's treasures. Turmoil in Europe may have also have contributed to the demise of the great expeditions. The Second World War brought a halt to such work. Some, such as Walter Emery and Jean-Philippe Lauer, picked up where they left off when the war was over, but the new excavations were often on a different scale.

Years	Monument	Site	Excavator
1887–88	Senwosret I's pyramid	Illahun	W.M.F. Petrie
1888–89	Amenemhet III's pyramid	Hawara	W.M.F. Petrie
1891	Sneferu's pyramid	Meidum	W.M.F. Petrie
1894	Senwosret I's pyramid	Lisht	J.E. Gautier and G. Jéquier
1894–95	Amenemhet II's pyramid		
	Senwosret III's pyramid		
	Amenemhet III's pyramid	Dahshur	J. de Morgan
1896–7	Archaic royal tombs	Abydos	E. Amélineau
1898–1901	Niuserre's sun temple	Abu Ghurob	L. Borchardt and H. Schaeffer (Baron von Bissing Expedition, DOG)
1899–1900	Archaic royal tombs	Abydos	W.M.F. Petrie (EES)
	Ahmose's pyramid	Abydos	A. Mace
1900	Layer Pyramid	Zawiyet el Aryan	A. Barsanti (SAE)
	Unas's mortuary temple	Saqqara	A. Barsanti (SAE)
1901	Ahmose's pyramid	Abydos	T. Currelly (EES)
	Djedefre's pyramid	Abu Roash	M. Chassinat
1902–08	Sahure's pyramid		
	Neferirkare's pyramid		
	Niuserre's pyramid	Abusir	L. Borchardt (DOG)
1902–32	Western Field	Giza	G.A. Reisner (Phoebe Hearst Expedition HMFA)
1903–7	Mentuhotep I's tomb	Deir el-Bahri	E. Naville and H.R.Hall (EEF)
1904–5	Unfinished Pyramid	Zawiyet el Aryan	A. Barsanti (SAE)
1905–08	Teti's pyramid	Saqqara	J.E. Quibell (SAE)
1906–10	Menkaure's pyramid	Giza	G.A. Reisner (HMFA)
1906–34	Senwosret I's pyramid	Lisht	A.M. Lythgoe, A.C. Mace and A. Lansing (MMA)
1909–10	Khafre's pyramid	Giza	U. Hölscher (von Sieglin Expedition)
	Sneferu's pyramid	Meidum	W.M.F. Petrie and G.A. Wainwright (EES)
1910	Amenemhet III's pyramid	Hawara	W.M.F. Petrie
1910–11	Layer Pyramid	Zawiyet el-Aryan	G.A. Reisner and C. Fisher (HMFA)
	Mazghuna pyramids	Mazghuna	E. Mackay (under Petrie)
1911–31	Mentuhotep I's tomb	Deir el-Bahri	H. Winlock (MMA)
1912–14	Western Field	Giza	H. Junker (DAI)
1913	Senwosret I's pyramid	Illahun	W.M.F. Petrie and G. Brunton (EEF)
1913–16	Nubian pyramids	Kerma	G.A. Reisner (HMFA)
1915–23	Nubian pyramids	Gebel Barkal	G.A. Reisner (HMFA)
1916–18	Nubian pyramids	Nuri	G.A. Reisner (HMFA)
1918–19	Nubian pyramids	El-Kurru	G.A. Reisner (HMFA)
1920	Amenemhet I's pyramid	Lisht	A.C. Mace (MMA)
1920–22	Teti's pyramid	Saqqara	C.M. Firth and V. Loret (SAE)
	Pyramids of Khuit and Iput	Saqqara	C.M. Firth and V. Loret (SAE)
1920–23	Nubian pyramids	Meroe	G.A. Reisner (HMFA)
1920/2–38	Khufu's pyramid	Giza	Various SAE and Selim Hassan (SAE)
1924	Shepseskaf's mastaba	S. Saqqara	G. Jéquier (SAE)
1924–32	Eastern Field	Giza	G.A. Reisner (HMFA)
1925–35	Western Field	Giza	H. Junker (Vienna Academy)
1926–35	Sphinx	Giza	E. Baraize (SAE)
1926–36	Pepi II	Saqqara	G. Jéquier (IFAO)
1926–39	Djoser's Step Pyramid	Saqqara	C.M. Firth and J.P Lauer (SAE)
1928–29	Userkaf's pyramid	Saqqara	C.M. Firth (SAE)
1929	Unas's mortuary temple	Saqqara	C.M. Firth (SAE)
1929–30	Sneferu's pyramid	Meidum	A. Rowe (UMP)
1929–31	Khendjer's pyramid	S. Saqqara	G. Jéquier
	Anonymous pyramid	S. Saqqara	G. Jéquier
1929–35	Central Field	Giza	S. Hassan (CU)
1936–38	Sphinx	Giza	S. Hassan (SAE)
1936–39	Unas's mortuary temple	Saqqara	J.-P. Lauer (SAE)
1936–56	1st dynasty mastabas	Saqqara	W. Emery (EES)
1937–38	Unas's causeway	Saqqara	S. Hassan (SAE)
1937–49	Unas's pyramid	Saqqara	A.H. Hussein and S. Hassan (SAE)
1945	Djedkare-Isesi's pyramid	S. Saqqara	A.H. Hussein (SAE)
1945–49	Sneferu's Bent Pyramid	Dahshur	A.S. Hussein (SAE)
1950	Sekhemkhet's pyramid	Saqqara	Z. Goneim (SAE)

CU	*Cairo University*
DAI	*Deutsches Archäologisches Instituts, Abteilung Kairo*
DOG	*Deutschen Orient-Gesellschaft*
EEF	*Egypt Exploration Fund*
EES	*Egypt Exploration Society*
HMFA	*Harvard Museum of Fine Arts*
IFAO	*Institut Français d'Archéologie Orientale*
MMA	*Metropolitan Museum of Art*
SAE	*Service des Antiquités de l'Égypte*
UMP	*University Museum, Pennsylvania*

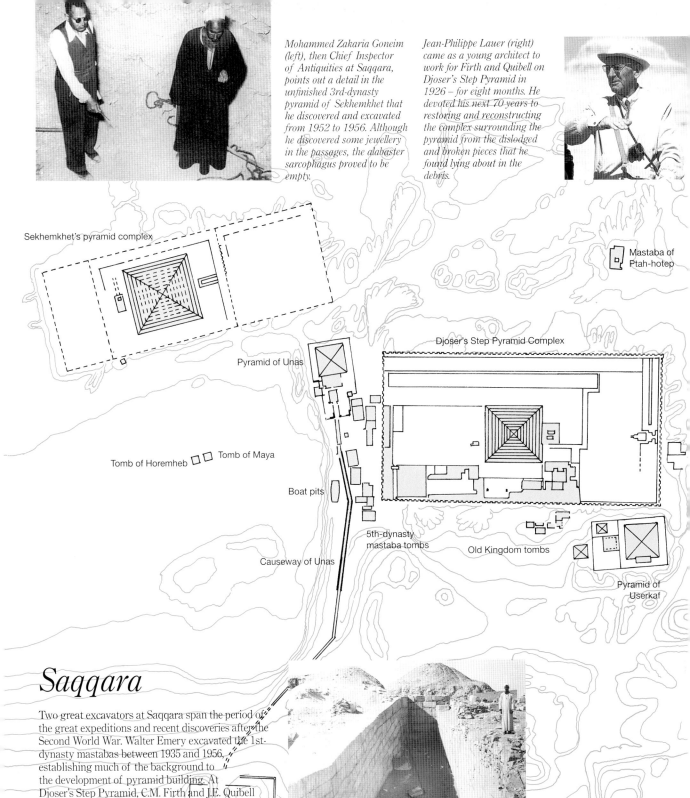

Mohammed Zakaria Goneim (left), then Chief Inspector of Antiquities at Saqqara, points out a detail in the unfinished 3rd-dynasty pyramid of Sekhemkhet that he discovered and excavated from 1952 to 1956. Although he discovered some jewellery in the passages, the alabaster sarcophagus proved to be empty.

Jean-Philippe Lauer (right) came as a young architect to work for Firth and Quibell on Djoser's Step Pyramid in 1926 – for eight months. He devoted his next 70 years to restoring and reconstructing the complex surrounding the pyramid from the dislodged and broken pieces that he found lying about in the debris.

Sekhemkhet's pyramid complex

Mastaba of Ptah-hotep

Pyramid of Unas

Djoser's Step Pyramid Complex

Tomb of Horemheb □ □ Tomb of Maya

Boat pits

5th-dynasty mastaba tombs

Old Kingdom tombs

Causeway of Unas

Pyramid of Userkaf

Saqqara

Two great excavators at Saqqara span the period of the great expeditions and recent discoveries after the Second World War. Walter Emery excavated the 1st-dynasty mastabas between 1935 and 1956, establishing much of the background to the development of pyramid building. At Djoser's Step Pyramid, C.M. Firth and J.E. Quibell were the first to undertake scientific exavation of the pyramid's superstructure, though the underground complex had been explored in the previous century. In 1926 they were joined by J.-P. Lauer, who has worked at the site ever since – with interruptions for the Second World War.

To the south of the causeway of the pyramid of Unas are two boat pits alongside one another. They are lined with fine Turah limestone.

C.M. Firth, assisted by James Quibell, began investigation of Djoser's Step Pyramid complex at Saqqara in 1924. Season after season brought finds such as a statue of Djoser in the serdab chamber (p. 90). A vast complex of courtyards and stone buildings, many carved in imitation of natural forms, was gradually revealed. Firth saw the need for the analytical skills of an architect and Jean-Philippe Lauer was assigned to the excavation. The photograph shows an aerial view of the Step Pyramid complex at the onset of the campaign of 1933.

3rd-dynasty cemetery

3038

3035

3036

3357

3471

1st-dynasty mastabas

2185

3500

3503

3505

3504

6th-dynasty mastaba tombs

Pyramid of Teti

Pyramid of Iput

3506

3507

Pyramid of Khuit

Pyramid of Merikare?

N

0   200 m

0   600 ft

(Left to right) The Step Pyramid of Djoser, the pyramid of Userkaf, and the pyramid of Teti with the ruins of its funerary temple.

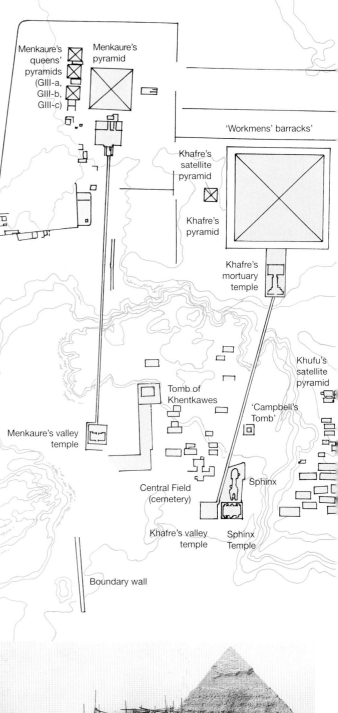

Menkaure's queens' pyramids (GIII-a, GIII-b, GIII-c)

Menkaure's pyramid

'Workmens' barracks'

Khafre's satellite pyramid

Khafre's pyramid

Khafre's mortuary temple

'Covington's Tomb'

Khufu's satellite pyramid

Tomb of Khentkawes

'Campbell's Tomb'

Menkaure's valley temple

Central Field (cemetery)

Sphinx

Khafre's valley temple

Sphinx Temple

Boundary wall

Giza

During the season of 1901–02, Gaston Maspero, Director-General of the Antiquities Service, asked the Italian, German and American missions to divide up the Giza necropolis between them for excavation. When lots were drawn for the Western Cemetery, George Reisner of the Harvard-Boston Expedition was awarded the northernmost of three strips. He later inherited the southern strip when Ernesto Schiaparelli gave up the Italian concession. Herman Junker of the German Archaeological Institute in Cairo drew the middle strip. Reisner's concession at the Eastern Cemetery ended at the ridge that forms the northern boundary of the Sphinx 'amphitheatre'. Finally, Reisner's concession included the pyramid of Menkaure, with its mortuary and valley temples and the small pyramids of his three queens. Khafre's pyramid complex was conceded to the Germans who excavated the pyramid and valley temple under Uvo Hölscher in 1909. The Sphinx itself, and the area in front, was excavated by the Antiquities Service under Emile Baraize from 1925 to 1934, and then by Selim Hassan from 1936 to 1938.

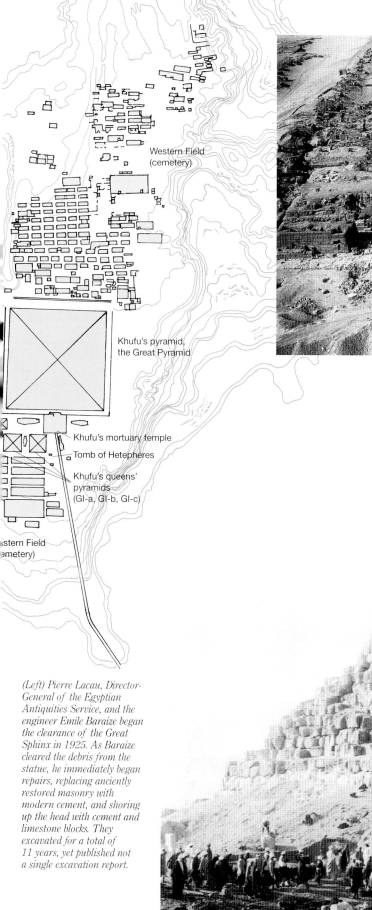

Western Field
(cemetery)

Khufu's pyramid,
the Great Pyramid

Khufu's mortuary temple

Tomb of Hetepheres

Khufu's queens'
pyramids
(GI-a, GI-b, GI-c)

stern Field
emetery)

→ N

0   200 m

0   600 ft

*The Western Cemetery
(above). Set out on a plan laid
down at the time of Khufu,
its mastaba tombs were built
on streets and avenues and
assigned to high 4th-dynasty
officials. Notables from the
5th and 6th dynasties,
expanded the field to the foot
of Khufu's pyramid. At the
end of the pyramid age,
smaller tombs and shaft
graves were dug into the
streets and avenues of
mastabas of their forebears.*

*(Left) Pierre Lacau, Director-
General of the Egyptian
Antiquities Service, and the
engineer Emile Baraize began
the clearance of the Great
Sphinx in 1925. As Baraize
cleared the debris from the
statue, he immediately began
repairs, replacing anciently
restored masonry with
modern cement, and shoring
up the head with cement and
limestone blocks. They
excavated for a total of
11 years, yet published not
a single excavation report.*

*Reisner's excavation of
'Queens' Street', along
Khufu's three queens'
pyramids, would lead his
crew to the unmarked tomb
of Hetepheres, the mother
of Khufu.*

Recent Discoveries

Although the foundations of pyramid studies were laid by the great expeditions, we have learned a great deal from excavations and surveys carried out since the end of the Second World War. Major expeditions have been initiated, but much work has also been done simply documenting and conserving massive quantities of material uncovered by earlier expeditions. Today we reclear sites and re-examine results, or excavate to fill specific gaps (such as the North Pyramid at Dahshur or Raneferef's pyramid at Abusir). We also excavate to learn more about the social and economic conditions that inspired pyramid building and made it possible.

Work was resumed immediately after the war by Walter Emery at North Saqqara, excavating the Archaic mastabas. In 1945 J.-P. Lauer returned to the Djoser complex. Abdelsalam Hussein, for the Antiquities Service, began the Pyramids Study Project, with the aim of systematically surveying, clearing, documenting and conserving all the major pyramids. After Hussein's death, Ahmed Fakhry took on the project, which was never completed. Between 1963 and 1975 Vito Maragioglio and Celeste Rinaldi undertook a comprehensive archi-

tectural survey of pyramids from the Old through the Middle Kingdom. They used earlier publications and their own visual inspections and measurements and published eight volumes, in which they meticulously described each pyramid.

The German Archaeological Institute embarked on a study of Middle Kingdom architecture in 1976. Its director, Dieter Arnold, moved to the Metropolitan Museum of Art, New York, in 1984, but continued his work and resurrected the museum's Lisht expedition. At Abusir, the Czech Institute of Egyptology, University of Prague, under Zbynek Zaba and later Miroslav Verner, examined the pyramids in detail. Rainer Stadelmann began an investigation of Old Kingdom Dahshur, while the French Archaeological Mission to Saqqara initiated a full examination of the 5th- and 6th-dynasty pyramid complexes. At Giza Zahi Hawass excavated and cleared several areas: the far Western Cemetery, Menkaure's pyramid, the so-called Workers' Cemetery, the eastern side of Khufu's pyramid and east of Khafre's valley temple.

Modern technology and the pyramids

A wide range of modern techniques is increasingly being brought to bear on probing the pyramids, often to answer very targeted questions. For instance, in the 1980s R. and D. Klemm surveyed quarries throughout Egypt with the aim of determining the sources of stone for the pyramids from Abu Roash to Meidum by means of trace analysis. And in 1984 we radiocarbon dated 64 samples of organic material extracted from the pyramids and associated structures. The dates, after calibration,

The chambers of Raneferef's unfinished pyramid at Abusir in the course of excavation by the Czech Mission at this pyramid field. Behind is Neferirkare's pyramid, with stages of its construction clearly visible.

were on average 374 years earlier than one of the major accepted chronologies. During the 1995 season more than 300 samples were collected from monuments ranging from the 1st-dynasty tombs at Saqqara to Djoser's pyramid, the Giza pyramids, a selection of 5th- and 6th-dynasty pyramids and Middle Kingdom pyramids. These dates will shed new light on Egyptian chronology.

Khufu's pyramid in particular has been investigated by a battery of modern scientific survey techniques. In 1986, at the request of Ahmed Qadry, President of the Egyptian Antiquities Organization (EAO), two French companies undertook a microgravimetric study of the pyramid. The technique, normally used for assessing the foundations of dams and nuclear power plants, measures the density of structures. Results indicated that the pyramid's macrostructure consists of 34 major 'blocks' with a low-density block near the top, and blocks of heterogeneous density below. This might correlate with the mastaba-like chunks of masonry in the cores of Khufu's queens' pyramids and Menkaure's pyramid. Analysis of the microstructure found an anomaly west of and below the horizontal passage to the Queen's Chamber.

Gilles Dormion and Jean-Patrice Goidin, two French architects associated with this study, drilled three small holes in the passage to investigate the anomaly. The holes penetrated through compact limestone, limestone debris and mortar, and sand, then more limestone debris. The fact that in one drill hole the end of the sand was not found, prompted speculation of a hidden chamber. It is more likely that the layers are simply the packing between the limestone walls of the passage and the core masonry of the pyramid. In 1987 a Japanese team from Waseda University (Tokyo), led by Sakuji Yoshimura, carried out a remote sensing survey of Khufu's pyramid. The Japanese team confirmed the same anomaly and they also recorded data that suggested to them the possibility of a tunnel entering the pyramid under the south side.

In 1990 a French team of Jean Kerisel, Jean-Bruno-Kerisel and Alain Guillon studied air pollution inside the King's Chamber and subtle evidence that it is sinking towards the south. On this side the great granite roof beams show pronounced cracks. Jean Kerisel returned in 1992 to investigate the Subterranean Chamber with ground penetrating radar and microgravimetry. In 1995 he obtained permission to drill into its bedrock floor in search of a cavity but none was found.

Perhaps the most widely reported investigation took place in 1992. In an official project of the German Archaeological Institute in Cairo, under its director Rainer Stadelmann, and the Supreme Council for Antiquities, robotics expert Rudolf Gantenbrink mounted a miniature video camera on a wheeled robot and sent it up the 'air shafts' of the King's Chamber. The next year he sent a new

version, Upuaut II, into the southern 'air shaft' of the Queen's Chamber. The robot crawled 65 m (213 ft) up a 45° slope when it was stopped by a smooth limestone plug from which two copper pins projected. A small fragment of copper lay on the floor just in front. The find was labelled a 'door' though in fact nothing larger than a small rat could get through it, so perhaps slab is a better description.

The Sphinx has also been intensively investigated. In 1978, SRI International of California, with the EAO's Science Section, conducted a remote sensing, subsurface survey of the Sphinx sanctuary and temple. A preliminary survey in collaboration with Ain Shams University in 1977 found various anomalies: one – in front of the forepaws – suggested 'a cavity or shaft'. The SRI team conducted a more detailed resistivity survey and results were checked with acoustical sounding. The team investigated confirmed anomalies by core drilling and direct observation with a borescope camera. Five holes were drilled, but the researchers found no significant cavities other than those that occur naturally in limestone.

A team connected with the SRI International Science and Archaeology Project at Giza, under my direction, cleared the floor of the Sphinx sanctuary and with Zahi Hawass I carried out excavations in the northeast corner of the Sphinx sanctuary. In 1979–83 I was Field Director and then Director of a five-year project to provide scale architectural drawings of the Sphinx and its site. Each individual stone of the masonry layers on the Sphinx was documented (p. 128). The drawings became essential for the EAO's work on the Sphinx from 1988.

(Above) A team from Waseda University in Khufu's Queen's Chamber. (Below) Ulrich Kapp of the German Archaeological Institute who contributed to the Sphinx survey by the American Research Center in Egypt.

Recent Pyramid Explorations

Years	Monument	Site	Investigator
1951–52	Sneferu's Bent Pyramid	Dahshur	Ahmed Fakhry (SAE)
1951–70	Teti's pyramid	Saqqara	MAFS
1954	Khufu's boat pit (east)	Giza	K. el-Malakh (EAO)
1955–57	Userkaf's sun temple	Abusir	H. Ricke (Swiss and German Institutes)
1960	Khafre's satellite pyramid	Giza	A. Hafez Abd el-'Al
1961–69	Khufu's complex	Giza	H. Messiha
1963–67	Sekhemkhet South Tomb	Saqqara	J.P. Lauer
1963–present	Nubian pyramids	Sedeinga	M.S. Girogini/A. Labrousse
1965–67	Sphinx Temple	Giza	H. Ricke and G. Haeny, Swiss Institute
1966–71	Pepi I's pyramid	Saqqara	MAFS
1966–73	Mentuhotep I's tomb	Deir el-Bahri	D. Arnold (DAI)
1967	Khafre's pyramid	Giza	L. Alvarez (UC, Berkeley, Ain Shams and EAO)
1968–88	Pepi I's mortuary temple	South Saqqara	MAFS
1971–72	Merenre's pyramid	South Saqqara	MAFS
1971–73	Settlement dump	Giza	K. Kromer (Austrian Institute)
1972–73	Pyramid tombs	Tabo, Napata	Ch. Maystre (CEOUG)
1974–76	Unas's mortuary temple	Saqqara	MAFS
1974–78	Giza pyramids	Giza	SRI International, remote sensing
1976	Tombs of the Intefs	Luxor	D. Arnold (DAI)
1976–78	Userkaf's mortuary temple	Saqqara	J.-P. Lauer and A. Labrousse (MAFS)
1976–83	Amenemhet III's pyramid	Dahshur	D. Arnold (DAI)
1977	Khentkawes's pyramid	Abusir	M. Verner (Czech Mission)
1977–78	Sphinx	Giza	M. Lehner and Z. Hawass (EAO)
1977–present	1st-dynasty royal tombs	Abydos	G. Dreyer and W. Kaiser (DAI)
1977–present	Sneferu's North Pyramid	Dahshur	R. Stadelmann (DAI)
1978	Sphinx	Giza	SRI International/EAO
1978–79	Provincial pyramid	Elephantine	German and Swiss Institutes of Archaeology
1979–83	Sphinx	Giza	J. Allen and M. Lehner (ARCE)
1979–present	Pyramids of Meroe	Meroe	F. Hinkel
1980	Unfinished Pyramid	Abusir	M. Verner (Czech Mission)
1980–81	Sinki pyramid	South Abydos	N. Swelim and G. Dreyer
1981	Seila pyramid	Seila	Univs. of California, Berkeley/ Brigham Young Univ.
1981–87	Raneferef's pyramid	Abusir	M. Verner (Czech Mission)
1982	Pyramid of Tia and Tia	Saqqara	G. Martin (University College, London)
1982–85	Userkaf's pyramid	Saqqara	Ali el-Khouli (EAO)
1984	Sneferu's pyramid	Meidum	Ali el-Khouli (EAO)
1984–86	Nefermaat's mastaba	Meidum	Ali el-Khouli (EAO)
1984–88	'Private' pyramids	Saqqara	S. Tewfik (Cairo University/EAO)
1984–89	Senwosret I's pyramid	Lisht	D. and D. Arnold (MMA)
1985	Lepsius 'Pyramid' I	Abu Roash	N. Swelim
1985–present	Archaic enclosures	Abydos	D. O'Connor and W.K. Simpson (Univ. of Pennsylvania/Yale Univ.)
1986	Sneferu's Bent Pyramid	Dahshur	J. Dorner

Excavation under way on the eastern side of Sneferu's North Pyramid at Dahshur in 1983. Rainer Stadelmann of the German Archaeological Institute has studied the pyramid in detail. To the right can be seen intact casing blocks, some restored.

Years	Monument	Site	Investigator
1986	Lepsius Pyramid L (50)	Dahshur	R. Stadelmann (DAI)
1986	Khufu's pyramid	Giza	A. Qadry, microgravimetric survey
1986	Khufu's pyramid	Giza	G. Dormion and J.P. Goidin
1986	Djedkare-Isesi's pyramid	South Saqqara	S. el-Nagar
1986	Pepi I's satellite pyramid	South Saqqara	A. Labrousse
1986–91	Workers' installations	Dahshur	R. Stadelmann (DAI)
1986–present	Mastaba field	Dahshur	R. Stadelmann (DAI)
1987	Khufu's pyramid	Giza	S. Yoshimura (Waseda Univ., Tokyo)
1987	Sphinx	Giza	S. Yoshimura (Waseda Univ., Tokyo)
1987	Seila pyramid	Seila	N. Swelim and Brigham Young Univ.
1987	Khufu's boat pit (west)	Giza	National Geographic
1988–95	Pepi I's queens' pyramids	South Saqqara	MAFS
1988–89	'Workmen's barracks'	Giza	M. Lehner (Yale Univ.)
1988–present	Settlement remains	Giza	M. Lehner (Oriental Inst./ Harvard Semitic Mus.)
1988–present	Sphinx	Giza	SCA
1988–present	Senwosret II's town	Illahun	N. Millet (ROM)
1989	Settlement	Giza	Z. Hawass and M. Jones (AMBRIC/ SCA)
1990	Khufu's valley temple	Giza	Z. Hawass (SCA)
1990	Khufu's pyramid	Giza	J. Kerisel, J.-B. Kerisel and Alain Guillon
1990	Sphinx	Giza	UNESCO
1990–91	Lepsius Pyramid XXV (25)	Abusir	M. Verner (Czech Mission)
1990–present	'Workers' cemetery'	Giza	Z. Hawass (SCA)
1990–present	Gisr el-Mudir	Saqqara	I. Mathieson and H. Smith (Nat. Mus. of Scotland)
1990–present	Senwosret III's pyramid	Dahshur	D. Arnold (MMA)
1991	Sphinx	Giza	R. Schoch, T. Dobecki and J.A. West
1991	Unas's valley temple	Saqqara	A. Moussa and A. Labrousse (MAFS)
1991	Amenemhet I's pyramid	Lisht	D. Arnold (MMA)
1991–97	Pyramids of Iput and Khuit	Saqqara	A. Labrousse and Zawi Hawass (SCA)
1991–present	Dra Abu el-Naga	Luxor	D. Polz (DAI/UCLA)
1992	Sphinx	Giza	I. Marzouk and A. Gharib
1992	Eastern Field	Giza	Z. Hawass (EAO)
1992	Khufu's Queens' pyramids	Giza	Z. Hawass (EAO)
1992	Ninetjer's galleries	Saqqara	P. Munro (Berlin and Hanover Univ. Mission)
1992	Sahure's pyramid	Abusir	Z. Hawass
1992–93	Unas's causeway	Saqqara	A. Moussa (EAO) and A. Labrousse (MAFS)
1992–95	Khufu's pyramid	Giza	J. Kerisel
1993	Khufu's satellite pyramid	Giza	Z. Hawass
1993	Khufu's pyramid	Giza	R. Stadelmann and R. Gantenbrink (DAI)
1993	Neferhetepes's complex	Saqqara	J.P. Lauer and A. Labrousse (MAFS)
1993–present	Djedefre's pyramid	Abu Roash	Giza Pyramids Inspectorate/IFAO/ Univ. of Geneva
1993–present	Ahmose I's pyramid	Abydos	S. Harvey Pennsylvania/Yale Univ. Expedition
1994	Senwosret III's temple	Abydos	J. Wegner Pennsylvania/Yale Univ. Expedition
1995–96	Khafre's valley temple	Giza	Z. Hawass (SCA)
1995–96	Lepsius Pyramid XXIV (24)	Abusir	M. Verner (Czech Mission)
1996	Menkaure's pyramid	Giza	Z. Hawass (SCA)
1997	Queen Khuit's pyramid	Saqqara	Z. Hawass (SCA)

Zahi Hawass surveys the burial chamber of Khufu's satellite pyramid, which he discovered in 1993. Hawass also found the capstone of the small pyramid.

In 1987 the Japanese applied the electromagnetic sounding technique to the Sphinx. They believe they found evidence of a north–south tunnel under the Sphinx, a water pocket below the surface near the south hind paw and another cavity near the north hind paw. Both rear anomalies are probably part of the 'main fissure' that cuts through the Sphinx site. Robert Schoch (Boston University), Thomas Dobecki and John Anthony West carried out a survey in 1991 of the Sphinx using seismic methods to support a theory that it predates the 4th dynasty. But in 1992 Imam Marzouk and Ali Gharib of the Egyptian National Research Institute of Astronomy and Geophysics carried out a study of the ground below the Sphinx using shallow seismic refraction and found no evidence of cavities.

Unlike the other two Giza pyramids, the base of Menkaure's pyramid was never freed from debris. In 1996 Zahi Hawass began to clear its west and south sides and found an unfinished statue, which was roughly shaped from granite in the Ramessid period. The discovery fits other evidence that New Kingdom pharaohs quarried the Giza pyramids for stone. In September 1996 the team uncovered a row of large limestone foundation blocks laid on end along the south side of the pyramid.

A lthough each pyramid featured the same square base and diagonals rising to a centre point, the ruined pyramids show considerable variation. This is because of the way the ancient Egyptians built the inner core. The pyramid builders had to finish off each pyramid with smooth faces and straight lines; in most cases they did so with a casing of fine white limestone blocks tightly joined to make a continuous smooth plane on each of the four faces. But the core could be accretion layers of stone and clay that leaned inward on the pyramid; or stone blocks and boulders that were roughly piled without regular courses; or stone rubble inside rough stone and clay retaining walls; or mudbrick. Over the ages, as later peoples tore off the fine limestone of the outer casings for buildings elsewhere, the cores were exposed to the elements.

The variability between pyramid cores and all other features – temples, causeways, subsidiary pyramids and tombs of retainers – makes it obvious that we cannot understand the methods of pyramid building, or assess the historical significance of pyramids, by assuming a generic model for all pyramids. The building methods, the social organization and the economy of pyramids must have varied with the variation in the architecture. A catalogue of pyramids then is of greater interest than just the satisfaction of a stamp-collecting kind of iteration. The catalogue illustrates the shape of pyramid history in ancient Egypt, showing us patterns that are clues to the development of one of the world's earliest great civilizations.

The pyramids of Giza, seen from across the desert to the south.

III   THE WHOLE PYRAMID CATALOGUE

Origins of the Pyramid – Hierakonpolis

Reconstruction of a reed and wood shrine in the form of the Per Wer *or 'Great House'. This type of structure may have stood on the Nekhen mound.*

Temple and mound

To the ancient Egyptians the mounds that covered their protodynastic graves may have been an image of the primeval mound, the fertile land from which all creation grew. Thus priests 'planted' the king's body in the earth mound of his grave, and, like new seedlings on the first mounds of earth to emerge from the annual Nile flood, he would rise again. At Hierakonpolis we find the earliest association of king, mound and Horus, god of kingship. The Greek name of the site means 'City of the Falcon', the symbol of Horus; its ancient name was Nekhen. Archaeological evidence suggests it was an important predynastic centre, perhaps a kind of capital of southern Egypt. Close to the beginning of the 1st dynasty (*c.* 2900 BC), settlements scattered across the low desert and up into the Wadi Abu Suffian – the valley that cuts the high desert cliffs – coalesced to form the walled town of Nekhen.

In one corner of the town is an enclosure surrounded by mudbrick walls, within which is Egypt's oldest known temple mound. It is here that basic concepts of Egypt's divine kingship appear to have originated. Excavations by J.E. Quibell in

The pavilion shown in front of the shrine structure (below, left) is based on the festival pavilion of Narmer depicted on the 1st-dynasty ceremonial macehead found in the Main Deposit (left). Access to the top of the mound of Nekhen may have been by a similar staircase, although the ceremony depicted was probably conducted at Buto.

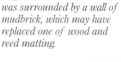

(Right) The sacred enclosure was surrounded by a wall of mudbrick, which may have replaced one of wood and reed matting.

(Below) Map showing the location of Giza, Saqqara, Abydos and Hierakonpolis.

(Below) Two life-sized statues of kneeling attendants. One, made of limestone had deteriorated considerably because of the wet soil conditions. They may have stood either side of the entrance passage.

(Above) Door socket in the form of a prisoner with his hands tied behind his back.

Giza
Saqqara

Abydos

Hierakonpolis

0   100 km
0   60 miles

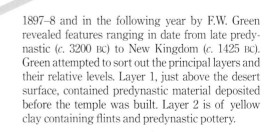

1897–8 and in the following year by F.W. Green revealed features ranging in date from late predynastic (*c.* 3200 BC) to New Kingdom (*c.* 1425 BC). Green attempted to sort out the principal layers and their relative levels. Layer 1, just above the desert surface, contained predynastic material deposited before the temple was built. Layer 2 is of yellow clay containing flints and predynastic pottery.

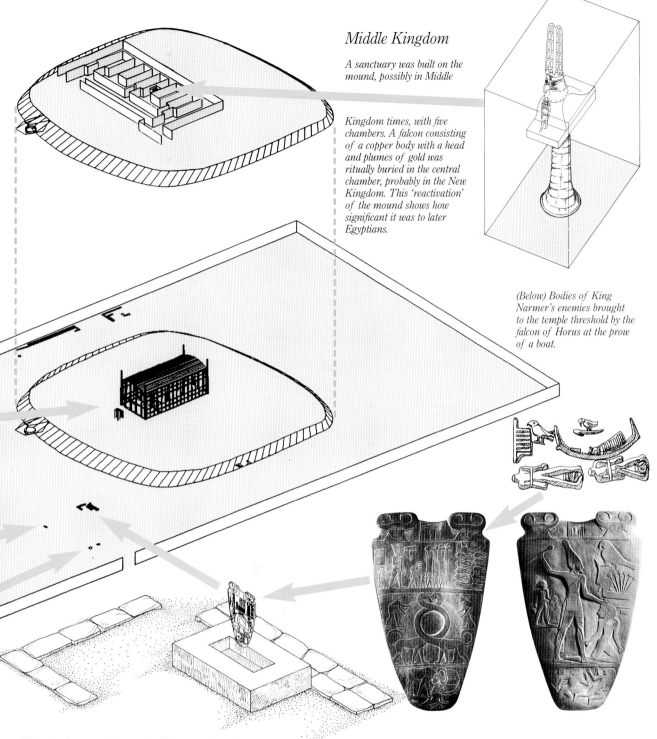

A sanctuary was built on the mound, possibly in Middle

Kingdom times, with five chambers. A falcon consisting of a copper body with a head and plumes of gold was ritually buried in the central chamber, probably in the New Kingdom. This 'reactivation' of the mound shows how significant it was to later Egyptians.

(Below) Bodies of King Narmer's enemies brought to the temple threshold by the falcon of Horus at the prow of a boat.

The circular mound, contained by a revetment, or retaining wall, of coarse sandstone blocks laid in horizontal courses, was built on top of Layer 2. It measures 49.26 m (162 ft) across, with the courses stepped at an angle of 45°. We do not know its original height because the top of the mound was probably cut down when later buildings were erected. A temple was built around the mound, probably near

The Narmer palette, of greywacke (dark green slate) commemorates the victories of King Narmer, whose name is inscribed within the serekh. One side shows the king, wearing the red crown of Lower Egypt in a triumphal procession. The strange long-necked beasts may represent the two halves of the country now forcibly united. The other side shows a kneeling prisoner, probably a Lower Egyptian, being smitten by the king who here wears the the white crown of Upper Egypt.

Main Deposit

Maceheads, including
  Narmer
  Narmer 'Wedding'
Palettes, including
  Narmer palette
  'Two Dog' palette
Flint knives
Archaic statuette of
  Khasekhemwy
Ivory wands
Small carved ivory and
  faience votive figures
Animal figurines,
  including scorpions or
  scorpion tails and
  monkeys, birds, frogs,
  dogs, hippopotamuses,
  a boar, gazelle
Stone and faience vessels
Model vessels
Pottery vessels
Stelae fragments

*The Rites of the Mound of
Jemme are depicted at the
Edifice of Tarhaqa and the
Temple of Osiris Heka Djet
at Karnak. The falcon perches
on the lotus sprouting from
the mound, the risen form
of the falcon 'planted' in the
Hierakonpolis mound.*

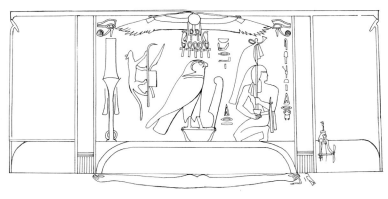

the beginning of the 1st dynasty on the evidence of Layer 3, which surrounded the mound and contained abundant charcoal and fire reddened earth, as well as pottery sherds of the protodynastic period and 1st dynasty. These traces of a conflagration suggest that the structures consisted of reed matting and wood, the traditional type of architecture that was imitated in stone by Djoser in his pyramid complex.

The mound must have been a 'high place' for a chapel in the form of the *Per Wer*, 'the Great House', which was the name of the national shrine of southern Egypt at Hierakonpolis. As the mound was the highest place in both town and temple, a temporary shrine for the ruler might have been set up on ritual occasions. One such shrine is depicted on the Narmer macehead from the Main Deposit, a collection of objects found immediately outside the mound, to the northeast. These constitute some of the oldest and most archetypal icons of kingship ever discovered in Egypt.

The Main Deposit

This mysterious cache consists of many objects, including flint knives, small and large decorated stone maceheads, faience figurines, slate palettes and a concentrated heap of ivory figurines and wands. Almost all are in the style of the protodynastic and Archaic (early dynastic) periods. Green thought that the cache lay upon or within Layer 3.

Without doubt, the Narmer Palette is the most striking object in the cache – both a monument of early Egyptian kingship and a blatant pictorial statement of the forcible union of southern with northern Egypt. It is named after the king who is written with the hieroglyph of the catfish (*nar*) and chisel (*mer*) in the *serekh* panel (the stylized palace façade used for royal names). Narmer was a king of the protodynastic period who preceded Hor-Aha, probably the first king of the 1st dynasty.

A few clues suggest that the palette was found almost in its original position, close to the entrance of the Archaic temple. It lay near a slotted limestone slab and pavement and 9 m (30 ft) west of a limestone door jamb with a basalt pivot socket in the form of a prisoner with hands bound behind his back. This is generally the place – towards the

south end of the east side – of the later temple entrance, and, significantly, it corresponds to the location of the entrance to Djoser's complex. To the northeast Quibell found life-sized statues of kneeling attendants.

Another object in the deposit was the great limestone macehead showing Narmer seated at the top of a stairway at some kind of ceremony. The scene is thought by some to represent an occasion that took place at Buto, a predynastic Delta capital and northern counterpart of Nekhen. However, it is tempting to see the stairway to the raised platform as a stylized rendering of a mound like that at Nekhen, which must have had a stairway or other form of access, though no evidence for one was found.

The mound in mythology

Later Egyptians certainly believed that the mound at Hierakonpolis was extremely special to the cult of Horus. They built a sanctuary centered on the mound, possibly in Middle Kingdom times, consisting of five chambers – recalling the five niches that became standard for the sanctuaries of pyramid temples from the time of Khafre onwards. In the central chamber a beautiful falcon fashioned of copper plate with a head and plumes of gold was ritually buried in an upright position on a standard. This carefully designed burial made the mound a virtual tomb of the sacred cult of Horus of Nekhen, and reactivated the late predynastic shrine. It was a symbolic replanting of the divine seed of the deity, who would emerge from the mound which, to the Egyptians of the dynastic period, must have seemed to date back to the beginning of time.

Egyptian literature about the Afterlife is replete with references to divine mounds. The oldest of all, the Pyramid Texts (p. 31), refer to the Creator, Atum, rising as a mound in the enclosure of Heliopolis. In a sense, every Egyptian temple of later times was the primeval mound situated in the middle of its own defined sacred place. In the New Kingdom 'Rite of the Mound of Jemme' a gigantic pair of arms, one belonging to Geb, the primordial earth-god, and the other to Horus, god of kingship, lifts up a large mound. A lotus, symbol of rebirth, springs from the mound and provides a perch for the Horus falcon and the feather of truth, Maat. The scene represents the transfiguration of Amun, in this case into the falcon as a sun symbol and keeper of Maat, the concept of order in the universe. In the Old Kingdom, the pyramid was the mound of transformation and the pharaoh was the keeper of Maat.

The mound at Hierakonpolis can therefore be seen as closely prefiguring the Rite of Jemme, and as such it symbolizes a basic concept behind the greatest sacred mounds that the Egyptians ever constructed – the Old Kingdom pyramids.

The ancient Egyptians believed that the first pharaohs hailed from This, of which Abydos was the religious centre. At Abydos the high desert cliffs form a great bay bisected by a V-shaped ravine. Egypt's earliest kings may have seen this cleft as a passage into the Afterlife, for they built their tombs below it on a spur extending from the rocky cliffs and overlooking the wadi that runs to the edge of the cultivation. Modern Egyptians call this burial ground Umm el-Qa'ab, 'Mother of Pots', because of the enormous mounds of fragments of pottery left by ancient Egyptian pilgrims.

For several generations before the 1st dynasty it had been a tradition for local rulers to place their tombs far out in the desert near passages through the high cliffs. For example, protodynastic rulers of Hierakonpolis built their tombs in the Wadi Abu Suffian, where Michael Hoffman discovered them. These tombs must have been built about the same time as the Nekhen temple mound (p. 72).

At Umm el-Qa'ab, Gunter Dreyer has revealed how a constellation of royal tombs developed from a galaxy of graves reaching back into the pre-dynastic period, Cemetery U, forming a remarkable record of state formation. In the midst of the crowded small pit-tombs, larger mudbrick chamber tombs stand out. Tomb Uj is the largest, with a burial chamber that once housed a wooden shrine. Inside, Dreyer found an ivory *heqa* sceptre, the very hieroglyph for ruler. The tomb is a model of a house, with 12 chambers, a central court and symbolic slit-doors to magazines containing hundreds of Egyptian and imported Palestinian pots. Some of Egypt's earliest hieroglyphs show that great revenues already flowed to the ruler buried here from provincial estates and beyond. The tomb as replica of the 'great house' provisioned by the entire land carries on into the Old Kingdom pyramids.

Between Uj and the tomb of Hor-Aha, about 150 years later, is open space except for 11 rectangular tombs. Three, each consisting of two brick-lined pits, belong to the kings of 'dynasty 0', who ruled Egypt during its gradual unification – Iri-Hor, Ka

Royal Tombs at Abydos

and Narmer. Then suddenly, near Narmer's small tomb, is the startlingly larger and more complex tomb of Hor-Aha, equated by some with Menes, first king of the 1st dynasty.

Hor-Aha's tomb was built in stages, as were so many later mastabas and pyramids. It began as a double chamber-tomb but ultimately consisted of three large mudbrick-lined pits. The king may have been buried in the central one, the brick lining of which served as a protective shell around an inner wooden chamber. Forming an entourage for the king are 34 small pits – the graves of courtiers who were possibly sacrificed. Analysis of human bones shows them to be almost all of males, no older than 25. Curiously, the bones around the last chamber were those of young lions.

The tomb of the next king, Djer, was the largest 1st-dynasty burial at Abydos. Its roofed space of 12 x 13 m (39 x 43 ft) was probably the limit that could be covered by timber, matting and mud. Djer

(Right) Tomb Uj, of a local late predynastic ruler, in which Gunter Dreyer found some of Egypt's oldest hieroglyphs and hundreds of imported Palestinian vessels. Even at this early stage, the tomb is a simulacrum of a great house, provisioned from afar.

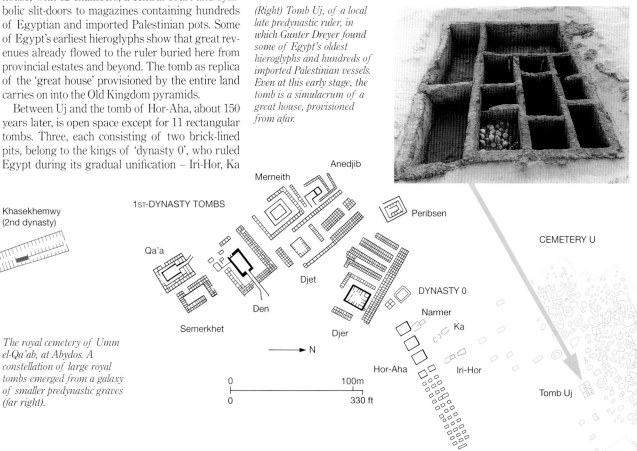

The royal cemetery of Umm el-Qa'ab, at Abydos. A constellation of large royal tombs emerged from a galaxy of smaller predynastic graves (far right).

Khasekhemwy (2nd dynasty)

1ST-DYNASTY TOMBS

Merneith

Anedjib

Peribsen

Qa'a

Djet

CEMETERY U

Den

Semerkhet

Djer

DYNASTY 0

Narmer

Ka

N

Hor-Aha

Iri-Hor

Tomb Uj

0 — 100m

0 — 330 ft

Retainers graves around the tomb of King Den, where priests, dwarfs and women of the royal household were buried. Their large numbers and the fact that many were marked with stelae is one argument that the cemetery at Abydos (shown in the map below, based on Petrie) is the true royal 1st-dynasty burial ground. The tombs included elements oriented to the southwest – the direction of a great cleft in the high cliffs surrounding the Abydos bay.

has 318 attendant graves, many marked with stela. Of 97 inscribed stelae, 76 belonged to females, 11 to males and 2 to dwarfs. These were probably service staff, priests and entertainers of the king's house and not high officials, who were drawn from the king's immediate family, and may have been buried in the large niched mastabas at Saqqara (p. 78).

How were the graves marked?

At least from the time of Djer, stone stelae, with the name of the ruler in a *serekh*, were set up near royal graves, probably on the east side. But scarcely any other evidence of a tomb superstructure has been found. Discussion has focused on the tomb of Djet, where the thick walls of the tomb supported a thinner wall retaining a mound of sand. Reconstructions range from a low mound to a great stepped mastaba. All, however, run into the difficulty that, as Petrie recognized and as Dreyer confirmed, the top of the mound would have been below the desert surface, possibly concealed by a second roof.

Dreyer suggests that the hidden tumulus above the burial chamber but below the desert surface fulfilled a magical role as the primeval mound ensuring resurrection. He postulated a second mound above the buried tumulus – about 1.5 m (5 ft) high above Djer's tomb and only 20 to 40 cm (8 to 16 in) high above Den's – based on the supposition that a royal tomb must have been marked by more than a pair of stelae, and also because this would have utilized the excess sand from digging the grave.

A clue to the superstructures may lie in Hoffman's study of Tomb 1 of a protodynastic ruler at Hierakonpolis. Careful excavation around the rectangular mudbrick-lined pit revealed the existence of a wood-pole and reed-mat shrine, surrounded by a similarly built enclosure wall. Could such a superstructure have existed above the royal tombs at Umm el-Qa'ab? The wood and reed-mat shrine would have replicated the wooden shrine in the burial chamber, just as the surface mound replicated the subterranean one.

Gunter Dreyer reconstructed the tomb of Djet as a double mound. It was marked by a stela showing Djet's name inside a wood-frame and reed-mat palace façade. Was it also covered by a wood and reed shrine, as reconstructed for Tomb 1 at Hierakonpolis?

Proto-false door

Umm el Qa'ab
royal cemetery:
late predynastic,
1st–2nd dynasty
(see p. 75)

New Kingdom
temples

2nd-dynasty
royal enclosures

Osiris temple

N

0   800 m

0   2500 ft

Developments in tomb architecture

Seven kings and one queen (Merneith) of the 1st dynasty built tombs at Abydos, expanding roughly towards the southwest, the direction of the great ravine. The wall of the mound over Djet's tomb has an overlap at the southwest corner, making a false flap-door corresponding to a niche in the tomb below – a precursor to the classic false door. Dreyer ascertained that a second stairway and chamber added to the southwest of Den's tomb was for a statue of the king, making this a prototype of the *serdab* chambers in Old Kingdom tombs.

As rulers continued to build their tombs at Abydos the main pit became deeper and the wood shrine around the burial chamber was fitted closer to its walls, leaving no space for magazines. Petrie summarized other principal changes:

'By Merneit[h] these [offering] chambers were built separately [round the burial chamber]. By Den an entrance passage was added, and by Qa the entrance was turned to the north. At this stage we are within reach of the early passage-mastabas and pyramids.'

A break in the sequence at Abydos for the 2nd dynasty makes tracing royal tomb development into the pyramid age difficult. No tomb has been found here for Hetepsekhemwy, the successor of Qa'a in the traditional king list and the first king of the 2nd dynasty. However, one of two enormous sets of underground galleries at Saqqara is ascribed to him. The last king of the 2nd dynasty, Khasekhem, changed his name to Khasekhemwy, 'The Appearance of the Two Powers' apparently after the conclusion of civil strife. His tomb at Abydos is a marked departure from the square pit-tombs, consisting of a long, irregular pit, divided into 40 magazines.

Valley funerary enclosures

At the juncture of the wadi with the cultivation, the 1st- and 2nd-dynasty kings built the second element of their tomb complexes at Abydos – a huge

The large royal enclosures of 2nd-dynasty kings simulated wood-frame and reed-mat structures in plastered and painted mudbrick.

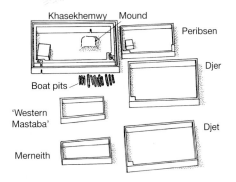

rectangular court. The earliest examples are now defined by the surrounding subsidiary burials, but later ones have niched mudbrick enclosure walls. Khasekhemwy's is the largest, covering over 5,000 sq. m (53,820 sq. ft). Such structures, with their niched façades, may be models of the palace enclosure of the living king (the style is often called 'palace façade'). Most are practically empty, but those of Khasekhemwy and Peribsen have a small building that sits askew inside the entrance at the southeast corner. This may have housed the king's statue or offerings made to him.

One interpretation sees these enclosures as full-scale replicas of the open courts for royal display in the palace. Another view is that, located at the edge of the cultivation, they perhaps played a role similar to the valley temples of the pyramids, in which case the wadi forms a kind of natural causeway to the mounded tombs. Perhaps, like the valley temples, the enclosures were associated with the 'purification tent' and 'mortuary workshop' (p. 25). In both form and location of the entrances, the enclosures can also be seen as the precursor to the niched wall that surrounds Djoser's complex, while the mounded grave moves inside the enclosure as the stone mastaba and, finally, the Step Pyramid.

Can these structures be precursors of both valley temple and pyramid enclosure? Both were masonry replicas of structures in less durable materials that veiled, and at the same time revealed, something royal and divine. When painted, the enclosure of Khasekhemwy, like the Saqqara mastabas, represented screen walls made of wood frames and colourful reed mats. In plastered and painted mudbrick, it was a more solid version of other Abydos enclosures that had perished (as, perhaps, did the tomb superstructures at Umm el-Qa'ab), leaving only the rectangles of subsidiary graves.

David O'Connor recovered traces of the floor of Khasekhemwy's enclosure. Near the centre he found a short line of bricks laid at an angle, suggesting the upward spring of a vault or tumulus. O'Connor suspects that these are the remains of a mudbrick mound – a 'proto-pyramid'. He compares the mound within the rectangle to the temple at Hierakonpolis and the Djoser enclosure. Even more dramatic was the discovery of a row of 12 buried boats, east of Khasekhemwy's complex. Each wooden boat is contained in a mudbrick casing, plastered with mud and whitewashed. Lengths vary from 19 to 29 m (69 to 95 ft). This ghostly fleet strengthens the comparison of these valley enclosures to pyramid temples, which were docking places to the Netherworld.

With Khasekhemwy we are only years away from the 3rd dynasty, Djoser and the first great stone pyramid complex. But before Djoser, we must come to terms with the curious possibility of another royal cemetery of the first two dynasties at Saqqara.

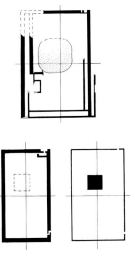

After he had found a row of bricks that may have belonged to a mound inside Khasekhemwy's valley enclosure (bottom left), David O'Connor reconstructed the 'proto-pyramid' slightly north and west of centre, a position occupied by the temple mound at Hierakonpolis (top) and Djoser's Step Pyramid (bottom right) in their respective enclosures. They also have in common entrances at the far south end of the east side and the east end of the north side (the first phase of Djoser's enclosure). The enclosures are not shown to scale.

Archaic Mastabas at Saqqara

Both literary tradition and archaeological discoveries inform us of a moment 4,900 years ago when the conquering overlords from the Qena Bend moved their administration of the Two Lands northwards to just below the apex of the Nile Delta. They called their new capital 'The Wall' – more familiar to us as Memphis. Towards the end of the 2nd dynasty it was known as *Ineb Hedj*, 'The White Wall'. Both the name and its hieroglyph suggest that it was a fortified enclosure with a series of bastions. The British Memphis Project is finding evidence that the oldest settlement was close to the North Saqqara escarpment. Directly across the Nile, thousands of Archaic tombs at Helwan indicate a missing settlement on the east. The twin towns must have formed the jambs of the 'gateway to the Delta', as Memphis would later be known.

The 1st-dynasty cemetery of high officials on the plateau edge at North Saqqara. Emery concluded they belonged to kings and queens, but names of certain officials were found on sealings or other texts associated with the tombs.

On the west side, a wide wadi rises like a natural ramp up into the Saqqara plateau from an old lake basin northwest of where the Archaic settlement may lie buried. Like the wadi at Abydos, this was a path from the land of the living to the realm of the dead. Flanking this route, along the very edge of the high cliff towering above the town, Egyptians of the 1st dynasty built a string of large mastabas with niched façades.

Monarchs or nomarchs?

Walter Emery excavated most of these mastabas between 1936 and 1956. As his excavations progressed, the sophistication and size of the deeply recessed, niched mastabas presented a real contrast to the contemporary royal tombs at Abydos, which were mostly variations of pit-graves. The niching of the mastabas is similar to that on the earliest *serekh* panels, the stylized representations of the palace-façade enclosure bearing the king's Horus name. So do the Saqqara tombs belong to kings and queens? Not on the basis of the niching alone, for it occurs on a wide range of Archaic tombs and seems to have generally designated high status.

At first Emery saw the Saqqara mastabas as the tombs of nobles and assigned mastaba 3035 to an official called Hemaka, the name found on sealings along with that of King Den. As he continued to excavate, however, he ascribed the tombs to royalty, not only because of their size and façades, but because of their contents. On jar sealings in mastaba 3357 he found only the name of the first king of the 1st dynasty, Hor-Aha – concluding therefore that this was his tomb. Other large mastabas contained seal impressions of almost all the other 1st-dynasty kings, and stone vessels with the names of the queens Merneith and Herneith.

This left scholars with two sets of apparently royal tombs: one at Saqqara, near the new capital, the other at Abydos, legendary homeland of the 1st dynasty. Some therefore thought that the tombs at

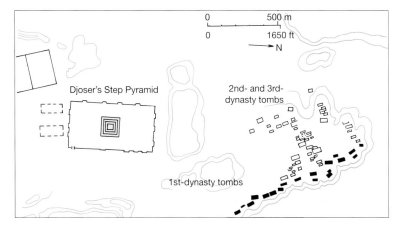

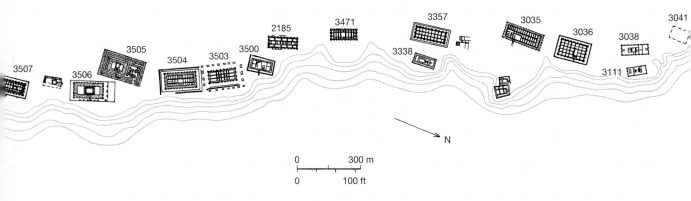

Abydos were symbolic, false tombs, or cenotaphs, to ensure the presence of the king's spirit in the old home ground during the Afterlife. In later times it was the practice for élite Egyptians to build cenotaphs at Abydos, the cult centre of Osiris.

On the other hand, others view Abydos as the true royal cemetery and see the Saqqara mastabas not as royal cenotaphs but as tombs of high officials. Seal impressions of such people, who held titles like Nomarch, Governor, Councillor, Treasurer, and 'Ruling in the King's Heart', are found almost as commonly as those of kings. Moreover, Emery recovered the stone stela of a man named Merka near a large niche or false door of mastaba 3505. Merka was a nomarch (*Adj-mer*), Captain of the Royal Ship and Controller of the Palace. He was also an *Iry Paat*, 'one of the *paat*', a class of patricians.

(Left) The inscribed panel from the stela of Merka, a high official, found near the main niche at the south end of mastaba 3505. Some see it as conclusive evidence that the large mastabas at North Saqqara belong to holders of high office under the kings, and not to the kings themselves.

(Below, left and centre) Modelled cattle skulls with real horns surround mastaba 3504, possibly a symbolic herd. Such skulls were found also at other mastabas, but in fewer numbers.

As for the argument that the Saqqara mastabas are bigger and therefore must be royal tombs, when the Abydos pit-graves are combined with the valley enclosures they present a total arrangement that is larger than the Saqqara mastabas. The presence also at Abydos of extraordinarily large groups of retainers' burials with their many small stelae, as well as the large stelae of rulers, all point to Abydos as the true burial ground.

Symbolic architecture

The Saqqara mastabas are massive structures comparable to fortified city walls, which some see as the inspiration for their façades. But when we consider the decoration painted on the plastered surface of the niched walls, it is apparent that the builders also had something else in mind. Recessed panels are painted yellow to imitate wood, while the forward, broadest faces are painted in varied patterns of squares, crosses and lozenges. These are the patterns of woven mats that the 1st-dynasty builders knew from their daily lives. They were simulating the wood-frame and woven reed-mat structures such as formed the *Per Wer* and the *Per Nu*, the predynastic shrines that became emblematic for Upper and Lower Egypt.

Like later false doors, which were abbreviated versions of these niched façades, the broader niches of the mastabas were contact points between this world and the Netherworld. Tucked into several niches of mastaba 3503 – which some still ascribe to Merneith, but which contained sealings of an official, perhaps Seshemka – Emery found offering dishes still in place after nearly five millennia. Even more dramatic, and peculiar to the 1st-dynasty mastabas of North Saqqara, are hundreds of clay ox heads with real horns attached – for instance arranged along the bench and in the recesses of mastaba 3504, ascribed to Djet but associated with sealings of an official named Sekhemka. These may represent offerings or a living herd.

(Above) Saqqara mastaba 3505; (below) the Abydos tomb and valley enclosure of Qa'a

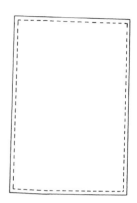

One argument in favour of the Saqqara mastabas being the royal tombs is their size. However, when the total arrangement of tomb and valley enclosure at Abydos is combined, they comprise a much greater area.

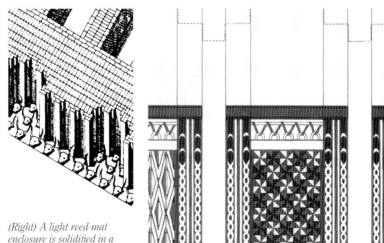

(Right) A light reed-mat enclosure is solidified in a painted mudbrick mastaba.

Egyptologists have long been frustrated by a lack of precedent for this earliest monumental architecture with its sophisticated exterior decoration. We may be missing a long evolution of fortifications, towns and tombs of early Delta communities, such as Buto, largely unexcavated. But it is important to realize that the mastabas, like the Abydos valley enclosures, are *simulacra* – models whose false doors were too narrow and low to have been exact copies of real doors. The elaborate niching of this fictive architecture accentuated the painted rendering of reed mats and wood frame. It was a way to 'show the construction' of the skeletal system while freezing it for eternity in mudbrick. Some burial chambers had real posts and reed mats on the walls – the 'inside' of the 'reed shrine'.

Pyramid Precedents

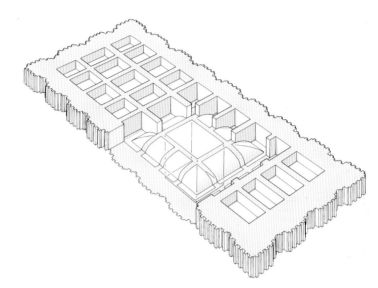

Mastaba 3507 with an interior vaulted tumulus over the burial chamber. Above the substructure of the standard mastaba, the interior was divided into a chequerboard pattern of smaller magazines that sometimes contained additional burial goods.

Changes in the design of the 1st-dynasty mastabas at Saqqara do suggest incipient forms of elements of the later pyramids, an aspect that still convinces some Egyptologists that they are royal tombs. North of mastaba 3357, ascribed to Hor-Aha, are a set of model buildings and two large terraces extending up to walls lining a boat pit. The whole looks like a simulated quay or dock with goods off-loaded and stored in the model buildings. Could this arrangement be a precursor to the mortuary temple, such as on the north side of Djoser's Step Pyramid? Mastaba 3505 (ascribed to Qa'a, but probably belonging to Merka) has a more developed north chapel that is closer to Djoser's pyramid temple, although it also fits in the development of chapels of tombs of high officials.

It is in the very core of the mastabas that features develop which appear to be compelling precedents for the later pyramids. In mastaba 2185 we see for the first time great stone beams over the burial chamber. Mastabas 3036 and 3035, belonging to the officials Ankhka and Hemaka, have a stepped entrance corridor built into a sloping trench that approaches the burial chamber from the east. The corridors feature the first portcullis grooves and slabs, the sliding stone door that would be used in pyramid passages throughout the Old Kingdom. As well as improving security, these arrangements have the functional advantage of allowing the burial chamber and magazines to be entered for the funeral even after they had been sealed by the superstructure. Earlier mastabas must have been built after the occupant had been interred and could not be re-entered.

In mastaba 3507, Emery found a low rounded tumulus above the burial chamber. Set within the rectangular niched wall enclosure, the mound completed the basic pattern of the early Hierakonpolis temple and the later Djoser complex. In mastaba 3357, reed mats stuck on the walls perhaps imitated the interior of a reed enclosure – a forerunner of Djoser's apartments below his pyramid, where the reed mats are rendered in blue faience tiles.

But it is in mastaba 3038, from the reign of Adjib, that we find the closest precedent to Djoser's Step Pyramid. The entire substructure, in a 4-m (13-ft) deep rectangular pit, had mudbrick walls rising to a height of 6 m (19 ft). Three sides of this structure were then built out to form eight shallow steps rising at an angle of 49°. This would have been an oblong step pyramid except the remaining side was left uncovered. In the final building phase a niched enclosure wall was erected all round and the area within entirely filled with sand, thus completely burying the stepped mound.

When Emery stripped away the niched mastaba to reveal the stepped mound, Egyptologists were struck by its similarity to the image of a stepped mound associated with the name of King Adjib etched on pottery, stone vases and ivory tablets from both Saqqara and Abydos. On top of Adjib's mound is a stela with hieroglyphs that read 'Protection around Horus' (i.e. the king). Could this innovative stepped mound buried inside mastaba 3038 have been so renowned that it became closely associated with King Adjib?

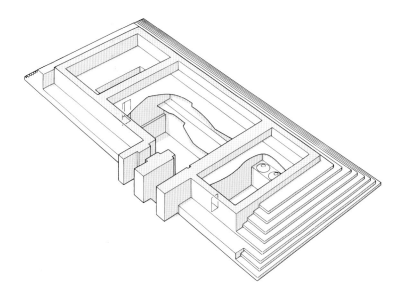

The image of a stela, which reads 'Protection around Horus', on a stepped mound, along with the name of the 1st-dynasty pharaoh Adjib.

The stepped tumulus inside the niched mastaba 3038 (above and right), associated with sealings of Adjib. A chamber with granaries was located to one side of the central burial chamber.

(Below) Mastaba 3505, showing the descending entrance staircase that was blocked by large stone portcullis slabs. As well as the burial chamber, side chambers were probably magazines.

(Left) A view into the interior of mastaba 3500, with the great stone portcullis slabs still blocking the entrance passage.

81

Saqqara: An Overview

A view of the Saqqara pyramid field from Giza.

The Saqqara plateau hosted 11 royal pyramids, more than any other site in Egypt. This is not counting the satellite pyramids, queens' pyramids and Shepseskaf's mastaba. In the midst of the pyramids were the many hundreds of tombs of officials great and small, ranging in date from the 1st dynasty to the Coptic period. The entire necropolis extends across the central plateau for 2.5 km (1½ miles) from the northern tip of the row of 1st-dynasty tombs to south of the pyramid complex of Sekhemkhet, and for the same distance from the eastern escarpment to the enigmatic great empty enclosure, the Gisr el-Mudir, west of Djoser's pyramid. If we include the pyramid fields of Abusir to the north, and South Saqqara, its natural extensions, the necropolis is over 7.5 km (4 miles) long.

This city of the dead in stone and sand is the otherworldly counterpart of the living city of Memphis. Memphis migrated southwards to stay ahead of the sands drifting in from the desert as the climate became increasingly drier throughout the Old Kingdom, and to follow the Nile as it retreated eastwards. As the city moved so did the necropolis up on the high desert.

The centrepiece of the Saqqara tableau is the Step Pyramid of Djoser (the Horus Netjerykhet). When the king's builders began this unprecedented creation in stone, the site may have already been a royal reserve. Immediately south, there are two large sets of underground galleries, over 130 m (427 ft) long and entered by passages from the north. On the basis of seal impressions found within them, they are considered to be the tombs of the first and third kings of the 2nd dynasty – Hetepsekhemwy and Ninetjer, both of whom, unlike Peribsen and Khasekhemwy later in the dynasty, did not have tombs at Abydos. The tombstone of the second king of the 2nd dynasty, Raneb, was found in the area, suggesting that another royal tomb remains to be found.

Stadelmann believes that the galleries were once topped by long mastabas, similar to Djoser's South Tomb. He also links these tombs with the huge empty rectangles formed by low walls further west, out in the desert. According to Stadelmann, these empty precincts are the counterparts to the valley enclosures of Peribsen and Khasekhemwy at Abydos, although here the sacred precincts are farther west into the desert whereas at Abydos they are east of the royal tomb and down near the cultivation. Others date the rectangles to the 3rd dynasty.

Why are Djoser's and Sekhemkhet's pyramids and these mysterious empty rectangles so far out into the desert? If we look at the map of Saqqara with south at the top as the ancient Egyptians viewed their world, we see that the Abusir Wadi is a natural causeway connecting the floodplain below the northern point of the Saqqara Plateau to the front of the Djoser and Sekhemkhet enclosures, and the two anonymous royal rectangles. At the mouth of the wadi there may have been a lake, perhaps forming a harbour just beside the early settlement at the foot of the escarpment.

Pyramid builders abandoned Saqqara for almost the entirety of the 4th dynasty as the clamour of building jumped south to Meidum then to Dahshur, during Sneferu's reign, and was thereafter focused on Giza for three generations. Only with the passing of that dynasty, around 2472 BC, did Shepseskaf come back to build his giant stone mastaba at South Saqqara.

Return to Saqqara

Userkaf, the first king of the 5th dynasty, returned to the heart of central Saqqara and built his pyramid squarely beside the east wall of the Step Pyramid enclosure, at its far north end. This position must have been very important to the king. Locating his pyramid here, he had to straddle a depression, perhaps part of the so-called moat that surrounds the Step Pyramid enclosure.

The 5th-dynasty pyramid complexes at Saqqara each required access to the valley floor via a causeway. Ideally this would run through a natural wadi that sloped gradually enough to avoid the need for a huge foundation ramp. This determined where the builders could situate a pyramid complex. New evidence recovered by the British team at Memphis and Saqqara indicates another determining factor. Each complex may have been situated to take advantage of natural lakes along the desert edge. Such lakes were left after the annual floods receded or were stranded as the course of the Nile moved. Userkaf's causeway, never excavated, probably ran through the wadi that now contains the tourist road up to the plateau.

The four kings who followed Userkaf built their pyramids in a cluster at Abusir. Again, the lake in the Abusir 'bay' could have furnished a common harbour. As the kings added to the Abusir pyramid cluster they followed a practice that we have seen in the 1st-dynasty royal cemetery at Abydos, and also at central Saqqara and Giza, that is to extend in a general southwest orientation.

Near the end of the 5th dynasty Djedkare-Isesi built his pyramid at South Saqqara on a point overlooking the mouth of the prominent Wadi el-Tafla, which probably furnished a low, ponded area suitable for a pyramid harbour.

Unas built his pyramid close against the Step Pyramid enclosure, at the far west end of the south side. Like two guard posts, the pyramids of the first (Userkaf) and last (Unas) kings of this dynasty flanked the precinct of their ancestor, Djoser. As with Userkaf, the selection of the site for his pyramid must have been of considerable importance to Unas, since it required that he build an extremely long causeway to reach the floodplain. It ran through a minor wadi to yet another of the natural lakes along the desert edge.

When Teti, first pharaoh of the 6th dynasty, built his pyramid northeast of Userkaf's, a necklace of pyramids from the 3rd, 5th and 6th dynasties extended diagonally from northeast to southwest across the central Saqqara plateau. The orientation is approximate, although a line can be drawn connecting the northwest corner of the pyramid of Sekhemkhet, the pyramid of Unas (but off centre), the southeast corner of Djoser, the southeast corner of Userkaf and the centre of Teti. A small pyramid, almost destroyed (of Merikare or Menkauhor), east of Teti's extended the line of pyramids a little farther northeast to the edge of the escarpment.

Pepi I and two of his sons, Merenre and Pepi II, returned to South Saqqara and built their pyramids on the shoulders of the Wadi el-Tafla. This part of Saqqara lines up with the principal ruins of Memphis dating to the Middle and New Kingdoms. The Greek name Memphis probably derives from the name of Pepi I's pyramid, *Men-nefer Pepi*, 'The Perfection of Pepi Endures'. His pyramid town may be located under the modern village of Saqqara. Pepi II chose to build his pyramid close to the mastaba of Shepseskaf. After Pepi II, the pharaohs would build no major pyramid complexes for more than 150 years. The pyramid of an 8th-dynasty ruler, Ibi, and that east of Teti's, if it belongs to Merikare and so dates to the 9th dynasty, were the last pyramids built at Saqqara. These small pyramids were the final gasps of the Old Kingdom pyramid age.

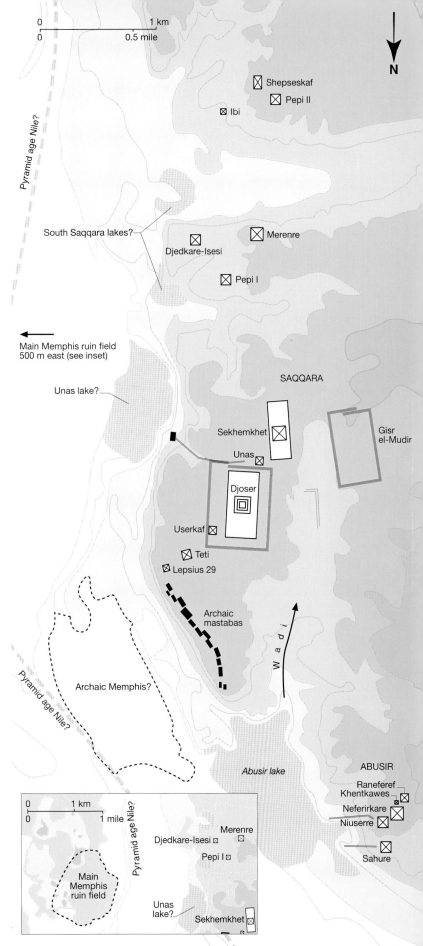

Djoser's Step Pyramid Complex

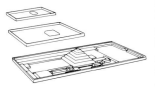

Stages in the evolution of the pyramid: from Khasekhemwy's mound within an enclosure at Abydos (top), to Djoser's simple mastaba within a rectangular stone enclosure (centre) at Saqqara, which was then covered by his great Step Pyramid.

(Opposite page) A unique pyramid complex: the success of Djoser is echoed through later antiquity in the tradition that this king, and his architect, Imhotep, were the inventors of stone architecture. We see many familiar forms for the first time here: the first colonnade, the first hypostyle, portico, life-sized statues, torus-moulding and cavetto cornice, and, of course, the first pyramid. Many structures in the complex survived as members of the hieroglyphic sign-list of sacred buildings, a 'vocabulary of forms'. The 3rd-dynasty builders inherited many of these forms from predynastic wood and reed structures and petrified and perpetuated them in the Step Pyramid complex. They left the doors of the complex open forever, inviting later generations of kings and their designers to come in and to see, and to build their own variations. The actual entrance colonnade, now restored, is shown opposite, bottom left.

It would be hard to overemphasize the dramatic leap in architectural size and sophistication represented by Egypt's first royal stone complex, the Step Pyramid of Djoser at Saqqara. Djoser is the name given to this king by New Kingdom visitors to the site over a thousand years later. But the only royal name found on the walls of the complex is the Horus name, Netjerykhet. In 1996 Dreyer found Netjerykhet's mud sealings at Khasekhemwy's Abydos tomb, suggesting a direct link between them. As for the monumental record, prior to Djoser the most common material for large buildings was mudbrick.

Then, within Djoser's 19-year reign (2630–2611 BC), his architect Imhotep, Chancellor and Great Seer (i.e. high priest) of the sun god Ra, built the Step Pyramid and its huge enclosure. A limestone wall, 10.5 m (34 ft) high and 1,645 m (5,397 ft) long, contained an area of 15 ha (37 acres), the size of a large town in the 3rd millennium BC. Within was a vast complex of functional and dummy buildings, including the Pavilions of the North and South, large tumuli and terraces, finely carved façades, ribbed and fluted columns, stairways, platforms, shrines, chapels and life-sized statues. There was even a replica of the substructure, the South Tomb. The centrepiece was the Step Pyramid, rising in six steps to a height of *c.* 60 m (197 ft), containing 330,400 cu. m (11,668,000 cu. ft) of clay and stone.

The Step Pyramid complex is such a basic template of Egyptian art and architecture that it is easy to take it for granted. But the implications of the architecture for changes in the government of Egypt and political control of people's lives are astounding. Consider one of many facts about the complex that has major implications for human labour: the builders did not form the recesses of the huge stone enclosure wall before they laid the blocks, as modern masons would. Instead they hand-carved each recess into the face of the already laid masonry, an enormous task since there were 1,680 recessed panels on the bastions and dummy doorways, each panel more than 9 m (30 ft) tall.

Building in stages

The pyramid was built in stages, progressing from an initial square mastaba to the final six-step pyramid. According to Jean-Philippe Lauer, the main excavator of the site, there were six stages (M_1 - M_2 - M_3 - P_1 - P_1' - P_2). Assuming that this is correct

(Rainer Stadelmann has modified this scheme), we get a major expansion every three years, if we divide the six stages into the 19 years of Djoser's reign. Even doubling his reign to 38 years – conceivable if the 19 years were biennial taxation years – gives us a major alteration every six years.

When the builders began to transform the mastaba into the first pyramid they built a crude core of roughly shaped stones with a fine limestone casing and a layer of packing in between. This technique had been used also for the mastabas. But now there was a profound difference: they abandoned horizontal beds and began to build in accretions that leaned inwards. They also used bigger and better blocks that they no longer needed to pack with large amounts of mortar of tafla – the local tan-coloured desert clay. Instead, the clay was used only as an aid to setting each block on a bed that inclined with the accretion layer.

The Egyptians also built the surrounding structures and enclosure in stages. Werner Kaiser pointed out that the first, smaller, stage, is similar to the Abydos valley enclosure of Khasekhemwy. Djoser's original mastaba is off-centre in the first enclosure, like the mound O'Connor hypothesizes for Khasekhemwy's enclosure, and that within the enclosure at Hierakonpolis (p. 77).

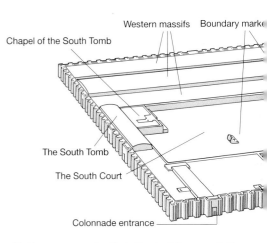

Chapel of the South Tomb — Western massifs — Boundary marke[r]
The South Tomb
The South Court
Colonnade entrance

Evidence suggests that the builders partially buried the dummy structures of Djoser's enclosure – the Pavilions of the North and South, the South Tomb and Sed Chapels – almost immediately after they built them in the first stage. Likewise they encased the king's mastaba in fine limestone in the first stage and then only a few years later entirely covered it with the Step Pyramid – an act which, if Stadelmann is right, they may have planned from the beginning. The half-submerging of the dummy buildings must have signified the chthonic, underworld aspect of existence after death. And the full envelopment of the mastaba conforms to the pattern of early Egyptian monuments that successive stages conceal earlier ones. Tomb building appears

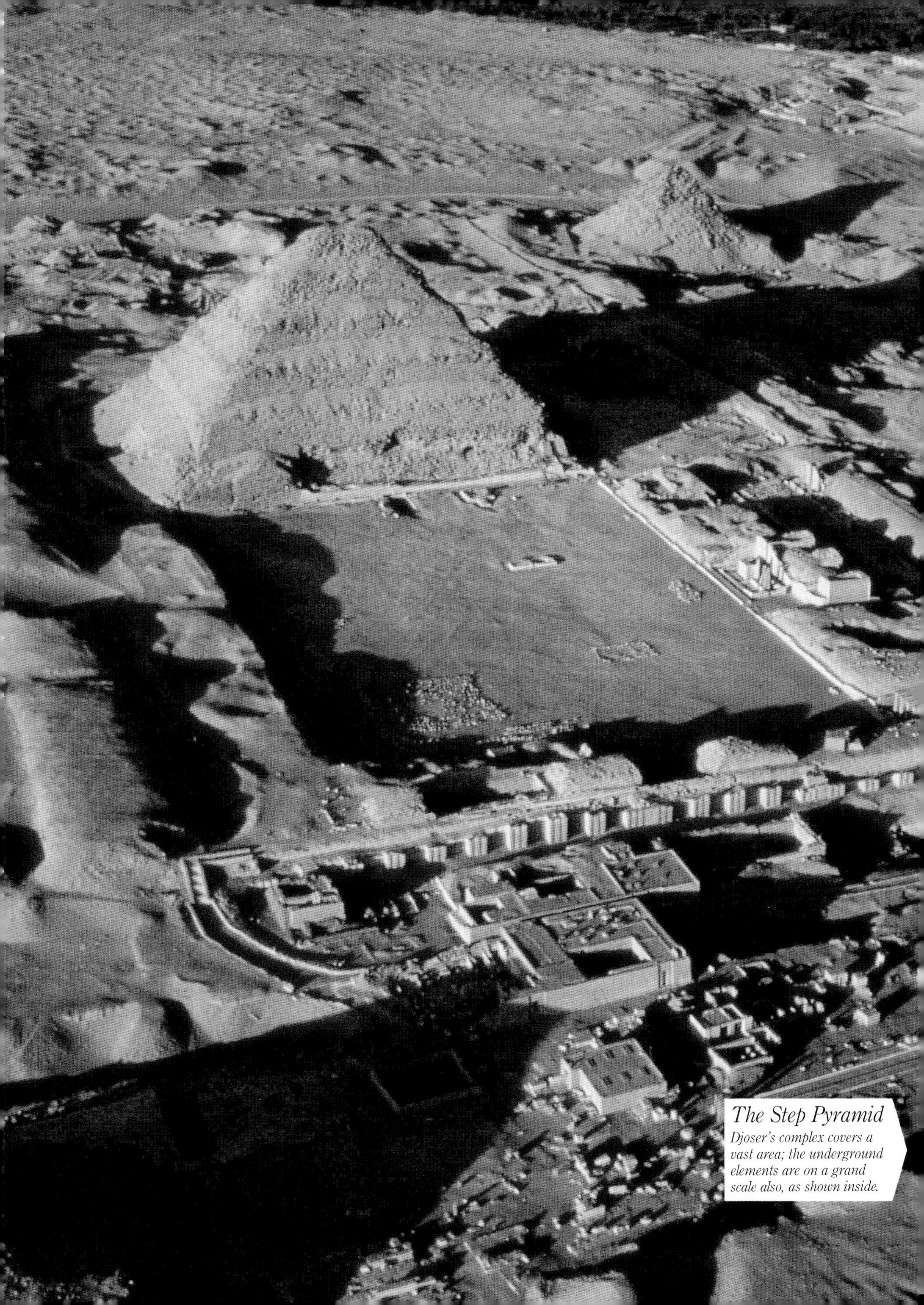

The Step Pyramid
Djoser's complex covers a
vast area; the underground
elements are on a grand
scale also, as shown inside.

Inside the Step Pyramid

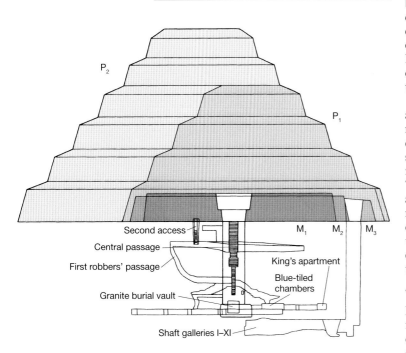

Profile view of the Step Pyramid, looking north, showing the stages in the building of the superstructure, and tangle of shafts, galleries and chambers of the substructure.

The above-ground elements of Djoser's pyramid complex are only one part of the story. Below, the Egyptians created an underground structure on a scale previously unknown, quarrying out more than 5.7 km (3½ miles) of shafts, tunnels, chambers, galleries and magazines. The only precedent is the 2nd-dynasty royal underground galleries a short distance south of the Djoser complex, one of which is assigned Hetepsekhemwy. In fact, Djoser's Western Galleries are almost aligned with Hetepsekhemwy's, but are several orders of magnitude larger; they are also the least explored part of the pyramid's substructure. A central corridor and two parallel ones extend over 365m (1,198 ft), connecting 400 rooms. These and other subterranean features – impressive enough – surround one of the most complicated tangles of tunnels and shafts the Egyptians ever created, below the pyramid itself.

A great Central Shaft, 7 m (23 ft) square and 28 m (92 ft) deep, was dug for the burial chamber. To remove waste as the shaft got deeper, a descending corridor was built, joining the shaft from the north. Above and around it masons were building mastaba M_1. Others began work on the king's burial vault at the bottom, bringing in materials by the descending corridor. The final vault was of granite, but Lauer found evidence that there had been an earlier one with walls of alabaster and a pavement of diorite or schist. Numerous fragments of these costly materials were found packed around the vault. But most interesting were limestone blocks with large five-pointed stars in low relief. These blocks, which

had been reused with their decoration hidden or neglected, must have formed the roof of the first burial vault – the earliest known example of a star ceiling. This motif, one that the Egyptians placed over royal tomb chambers for centuries, embodies one of the paradoxes of the pyramids. Djoser may lie after death underground, under millions of tons of masonry, but the roof of the chamber is 'open' to the night sky, to which his soul is free to fly.

The fact that this burial vault was scrapped and another built parallels the multiple buildings and rebuildings above ground. When it was decided to expand the mastaba into a pyramid, the new superstructure covered the descending corridor and made it impossible to keep the central shaft open. They were filled and covered with masonry and another way had to be contrived to bring in the royal body. A new access was built, beginning as an open stairway trench north of the pyramid temple, while the centre of the descending corridor was left open. In the narrowest parts of the new access there was no room for anything wider than a metre.

The granite vault

Djoser's final resting place was a vault consisting of four courses of well-dressed granite blocks, its only opening a cylindrical aperture towards the north end. Once the royal remains were laid to rest, the hole was blocked with a granite plug weighing 3.5 tons, with four grooves to guide the ropes used to lower it. Above the burial vault the builders had created a small room to give them space to lower the plug. Nothing of this remained for modern archaeologists – it must have been destroyed by ancient explorers who emptied the shaft, probably in the 26th dynasty – but the form of this 'manoeuvre chamber' could be worked out on the basis of the one found intact in the South Tomb.

Space inside the vault was restricted, and Lauer believes the body was placed in a gilded wooden box. Once body and granite plug were in place, the

descending corridor was filled. Djoser's body was now packed like the core of a battery and no doubt those who succeeded him believed his remains, buried in the heart of the pyramid, rendered the structure fully charged. Mummy parts were retrieved from the vault: underneath outer coarse linen, a finer linen had been used to model tenons and bones – a technique characteristic of the most ancient mummies of the Old Kingdom. However, recent radiocarbon dating shows them to be many centuries younger than Djoser.

The king's subterranean palace

Well before the expansion of the mastaba into the pyramid, masons were at work on passages surrounding the central shaft. To the north, west and south, they tunnelled long armatures ending in transverse galleries, from which they began to cut crude perpendicular magazines. A stairway from the descending corridor took a series of turns and corridors, ending in an eastern chamber. Here, craftsmen were far advanced on an exquisite decoration of faience and limestone. Rows of blue faience tiles with raised bands of limestone simulate a reed-mat structure – perhaps the king's palace. Blue also evokes the watery associations of the Egyptian Netherworld. The decoration was organized into six panels. Three on the north side were topped by an arch supported by simulated *djed* pillars. One contained the real doorway; the limestone frame bore the name and protocol of Netjerykhet (Djoser). Three southern panels framed false door stelae, showing Djoser performing a ritual run and visits to shrines. This chamber was never completed – the builders left the east wall roughly hacked from the rock and the decorators seem to have finished in a hurry. All four walls of two further chambers were covered with the blue-tile inlay and the doorways were framed with Djoser's name. These must represent the inner private rooms of the palace.

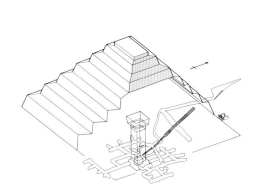

Djoser's underground complex of passages, stairways and chambers is one of the most complex under any pyramid. Not all the robbers' tunnels are shown here. The diagram (left) shows how the main substructure perspective relates to the pyramid.

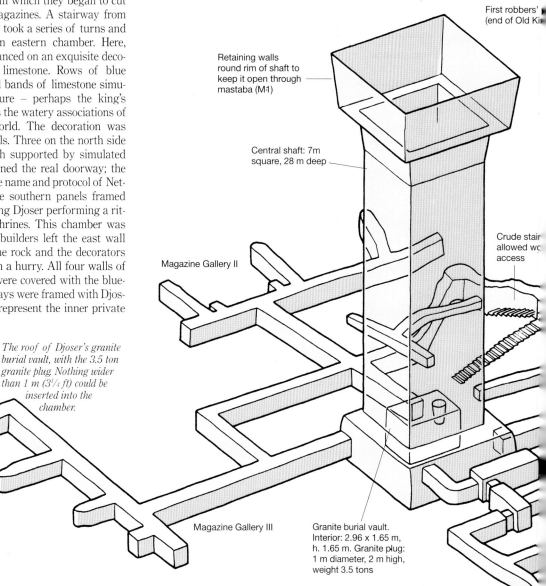

The roof of Djoser's granite burial vault, with the 3.5 ton granite plug. Nothing wider than 1 m (3¼ ft) could be inserted into the chamber.

First robbers'
(end of Old Ki

Retaining walls round rim of shaft to keep it open through mastaba (M1)

Central shaft: 7m square, 28 m deep

Crude stair allowed wc access

Magazine Gallery II

Magazine Gallery III

Granite burial vault. Interior: 2.96 x 1.65 m, h. 1.65 m. Granite plug: 1 m diameter, 2 m high, weight 3.5 tons to have been part of a larger ceremonial cycle, an act of consolidation and renewal that necessitated burying finely crafted structures. The Egyptian penchant for simulation receives one of its greatest expressions here. The stone enclosure wall imitates one of mudbrick; the ceiling stones of the entrance passage, the Sed chapels and the Pavilions of the North and South imitate wooden log beams; traces of paint indicate that many façades and pillars in fine limestone were painted red to imitate wood.

With certain elements, it was enough that their form – their image – was present in the façade; the interior could be abbreviated. Yet not all the buildings in the Djoser complex are dummy façades. Lauer has distinguished between functional versus fictional structures. The fictive architecture served the king's *ka* in the Afterlife. The functional may have been necessary for the actual conduct of the funeral ceremonies. Djoser's funeral cortège could have negotiated an elaborate course through the buildings, a statue of the king at every major turn symbolically allowing the procession to pass. But, given the fact that many entrances and passages are scarcely wider than 1 m (3¼ ft), it would have been far more convenient to bring the royal body and its accoutrements into the complex by way of a ramp over the enclosure in its northeast corner.

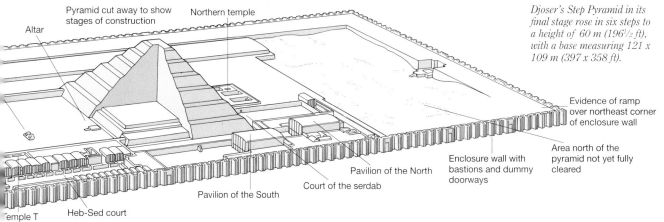

Djoser's Step Pyramid in its final stage rose in six steps to a height of 60 m (196½ ft), with a base measuring 121 x 109 m (397 x 358 ft).

Pyramid cut away to show stages of construction

Northern temple

Altar

Evidence of ramp over northeast corner of enclosure wall

Area north of the pyramid not yet fully cleared

Enclosure wall with bastions and dummy doorways

Pavilion of the North

Court of the serdab

Pavilion of the South

Heb-Sed court

Temple T

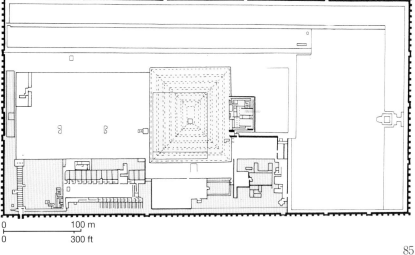

0   100 m
0   300 ft

N

Djoser's statue in its serdab (below), representing the king emerging from his private Netherworld apartment below the pyramid.

With eyes once inlaid with rock crystal, Djoser's statue (above) gazed out through peep-holes in the serdab box, tilted upwards 13° to the northern sky where the king joined the circumpolar stars, his brethren. A replica statue now occupies the serdab.

The eastern shafts and galleries

Yet another, deeper substructure below the pyramid was begun when it was still a mastaba. Eleven vertical shafts were dug, from the bottom of which long galleries extend to the west. Galleries I–IV were used as tombs: two intact alabaster sarcophagi and fragments of others were found. The end of Gallery III widened into a room, cased with fine limestone, where the hip-bone of an 18-year-old woman was found. A seal impression gave the Horus name of Djoser and, tantalizingly, the titles 'Treasurer, Chief Lector Priest and Builder of Nekhen' – the first two were held by Imhotep. Recent radiocarbon dating deepens the mystery of Djoser's tomb once more: one set of female remains dates to generations before Djoser's time.

Galleries VI–IX contained a remarkable collection of stone vessels. Stacks of plates and cups – mostly of alabaster but also of other fine stones – added up to a staggering total of around 40,000 vessels. Many bore inscriptions revealing that the majority were not made for Djoser, but probably belonged to his royal ancestors. Perhaps, like the female remains that date so early, the vessels were salvaged from the already plundered 1st-dynasty mastabas at Saqqara. The Step Pyramid was not only a vocabulary of forms passed on to the future, but also a repository of the past.

Once painted to bring it to life, Djoser's original statue is now in the Cairo Museum. It is inscribed with his name, as King of Upper and Lower Egypt, heir of two crown goddesses, Nekhbet (south, vulture) and Wadjet (north, cobra), Netjerykhet of gold.

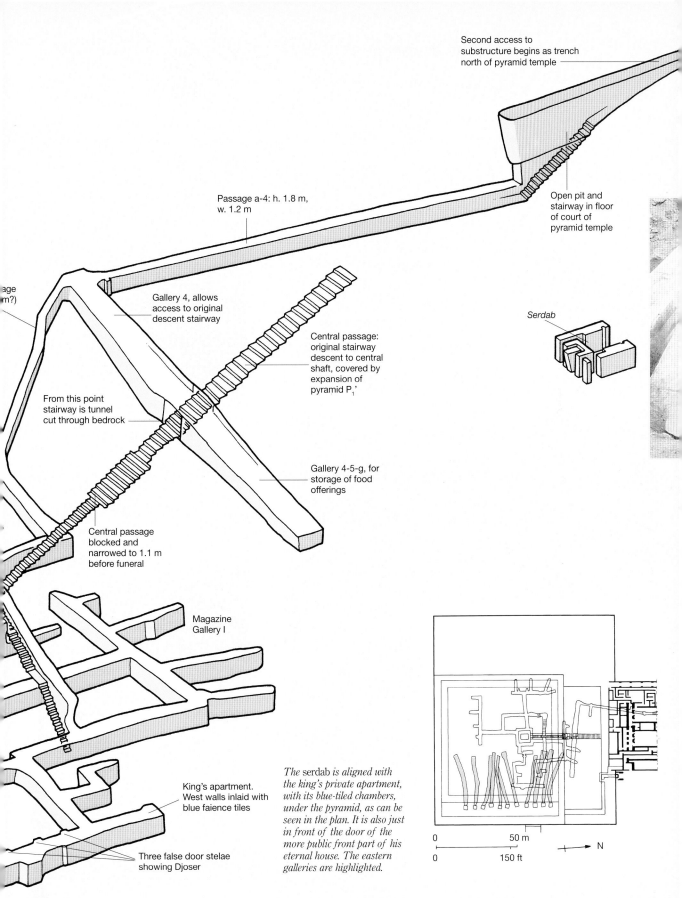

Second access to
substructure begins as trench
north of pyramid temple

Passage a-4: h. 1.8 m,
w. 1.2 m

Open pit and
stairway in floor
of court of
pyramid temple

age
m?)

Gallery 4, allows
access to original
descent stairway

Serdab

Central passage:
original stairway
descent to central
shaft, covered by
expansion of
pyramid P$_1$'

From this point
stairway is tunnel
cut through bedrock

Gallery 4-5-g, for
storage of food
offerings

Central passage
blocked and
narrowed to 1.1 m
before funeral

Magazine
Gallery I

King's apartment.
West walls inlaid with
blue faience tiles

The serdab *is aligned with
the king's private apartment,
with its blue-tiled chambers,
under the pyramid, as can be
seen in the plan. It is also just
in front of the door of the
more public front part of his
eternal house. The eastern
galleries are highlighted.*

Three false door stelae
showing Djoser

0   50 m

0   150 ft

N

The South Tomb

By all Egyptological reckoning the Step Pyramid itself is a functional royal tomb. But in Djoser's complex, in addition to the Step Pyramid, we find the enigmatic South Tomb. Below it the builders replicated three essential features of the substructure of the pyramid: the descending corridor; central shaft with the granite vault; and the king's palace with its blue-tiled chambers. As under the pyramid, the builders blocked the descending corridor except for a narrow stairway to allow them to bring in whatever it was they placed in the vault. About halfway down the corridor a side chamber was found filled with large jars. On top of these the workmen had left a wooden stretcher, box and posts from a baldachin that resemble those of Hetepheres's cache at Giza (p. 117).

Robbers had done far less damage to the South Tomb than the pyramid itself, so excavators found the manoeuvre chamber intact. The walls were of large limestone slabs and the underside of the stone ceiling beams had been rounded to imitate palm logs. As in the pyramid (though here at the south rather than the north end), the burial chamber was

entered by a round aperture. Remarkably, the wooden beam used to lower the granite plug was still in place with traces left by the ropes still visible. Incorporated into the masonry of the manoeuvre chamber were blocks of fine limestone with relief-carved stars – remains of a previous vault.

The granite vault is similar to the one under the pyramid, but it is much smaller, and its interior was covered in green traces of copper. What was placed in this vault, too small for a human burial? Various suggestions have been made: that it was a fictive tomb for a ritual death during the Heb-Sed ceremonies when the king renewed his vital forces; that it was the home of the king's *ka*; that it was the burial place of the royal placenta, preserved from birth until death; that it was for the burial of the crowns; or that it was a symbolic reference to the old tombs at Abydos, be they actual or fictive burial places. Lauer thought it might have been for the king's internal organs, removed during mummification, though in later times the canopic chest containing these was placed in the same chamber as the body.

The entire South Tomb complex may have been intended for the king's *ka*, and the Egyptians often gave the *ka* special funerary treatment by the separate interment of a statue. There is compelling evidence that Khafre's satellite pyramid was used for a statue burial. The South Tomb may thus be seen as the precursor of later satellite pyramids. The wooden stretcher, box and poles found in the magazine in the South Tomb may be the ritually disassembled parts of the apparatus used to carry such a statue.

All indications point to the fact that the South Tomb was finished first: the king's inner palace is far more complete than that of the pyramid. Chamber I has six panels identical to those under the pyramid, with blue faience tiles laid on a limestone backing imitating reed-mat façades with a vaulted top supported by *djed* columns. One contained the real door from the vestibule. In another chamber (II) three more panels contain false door stelae, while the fourth contains the real door exiting to a short corridor. Two more chambers are covered, like their counterparts under the pyramid, with blue faience inlay. The blue-tiled chambers are one of the most impressive features of the Djoser substructure. Yet the product of this extraordinary care and craftsmanship was never intended to be seen by living eyes; it was meant instead to ensure something in the king's existence after death. The clue to what that was lies in the false door stelae, which form the pictorial and textual determinative to the entire underground complex. In the darkest, most inaccessible place the Egyptian builders could devise, they used the best of their nascent abilities in relief art and text to depict the king in perpetual communication, not so much with his living subjects, as with the *netjeru*, the gods and denizens of the Netherworld, where the king's mat palace was now part of the watery, sacred region of primeval reed shrines.

King Djoser performing the ceremonial heb-sed run, holding the household deed – to the whole of Egypt. This is one of the false door stelae in the blue-tiled chambers of the South Tomb. Three stelae were located under the main pyramid, and three under the South Tomb.

Djoser Underground

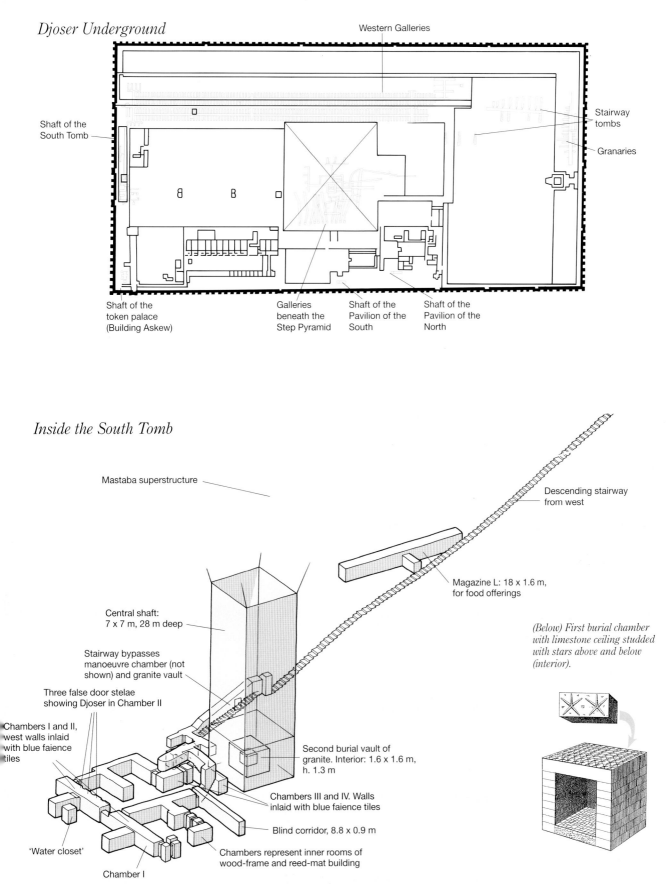

Western Galleries

Stairway tombs

Granaries

Shaft of the South Tomb

Shaft of the token palace (Building Askew)

Galleries beneath the Step Pyramid

Shaft of the Pavilion of the South

Shaft of the Pavilion of the North

Inside the South Tomb

Mastaba superstructure

Descending stairway from west

Magazine L: 18 x 1.6 m, for food offerings

Central shaft: 7 x 7 m, 28 m deep

Stairway bypasses manoeuvre chamber (not shown) and granite vault

Three false door stelae showing Djoser in Chamber II

Chambers I and II, west walls inlaid with blue faience tiles

Second burial vault of granite. Interior: 1.6 x 1.6 m, h. 1.3 m

Chambers III and IV. Walls inlaid with blue faience tiles

Blind corridor, 8.8 x 0.9 m

'Water closet'

Chambers represent inner rooms of wood-frame and reed-mat building

Chamber I

(Below) First burial chamber with limestone ceiling studded with stars above and below (interior).

93

The Short Life of Step Pyramids

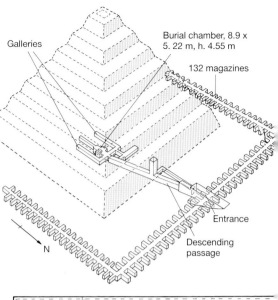

Galleries

Burial chamber, 8.9 x 5. 22 m, h. 4.55 m

132 magazines

Entrance

Descending passage

N

It might perhaps be expected that a long line of comparable step pyramid complexes would follow Djoser's. But while many specific elements were borrowed by later generations, the rectangular step pyramid complex did not endure.

Sekhemkhet's Buried Pyramid

The pyramid of Sekhemkhet at Saqqara, southwest of Djoser's, was an attempt to build another such complex, but it was abandoned soon after it was begun. In the Turin Papyrus Djoser's successor, Djoserty, is given a reign of only six years. This accords well with his identification as the king with the Horus name Sekhemkhet, whose pyramid never rose above the surface of its rectangular enclosure. It has been called simply the 'buried pyramid' but its base dimensions and the angle of incline suggest that it was probably intended to rise about 70 m (230 ft), in seven steps – higher than Djoser's.

In building the pyramid the masons used the same technique as Djoser's: accretions leaning inwards by 15°, with sloping courses of stone laid at right angles to the incline. As the pyramid was unfinished it never received its limestone casing, but considerable progress was made on the substructure. An unfinished set of galleries forms a U-shape around the pyramid underground.

At the end of the entrance corridor, past three sets of blocking that appeared intact, and under the dead centre of the pyramid, the excavator, Zakaria Goneim, found the burial chamber. Roughly rectangular, it was left unfinished. Corridors led to galleries, again unfinished, that may have been part of a planned 'apartment', like that built for Djoser.

Despite its unfinished state, Sekhemkhet's pyramid contains a curious mystery – a blocked burial chamber containing a unique sealed sarcophagus (below) that was absolutely empty.

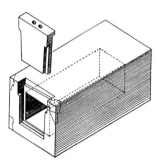

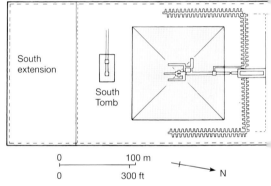

South extension

South Tomb

0   100 m
0   300 ft

N

In the centre of the chamber lay an alabaster sarcophagus. On top were two bands of plant material, possibly a funerary wreath. Analysis, however, proved it to be bark and decomposed wood. The sarcophagus is unique in being made of a single piece of stone with a sliding door at one end. It was only with great difficulty that the excavator raised the panel – which he described as sealed with mortar – to find the sarcophagus empty. Some dispute whether the tomb was unviolated, but Goneim was sure it remained as the builders had left it.

Sekhemkhet's South Tomb was also discovered – or rather its foundations and part of a destroyed mastaba, as this too was never completed. A wooden sarcophagus with the remains of a two-year-old child, as well as stone vases and jewellery of 3rd-dynasty date, were found at the end of a simple widening of the entrance corridor. Something happened at court that ended work on the most important monument in the land. But the child in the South Tomb is not Sekhemkhet. He reigned six years and is shown in adulthood in a relief at Wadi Maghara in Sinai. The mystery remains unsolved.

The Layer Pyramid of Zawiyet el-Aryan

Another 3rd-dynasty king attempted – and failed – to complete a step pyramid complex. Less is known about the Layer Pyramid of Zawiyet el-Aryan than even Sekhemkhet's. It occupies a site about 7 km (4 miles) north of Saqqara, on a ridge above, but not far from, the floodplain. In this, the pyramid departed from the trend set by Djoser and Sekhemkhet who built far out in the desert.

The pyramid's superstructure is typical 3rd-dynasty masonry, consisting of 14 accretions, leaning inward against a central core. Each accretion layer was built with a dressed outer face, with coarser masonry backing and thick seams of clay as mortar. Completed, the pyramid would probably have risen in five steps to a height of 42–45 m (138–148 ft). No traces of casing were found, perhaps because this pyramid too was never finished.

(Left) Sekhemkhet's pyramid was intended as a step pyramid probably of seven steps, but was never finished. Its base length was 120 m (394 ft). A northward extension of the enclosure covered a wall of bastions and niches, cased in fine limestone, like Djoser's enclosure wall.

(Above) The Layer Pyramid of Zawiyet el-Aryan, perhaps belonging to Khaba, was also begun as a step pyramid. The inward-leaning accretions are visible in what remains today.

(Right) The Horus name of Khaba was found inscribed on vases in a mastaba near the pyramid.

White Wall

North extension

Its substructure is so similar to Sekhemkhet's that there can be little doubt that scarcely any time elapsed between the two. No trace of a burial was found and a side passage leads to galleries again clean and empty – as if the workmen had only just left. Perhaps, indeed, this was the case, with the premature death of the king. A clue to the identity of the king whose pyramid this was is the Horus name Khaba, found inscribed on stone vases in a mastaba north of the pyramid.

The base length of the uncompleted Layer Pyramid was 84 m (275 ft) and it was probably intended to rise to a height of up to 45 m (148 ft). It is entered by a flight of steps in an open trench. A sloping passage runs to the bottom of a vertical shaft from which an unfinished passage leads south. A lower passage also leads south to a stairway and horizontal passage to the burial chamber.

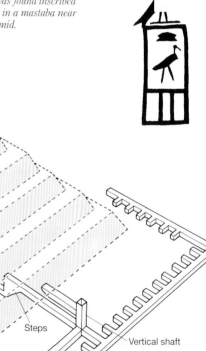

Burial chamber, 3.63 x 2.65 m, h. 3 m

Steps

Vertical shaft

Entrance stairway

32 magazines

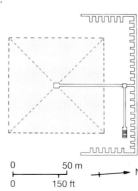

0   50 m

0   150 ft

N

The Enigma of the Provincial Step Pyramids

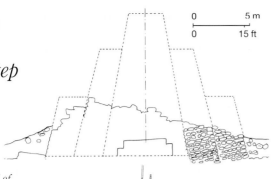

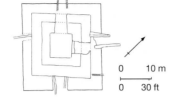

(Right) The step pyramid of Sinki, at Abydos. Excavated by Nabil Swelim and Gunter Dreyer, it had ramps and accretion marker bricks still in place. (Far right) The pyramid at Zawiyet el-Meitin. (Below) The pyramid at Seila.

Seven step pyramids are known in the provinces. The southernmost is on the island of Elephantine. Three more are near Ombos, Edfu and Hierakonpolis (at el-Kula). The next is at Sinki near Abydos. A solitary small pyramid is found in Middle Egypt at Zawiyet el-Meitin. Another, at Seila, overlooks the Fayum from atop the desert spur between it and the Nile.

The purpose of these small step pyramids is a mystery. It has been suggested that they mark the homelands of royal consorts, that they are the sacred places of Horus and Seth, or that they are symbols of the primeval hill. So far, none has been shown to have a burial chamber or ancillary buildings such as chapels. In 1987, the Brigham Young University Expedition did, however, find a fragmentary offering slab, two stelae – one of which was inscribed with the name of Sneferu, first king of the 4th dynasty – and scant traces of a mudbrick causeway on the east side of the Seila pyramid. This adds Seila to Sneferu's pyramid at Meidum and two at Dahshur. The five southern pyramids are different from the northern two, but their similarity to one another suggests that they were part of a single building programme by one king – perhaps Huni, father of Sneferu, to judge by a large granite cone inscribed with his name found at Elephantine. A further pyramid is tentatively ascribed to Huni. In 1985 Nabil Swelim surveyed a large rock knoll at Abu Roash that Lepsius had seen covered with mudbricks and numbered I. A passage in the north side slopes down to a chamber of the kind found in pyramids of the early 4th dynasty. Though it is unique for this period in being built of mudbrick, Swelim dates it to the end of the 3rd dynasty or the start of the 4th, and assigns it to Huni.

The small step pyramids may mark the locations of royal residences near, but outside, major religious and political centres. They would have been temporary residences occupied during visits of the king or his representatives during a journey through the land to collect taxes and give judgments. The pyramids spaced out along the provinces of Upper Egypt might also be connected with the early organization of the country into nomes (provinces).

These pyramids may therefore have been symbols of living sovereignty, hinting that the step pyramid stood for more than the royal tomb, the marker of a dead king. It is interesting that Huni took the pyramid to the provinces just before people and produce would be brought from the provinces to the core of the Egyptian nation for building the largest pyramids of all time.

The Provincial Pyramids

	Elephantine	Edfu South	El-Kula	Ombos	Sinki	Zawiyet el-Meitin	Seila
Orientation	17° NW	~ N	E–W	~ 12° NW	~ E–W	~ 20° NW	12° NW
Max. preserved height	5.1 m	5.5 m	8.25 m	c. 4.5 m	c. 4 m	4.75 m	6.8 m
Base length	Average 18.46 m 35.23 cubits	35–36 cubits	18.6 m 35.5 cubits	18.39 m 35.09 cubits	c. 35 cubits	On 2nd accretion: ~ 18.3 m, 35 cubits On 3rd accretion: 22.5 m, 43 cubits	On 3rd accretion: 25 m, 48 cubits
Slope angle	13°	~ 13°	< 11°	10°	? > 10°	~ 10 °	~ 14°
Steps	3	(3)	3	3?	(3)	3–4 respectively	4
King	Huni	? Huni	? Huni	? Huni	? Huni		Sneferu

Transition at Meidum

In many ways Meidum is the most mysterious of all the great pyramids. Embedded within the puzzles of this pyramid and its surrounding necropolis are distant events that transformed Archaic Egypt into the classic Old Kingdom pyramid age.

When Sneferu, the first king of Manetho's 4th dynasty, came to the throne in around 2575 BC, Djoser's was the only large royal pyramid that stood complete. Sneferu would become the greatest pyramid-builder in Egyptian history by constructing three colossal pyramids (at Meidum and the Bent and the North pyramids at Dahshur) and the smaller one at Seila – a total mass of stone that exceeds even that of his son Khufu, in the Great Pyramid at Giza.

Like Djoser's Step Pyramid, Meidum was built in stages, beginning with a step pyramid of seven steps (E1). Before the builders finished the fourth or fifth step, the king enlarged the project to a pyramid of eight steps (E2) which was completed in Sneferu's first 14 years. Previously it was suggested that Huni was responsible for this pyramid, based solely on the need to identify a large royal tomb for this king. However, the ancient name of Meidum, *Djed Sneferu* ('Sneferu Endures'), and the fact that Sneferu's name, unlike Huni's, appears in texts at the site, all point to the former as the builder of Meidum from start to finish.

In his 15th year on the throne Sneferu and his court moved to the area around Dahshur (p. 101). But then, during the last 15 years of his reign, according to Rainer Stadelmann, he sent his workers back to Meidum to fill out the original step pyramid as a true pyramid (E3). The pyramid at Meidum thus represents the very beginning and the end of Sneferu's pyramid-building programme.

Today Meidum consists of a three-stepped tower rising above a sloping mound of debris. The usual assumption is that the tower was left after the outer casing and packing that filled in the steps was quarried away. Indeed, Petrie recorded that the pyramid was still exploited as a quarry in his day. An alternative, and controversial, suggestion was that the tower and debris resulted from the collapse of the pyramid while it was under construction. Excavations, however, have now cleared away a large part of the debris and recovered various later remains but no 4th-dynasty ropes, timbers or workers' bodies – discounting the theory of a sudden collapse.

Construction techniques for the superstructure were initially in the old step pyramid style, with accretions of stone courses laid at an inward slope. Better quality stone, laid in more regular courses, was used for the outer faces of the accretions, and fine white Turah-quality limestone for the exterior surfaces of the steps.

(Below left) The first time the method of corbelling was used to roof a burial chamber was at Meidum. Like the eastern chapel, the chamber was left unfinished, lacking the fine dressing of the masonry.

(Below right) A cross-section of the pyramid at Meidum reveals the stages in its building and also the different styles of construction. Initially the masons used the traditional inward-leaning accretions, but more regular courses were employed for the final stage.

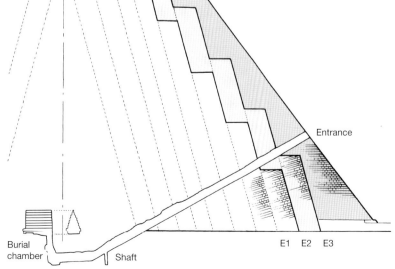

Entrance

Burial chamber

Shaft

E1 E2 E3

The small chapel on the east side of the pyramid was added when Sneferu's builders returned to create a true pyramid. However, when the pyramid was abandoned a second time the stelae in its court were left blank, perhaps because of the rise to power of the powerful and ambitious Khufu.

Inside the pyramid

The interior arrangement of the Meidum pyramid was an innovation and one that would become standard. A long passage from near the centre of the north face led to the burial chamber. Sneferu's workmen built the lower part of the passage in an open trench cut into the ground and filled with packing. This is not unusual, but they built the chamber at the approximate original desert surface and extended the narrow passage, which descended from the entrance, up into the body of the pyramid, opening about 16.6 m (54 ft) from the pyramid base, just above the first step.

Towards the bottom of the descending passage a short vertical shaft opens in the floor. A little beyond this, just before a horizontal section, a slot carved into the walls, floor and ceiling of the pas-

sage may have been for a door as fragments of wood were found here.

Two rooms or niches open off the corridor, probably for storing plugging blocks before they were used to seal the corridor. At its end is another vertical shaft leading up into the burial chamber. Cedar logs embedded in the masonry half way up the shaft may have been used to raise a sarcophagus into the chamber – or to facilitate its removal.

Sneferu's builders were evidently experimenting with ways to create a central room within the pyramid mass. In place of the thick granite beams that roof Djoser's vaults, they used a technique of corbelling for the first time, with each course of blocks above a certain height projecting inwards until the two walls almost meet. It is remarkably small, 5.9 m (19 ft) long and 2.65 m (9 ft) wide, perhaps intended as a kind of coffer in its own right, though it was never finished. Spanning the walls near the top of the chamber at the north end the workmen fitted more logs, one of which survives. These may also have assisted in raising the sarcophagus. But no trace of a sarcophagus was found in the chamber. Petrie recovered pieces of a wood coffin of 'the early plain style' at the bottom of the shaft, which are now in University College, London.

Burial chamber, 5.9 x 2.65 m, h. 5.05 m, corbelled

'Tower' visible today

Entrance

Eastern chapel, 9.18 x 9 m, h. 2.7 m

Vertical shaft, h. 6.5 m

N

Descending passage: 58 m long; 0.85 m wide; h. 1.65 m

Horizontal passage with two recesses for plug blocks

Transformations of a pyramid: from E1, a step pyramid of seven steps, to E2, a step pyramid of eight steps, to E3, a true pyramid with a slope of 51° 50' 35". Its base length was around 144 m (473 ft) and it was 92 m (302 ft) high. Meidum represents the beginning and end of Sneferu's reign, and the transition from the Archaic to the classic pyramid age. On the north side the long sloping passage to the burial chamber must have been planned from the outset.

The pyramid complex

A large rectangular enclosure wall, only traces of which survive, surrounded various elements of the pyramid complex that were also to become standard. On the south side of the pyramid a small satellite pyramid may have been completed, though it was badly destroyed when Petrie found it. Inside, a short sloping passage led to a burial chamber from the north. In the debris on the east side of the small pyramid a fragment of relief with the legs of a falcon was found, perhaps all that is left of a pair of stelae topped by the Horus falcon, like those in front of the satellite pyramid of the Bent Pyramid.

Another feature that would become standard is the causeway. Petrie's team excavated a long channel, running from the east-southeast in a straight line towards the pyramid centre, that they called the Approach. It is south of the final causeway and is perhaps an earlier version. Both are cut as channels into the bedrock and were paved with mud and had mudbrick sides. The causeway differed, however, in having completed side walls of limestone.

The royal necropolis

Meidum was the first newly established elite necropolis since Hor-Aha inaugurated the 1st-dynasty cemetery of officials at Saqqara. Just as the pyramid of Meidum is transitional from the step pyramid to the true pyramid, so the necropolis for which it is the centrepiece represents an unfinished transition from the old to the new.

The builders tried at first to replicate the pattern at Saqqara, with the king's funerary monument to the south and a series of large mastabas for high officials along the eastern escarpment to the north. Mastaba 16 belonged to Nefermaat, one of Sneferu's sons, and, close to the pyramid, was mastaba 17 – anonymous but probably the tomb of another prince. In addition there was an idea for a cemetery

better organized and set apart to the west of the pyramid. This was the seed of the concept that would find its fullest expression in Khufu's Western Cemetery at Giza. Most of the tombs, however, were left incomplete and unused with the move to Dahshur and the second abandonment of Meidum.

Return to Meidum: the true pyramid

It was probably in the 28th or 29th year of his reign that Sneferu ordered his workers to return to Meidum to transform the step pyramid into a true pyramid (E3) with a slope of 51° 50' 35", practically the same as Khufu's. They increased the length of the sides and extended the interior passage up through the added masonry, which was now laid in horizontal courses, first seen in the upper part of the Bent Pyramid at Dahshur (p. 102).

(Above) In the chapels of Nefermaat's mastaba (16) the artists experimented with tomb decoration. The figures were deeply cut and filled with coloured paste. This restored panel reads: 'He made his hieroglyphs in writing that cannot be erased.'

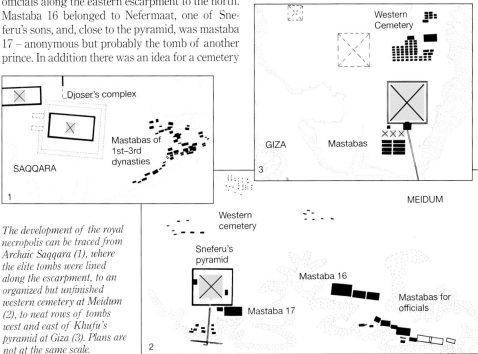

The development of the royal necropolis can be traced from Archaic Saqqara (1), where the élite tombs were lined along the escarpment, to an organized but unfinished western cemetery at Meidum (2), to neat rows of tombs west and east of Khufu's pyramid at Giza (3). Plans are not at the same scale.

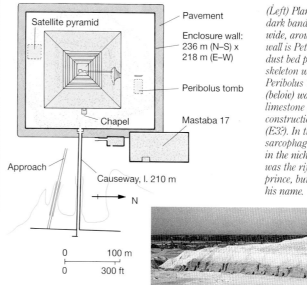

Satellite pyramid

Pavement

Enclosure wall:
236 m (N–S) x
218 m (E–W)

Peribolus tomb

Chapel

Mastaba 17

Approach

Causeway, l. 210 m

N

0   100 m
0   300 ft

(Left) Plan of Meidum: the dark band, 14.5 m (46 ft) wide, around the enclosure wall is Petrie's 'chip and stone dust bed pavement'. A female skeleton was found in the Peribolus Tomb. Mastaba 17 (below) was filled with limestone chips from the construction of the pyramid (E3?). In the granite sarcophagus which still stands in the niche at the west end was the rifled mummy of a prince, but we do not know his name.

(Above) Two round-topped stelae, the chapel and causeway of the Meidum pyramid. Had the stelae been inscribed, like similar ones at Dahshur, people approaching from the causeway would have seen the Horus falcons as if perched on the roof of the chapel. But the stelae were left completely blank.

(Below) The casing and packing stones of the E3 phase of the Meidum pyramid were laid horizontally.

Other elements appeared that, in more complex form, became customary in later pyramids. A small stone temple was built against the centre of the eastern base – so minuscule that it may have been a commemorative chapel to the king and not a true mortuary temple, because Sneferu finished the pyramid as a cenotaph rather than a tomb. The chapel's interior plan has the same winding passages found in front of the chapels of Djoser's Step Pyramid complex. In a small unroofed court were two round-topped stelae, 4.2 m (nearly 14 ft) tall.

A long causeway, cut into the bedrock and unroofed, reached from the pyramid enclosure to the valley floor. We might expect a valley temple at the lower end of the causeway, as with later pyramids, but the excavators found only long mudbrick walls. Given the unsophisticated forms of other elements at Meidum, the causeway may have led to a simple enclosure and landing platform.

The second abandonment?

Sneferu's two stelae in the eastern chapel were never inscribed with his *serekh* but were left completely blank – a fact that seems inexplicable given our understanding of the Egyptian belief that, devoid of a name, a monument (like a person) would have no identity. Perhaps it was the king's unexpected death and the ascent to the throne of an aggressive young prince, Khufu, that caused work to be frozen so suddenly. We can conjecture that the builders had finished the pyramid's third stage (E3) and only the fine dressing of the chapel walls and the stelae inscriptions remained to be completed.

If the pyramid was later stripped by looters, why did they spare the lower part of the casing and the stelae? Perhaps they had access to the upper part via ramps that the builders had left in place, never

having completed the filling out of the old step pyramid as a true pyramid. If so, the construction debris and embankments would have covered the lower, finer masonry that the robbers usually strip first. The appearance of Meidum today, in this case, would be that of a pyramid under construction, as well as one that has been partly stripped.

One significant, but overlooked, clue can be found in the two distinct types of debris. The lower type covered well-preserved casing, while the upper type corresponds to areas of casing that are badly weathered. From this it can be deduced that the lower layer was deposited soon after the casing was laid, while the upper part was deposited during and after pieces of casing were dislodged from higher up the pyramid and came crashing down. Could this lower debris include the remains of the original construction embankments?

In truth, because there has been so much stone robbing we simply do not know to what extent the builders finished the Meidum pyramid. Two steps seem to have disappeared between the visit of Shaykh Abu Mohammed Abdallah in 1117–19 and that of Norden in 1737, when the pyramid had three steps as today. In 1899 M.A. Robert, Inspector of the Register of Land Survey, ascended the Meidum pyramid to plant a pole for his survey. At the summit he had the impression that the highest step was never finished. Some inscribed Greek and three small hieroglyphs indicate that there was access to the top of the pyramid in ancient times. And Robert did not need to make a hole to plant his survey flag. In the centre of the top step there was already a hole, which has been interpreted as the socket for a rod that the builders planted for sighting diagonal lines as they raised the true pyramid mantle up and around the old step pyramid.

Dahshur

For whatever reason, in about the 15th year of his reign Sneferu abandoned Meidum and moved 40 km (25 miles) north to Dahshur. Here he founded another new necropolis – all the more unusual since Meidum itself represented the first time a royal necropolis had been laid out at a virgin site since the founding of Saqqara. One suggested motive for the move was Sneferu's desire to be closer to the apex of the Delta and to the increasingly important trade with Syria and the Levant.

At Dahshur Sneferu built two large pyramids – the Bent Pyramid and the North, or Red, Pyramid. The two are roughly aligned – the east side of the North Pyramid approximately lining up with the west side of the Bent Pyramid. A long causeway from the Bent Pyramid runs to what is often described as the first valley temple, but which in fact is some distance into the desert. Northeast of the Bent Pyramid a cemetery of mastabas was begun. Decorated with relief-carved chapels, the tombs were for the élite of Sneferu's court.

In 1986 Rainer Stadelmann excavated Lepsius pyramid number 50 (L). It is 250 m (820 ft) east of the North Pyramid, and consists of the base of a pyramid that was barely begun. On the east side were large limestone blocks and a brick ramp that may have been intended for building the subterranean apartment. The pottery in the vicinity appeared to be 4th dynasty.

Middle Kingdom pharaohs also chose Dahshur as the site for their pyramids, beginning with Amenemhet II. Those of Amenemhet III and Senwosret III are of mudbrick, and in some ways Amenemhet III's looks like a mudbrick version of the Meidum pyramid. Interestingly, just as Sneferu had serious structural problems when building his Bent Pyramid at Dahshur because of the unstable desert sand, gravel and clays it was founded on, so Amenemhet III, building on a similar surface, encountered subsidence and cracking. This probably explains why he built another pyramid at Hawara, just as Sneferu built a substitute pyramid to the north of the first at Dahshur.

Two of Sneferu's sons, Nefermaat and the anonymous prince of mastaba 17, were buried at Meidum. Another son, Kanefer, was buried in one of the cluster of tombs near the pyramid of Amenemhet II. These three sons should have inherited the throne which passed instead to Khufu – who may have been very young when he began to build his pyramid. This perhaps explains the confidence with which he started out on his gigantic programme at Giza.

Despite having built two giant pyramids at Dahshur, one of which was to be for his burial, Sneferu was apparently still not content and returned to Meidum to finish off his pyramid there.

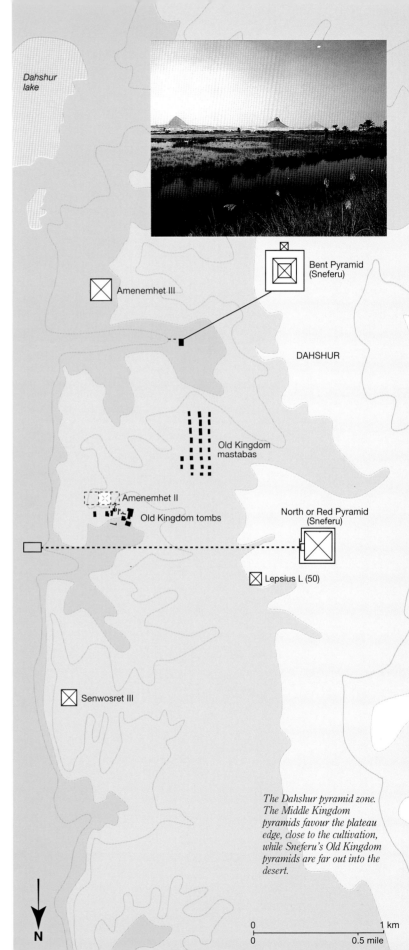

The Dahshur pyramid zone. The Middle Kingdom pyramids favour the plateau edge, close to the cultivation, while Sneferu's Old Kingdom pyramids are far out into the desert.

The Bent Pyramid

When Sneferu abandoned his step pyramid at Meidum and moved north to Dahshur, there was as yet no blueprint for a true pyramid. To us, with a clear image of the shape of the classic pyramid, with a slope of 52° or 53°, this may seem strange. It was, however, a time of great experimentation, comparable to the period when Djoser's architect Imhotep was building the Step Pyramid.

How the pyramid got its bend

The old step pyramids had faces that sloped about 72° to 78°, certainly too steep for a true pyramid. There is evidence within the core of the Bent Pyramid that it began as a far smaller pyramid with a slope of about 60°. But structural problems with subsidence soon set in. Emergency measures took the form of an added girdle around the stump of the pyramid, forming a slope of just under 55°.

These early stages were constructed using the traditional method of laying the courses with the stones sloping inward. Even at the reduced angle it appears that there were still major problems until, about half way up, the builders began to set the courses horizontally. It had become clear that the inward-leaning courses, far from aiding stability, actually increased the stresses on the pyramid.

The Bent Pyramid was then continued at a much decreased slope of around 43° to 44°, giving it a pronounced bend. It may have been at this point, before the upper part was finished, that the decision was taken to begin a new pyramid at North Dahshur. Around the same time, perhaps the 30th year of Sneferu's reign according to Stadelmann, work also began on the satellite pyramid.

Other changes in construction methods are discernible. Both core stones and casing stones are larger – the casing ones very much so – than in the 3rd-dynasty pyramids. However, no great care was taken to lay the internal masonry neatly. Substantial spaces between the stones are simply filled with limestone debris and even tafla in places. Gypsum mortar was just beginning to be used more frequently, which, unlike the desert clay mortar, had to be specially prepared using fuel. It was this combination of a lack of good mortar, carelessly laid blocks and, most importantly, the unstable desert surface, that caused the structural problems.

(Below) The sliding portcullis blocking system in the western passage, with the block in the open position. This is perhaps an indication that the higher chamber was originally built for Sneferu's burial.

With more preserved casing than most pyramids, the Bent Pyramid reveals that plunderers began stripping the fine limestone from the corners and from bottom to top, as is evident here.

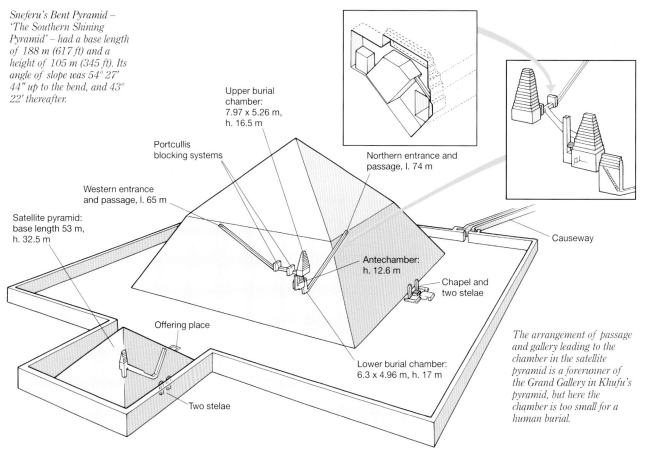

Sneferu's Bent Pyramid – 'The Southern Shining Pyramid' – had a base length of 188 m (617 ft) and a height of 105 m (345 ft). Its angle of slope was 54° 27' 44" up to the bend, and 43° 22' thereafter.

Upper burial chamber: 7.97 x 5.26 m, h. 16.5 m

Portcullis blocking systems

Northern entrance and passage, l. 74 m

Western entrance and passage, l. 65 m

Satellite pyramid: base length 53 m, h. 32.5 m

Causeway

Antechamber: h. 12.6 m

Chapel and two stelae

Offering place

Lower burial chamber: 6.3 x 4.96 m, h. 17 m

Two stelae

The arrangement of passage and gallery leading to the chamber in the satellite pyramid is a forerunner of the Grand Gallery in Khufu's pyramid, but here the chamber is too small for a human burial.

Inside the pyramid

The Bent Pyramid is unique in having two internal structures, with entrances on the north and west sides. From the north side a long, sloping passage leads to a narrow antechamber with an impressive corbelled roof. The burial chamber, also corbelled, is above this antechamber and was perhaps reached by a stairway or ladder. All this building, plus a vertical shaft on the precise central axis of the pyramid, would have taken place in a trench sunk into the original desert surface.

The second passage runs from the west side of the pyramid, through portcullis blocking systems, to another burial chamber, again with a corbelled roof. This is at a higher level than the first. Here once again, structural instability is evident as the chamber was completely shored up with balks and scaffolding of great cedar beams.

Some time after both chambers were constructed, a connecting passage was made between them. It was definitely built later as it was hacked through the masonry by someone who knew exactly where the two chambers were. We can only speculate why Sneferu decided to have this duplicate arrangement in his pyramid. One suggestion is that the western system may be a vestige of the South Tomb of Djoser, the long passage emphasizing once again a general southwest orientation, as in the 1st-dynasty royal burial ground at Abydos.

The pyramid complex

At the centre of the eastern side of the Bent Pyramid is a small chapel. As at Meidum the contrast between this tiny structure and the giant pyramid is very striking. Stadelmann points out that the small chapels of both Meidum and the Bent Pyramid were not part of the development of the large mortuary temples, rather they were intended to be simple shrines for pyramids that Sneferu completed as cenotaphs.

Initially the Bent Pyramid's chapel was a very simple affair composed of two walls of Turah limestone roofed with slabs, which was expanded by mudbrick walls. Within it was an offering place consisting of a slab that took the form of the hieroglyph for offering, '*hetep*', a stylized loaf of bread on a reed mat. Behind this, two round-topped stelae, the stumps of which remain, were formerly inscribed with the names of Sneferu.

A causeway, also with walls of Turah limestone, ran from the pyramid complex to what is often called the first valley temple – a beautiful small, rectangular structure. On the back wall were six statues of Sneferu striding forth. In front of and, curiously, blocking these statues were two rows of five rectangular pillars. A courtyard beyond had walls carved the earliest representations of the estates of the king bearing produce towards the statues of Sneferu (p. 228).

Sneferu's Bent Pyramid, with its satellite, looking northwest to southeast.

A stela from Sneferu's Bent Pyramid showing the seated figure of the king.

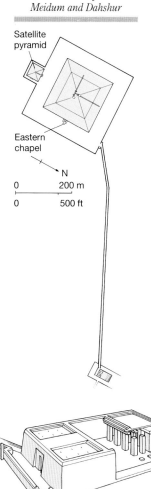

Satellite
pyramid

Eastern
chapel

N

0   200 m

0   500 ft

*The causeway reaches 210 m
(689 ft) to the 'valley temple'
of Sneferu's Bent Pyramid. In
fact the temple is not down in
the valley but far up a narrow
wadi that might have been
partially flooded during the
season of inundation. Two of
the king's name stelae stood
at the southern corners.*

This structure is in fact a combination of both mortuary and valley temple, with features that are developed later in both. It has the court, pillars and architectural statues found in later mortuary temples, and it is situated about halfway down to the valley. A second causeway probably ran from this to a dock or landing-stage.

In terms of both its masonry and internal structure, the satellite pyramid is an important link in the transition to the Great Pyramid of Khufu. It was built using the new method of laying courses horizontally. This, however, presented the masons with a new problem: the slope of the pyramid now had to be cut into the outer face of the casing stone. There is evidence that in the process of cutting and setting, the masons often accidentally broke off the sharp lower foot so that patches had to fitted. Its outer casing is built on a platform, which, on a sublime scale, is also found at the Giza pyramids. In recent years, thanks to Stadelmann's excavations, we have learned that Sneferu's North Pyramid was also built on a limestone platform.

The internal structure is in some ways an abbreviated version of the Great Pyramid's, with a descending and an ascending passage. A small notch in the ascending passage, where it increases in height to a miniature Grand Gallery, adds weight to the supposition that that structure in the Great Pyramid was indeed intended for the storage of plugging blocks. A wood piece fitted into the notch could be pulled by rope to release the plugs. Just as in the South Tomb of Djoser, the burial chamber of the satellite pyramid is far too small to have contained a human burial. It may instead have been for the ritual interment of a statue of the king.

On the east side of the pyramid was an offering place with two more round-topped stelae inscribed with Sneferu's name. On the north side, just below the entrance, there is a very curious emplacement or pit for some sort of cult activity – perhaps the burial of offerings.

The cult of Sneferu

By contrast with the pyramid-building kings of Giza, who seem to have been entirely ignored by Egyptians of the Middle Kingdom, the cult of Sneferu took root and prospered in succeeding periods. It was at the valley temple of the Bent Pyramid that this cult was focused. Why this was so is an interesting question. Perhaps it was because here at the Bent Pyramid we have a fully completed complex. Although Sneferu was probably not buried here, his name was completed on various stelae and so this was where his life continued. Ironically, this was also the pyramid complex that ran into severe structural problems and tested the builders' nerves to the greatest extent.

The North Pyramid

In around his 30th year on the throne, Sneferu abandoned the Bent Pyramid as his burial place, although, as at Meidum, he later completed it. Instead, he began work on the North, or Red, Pyramid which was built at the gentler slope of 43° 22' from the beginning. In many ways this was more elegant than the Bent Pyramid, where the builders obviously struggled and experimented with various solutions to the structural problems they were faced with. The North Pyramid shows none of this – it is a neatly planned and executed construction, built with an efficient use of materials.

Rainer Stadelmann has been working at North Dahshur for over a decade. In the course of his excavations of the debris at the base of the pyramid he found hundreds of pieces of the fine limestone casing. Many of these have graffiti inscribed on their rear faces by the work gangs. One from a corner bears the hieratic (shorthand hieroglyphic) inscription mentioning 'bringing to earth year 15'. This refers to counting year 15, which, if biennial, is equivalent to the 30th year of Sneferu's reign. Some 30 courses higher Stadelmann was able to place a casing stone dated only four years later – this gives us a very clear picture of the length of time it took to build such pyramids.

*The North, or Red, Pyramid
at Dahshur. The 'Shining
Pyramid' had a base length
of 220 m (722 ft) and a
height of 105 m (345 ft). Its
angle of slope was 43° 22'.*

Antechambers:
3.65 x 8.36 m,
h. 12.31 m

Burial chamber:
4.18 x 8.55 m, h. 14.67 m

Remarkably, Stadelmann also found pieces of the pyramid's capstone. This was a simple culmination of the structure – a block with no carving or inscription and made of good quality limestone rather than any costlier material. Its pieces were found near the base, rejected by those who were stripping the outer mantle of its fine limestone.

Inside the pyramid

The North Pyramid's substructure is a continuation of the developments seen at Meidum and the Bent Pyramid. From high up in the pyramid a long corridor descends to ground level. At this point are two almost identical tall antechambers with corbelled roofs of great finesse, technically far in advance of those at Meidum. A short horizontal passage leads from the second antechamber, high up to deter robbers, to a corbelled chamber, 15 m (50 ft) tall, built within the masonry of the pyramid. Fragments of human remains were found in the burial chamber, but it has not been ascertained whether or not they are from the royal mummy.

From Sneferu to Khufu we witness the struggle to raise the chamber from ground level into the body of the pyramid. Perhaps this is a reflection of the increasing identification of the king not just with the god Horus, who soars above all living creatures, but with the sun and its rays, of which the pyramid is a symbol.

The pyramid complex

Egyptologists eagerly anticipated the excavation of the mortuary temple at the North Pyramid. Pyramid chapels prior to this – at Meidum and the Bent Pyramid – were very small, simple structures, while that belonging to Khufu's Great Pyramid represented a huge leap in both scale and complexity. None the less, the mortuary temple of the North Pyramid – Sneferu's probable burial place – did not approach Khufu's in grandeur. Indeed, it seems to have been finished hurriedly, perhaps by Khufu at the time of his father's death.

Stadelmann was able to reconstruct the plan of the temple from the scant remains. There was a stone chapel on either side of an inner sanctuary which may have contained a false door stela. North and south of the temple, courtyards retained round sockets in the soil for potted plants or offerings made in connection with the funeral, features that seem far more ephemeral than the great stone Giza temples designed for long-term cults.

Although a few possible traces were found east of the mortuary temple, a substantial causeway appears never to have been built down to the valley temple. Rudimentary remains of the latter were seen at the end of the last century but have never been systematically excavated. It was here, however, that the decree of Pepi I was found, exempting the *khentiu-she* of the pyramid town from taxation, along with their fields, trees and wells – in this case it was the double pyramid complex of Sneferu. The lack of a causeway linking the two temples is perhaps further evidence of a hurried conclusion to the completion of the North Pyramid, which Stadelmann believes was Sneferu's final resting place.

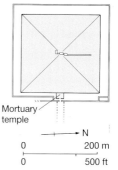

Mortuary temple

Sneferu's North Pyramid, with his Bent Pyramid in the background.

The mortuary temple of the North Pyramid was destroyed all but for traces at ground level. Its pyramidion or capstone was reconstructed in the temple's enclosure.

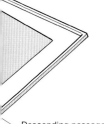

Descending passage, 62.63 m long

(Above) A fragment of casing from the base of the North Pyramid with the graffito 'bringing to earth the western corner [stone] [counting] year 15…two cubits', that is Sneferu's 29th to 30th regnal year.

Giza: An Overview

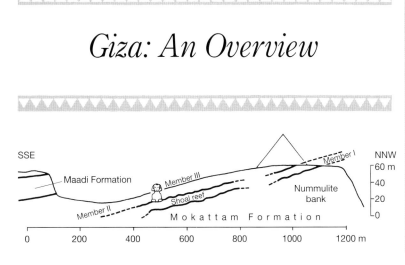

SSE

Maadi Formation

Member III

Member II

Shoal reef

Member I

NNW

60 m
40
20
0

Nummulite
bank

M o k a t t a m   F o r m a t i o n

0   200   400   600   800   1000   1200 m

The Giza Plateau consists of a plate of limestone called the Mokkatam Formation. Its regular surface is ideal for building and it was here that the 4th-dynasty Egyptians created the most carefully designed of the royal pyramid clusters. To the northwest is an embankment of fossils, called nummulites. Down the slope to the southeast a sequence of layers alternates hard and soft stone. The Egyptians cut away the softer layers to remove the harder layers in blocks for the pyramids, tombs and temples. Known as Member II and III, this stone is visible in the body and head of the Sphinx. Further south rises the Maadi Formation, containing many fissures, wadis and gullies. This area was quarried for stone and tafla (the natural desert clay) for pyramid support structures.

The pyramids at Giza were built over the span of three generations – by Khufu, his second-reigning son, Khafre, and Menkaure. Any overview of these colossal human achievements in stone must take into consideration the natural geology of the land they were built on. The southeast corners of the pyramids of Khufu, Khafre and Menkaure are nearly aligned on the great Giza diagonal that runs about 43° east of true north, almost perpendicular to the dip of the plateau. This follows what geologists call the strike of the Mokkatam Formation, that is, a line perpendicular to the slope. When you walk along the side of a hill without going up or down, you are following its strike. By aligning themselves to this, the builders ensured that the bases of the three main pyramids were at approximately the same level, although the base of Khafre's is about 10 m (33 ft) higher than Khufu's.

Some religious or cosmic impulse beyond the purely practical may also have influenced the ancient surveyors, though we can only speculate what it was. Perhaps the diagonal pointed northeast to Heliopolis, the home of the *ben-ben*, and southwest, in the direction of the Netherworld entrance of the first royal cemetery at Abydos.

It is certainly clear that at Giza, more than ever before, cardinality was a principal concern. Khufu's pyramid is laid out with its sides oriented almost exactly to true north – the greatest deviation is under 5', and the 4th-dynasty builders took pains to ensure that major parts of the pyramid complexes would align. The Giza diagonal line passes close to the diagonal of Menkaure's first subsidiary pyramid (GIII-a), the front of Khafre's mortuary temple and Khufu's first subsidiary pyramid (GI-a). The west sides of Khufu's and Khafre's pyramids are close to alignment with the fronts of the pyramid temples of Khafre and Menkaure respectively; and the south side of Khafre's pyramid aligns with the south wall of the Sphinx Temple. These alignments are out by just about the amount that we would expect from methods of sighting and measuring using long cords across a kilometre of sloping plateau. The great northeast–southwest Giza diagonal ends to the southwest at a small hillock of the Maadi Formation that may have been useful as a 'back sight' for the ancient surveyors, which they could use to align points across the plateau.

The formal symmetry of the pyramid complexes at Giza inspires many pyramid enthusiasts to look

The three pyramids at Giza. Their breathtaking accuracy and alignment has inspired much theorizing.

for more alignments, always with the suspicion of hidden meanings or lost treasures. A theory of Robert Bauval suggests that the Giza diagonal is inspired by the stars in the belt of the constellation Orion, which the Egyptians saw as a symbol of Osiris. But when the map of Orion is positioned over that of Giza and nearby pyramids, it is clear that there are stars in Orion for which there are no matching pyramids, and pyramids for which there are no stars in Orion, or any other constellation.

The classic pyramid complex

At Giza the pyramid reached its apogee and the standard features of the Old Kingdom pyramid complex – the mortuary and valley temple – were expanded and formalized. Sneferu's small chapel and inchoate valley temple at the Bent Pyramid, and his hastily finished pyramid temple at North Dahshur, are replaced by large, well-built temples with a vastly increased use of hard stone, pillars and statues. With Menkaure the size ratio between pyramid and temple changed in favour of a reduced pyramid and an enlarged temple. The causeways of the Giza pyramids reached nearly a kilometre east to valley temples close to the flood-plain. Khufu's was the longest and it may also have been he who built the huge southern boundary wall at the mouth of the Main Wadi. Wall and causeway defined an area of harbours, settlement and possibly a palace at the foot of the plateau (p. 230).

The cemeteries of mastaba tombs east and west of Khufu's pyramid, representing another advance in formal orthogonal design, are organized in the streets and avenues of a preconceived plan. Reisner excavated these cemeteries and saw the necropolis as a 'community of *kas*' for the court of Khufu to reign over in the Afterlife. Here is the realization of the unified cemetery begun west of the Meidum pyramid and the more loosely organized rows of mastabas east of Sneferu's Dahshur pyramids.

In such a rigid organization of space, with three giant pyramid complexes fitted into one necropolis, some delineation of borders was needed. While each pyramid stood within its own narrow enclosure, the Egyptians also divided the plateau into three huge rectangular precincts by means of stone and clay walls. These are still well preserved around the pyramids of Khafre and Menkaure, but much less so around Khufu's.

Over the course of three generations builders continued to position major architectural elements at Giza. Yet during this time work was interrupted in the reign of Djedefre, who went north to Abu Roash (p. 120), and perhaps during the few years of a king between Khafre and Menkaure who may have begun the unfinished pyramid at Zawiyet el-Aryan (p. 139). The last major royal sepulchre at Giza was the tomb of Khentkawes (p. 138). Her mastaba-like tomb had a large doorway opening to the mouth of the wadi that had been the main conduit for construction supplies. The channel that gave birth to the Giza necropolis thus became the approach to the tomb of the queen mother who perhaps gave birth to a new dynasty that moved its necropolis to Saqqara and Abusir.

A computer reconstruction of the Giza pyramids, with the possible harbour lapping at Khafre's valley temple and the Sphinx Temple.

A plan of the Giza plateau showing the major alignments and the many different elements that make up this classic pyramid cluster.

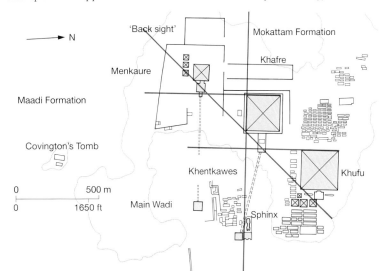

The Great Pyramid of Khufu

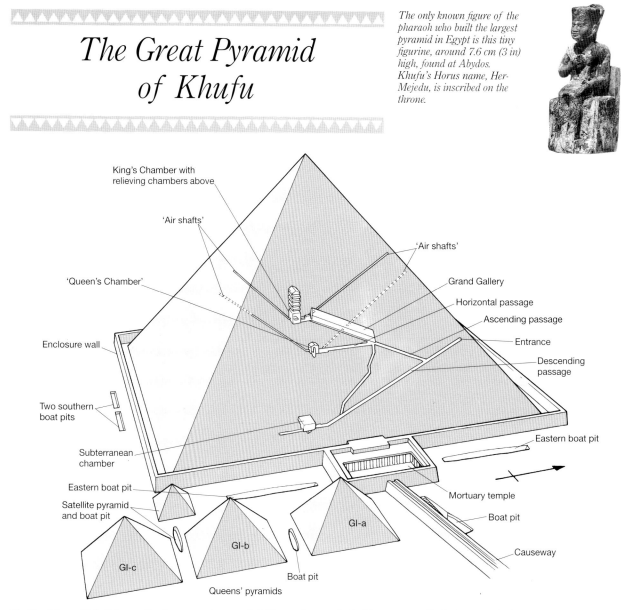

King's Chamber with relieving chambers above

'Air shafts'

'Air shafts'

'Queen's Chamber'

Grand Gallery

Horizontal passage

Ascending passage

Entrance

Descending passage

Enclosure wall

Two southern boat pits

Subterranean chamber

Eastern boat pit

Satellite pyramid and boat pit

Eastern boat pit

Mortuary temple

Boat pit

GI-a

Causeway

GI-b

Boat pit

GI-c

Queens' pyramids

The Great Pyramid, built by Khufu who came to the throne around 2551 BC, was called Akhet Khufu, *'The Horizon of Khufu'. Its base length is calculated as 230.33 m (756 ft) and it rose to a height of 146.59 m (481 ft), with an angle of slope of 51° 50' 40". Its orientation is 3' 6" off true north. In addition to this astonishing achievement, Khufu also built three queens' pyramids, boat pits and a satellite pyramid, only recently found.*

Sneferu may have ruled Egypt for nearly half a century, in which time he completed his three giant pyramids at Meidum and Dahshur. His son Khnum-khuf ('the god Khnum is his protection'), Khufu for short (Cheops in Greek), chose the Giza Plateau, 40 km (25 miles) north of Dahshur, to begin building his own pyramid complex. In terms of its size, the technical accomplishment of its construction, the great concern for cardinality and the organization it represents, Khufu's pyramid was another astonishing leap forward.

Rainer Stadelmann, in his study of the reigns of the early pyramid builders, concludes that, like his father Sneferu, Khufu reigned longer than the 23 years given him in the Turin Papyrus, compiled some 1,400 years later. Even with a reign of 30 to 32 years, the estimated combined mass of 2,700,000

cu. m (95,350,000 cu. ft) for his pyramid, causeway, two temples, satellite pyramid, three queens' pyramids and officials' mastabas, means that Khufu's builders had to set in place a staggering 230 cu. m (8,122 cu. ft) of stone per day, a rate of one average-size block every two or three minutes in a ten-hour day. If Khufu did not equal the total mass of his father's monuments, he came close in his single pyramid and far surpassed his father's pyramids in size and accuracy.

The Great Pyramid contains about 2,300,000 blocks of stone, often said to weigh on average *c.* 2.5 tons. This might be somewhat exaggerated; the stones certainly get smaller towards the top of the pyramid, and we do not know if the masonry of the inner core is as well-cut and uniform as the stone courses that are now exposed (the outer fine

The Great Pyramid
A computer reconstruction
of the Giza pyramids. The
interior of Khufu's pyramid
is explored overleaf.

Inside Khufu's Pyramid

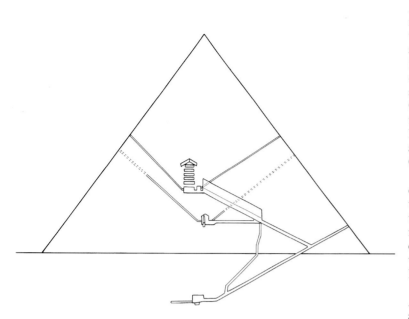

The passages and chambers inside the Great Pyramid: some argue that the Subterranean Chamber and so-called 'Queen's Chamber' were each in turn intended for the king's burial but were successively abandoned as plans changed. However, it is possible that the entire inner complex was conceived and built according to a unified plan. Old Kingdom pyramids frequently have three chambers. Here the two lower rooms were probably planned from the outset to cater for different aspects of the king's spiritual welfare.

Inside Khufu's pyramid we find developments that are unique in pyramid evolution and remarkable in the entire history of architecture. Many Egyptologists have long accepted Borchardt's suggestion that the pyramid's three chambers represent two changes in plan, with the abandonment of the Subterranean Chamber, believed to be the original intended burial chamber of the king, and then the Queen's Chamber, in favour of the King's Chamber. Several clues, however, combine to make it probable that all three chambers and the entire passage system were planned together from the outset. Three chambers seem to have been the rule for Old Kingdom pyramids.

From the original entrance – offset by 7.29 m (24 ft) east from the centre axis – the descending passage plunges down through the pyramid, ending in the Subterranean Chamber. This was the classic pyramid substructure: a corridor descending to a chamber at or below ground level, as seen at Meidum. But here, for the first time, the chamber was carved out of the solid bedrock, though it was never completed.

One of the real puzzles of this chamber is a small, rough passage leading south from one corner. Only one man could have fitted at the end of it, inching forward into the blind rock with hammer and chisel. Where was it intended to lead? If it was to another room, the Subterranean Chamber cannot have been for the king's burial, as this was always the last chamber of a series. Moreover, the Descending Passage is simply too small to

introduce a sarcophagus the size of that found in the King's Chamber.

The so-called Queen's Chamber (misnamed by Arab explorers) is higher up in the pyramid, reached via the Ascending Passage and a horizontal passage. It lies exactly on the east–west centre axis of the pyramid and was almost completely finished, with only the walls and floor still to be dressed down. The junction of the Ascending Passage with the horizontal passage leading into the Queen's Chamber was originally roofed. Evidence for this takes the form of holes for large beams for holding blocks that roofed the horizontal passage and provided a continuous floor from the Grand Gallery to the Ascending Passage.

The Queen's Chamber was therefore totally closed off – a characteristic of a *serdab*, a room for the *ka* statue – the king's spiritual double – such as the statue of Djoser sealed in a stone box at the north side of his Step Pyramid. With a total height of 4.7 m (15 ft 5 in), a corbelled niche in the east wall could certainly have contained a larger-than-life statue of the king.

After the cramped and difficult crawl up the Ascending Passage, about 1.05 m (3½ ft) wide and a little taller, the route to the King's Chamber suddenly opens out into the breathtaking Grand Gallery. At the top is what is known as the Great Step, followed by the antechamber and finally the King's Chamber. Entirely constructed out of red granite, this room is impressive for its simplicity and resonance.

Above the King's Chamber are five stress-relieving chambers, each with the same floor area as the respective chamber below. At the very top, the stones are cantilevered in the form of a pent roof to distribute the weight and stresses of the mountain of masonry above. This is an innovative and ingenious arrangement, for which there are few parallels and no precedent. Graffiti left by the work crews on the walls add a human element. Names of

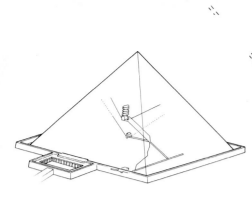

The **'air shafts'** extend like antennae through the body of the pyramid from both the King's and the Queen's Chambers. Those from the King's Chamber penetrate all the way to the outside, though very possibly the pyramid casing closed off these purely cultic shafts which may also have been originally plugged in the chamber.

'Air shafts' oriented to Orion

'King's Chamber', 10.5 x 5.2 m, h. 5.8 m

Antechamber

'Queen's Chamber', 5.8 x 5.3 m, h. 6 m

(Right) Rudolf Gantenbrink's robot, Upuaut II, carried a video camera up the southern shaft of the Queen's Chamber, just 20 cm (8 in) square. It was stopped after about 65 m (213 ft) by a fine limestone plug with two embedded copper pins.

(Below) The **Subterranean Chamber** lies 30 m (98 ft) below the plateau surface. It is reached by the Descending Passage, which slopes at an angle of 26° 34' 23" for 28.8 m (92 ft 6 in) through the pyramid masonry, and then another 30.3 m (99 ft 5 in) through the natural rock without deviating more than a centimetre in angle or orientation.

The so-called **Queen's Chamber** was certainly not for the burial of a queen. Very probably it was a sealed room for a special statue of the king, representing his ka or 'spiritual force'. This is suggested by the existence of a corbelled niche, 4.7 m (15 ft 5 in) high, on the east wall of the chamber, which may once have held such a statue. A square pit at its base was deepened by early treasure-seekers. The 'Queen's Chamber' lies exactly on the east–west centre axis of the pyramid. Its walls and pented ceiling are of fine limestone. A few objects were reportedly found in the northern airshaft in the late 19th century, now on display in the British Museum (inset, right).

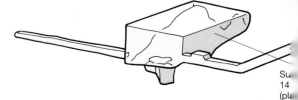

Su 14 (pl

During our survey of Khufu's pyramid, we noted that of a total of 921.44 m (3,023 ft) of original pyramid baseline, only 54.44 m (179 ft) remains, much of it badly worn, while only 212.48 m (697 ft) of the foundation platform survive. It is on the basis of these remnants that the amazing accuracy of the original building is reconstructed by surveyors.

Causeway, l. 739.8 m

N

0   200 m
0   500 ft

Computer-generated diagrams of Khufu's Great Pyramid, showing the complex internal structure.

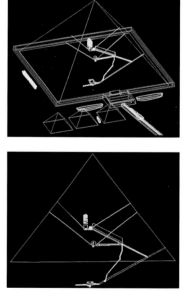

white Turah limestone casing was stripped off long ago). On the other hand some of the casing stones at the base may weigh as much as 15 tons, and the large granite beams roofing the King's Chamber and the stress-relieving chambers above it have been estimated to weigh from 50 to 80 tons. Such statistics, while repeated frequently, never cease to astound.

As for accuracy: the base is level to within just 2.1 cm (under 1 in); the average deviation of the sides from the cardinal directions is 3' 6" of arc; and the greatest difference in the length of the sides is 4.4 cm (1¾ in). Why such phenomenal precision? For the royal designers such exactitude may have been imbued with symbolic and cultic significance that now eludes us. A more practical explanation is that it may have been a response to the architectural disaster at the Dahshur Bent Pyramid. To avoid a repetition the builders founded the outer casing on a specially levelled platform constructed on the bedrock (p. 212) – leaving a low massif of natural rock inside the pyramid.

The Great Pyramid, like those built by Sneferu, consisted of casing and core stones, laid in horizontal courses, with packing blocks in between. Large quantities of gypsum mortar were poured into the often wide interstices between the core stones. Greatest precision was achieved in the fine outer casing; the core, which is what we see now, was less carefully laid, though it is still a marked improvement on the internal fabric of previous pyramids. At the corners and towards the top higher quality limestone was used because of the need for greater precision and control.

The pyramid complex

All the standard elements of the pyramid complex were present, though they have mostly since disappeared. The finished pyramid was surrounded by a Turah limestone wall, over 8 m (26 ft) high, enclosing a court, 10.2 m (33 ft) wide, paved in limestone. Access to this court could only be gained via the valley temple, causeway and mortuary temple.

The mortuary temple was demolished down to bedrock over the centuries. It is square and much larger than the small chapels associated with the Meidum and Bent pyramids. What remains is some black basalt pavement of an open court, sockets for the granite pillars of the surrounding colonnade and western recessed bay, and the bedrock cuttings for the outer wall. The walls were of fine limestone carved in relief. This is the first time we find granite and basalt combined to construct a truly large temple. There was an inner sanctuary and storage rooms, but it is not known whether the five statue niches and false door that became standard later were already part of the plan.

Khufu's causeway walls must have been covered with fine relief carving – as we know from the testimony of Herodotus and the discovery of a few carved pieces. Its foundations rose to an astonishing height of more than 40 m (131 ft) to carry the corridor from the edge of the plateau down to the valley temple. East of the escarpment these foundations were still extant at the turn of this century. A basalt pavement is probably the remains of the valley temple (p. 232). It is otherwise completely unknown and its form remains totally hypothetical.

As well as his own pyramid and temples, plus boat pits (p. 118), Khufu also built three pyramids for queens (p. 116), and cemeteries of mastabas – to the west for his highest officials and to the east for his nearest royal relatives – all laid out in a systematic, unified fashion. Khufu's satellite pyramid, perhaps for his *ka*, remained undetected until recently, when it was discovered by Zahi Hawass during cleaning operations. It is tiny, only 20 m (66 ft) per side, and has a T-shaped descending passage plus chamber. The side walls of the chamber lean inward, like a tent or canopied structure, a form that matches the galleries under the east side of Djoser's Step Pyramid.

The **King's Chamber**, *with the royal sarcophagus. Nine great granite beams stretch across the roof, each more than 5.5 m (18 ft or 10 cubits) long and weighing 25 to 40 tons. Never before had the Egyptians spanned such a wide space in stone. There are signs that the great beams had begun to crack even while the pyramid was under construction, although the Egyptians had created one of the most remarkable structures in architectural history to prevent it. When the priests made their final exit in 2528 BC, they sealed the tomb by sliding three portcullis slabs down slots in the side walls of the Antechamber.*

The red granite sarcophagus near the western wall of the King's Chamber was the final resting place of Khufu's body. The room itself is like a sarcophagus, lined with red granite and resonating with every murmur and footstep. The sacred room was probably already robbed of its contents some time between the end of the Khufu's reign and the collapse of the Old Kingdom (c. 2134 BC). Those who first violated the stone box and robbed the royal mummy probably made the prominent break in the corner of the sarcophagus in order to lift the heavy lid.

the workers are combined with that of the king – here Khnum-Khuf.

Khufu's sarcophagus was made of the same red granite as his chamber and is on the exact central axis of the pyramid. Petrie noted that the sarcophagus is fractionally wider than the doorway into the chamber and it would therefore have to have been put in place in the chamber as the pyramid was being built around it.

If the King's Chamber was the burial room and the Queen's Chamber was a statue *serdab*, what was the purpose of the Subterranean Chamber? Rainer Stadelmann suggests that its rough and unfinished state may represent the Underworld cavern. Rather than the first chamber to be built, it is possible that it was the last, and still under construction when the king died and work was frozen.

A symbolic function should also be attributed to the so-called 'air-shafts', which had nothing to do with conducting air. No other pyramid contains chambers and passages so high in the body of the masonry as Khufu's and so the builders provided the King's Chamber with small model passages to allow the king's spirit to ascend to the stars.

There are similar 'air-shafts' in the Queen's Chamber though here, mysteriously, they did not penetrate through the walls of the chamber itself. In 1872 an engineer called Waynman Dixon, working for Piazzi Smyth, knowing of the existence of such passages in the King's Chamber, searched for them in this chamber too. He tapped the wall till he found places that sounded hollow and broke through.

Recently these passages have been investigated by Rudolf Gantenbrink, working for Rainer Stadel-mann of the German Archaeological Institute in Cairo. He sent a small robot camera up the southern passage. It came to a halt, after about 65 m (214 ft), in front of a plugging block with two copper pins sticking out of it. Investigations halted at this point and the meaning of the block, and what, if anything, lies beyond, remain mysteries.

Sealing the tomb

When Khufu's priests and workmen left the King's Chamber for the last time, they sealed the tomb chamber by sliding portcullis slabs down three slots in the side wall of the antechamber. Then, as a second line of defence they released the huge granite plugging blocks stored in the Grand Gallery by knocking away the beams holding them. These slid down the ascending passage, thus blocking it.

The men probably made their escape by slipping down the so-called 'well' or 'service shaft' cut into the west wall at the bottom of the Grand Gallery. This was no robber's tunnel as some have believed, but was probably cut to conduct air down to the bottom of the descending passage, so that work could continue on the Subterranean Chamber. Once they arrived at the descending passage via the service shaft, the pyramid sealers could climb up past the plugged mouth of the ascending passage and out through the original entrance of the pyramid. They probably plugged the section of the descending passage from the mouth to its junction with the ascending passage – the third line of defence for the king's burial. The entrance in the face of the pyramid would have been sealed with a limestone block that the builders hoped – in vain – made it indistinguishable from the pyramid casing.

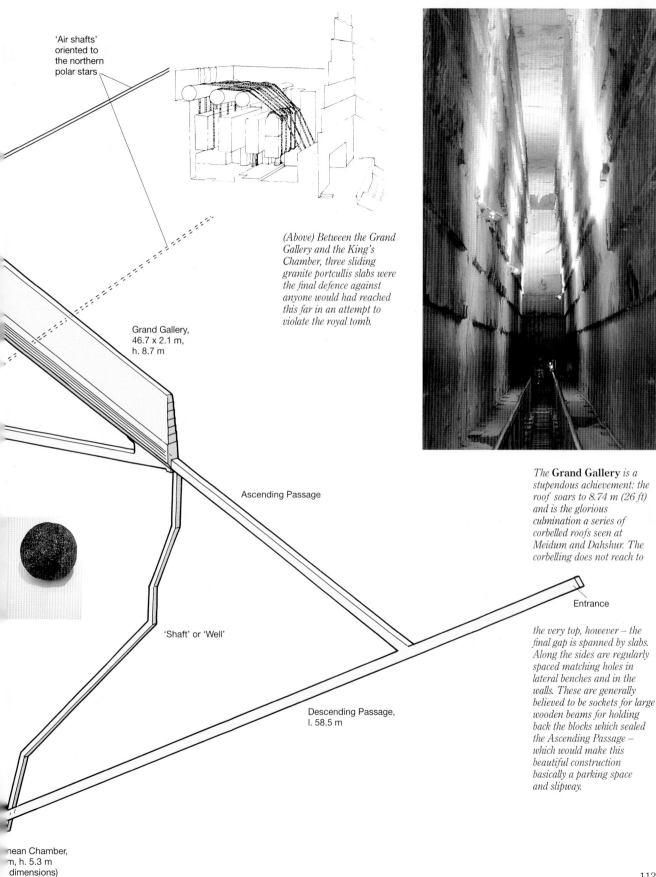

'Air shafts' oriented to the northern polar stars

(Above) Between the Grand Gallery and the King's Chamber, three sliding granite portcullis slabs were the final defence against anyone would had reached this far in an attempt to violate the royal tomb.

Grand Gallery, 46.7 x 2.1 m, h. 8.7 m

Ascending Passage

'Shaft' or 'Well'

Descending Passage, l. 58.5 m

Entrance

The **Grand Gallery** is a stupendous achievement: the roof soars to 8.74 m (26 ft) and is the glorious culmination a series of corbelled roofs seen at Meidum and Dahshur. The corbelling does not reach to the very top, however – the final gap is spanned by slabs. Along the sides are regularly spaced matching holes in lateral benches and in the walls. These are generally believed to be sockets for large wooden beams for holding back the blocks which sealed the Ascending Passage – which would make this beautiful construction basically a parking space and slipway.

nean Chamber, m, h. 5.3 m dimensions)

(Right) Khufu's eastern cemetery and queen's pyramids before the discovery of the satellite pyramid. This was found when Zahi Hawass removed the modern road visible in the photograph and cleaned the area.

(Below right) The remains of Khufu's satellite pyramid in front of the right-hand queens' pyramid. The boat pit between two of the queens' pyramids may in fact belong to the satellite pyramid, parked at its eastern side.

The Queens' Pyramids

Khufu built three pyramids for queens, labelled, north to south, GI-a, GI-b and GI-c. In contrast to the levelled foundation of his own pyramid, these accommodated the slope of the ground, so that their bases are neither level nor perfect squares. They may have been planned to an ideal length of 88–89 cubits, one-fifth of Khufu's, and, with a slope near 52°, each rose about a-fifth of its height. As with Khafre's, the bedrock for the bottom course of casing is cut to different heights and angles, so that the top of the first course could be levelled with a minimum of cutting.

Each queen's pyramid had a stepped internal nucleus. GI-a has thin stone retaining walls visible in its denuded top. Scrutiny of GI-c, the most complete, reveals three inner tiers or steps of mastaba-like chunks. Backing stones, equal in size and hue to the nucleus, obscure the tiers. Near the bottom is a packing layer, between core and casing, of small blocks of soft yellow limestone – seen on all three pyramids – and, finally, remains of fine limestone casing with exquisite joins.

All three have a passage on or near the centre axis, sloping to a chamber that makes a westward turn, probably for manoeuvring the sarcophagus. The burial chambers, west of the centre axis, were cut out of bedrock and lined with masonry.

Which queens?

The first pyramid to the north, GI-a, may have been for Hetepheres, thought to be the mother of Khufu (p. 117). GI-b might belong to a queen Meritetes, who lived through the reigns of Sneferu, Khufu and Khafre, based on an inscription found in the chapel of the first mastaba to the east, that of Kawab, an 'eldest son' of Khufu. One theory is that the male occupants of mastabas closest to the small pyramids were sons of the respective queens.

The southernmost pyramid, GI-c, could belong to a queen Henutsen, a name known only from much later, in dynasties 21–26, when the chapel at the centre of the eastern base of this pyramid was converted to a temple of the goddess Isis under the epithet 'Mistress of the Pyramids' (p. 38). All three pyramids once had similar chapels, smaller equivalents of the great mortuary temple of Khufu. But only that of GI-c survives with its walls intact, thanks to its conversion. The mortuary chapel of GI-a is now entirely missing, robbed down to bedrock, and only the foundations of GI-b remain.

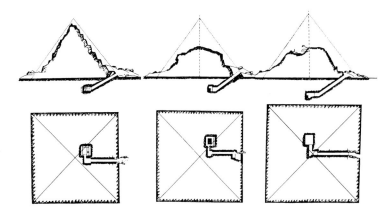

The Burial of Hetepheres

Queen's pyramid GI-a was begun 28 m (92 ft) east of its final position, as indicated by the beginning of its passage cut into the bedrock. Aligned with the abandoned pyramid on the north is the deep shaft belonging to Queen Hetepheres. In 1925, while George Reisner was absent in the United States, his photographer was setting up his tripod when one leg sank into the ground. Investigation led to the discovery of a sealed shaft and stairway. The shaft was extraordinarily deep (over 27 m or 89 ft) and was blocked with masonry from top to bottom – which took weeks to clear.

At the very bottom of the shaft was a chamber, where the excavators found a beautiful alabaster sarcophagus and, in a niche in the western wall, a small alabaster box with the string around it still in place and its sealing intact. This was the canopic chest for the queen's internal organs.

From the moment of discovery, however, it was apparent that this assemblage was a reburial, since the pottery was smashed and linen lay disintegrated among the remains of the boxes that had once contained it. Pieces of furniture that had been

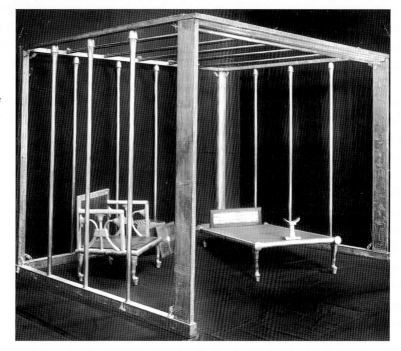

jammed into the chamber could be reconstructed from surviving gold foil although most of the wood had deteriorated. On top of the sarcophagus were beautiful long poles belonging to a canopy in the form of early papyrus bud columns. This canopy, if reassembled, would fit exactly into the chambers of the queens' pyramids. There were also the parts of two sitting chairs, a carrying chair, a tube for walking sticks, a headrest and two sets of silver bracelets. What we have here is the private boudoir of a queen.

The first name found in the tomb was that of Sneferu. But then other texts came to light that contained the name Hetepheres. She was called 'Mother of the King' and 'Daughter of the God' and it became evident that she was the wife of Sneferu and mother of a reigning king. Seal impressions included the name Her-Mejedu – the Horus name of Khufu.

The sarcophagus was empty and Reisner noted that the contents of the chamber were in the reverse order usually found in tombs. Why? Reisner thought that Hetepheres had originally been buried at Dahshur but her tomb had been violated and her body stolen. Khufu's men did not tell him of the missing body and he arranged for a reburial at Giza, in a deep, unmarked shaft for safety. Other explanations are possible, if not entirely satisfactory. I suggested that her body is missing because it was removed to the burial chamber in GI-a, after the first pyramid was begun and then abandoned, perhaps with a new set of equipment. The original shaft was then filled in and forgotten until stumbled on by Reisner's photographer some four-and-a-half thousand years later. Yet another line of speculation sees this unmarked burial (or reburial) of a queen mother's grave goods as an indication of disputes over the royal succession. It is not certain that Hetepheres was the mother of Khufu, who survived three older brothers.

Reconstruction of the burial assembly of Queen Hetepheres, based on Reisner's meticulous excavation of each individual fragment of the disintegrated remains. The great bed canopy was found dismantled.

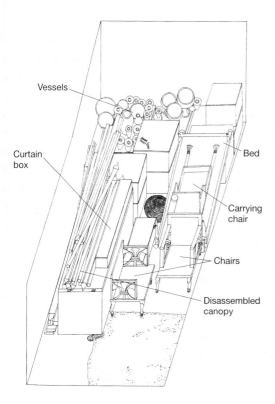

Vessels

Curtain box

Bed

Carrying chair

Chairs

Disassembled canopy

Hetepheres's reassembled canopy and items of furniture. On the front panel of the canopy was found the Horus name (below) Neb-Maat, 'Lord of Truth', that is Sneferu.

Khufu's Boats

The large number – and size – of boat-shaped pits east of Khufu's pyramid give it the appearance of a royal port authority or docking place on the journey from this world to the Netherworld. One pit is parallel to the causeway and therefore at the very threshold of the mortuary temple. On either side of the temple, to the north and south, are two even larger boat-shaped pits, possibly for boats to transport the king to stellar destinations. Next to the queen's pyramid (GI-a) is a fourth boat-shaped pit and, recently, a fifth has been found east of the newly discovered satellite pyramid, perhaps for the symbolic transport of the king's *ka* statue.

On the south side of the Great Pyramid are two further boat pits that are often discussed together with those mentioned above, but which in fact differ in one important respect. They are long, narrow and rectangular rather than boat-shaped, and they contain the disassembled parts of real boats.

The royal barques

The two southern boat pits were discovered in 1954, each covered by a roof of huge limestone slabs. When one of the slabs was raised from the first pit, the planking of a great boat was seen, completely dismantled but arranged in the semblance of its finished form.

The boat was removed from its pit, piece by piece, under the supervision of Ahmed Youssef, the master restorer who worked on Hetepheres's funerary furniture (p. 117). Made of cedarwood, the 1,224 separate parts had numerous U-shaped holes so that the boat could be 'stitched' together using ropes made of vegetable fibres. After many years of painstaking work, the boat was finally reassembled like a giant jigsaw, and is now housed in its own boat-shaped museum next to the pyramid. When reassembled the boat measures 43.3 m (142 ft) long. Its

prow and stern are in the form of papyrus stalks, the stern one bent over. It is thus a wooden replica of a type of papyrus reed boat perhaps dating back to the predynastic period – another example of the Egyptian fondness for simulating their earliest reed structures in more durable materials. A cabin, or inner shrine, is enclosed within a reed-mat structure with poles of the same papyrus-bud form that we see in the canopy of Hetepheres (p. 117).

The second boat pit, just to the west of the museum, was investigated in 1985 by a team from National Geographic with the Egyptian Antiquities authority. A hole was drilled through the limestone beams and a tiny camera inserted. It was hoped that the pit had been so well sealed that the air inside would have last been breathed by the ancient Egyptians, but there were obvious signs that this was not the case. However, it was ascertained that the pit did contain the disarticulated parts of a boat, lying in approximately their correct relative positions, though the pit was shorter than the fully-assembled boat would have been.

These southern boat pits do not seem to have been part of the symbolic layout of the whole Khufu complex but rather are a deliberate, ritual disposal. Significantly, the pits would have

Pyramid as port authority of the Netherworld: the eastern side of Khufu's Great Pyramid is occupied by the remains of his mortuary temple (of which just the basalt pavement survives), the foundation of his causeway, boat pits, queens' pyramids and mastaba tombs.

(Above) The existence of a second boat in the unopened boat pit was confirmed when a tiny camera was inserted.

When the first boat was restored (far right), signs for prow, stern, port and starboard, similar to phyle names in work gangs and temple priesthoods, were discovered on the planks.

been beyond the pyramid's enclosure wall, which is now missing. Both the pits are rectangular, rather than boat-shaped and are also too small to have contained the fully assembled boats – though the builders could easily have achieved this if they had wanted to. It appears therefore that the boats were intended to be dismantled and buried, but why?

The boats could have been symbolic transport mechanisms for the king to ascend to the heavens – westwards with the setting sun and eastwards with the rising sun – but the indications are that they fall into a different class of objects. Items connected with the royal funeral were considered in some sense highly charged. To neutralize them they were dismantled and buried separately, close to but outside the funerary precinct. Another example is the wood canopy for transporting a statue, found, ritually disassembled in an extra shaft outside Khafre's satellite pyramid (p. 126).

It seems probable, therefore, that these complete, but wholly disassembled, boats were connected with Khufu's final earthly voyage – to his pyramid.

Master craftsman Ahmed Youssef with the boat of Khufu that he reassembled after it had lain buried in a pit for 4,500 years.

The displacement of this boat is 45 tons. The maximum draft is 1.48 m (5 ft). It is 5.9 m wide with a total length of 43.3 m (142 ft). It was found in 1,224 pieces, comprising 656 major parts of the boat, all originally stitched together with rope, with several lines of mortice and tenon joints across the hull, as seen in the diagram (below left).

Djedefre at Abu Roash

The first Sphinx? The face of Djedefre in a magnificent dark purplish quartzite head found at Abu Roash. The king is shown wearing the nemes crown. The scant remains of the original surface behind the headdress turn outwards, suggesting the beginning of a lion body. Now in the Louvre, it is one of several magnificent pieces of sculpture found in the boat pit east of the pyramid of Djedefre.

The very pronounced alignments between the pyramid complexes at Giza show considerable concern for unity of design over three generations. An anomaly in this, however, is the pyramid built by

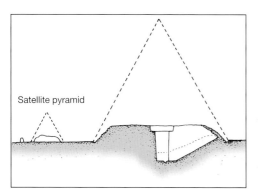

The work of the Franco-Swiss team at Abu Roash is revealing new details about Djedefre's pyramid. It was probably intended to be 106.2 m (348 ft) to a side. There is uncertainty about the exact angle of slope, with evidence for 48°, though it has been suggested it would have been nearer 52°. Its theoretical height is between 57 m (187 ft) and 67 m (220 ft).

Djedefre, Khufu's son and successor, 8 km (5 miles) to the north on a hillock overlooking the Giza plateau. By moving to this spot, Djedefre's pyramid was nearer due west of Heliopolis, centre of the sun cult, than Giza. Perhaps he was motivated by religious reasons since Djedefre is the first pharaoh we know to take the title 'Son of Re'.

It has been suggested that Djedefre's removal of his funerary monument from Giza, its destruction and Khafre's return to Giza indicate a split between the sons of Khufu and conflict over the succession. However, Djedefre's cartouche was found, with workers' graffiti, on the limestone beams covering Khufu's boat pit, showing that he oversaw his father's funeral. The French Institute/University of Geneva Abu Roash Expedition, begun in 1995 under Michael Valloggia, is finding little evidence of destruction dating from the Old Kingdom, rather it is from the Roman period.

Today nothing remains other than the stump of the core around a natural hillock. Core masonry and mortar adhere to the bedrock massif which would have been preserved in the middle of the pyramid, as in Khufu's and Khafre's. Great quantities of granite from the casing lie all around. A number of blocks have a 60° slope, indicating to some that Djedefre intended a step pyramid. Others have suggested that he was planning to build a mastaba, like the later tombs of Khentkawes and Shepseskaf. However, step pyramid accretions generally had a much steeper slope of 72–78° and the mastaba of Shepseskaf has an angle of 65°. So it was previously concluded that Djedefre was building a very steep pyramid, like the first stage of Sneferu's Bent Pyramid at Dahshur.

The Franco-Swiss excavations at the north corners and centre of the base of the pyramid have revealed a foundation bed with a 12° slope. If the casing blocks were laid at this angle, the pyramid slope is reduced to 48°, though the team suggests a range near 52°, which would conform to Sneferu's Meidum pyramid (E3) and Khufu's. This would mean that Djedefre's masons returned to inclining

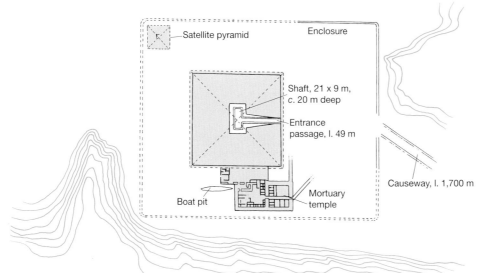

The enclosure of Djedefre's pyramid also departs from its counterparts at Giza. As a rectangle oriented north–south, it may be the first revival of the 'Djoser-type'. The mortuary temple is shifted north of the pyramid's east–west centre axis. The pyramid is located on a high plateau, approached by an extremely long causeway.

the casing, as in the bottom of Sneferu's Bent Pyramid, and as opposed to the finely levelled horizontal coursing of Khufu's casing. With the north baseline now accurately determined as 106.2 m (348 ft), the resulting theoretical height is between 57 m (187 ft), at 48°, and 67 m (220 ft), at 52°. We still do not know how far building progressed above some 20 granite courses at the base. Petrie found a fragment of a throne of a diorite statue, with the hieroglyphs for *Men..Ra*, most probably Menkaure. Stadelmann suggests that he undertook restoration work on the uncompleted pyramid.

Inside the pyramid

From Sneferu to Khufu we have seen a continual striving to build chambers higher in the pyramid body. Djedefre returned to the earlier concept and began his substructure as a colossal pit in the ground, 23 x 10 m (75 x 33 ft) and *c.* 20 m (66ft) or more deep. An access corridor was 49 m (161 ft) long and sloped at an angle of 22° 35'. The entrance passage and burial chamber were built into the corridor and pit. Scant remains of roofing masonry suggest that it was reminiscent of the earlier style of Djoser.

The pyramid complex

The Franco-Swiss team has now ascertained that there was an inner enclosure, 6 m (20 ft) from the north pyramid base, and widening on the east to contain the mortuary temple. Djedefre's mortuary temple appears hastily built. It is formed of rather thick fieldstone walls, finished with mudbrick to form compartments and chambers (chapels according to Stadelmann) around an open court east of the pyramid. This configuration is similar to workshops at Giza and elsewhere, and perhaps the structures were simply left when Djedefre died and

work on the pyramid stopped. Workshops and habitations also occupied the northeast corner of the inner enclosure. Just beside the northeast corner of the pyramid, layers of chips remained of a vast stoneyard for working pyramid blocks. Perhaps some of the walls were ancillary to the construction of the pyramid and were finished quickly as some kind of cult emplacement. A deep recess in the core masonry at the back of the 'temple' was perhaps for a false door.

A boat pit against the south side of the temple recalls the one just outside the entrance to Khufu's temple. A covered corridor led from the northeast entrance of the inner enclosure to the mouth of the causeway. Just outside this corridor, recent excavations discovered a cache of votive pottery. Similar caches have been found near the entrances to the temples or enclosures of the pyramids of Sneferu at Meidum and Dahshur, Menkaure, Shepseskaf's mastaba and Raneferef's pyramid. It indicates a sustained cult service for Djedefre.

The height of the knoll on which the pyramid was built, some 20 m (66 ft) higher than the Giza plateau, meant that an extraordinarily long causeway was needed to reach the valley – perhaps 1,700 m (5, 577 ft) long. The tentative, cursory and diminutive character of the pyramid is a striking counterpoint to the size of its causeway. Djedefre's pyramid was less than a quarter of the base area of his father's, Khufu, at Giza. Perhaps, already an elderly man when he came to the throne, Djedefre knew that he might not have many years left to complete his pyramid, and chose a smaller design – he is said to have reigned for only eight years.

Return to Giza: Khafre's Pyramid and the Great Sphinx

Khafre's pyramid was called 'Great is Khafre'. The simplicity of the chamber and passage system may reflect the builders' experience of problems in building chambers high in the body of the pyramids of Sneferu and Khufu. Its base length was 215 m (705 ft), rising to a height of 143.5 m (471 ft) at an angle of 53° 10'.

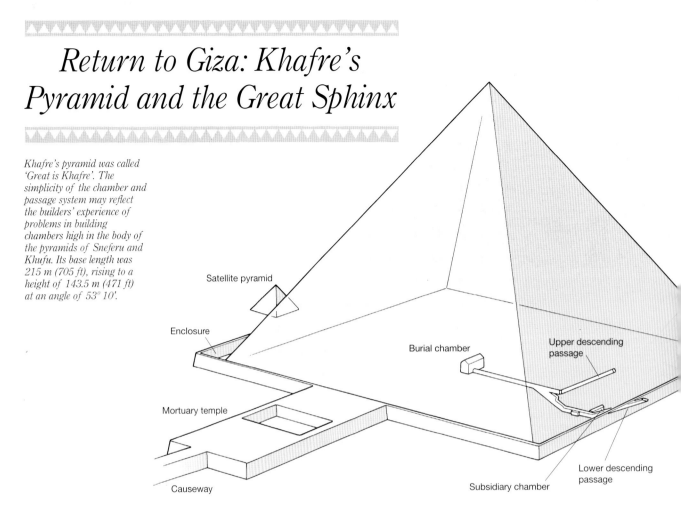

Satellite pyramid

Enclosure

Burial chamber

Upper descending passage

Mortuary temple

Causeway

Subsidiary chamber

Lower descending passage

The blocks of surviving casing at the top of Khafre's pyramid are not flush, suggesting they were cut to the pyramid's slope before setting. However, the unevenness may be due to settling when lower courses were robbed.

Djedefre was succeeded by Khafre, another son of Khufu. Two older brothers had been in line for the throne before Khafre and we might perhaps imagine him as a rather young man – youth, at least, could account for the extraordinary confidence he showed in laying out a square 215 m (705 ft) to a side, to form the base of a pyramid that stood shoulder to shoulder with his father's. Khafre's pyramid is in fact the smaller of the two, but he disguised this by founding it on bedrock some 10 m (33 ft) higher. It also has a slightly sharper angle of slope, 53° 10' to Khufu's 51° 50' 40". A very slight twist can be discerned at the top, introduced because the four corner angles were not quite aligned correctly to meet at the apex.

The pyramid

The pyramid was founded on a terrace which the ancient builders cut down by *c.* 10 m (33 ft) below the original bedrock surface to the northwest, but built up with large blocks of masonry at the opposite, southeast, corner. This compensated for the natural *c.* 3–6° slope of the Mokattam Formation. Apart from the bottom course of outer casing in granite, the pyramid was cloaked in Turah limestone. Only the upper quarter of the casing remains – apparently a reflection of the robbers' practice of stripping first the corners and base and then working upwards. Just beneath the lowest surviving course of casing stones, a band of regular stepped core stone is visible. The rest of the surface down to the base – the greater part of the pyramid – consists of very rough, irregular, loose stones.

What is this loose lower band? Is it packing between core and casing, exposed when the casing was torn away? That seems likely until, climbing the corners of the pyramid, one sees that this irregular masonry seems to continue for some depth into the pyramid body. The discontinuity might indicate different building styles, perhaps even a hiatus and then resumption of building. Alternatively, the core masonry may simply have been laid in a more regular fashion towards the top in order to allow the builders greater control (p. 222).

The casing stones at the top of the pyramid are much smaller – about 1 cubit thick (*c.* 50 cm/20 in) – than the casing stones which survive at the bottom of Khufu's pyramid and those of his queens. Their

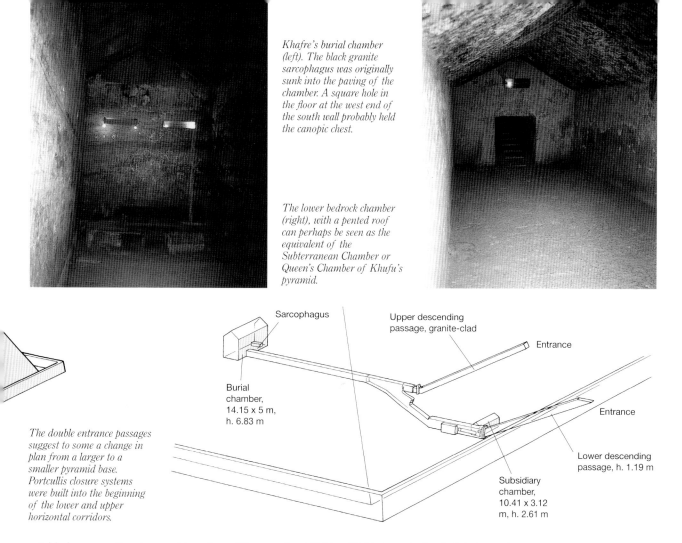

Khafre's burial chamber (left). The black granite sarcophagus was originally sunk into the paving of the chamber. A square hole in the floor at the west end of the south wall probably held the canopic chest.

The lower bedrock chamber (right), with a pented roof can perhaps be seen as the equivalent of the Subterranean Chamber or Queen's Chamber of Khufu's pyramid.

Sarcophagus

Upper descending passage, granite-clad

Entrance

Burial chamber, 14.15 x 5 m, h. 6.83 m

Entrance

Lower descending passage, h. 1.19 m

Subsidiary chamber, 10.41 x 3.12 m, h. 2.61 m

The double entrance passages suggest to some a change in plan from a larger to a smaller pyramid base. Portcullis closure systems were built into the beginning of the lower and upper horizontal corridors.

outside faces are often staggered by a few millimetres rather than flush. This might suggest that at this level the outer slope was cut into the blocks before they were laid, due to reduced working space. What we can say with confidence about these masonry variations is that even now – and Khafre's was the fifth of the giant pyramids – pyramid-building techniques were still largely *ad hoc*.

Among its many meanings, the pyramid was conceived as a port from which the voyage to the Netherworld began. The broad terrace to the east of Khafre's pyramid is made of massive limestone blocks weighing up to hundreds of tons. Huge limestone piers project beyond the northeast and southwest corners of the terrace, looking like slipways or giant docks. Five narrow boat-shaped trenches carved into the natural rock extend into the recesses between the two piers and the mortuary temple.

Inside Khafre's Pyramid

Khafre's pyramid contains two descending passages. One begins in the body of the masonry,

about 11.54 m (38 ft) above the level of the base; the other runs from in front of the base line at ground level, near the centre of the northern side. Like almost all pyramid passage systems, its does not align with the centre axis of the pyramid, in this case lying a little more than 12 m (39 ft) to the east. It has been suggested that the pyramid was originally intended to be larger, or that its north base line was first planned to be 30 m (98 ft) further north, so that the lower passage, like the upper one, would have been entirely within the body of the masonry. But it is hard to imagine that there was an earlier plan for a larger pyramid, such is the sculpted unity of the pyramid terrace, enclosure wall and pyramid base. What we are seeing is more likely evidence of a vacillation between two different passage systems in the course of building.

The lower passage descends at an angle to a horizontal corridor, 1.7 m high (*c*. 5 ft 8 in). A subsidiary chamber opens off the horizontal section, cut out of the bedrock and with a pented roof. The purpose of this chamber is not entirely clear. It may have been a *serdab* chamber, equivalent to the misnamed 'Queen's Chamber' in the Great Pyramid.

Alternatively it may have been simply used for storing offerings. At the end of the horizontal section an ascending passage rises, reaching an intersection with the other passage, itself descending to the bedrock from high up in the masonry of the pyramid.

Since the bedrock was left nearly 10 m (33 ft) high in the northwest corner of the pyramid while the tops of the burial chamber's walls are at the level of the pyramid terrace, the chamber must have been built in a pit similar to that in Djedefre's pyramid at Abu Roash, though not as deep. The roof of the burial chamber is composed of pented, limestone beams like the 'Queen's Chamber' and the uppermost of the five relieving chambers above the burial chamber in the Great Pyramid.

The sarcophagus

The burial chamber is at a right-angle to the axis of the passage system, putting the sarcophagus in this case very close to – but not directly on – both the north–south and the vertical axes of the pyramid. Khafre's sarcophagus is of black, hard granite, half embedded in the very thick paving which once covered more of the chamber floor. Its lid lay in two pieces. A pit cut into the floor of the chamber probably held the canopic chest – the first example of this found in a pyramid. Its lid would have been formed by one of the paving slabs of the floor.

Belzoni, having rediscovered the entrance to the upper passage, made his way into this chamber in 1818 but found to his disappointment that he was not the first to enter it in post-pharaonic times. Curiously, bones found in the sarcophagus turned out to be those of a bull. In a much later period bulls were buried as symbols of the pharaoh himself or of Osiris. Rainer Stadelmann has suggested that these bones were probably an offering thrown into the sarcophagus at some unknown later date by intruders, long after the king's body had been robbed and lost.

Khafre's mortuary temple, causeway foundation and valley temple are the best preserved of the three Giza complexes. Khafre added the Great Sphinx and its temple.

The burial chamber of Khafre's pyramid must have been built in a pit cut into the bedrock massif.

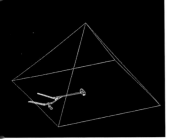

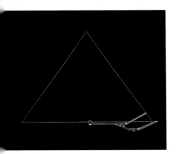

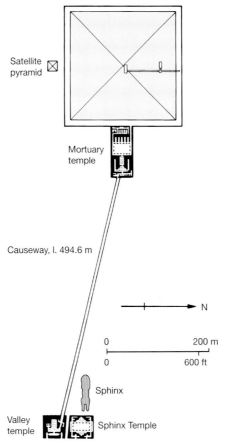

Satellite pyramid

Mortuary temple

Causeway, l. 494.6 m

N

0   200 m
0   600 ft

Sphinx

Valley temple   Sphinx Temple

The Pyramid Complex

The mortuary temple

Khafre's mortuary temple marks a real architectural advance – being both larger than previous examples and for the first time including all five elements that were to become standard. It consists of a fore part, forming an entrance to the main court, and a back part. The fore part was constructed of megalithic blocks of limestone, quarried nearby. The use of huge blocks to form the cores of the walls, which were then encased with finer quality stone, was introduced by Khafre. The inside of his mortuary temple was almost entirely lined with granite.

The causeway enters the mortuary temple near the south end of the front. Immediately to the left were two granite chambers and at the other end of a corridor running along the front of the temple were four more chambers, lined with alabaster. In the fore part of the temple the entrance hall consisted of two sections, one transverse with recessed bays and the other rectangular. The roofs of both were supported by columns made of single blocks of granite. A long, narrow, slit-like chamber branches off from each end of the first hall. It has been suggested that huge statues of the king once stood at the back of these dim passages.

The reigns of Khafre and to a lesser extent Menkaure saw an explosion of statue making – the size and number of Khafre's statues were unparalleled until the New Kingdom, almost 1,200 years later. But while hundreds of pieces of smaller statues have been found, no fragments of any larger ones remain from the mortuary temple, though there were over 52 in Khafre's complex of life size or larger. This is because they were removed intact by royal order, possibly in the 18th dynasty or by Ramesses II, and recycled for other royal projects.

Next in sequence came the open court, the pillars of which, encased in granite, were so broad that they formed piers around the courtyard. In front of them were 12 granite statues standing in pits or sockets in the white alabaster floor. Hölscher suggested that these were standing statues of the king in the form of Osiris. But Herbert Ricke argued for seated statues of the king wearing the *nemes* scarf. Our excavations of the 'workmen's barracks' west of Khafre's pyramid produced a clue suggesting that we should reconsider the form of these statues. These galleries turned out to be not living quarters but a royal workshop (p. 238). Among the finds was a fragment of a model of the king wearing the

crown of the south, with a back pillar painted to imitate granite. The pillar projects in an upside-down 'L' over the crown, as did the colonnade roof over the pillars of the court of Khafre's mortuary temple. Intriguingly, we have a series of striding royal statues wearing the crown of the south, usurped by Ramesses II but made much earlier. Their bases fit closely the sockets around the court of the Khafre mortuary temple. Further study should confirm whether or not these derive from here.

The inner walls of the court may have been decorated with reliefs above a certain height. Beyond the court were five niches, now badly destroyed, for more statues of the king. Behind them are five storerooms, perhaps for the offerings made to these five statues. At the very back of the temple, against the pyramid itself, was the inner sanctuary, probably with a false door niche. A stairway-ramp in the northeast corner of the temple climbed up to the roof, while from the northwest corner of the pillared court a corridor led to the paved pyramid enclosure. Outside the temple were five boat-pits, two on the north and three on the south, and possibly a sixth was planned. They are carved into the rock in a boat shape; two still retain roofing slabs.

The valley temple

Down the causeway Khafre's valley temple, marvellously well preserved, unlike the mortuary temple. Its major chambers are in fact very similar to the fore part of Khafre's mortuary temple. This is not surprising, since, as a gateway or portal to the whole complex, it more or less encapsulates, within a single temple, the architectural pattern of an entrance.

Five Features of Mortuary Temples

Five standard features of later mortuary temples were first found in Khafre's:
1 an entrance hall;
2 a broad columned court;
3 five niches for statues of the king;
4 five storage chambers;
5 an inner sanctuary – a pair of stelae, a false door or a combination of both.

The five niches may relate to the completed five-fold titulary of the king, or the five phyles. The Abusir Papyri indicate that in the 5th dynasty, three of the niches held statues of the king as ruler of south and north Egypt, and as Osiris.

A view into the interior of Khafre's valley temple, with granite lining, pillars and lintels intact. The corridor on the right is the continuation of the causeway into the temple.

(Below) Twenty-three statues of Khafre were placed around the T-shaped hall of his valley temple, lit only by narrow slits in the walls at ceiling height.

The diorite statue of Khafre, found by Mariette in the valley temple vestibule. The wings of the Horus falcon are folded around the king's headdress in a gesture of protection. It was one of 23 that originally would have lined the T-shaped hall of the valley temple.

(Below) A reconstruction of the statue-carrying shrine found in pieces under Khafre's satellite pyramid, shown here on a transport sled. A depiction of such a sled and statue shrine is shown in a relief from the tomb of Queen Meresankh III (below right).

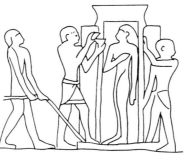

A quay or revetment in front of the Sphinx Temple was revealed by drillings, as much as 16 m (52 ft) deep. It probably continues south in front of the valley temple, from which point ramps lead to the two doors of the temple – perhaps symbolizing the duality of Upper and Lower Egypt. In 1995 Zahi Hawass recleared the area, revealing that the ramps cross over tunnels framed within mudbrick walls that formed a narrow corridor or canal running north–south. In front of the Sphinx Temple the canal runs into a drain leading northeast, probably to the quay buried below the modern tourist plaza. Both entrances were flanked by a pair of lions or, more likely, sphinxes, 8 m long (26 ft long). All that remains are shapes described by lever sockets and the cuttings for the statue bases.

The valley temple was built of megalithic core blocks sheathed in red granite. The temple entrances were closed with huge single-leaf doors, probably of cedarwood. Between the two entrances runs the vestibule. Here the walls were of simple red granite, originally polished to a lustre, and the floor was paved with white alabaster. A door then led to a T-shaped hall, which constituted the greater part of the valley temple. This again was sheathed with polished red granite and white alabaster, and its roof was supported by 16 single-block granite pillars, many still in position today.

A kind of internal cosmic circuit was incorporated into Khafre's valley temple, comparable to the larger symbolic circuit of the pyramid complex as a whole. This circuit began in the cross-bar of the T-shaped hall. Dim and mysterious, the only light came through narrow slits at the top of the walls. Statues of Khafre sat in pits along the walls. There are 23 statue bases, though the one at the centre of the leg of the T-shaped hall is wider and perhaps was counted twice, making 24 in total. Were fumigations and libations performed to a statue of Khafre for every hour of the day and night? Or did the statues represent the deified parts of the royal body, as H. Ricke and S. Schott thought?

The statue sequence continued along the cross-bar of the 'T' and ended at a doorway leading to a corridor from which a stairway ramp wound clockwise up and over the roof of the corridor and exited on to the roof of the valley temple. On the south side of the roof was a small courtyard, positioned directly over six storage chambers, arranged in two storeys of three, embedded in the core masonry of the T-shaped hall. The court represented an 'above', open to the sun, while the chambers were the 'below', a dark and chthonic aspect of the temple.

Symbolic conduits lined with alabaster, a material especially identified with purification, run from the temple's roof-top courtyard down into the deep, dark chambers. The statue sequence starts just outside the door to these chambers from the T-shaped hall. The symbolic circuit runs through the entire temple, taking in both the chthonic and the solar aspects of afterlife beliefs and of the embalming ritual, for which the valley temple was the stage according to some Egyptologists (p. 25).

The satellite pyramid

Pyramid GII-a, the satellite pyramid of Khafre, has been almost completely eradicated by stone robbers – only the outlines of the foundations and a few core blocks now remain, positioned on the centre axis of Khafre's pyramid. Satellite pyramids are thought to derive from the south tomb of Djoser and may have been for the burial of statues dedicated to the *ka*, the king's spiritual double and vital force. Khafre's satellite pyramid furnished evidence to support this. It has two descending passages, the second on the centre axis of the pyramid but out beyond its base. This passage extends beneath the pyramid, ending in a dead-end and a small niche. In this niche was a wooden box containing pieces of wood that had once formed an item of furniture. Reassembled by Ahmed Youssef, this turned out to be a frame of cedarwood in the form of a *sah netjer*, or divine booth, which had been deliberately – ritually, it seems – chopped into regular-sized pieces. In tomb scenes, for example one from the tomb of Khufu's granddaughter Meresankh, the *sah netjer* is depicted holding the queen's statue as it is ritually drawn along towards the tomb.

The Great Sphinx

The largest of the hundreds of statues built in Khafre's reign, the Sphinx was the first truly colossal piece of sculpture in ancient Egypt. The lion body is carved to a scale of 22:1 and the head 30:1. Egyptians would not carve statues of such proportions again until the reigns of New Kingdom pharaohs like Amenhotep III and Ramesses II, some 1,200 years later.

Location and geology

The Sphinx was carved from the natural bedrock at the very base of Khafre's causeway. The rectangular secondary enclosure wall which surrounds Khafre's pyramid complex would, if extended eastwards, take in the Sphinx. The south side of the Sphinx ditch forms the northern edge of Khafre's causeway as it runs past the Sphinx and enters Khafre's valley temple – the close association of the Sphinx with Khafre's valley temple makes it most probable that the Sphinx was carved for Khafre.

Close study by geologist Thomas Aigner of the geological layers in the Sphinx and the individual stones of Khafre's temples enabled us to unravel the sequence of quarrying and building that created this complex. The valley temple was probably composed of huge blocks quarried from the layers that run through the upper part of the Sphinx body. The standard large core blocks in the Sphinx temple, with a soft yellow band between two harder bands, came from just below chest height in the Sphinx body.

Design and iconography

The lion was a solar symbol in more than one ancient Near Eastern culture. It is also a common archetype of royalty. The royal human head on a lion's body symbolized power and might controlled by the intelligence of the pharaoh, guarantor of cosmic order, or *maat*. The sphinx, in the design achieved by the time of the Great Sphinx, survived for two-and-a-half millennia in the iconography of Egyptian civilization. The *nemes* headdress was the particular way of folding the scarf that was exclusive to Egyptian kings. The flaring sides of the royal *nemes* scarf replaced the lion's mane to bring the human head into proportion with the lion's chest.

The Great Sphinx, however, has a smaller head and headdress in relation to the lion body than in the classic sphinx form, and a considerably elongated body. It is not a question of the head being recarved, and cut down out of proportion; the lion body by itself is too long. The explanation seems to lie in the specific geology of the location. Huge fissures cut through Members I and II – the bottom two of the three geological layers from which the Sphinx is carved (p. 106). The greatest of these fissures runs right across the thinnest part of the Sphinx's body. As they isolated the block of stone that was to become the statue, the Egyptians encountered this serious defect and realized that it would prevent them from finishing off the curve of the rump and the haunches, the hind paws and the tail. It is quite likely that they elongated the body to compensate for it.

The Great Sphinx stands guard before the pyramid of Khafre, for whom this fusion of man and lion was sculpted in about 2500 BC. Towering 20 m (66 ft) above the spectator, it was the first truly colossal royal sculpture in the history of ancient Egypt, seen here looking across the limestone core blocks of the temple dedicated to it.
The different geological layers the Sphinx was carved from (p. 106) account for the variation in preservation of its parts. The head was carved from a much better building stone (Member III) than the soft layers of the body (Member II), while the base is carved from a petrified hard shoal and coral reef (Member I).

The builders of the Sphinx began by quarrying a U-shaped ditch, then sculpting the lion body from the reserved bedrock block. Stone was removed in the form of colossal blocks which were used to build the core walls of the valley temple (the upper layers) and the Sphinx Temple on a lower terrace to the east.

The Sphinx Temple

The floor of the Sphinx Temple is *c.* 2.5 m (*c.* 9 ft) lower than the Sphinx terrace, cut down into the hard stone of Member I. The temple seems to be specifically dedicated to the Sphinx, but we know very little about it because there are no known Old Kingdom texts that refer to either the Sphinx or its temple. By the time that a cult of the Sphinx was activated in the 18th dynasty, the Old Kingdom temples at Giza had long been abandoned.

Khafre's builders did not complete the Sphinx Temple, leaving the exterior without its intended granite casing, which perhaps explains the absence of priests and priestesses dedicated to its service among the Old Kingdom tombs at Giza – temple

service may never have begun. Twenty-four red granite pillars formed a colonnade and ambulatory around a central courtyard. The court is an almost exact copy of that in Khafre's mortuary temple, with colossal royal statues before huge pillars made of core blocks of locally quarried limestone. But here there are 10 rather than 12 statues, perhaps because of limitations of space. The court statues sat in sockets cut in the floor in front of each pillar, bringing the base of the statue flush with the alabaster paving covering the bedrock floor. Each court pillar was encased in red granite to match the statues. We can only make educated guesses about architectural symbolism in a text-less temple. Ricke, who studied this temple (1967–70) was keen

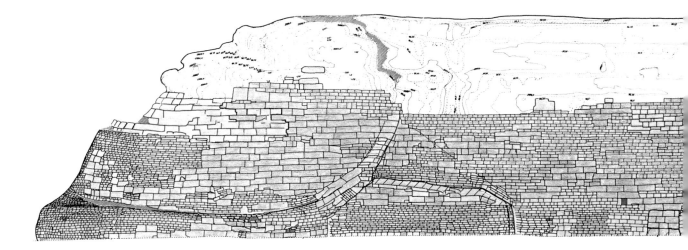

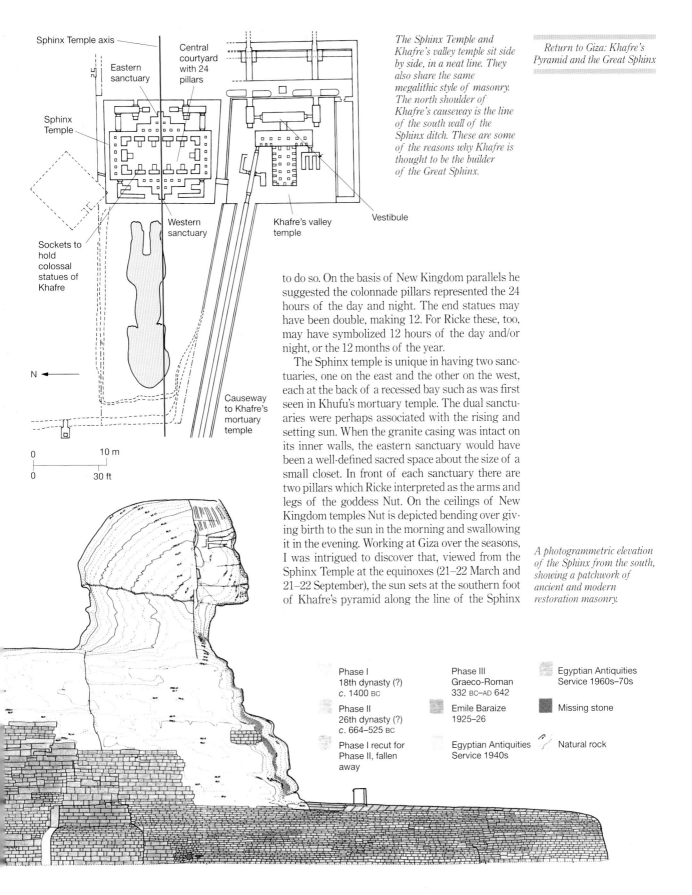

Sphinx Temple axis

Central courtyard with 24 pillars

Eastern sanctuary

Sphinx Temple

Western sanctuary

Sockets to hold colossal statues of Khafre

Khafre's valley temple

Vestibule

N

Causeway to Khafre's mortuary temple

0   10 m

0   30 ft

The Sphinx Temple and Khafre's valley temple sit side by side, in a neat line. They also share the same megalithic style of masonry. The north shoulder of Khafre's causeway is the line of the south wall of the Sphinx ditch. These are some of the reasons why Khafre is thought to be the builder of the Great Sphinx.

to do so. On the basis of New Kingdom parallels he suggested the colonnade pillars represented the 24 hours of the day and night. The end statues may have been double, making 12. For Ricke these, too, may have symbolized 12 hours of the day and/or night, or the 12 months of the year.

The Sphinx temple is unique in having two sanctuaries, one on the east and the other on the west, each at the back of a recessed bay such as was first seen in Khufu's mortuary temple. The dual sanctuaries were perhaps associated with the rising and setting sun. When the granite casing was intact on its inner walls, the eastern sanctuary would have been a well-defined sacred space about the size of a small closet. In front of each sanctuary there are two pillars which Ricke interpreted as the arms and legs of the goddess Nut. On the ceilings of New Kingdom temples Nut is depicted bending over giving birth to the sun in the morning and swallowing it in the evening. Working at Giza over the seasons, I was intrigued to discover that, viewed from the Sphinx Temple at the equinoxes (21–22 March and 21–22 September), the sun sets at the southern foot of Khafre's pyramid along the line of the Sphinx

A photogrammetric elevation of the Sphinx from the south, showing a patchwork of ancient and modern restoration masonry.

Phase I
18th dynasty (?)
c. 1400 BC

Phase II
26th dynasty (?)
c. 664–525 BC

Phase I recut for
Phase II, fallen
away

Phase III
Graeco-Roman
332 BC–AD 642

Emile Baraize
1925–26

Egyptian Antiquities
Service 1940s

Egyptian Antiquities
Service 1960s–70s

Missing stone

Natural rock

Computer Modelling the Sphinx

What did the Sphinx originally look like? To find the answer I first spent five years (1979–83) mapping the Sphinx, assisted by Ulrich Kapp of the German Archaeological Institute who produced front and side view drawings with photogrammetry. An overhead view was painstakingly mapped by hand with measuring tape. More recently computers have been brought in to digitize the maps and create a 3-D wireframe model. Some 2.5 million surface points were then plotted to put 'skin' on the skeletal view.

temple axis. In ancient times it would have passed over the western colonnade, across the court and into the eastern sanctuary, possibly illuminating any cult image within. At the very same moment the shadow of the Sphinx and the shadow of the pyramid, both symbols of the king, become merged silhouettes. The Sphinx itself, it seems, symbolized the pharaoh presenting offerings to the sun god in the court of the temple. It was during the brief reign of Khafre's predecessor, Djedefre, that the fifth, 'son of Re', element of the king's name emerged. The first true sun temples were built later, in the 5th dynasty, but the Sphinx Temple must be counted as the first solar-oriented temple associated with an Old Kingdom pyramid complex.

At the summer solstice the sun sets in the same place on the horizon for three days before its setting position begins to move back towards the south again. During those three days, viewed from the Sphinx Temple, it sets mid-way between the two largest Giza pyramids. Whether by chance or by design, the pattern this forms is the hieroglyph for horizon, *akhet*, the sun between two mountains, writ very large indeed across the Giza skyline. *Akh* meant 'to glorify'; *akhet* was 'the place of glorification where the sun sets' and also a circumlocution for 'tomb'. *Akhet*, or horizon, was the name given to the Great Pyramid of Khufu and, in certain textual contexts, also to the entire Giza necropolis.

Restoring the Sphinx

Repair work on the Sphinx began some three-and-a-half millennia ago and has continued throughout the statue's history. The worst deterioration – patches where the masonry flakes and crumbles – affected Graeco-Roman and modern repairs from 1926 to 1988. Major excavations were begun in 1926 under the supervision of the French engineer Emile Baraize. Unfortunately, his 11 years of work were never published and many different phases of architecture around the Sphinx were dismantled without ever being properly documented. Prior to the massive reconstructions of the veneer masonry from 1981 onwards, the Roman restoration consisted of small brick-sized stones, seen for instance on the paws. Baraize reset much of it that he found tumbled. This relatively soft white limestone deteriorated badly. The soundest restoration work dates to the pre-Roman pharaonic period, when the ancient Egyptians chose large limestone slabs (oldest phase of restoration) and in general selected durable masonry which developed a brown protective patina.

What is the date of the oldest repairs? The answer lies tucked between the forepaws of the Sphinx in the shape of the scant remains of a small, open-air chapel built in the 18th dynasty by Thutmose IV. The chapel was excavated by Caviglia in 1816 (p. 48), when it was in a much more

There was no need to add a face to our reconstruction of the Sphinx since it already has one, minus the nose. This single element was added by overlaying an alabaster face of Khafre in the Boston Museum of Fine Arts, whose features closely matched those of the Sphinx. The profile of the nose was taken from the famous diorite statue of Khafre (far left). The computer model was then used to reconstruct the Sphinx as 18th-dynasty Egyptians might have done: they restored the lion body with masonry cladding and very possibly added a statue of a pharaoh, perhaps Amenhotep II. It was his son, Thutmose IV, who carried out the restoration. When he became king he added a granite stela which became the centrepiece of a chapel between the forepaws. We drew the Sphinx over the photogrammetric elevations, then contoured it so the computer could produce a three-dimensional image.

131

In the upper part of his 'Dream Stela', set up in the embrace of the Sphinx (opposite), Thutmose IV makes an offering to the Sphinx in the form of the god Horemakhet.

In the New Kingdom the Sphinx was seen as an image of the sun god, and it is possible that this was what was intended also when it was created in the 4th dynasty. Another interpretation is that the Sphinx originally represented the king as a presenter of offerings to the sun god in the open court of the Sphinx Temple.

complete condition than today. The centrepiece of its back wall is a granite stela, weighing 15 tons and 3.6 m (12 ft) tall, erected by Thutmose IV and dated to the first year of his reign, 1401 BC. Called the Dream Stela, this commemorates his accession to the throne and tells the story of how, as a young prince (though not crown prince) on a hunting expedition in the vicinity of the Sphinx, he fell asleep in the shadow of the statue's head – indicating that sand then lay up to its neck. While he slept, the Sphinx, as the embodiment of the sun (and primeval king) in all its aspects – Khepri-Re-Atum – appeared in a dream and offered him the throne of Upper and Lower Egypt in return for repairing its body and clearing the sand. The text breaks off, but at the top of the stela Thutmose etched a scene of himself giving offerings and libations to the Sphinx. The Dream Stela is compelling evidence for dating the oldest restoration work to the reign of Thutmose IV, about 1,100 years after Khafre, not only because of its story, but because the limestone blocks framing the stele are uniform with the restoration on the Sphinx's paws and chest.

Thutmose's granite stela has made other, less constructive, contributions to Sphinx studies. It depicts the Sphinx couchant upon a high pedestal with a door in the bottom. This is most likely simply an artistic motif to bring the recumbent Sphinx to a height equal with the shoulder and head of the king. However, that has not stopped it nurturing the persistent legend that beneath the Sphinx there is a hidden passage or temple.

In origin, the stela is a reused lintel of a doorway from Khafre's mortuary temple. Given the enormity of the lintel, it probably derives from the temple entrance at the upper end of the causeway. In fact the pivot sockets on the back of the stela match those in the threshold of the temple. Given also the match of the earliest restoration stones to what is left of those of the walls of the causeway, it appears that the masonry of Khafre's complex was stripped in the 18th dynasty. This continued into the 19th dynasty. It may seem strange or unlikely that pharaohs would strip the temples of *Horus-User-ib*, Khafre, to resurrect the cult of the Sphinx as Horus-in-the-Horizon, *Horemakhet*. But since every pharaoh was a new incarnation of the god Horus, perhaps their individual monuments were regarded as simply the communal property of Horus.

When its cult was reactivated in the 18th dynasty, the Sphinx became the focus of a great mudbrick complex, a kind of royal national park around the ruins of Khafre's 4th-dynasty temples. Amenhotep II built a temple on the higher terrace northeast of the Sphinx in the first year of his reign, dedicated to the Sphinx as Horemakhet. Behind Khafre's valley temple was the resthouse of the pharaoh Tutankhamun and in front there was a typical Amarna-style villa, probably also a royal resthouse. A broad viewing platform and stairway fronted the Sphinx. Scores of stelae commemorate the visits of royalty, princes, kings and commoners during the 18th dynasty and later New Kingdom. Several show a royal statue standing between the paws of the Sphinx, just at the base of its chest and in the protective embrace from the rear. This was a very typical 18th-dynasty configuration. Behind Thutmose's stele, not only is there room for such a statue, but there is a huge block of masonry which could have served as a plinth for a statue 6–7 m (20–23 ft) in height – colossal in its own right.

New Kingdom inscriptions refer to the Sphinx sanctuary as *Setepet*, 'The Chosen'. In their first year of rule, pharaohs came to the chapel between the forepaws to make dedications to the Sphinx and to be ordained and confirmed in their position. In so doing, they participated in a hypostasis of royal power from living pharaoh to the ancestral king of the 18th dynasty (probably Amenhotep II), through ancient kings like Khufu and Khafre and ultimately to Horemakhet, the primeval god-king whose image towered above them in the form of the Sphinx.

Menkaure's Pyramid

Menkaure's pyramid was named 'Menkaure is Divine'. Smaller than his predecessors' pyramids at Giza, its has a base area of 102.2 x 104.6 m (335 x 343 ft). It rose to around 65 m (213 ¼ ft) at an angle of 51° 20' 25". The two descending corridors may indicate that it was planned to be much smaller, or that a passage had been intended to open as high on the exterior of the pyramid as Khufu's. Stadelmann accounts for the upper passage as a conduit for air for the builders.

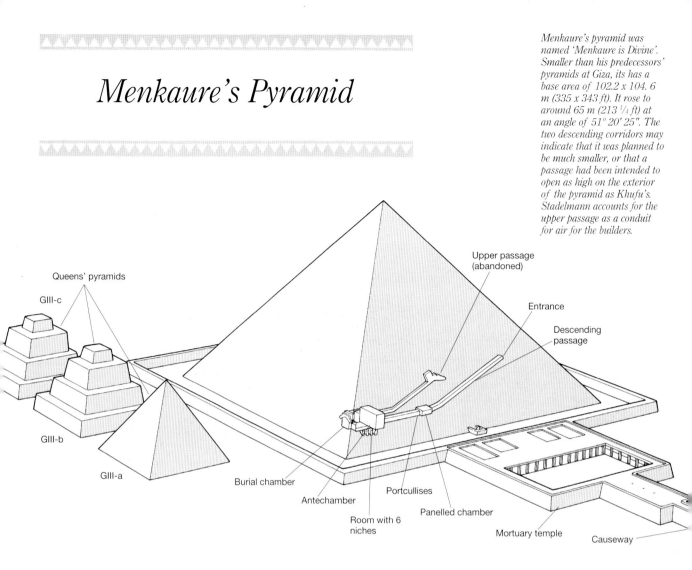

Queens' pyramids

GIII-c

GIII-b

GIII-a

Upper passage (abandoned)

Entrance

Descending passage

Burial chamber

Antechamber

Room with 6 niches

Portcullises

Panelled chamber

Mortuary temple

Causeway

Menkaure's queens' pyramids present some fascinating evidence. The eastern one was finished in granite and limestone casing. It has the T-shaped substructure of a satellite or ka-pyramid and it lies close to the centre axis of the main pyramid. It did, however, contain a granite sarcophagus and it had an eastern chapel, suggesting it was re-used for a queen's burial (although it has been suggested as the place for the king's mummification). The other two small pyramids were either built intentionally as step pyramids or left unfinished, which suggests that, at least here, core and casing did not rise together.

When archaeologists drew lots for excavating Giza on the balcony of the Mena House Hotel in 1899, the concession for Menkaure was won by George Reisner. He knew beforehand that, while the smallest of the three Giza pyramids, its temples could provide the richest finds (his assistant, Arthur Mace, had reconnoitered the site). Indeed, Menkaure's pyramid offered a uniquely complete pyramid profile. Reisner, ahead of his time in recording and excavation technique, was able to reconstruct much of the story of this pyramid: he could study the pyramid and its burial chamber, the queens' pyramids, the mortuary temple, the causeway and the valley temple. Because Menkaure died after at least 26 years of rule, leaving his complex unfinished, its remains represent a very revealing 'frozen' moment. The work was completed in mudbrick, apparently in haste, by his successor Shepseskaf.

The upper part of the pyramid was finished in traditional Turah limestone. At the bottom, 16 courses of red granite casing were left undressed,

(Right) The east–west rectangular chamber, hewn from the bedrock, has been seen as an earlier burial chamber, with the niche at its west end for the sarcophagus. Indeed, the niche resembles bed-niches in ancient Egyptian houses. A passage at the back leads to the space above the granite ceiling beams of the lower chamber.

Antechamber, 14.2 x 3.84 m, h. 4.87 m

apart from token patches around the entrance to the pyramid and behind the inner mortuary temple. Along with the actual burial, freeing the pyramid face seems to have been an integral part of activating the tomb. Handling bosses are still visible on many of the undressed granite blocks.

Menkaure's pyramid lies at the far end of the Giza diagonal and on the very edge of the Mokattam Formation, where it dips down to the south and disappears into the younger Maadi Formation. Its base area is less than a quarter of that of the pyramids of Khafre and Khufu, and with an original height of 65–66 m (213–16 ft), it represents about 1/10 of the building mass of Khufu's pyramid. The ancient builders were perhaps running out of room at Giza for another huge pyramid. However, there were doubtless other forces at work. One speculation is that as the son of the sun god, pharaoh had now to place more emphasis on temples and their endowments, and less on the pyramid as the marker of his personal tomb. In a process already evident in the reign of Khafre – and which continued throughout the Old Kingdom – while the pyramid shrank, the mortuary temple expanded in size and in the complexity and expense of its decorations. In spite of its reduced size, however, Menkaure's complex used a great deal of granite, which was always more costly to quarry and transport than the softer limestone.

Inside the pyramid

The entrance lies about 4 m (13 ft) above the base of the north side of the pyramid. A descending passage slopes down at an angle of 26° 2' for 31 m (102 ft) to a horizontal chamber, where there is a series of panels carved with a repeated very tall and stylized false door motif. This is the first purely decorative element inside a pyramid since Djoser's. The lintel spanning the entrance to the horizontal passage is carved as a drum roll representing the rolled up reed-mat curtain. A horizontal passage with three portcullises leads from here to a rectangular antechamber, oriented east–west, with the east end

(Below left) The east–west rectangular chamber, which some see as an earlier burial chamber, was probably constructed to help manoeuvre the granite lining of the actual burial chamber (below centre) and to insert the huge granite beams of its ceiling. These were carved in an imitation of a curved vault.

(Below) In Menkaure's granite-lined burial chamber Howard Vyse found his beautiful dark stone sarcophagus, carved with niches and panelling. It was removed to be taken to England, and was lost when the ship carrying it sank.

(Bottom) The rough-hewn 'cellar' with six niches may derive from Khufu's subterranean chamber. It may also may be a precursor of the standard three-niche eastern room in 5th- and 6th-dynasty pyramids. which was probably used to store the food offerings for the royal ka.

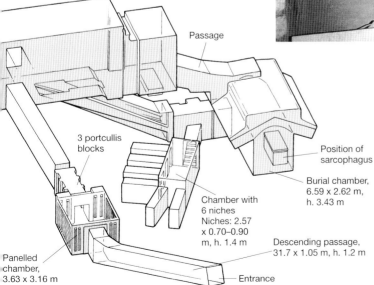

Passage

3 portcullis blocks

Position of sarcophagus

Chamber with 6 niches
Niches: 2.57 x 0.70–0.90 m, h. 1.4 m

Burial chamber, 6.59 x 2.62 m, h. 3.43 m

Descending passage, 31.7 x 1.05 m, h. 1.2 m

Panelled chamber, 3.63 x 3.16 m

Entrance

(Below and opposite) Menkaure's mortuary temple included the five elements that appeared in Khafre's: an entrance hall; broad court; statue niche; storage chambers; and inner sanctuary, though the five statue niches were possibly replaced by a single colossus of Menkaure. In his valley temple Reisner found several very fine statues of Menkaure accompanied by the goddess Hathor and nome deities, and also one (shown with its findspot) with one of his queens.

directly under the vertical axis of the pyramid. Another passage opens in the wall of the chamber directly above the point where the horizontal passage enters. After a short horizontal section, this passage slopes up into, and stops, in the pyramid core. The upper passage was probably abandoned when the floor of the antechamber was lowered.

A short passage slopes westwards from the middle of the floor of this antechamber, leading down to the burial chamber. On the right of the passage is another chamber with four deep niches in the east wall and two in the north. Similar chambers appear in the later mastaba of Shepseskaf and may be forerunners of the three chambers to the left (or east) in the standardized substructure of 5th- and 6th-dynasty pyramids.

At the end of the passage, the burial chamber was constructed within a rectangular space carved out of the bedrock and entirely encased in granite. Its ceiling has the appearance of a round barrel vault, but it was carved into the undersides of huge slabs of granite laid in the form of a pented roof. Inside Vyse found a beautiful dark sarcophagus with recessed or 'palace façade' panelling. It was empty and its lid was missing, although fragments of the latter were found, along with the bones and wrappings of a male body in the upper chamber. Unfortunately, the sarcophagus was lost at sea on the ship *Beatrice*.

The sarcophagus contained a mystery – a wooden coffin inscribed for Menkaure as though it was the coffin in which he was laid to rest. But its style dates it to the Saite period at the very earliest. Radiocarbon dating has proved that the human bones found in the upper chamber date to the Christian period. Recent radiocarbon dating of mummy parts from Djoser's burial vault show them to be much later than the 3rd dynasty, while female bones from under the Step Pyramid date centuries earlier than Djoser. Such findings suggest that burial practices in pyramids were more complex than we can appreciate.

The queens' pyramids

Three queens' pyramids were built to the south of Menkaure's pyramid. Below the eastern one was a T-shaped substructure, suggesting it was initially begun as a

satellite pyramid and was later taken over as a burial place for one of Menkaure's queens, perhaps Khamerernebty II. All three queens' pyramids had mudbrick chapels and presumably all received burials of queens; the body of a young woman was found in the burial chamber of the middle pyramid.

The mortuary temple and causeway

Menkaure began his mortuary temple, as had Khafre, with core blocks of limestone that were quarried locally. The largest of these, found at the northwest corner of the temple, is the heaviest known at Giza, weighing over 200 tons. Archaeological evidence suggests that building in stone ceased abruptly and the entire temple was finished in mudbrick by Shepseskaf, Menkaure's successor. The original intention was to encase the temple in granite. In the north corridor we see very clearly how work was progressing. Menkaure's masons had just started bringing in a series of granite blocks on both sides of the corridor. They were cutting back the large limestone core blocks to ensure that the front faces of the granite blocks were flush. The unfinished granite casing was concealed by a casing of mudbrick which was plastered and whitewashed. Though it has all disappeared today, when Reisner stripped away the mudbrick casing he found bright red paint on these core blocks marking levelling lines, measurements and the names of the work gangs.

Among the finds in the mortuary temple were fragments of royal statues. These included the head, chest, lap, knees and shins of a larger-than-life alabaster statue of Menkaure that must have been the centrepiece of his entire complex. Originally it stood at the back of a tall and narrow east–west hall at the end of the centre axis of the temple. From here, the king looked across the open court, through the entrance hall, and down the line of the causeway to the land of the living. Behind the great statue, on the other side of the back wall of the mortuary temple, at the base of the pyramid, there was probably a false door.

The statue represented the king emerging through the false door, symbolic portal to and from the underworld of the pyramid. There he received the offerings brought to him as head of his household for eternity and projected his divine force through the pyramid complex and out into the Nile Valley for the good of all Egypt.

Had Menkaure's pyramid complex been completed, the causeway would have been walled and roofed and extended all the way down to the valley temple. It is conventionally stated that Shepseskaf completed the causeway, but in mudbrick rather than limestone. However, it does not stretch beyond the point where it meets the west side of the old Khufu quarry. From this point down to the valley temple the causeway was probably never more than a construction ramp for delivering stone.

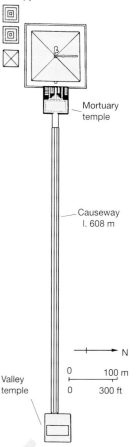

Menkaure's pyramid, with the great gash in its north face made by Othman in AD 1196. Below it, some intact granite casing is visible.

Queens' pyramids

Mortuary temple

Causeway
l. 608 m

N

0   100 m
0   300 ft

Valley temple

The valley temple and pyramid town

To find the valley temple, Reisner projected the axis of the causeway from the entrance hall of the mortuary temple. His first pit brought to light one of the most marvellous pieces in the entire history of ancient Egyptian art: the dyad of Menkaure striding forth in the embrace of his principal queen, Khamerernebty II.

The valley temple lies at the mouth of the main wadi, closing what had been the principal conduit for construction materials brought to Giza for three generations. Evidently it was clear to Menkaure's builders that this was to be the last of the large complexes at Giza. The temple was built in two phases. First, the foundations were laid out by Menkaure in huge, locally quarried limestone blocks, and later the temple was completed in mudbrick by Shepseskaf. Then, in the 6th dynasty, probably during the reign of Pepi II, it was completely rebuilt after it had suffered grievously from flooding.

In the temple's small offering space Reisner found the bases of four alabaster statues of Menkaure. Further back in the very inner sanctuary, he found the remains of other statues. And in the magazines flanking the rear central sanctuary were the triads of Menkaure, which also rank among the greatest pieces of ancient Egyptian art. Each of these shows the king wearing the tall conical crown of the south, striding forth in the embrace of two gods, one the goddess Hathor, the other a deity representing one of the Egyptian nomes.

In some of the earliest stratigraphic excavation in Egypt, Reisner retraced the process by which the houses of the pyramid town first crowded up against the front wall of the temple and then began to be built over the wall, invading the courtyard of the temple (p. 232). The pyramid town became a kind of sacred slum, expanding as the numbers of its tax-exempt inhabitants increased. So we begin to detect the discrepancy between royal intention for the pyramid complex and popular reality. At the back of the valley temple Reisner found an offering place still in position with ash from the last offerings made to the few statues kept intact in dark inner chambers.

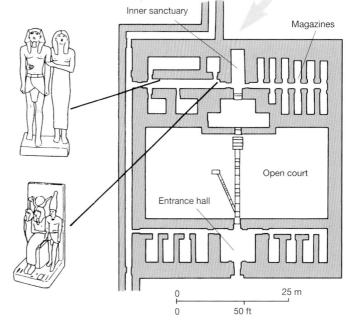

Inner sanctuary

Magazines

Open court

Entrance hall

0   25 m
0   50 ft

The Passing of a Dynasty

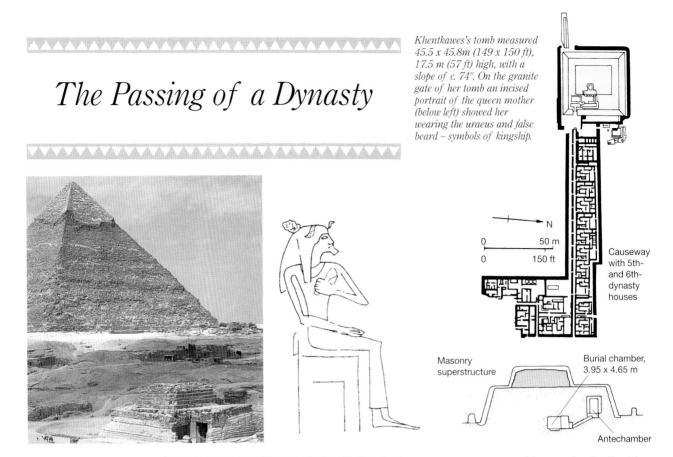

Khentkawes's tomb measured 45.5 x 45.8m (149 x 150 ft), 17.5 m (57 ft) high, with a slope of c. 74°. On the granite gate of her tomb an incised portrait of the queen mother (below left) showed her wearing the uraeus and false beard – symbols of kingship.

N

0   50 m
0   150 ft

Causeway with 5th- and 6th- dynasty houses

Masonry superstructure

Burial chamber, 3.95 x 4.65 m

Antechamber

Like her name, 'In-Front-of-Her-Kas' (i.e. her ancestors), the bedrock tomb of Khentkawes stands before the pyramids of her pharaonic lineage, Khufu, Khafre and Menkaure. With a mastaba-like superstructure and chapel doors open wide to the eastern approach that was flanked by her 'pyramid' town, this queen mother closed the Giza line and may have helped give birth to the 5th dynasty.

Her pyramid town consisted of 10 modular houses along her causeway. At the west end a larger 'house' with thicker walls may have been part of her wabet (p. 26). The southern extension, consisting of separate buildings, a court with granaries, terraces and a tunnel under the causeway, was for administration, possibly a token royal residence.

The Tomb of Khentkawes

In the course of excavations of the Giza Central cemetery in 1932–3, Selim Hassan investigated a strange tomb. Once assumed to be that of Shepseskaf, it in fact belonged to Khentkawes, a female ruler of the end of the 4th dynasty. Her remarkable tomb has a base consisting of a large cube of bedrock reserved as the stone around it was quarried for the great pyramids. On top of the cube is a masonry structure resembling a mastaba. Khentkawes's name was found on a great granite gate, itself extraordinary as an entrance to such a royal tomb. The lower bedrock section was encased in fine Turah limestone at the steep slope of about 74°, the same as the accretion layers of the earlier step pyramids. The top masonry is slightly vaulted, like Shepseskaf's mastaba.

The interior, though badly damaged in ancient times, has some similarities with Menkaure's. From a granite-lined hall hewn into the bedrock cube a short, sloping passage leads down to an antechamber, a set of magazines and a burial chamber constructed in granite. As with other royal pyramids, the tomb has a boat pit, near the southwest corner – once again the direction that was so important from the 1st-dynasty tombs at Abydos.

One of the most interesting aspects of this pyramid is its associated settlement. The queen's memory was preserved by people who lived in a series of houses in one of the oldest planned urban structures in Egypt. These houses were arranged in a linear settlement along Khentkawes's causeway and to the south in an L-shape. There are hints that the southern extension comprises an important house, perhaps even a token palace. Immediately southwest of this block is an enclosure of walls and rooms that Selim Hassan called the valley temple of Khentkawes. Merging into the front of Menkaure's valley temple, it is, in fact, an extension of Menkaure's pyramid town enclosed by a thick wall. The pivot socket of its northern gateway was formed by the base of a statue of Khafre, with the pivot hole in one of the royal feet.

The tomb is at the edge of the wadi that was the conduit for the building projects at Giza over three generations. By positioning her tomb at its mouth, Khentkawes, the queen who may have been transitional to the kings of the 5th dynasty, symbolically closed the passage to the great Giza necropolis.

On the tomb's granite gate Selim Hassan found a title that translates either as 'The Mother of Two Kings of Upper and Lower Egypt' or 'The King of Upper and Lower Egypt and Mother of the King of Upper and Lower Egypt'. The mystery deepened when Miroslav Verner found a pyramid of a Khentkawes with the same titles at Abusir (p. 145). Both ruled as kings in their own right but seem to be a generation apart.

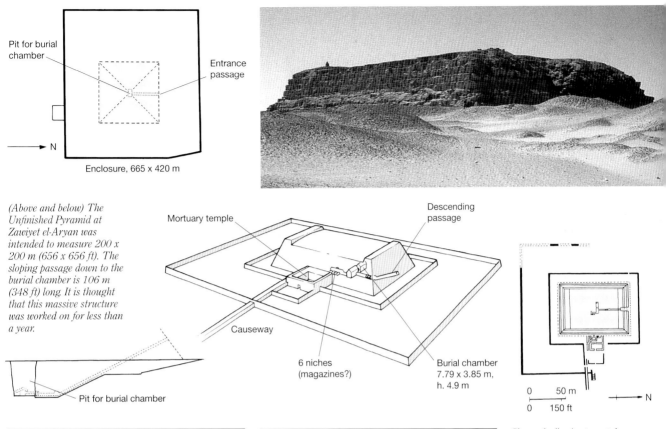

Pit for burial chamber

Entrance passage

N

Enclosure, 665 x 420 m

(Above and below) The Unfinished Pyramid at Zawiyet el-Aryan was intended to measure 200 x 200 m (656 x 656 ft). The sloping passage down to the burial chamber is 106 m (348 ft) long. It is thought that this massive structure was worked on for less than a year.

Mortuary temple

Descending passage

Causeway

6 niches (magazines?)

Burial chamber 7.79 x 3.85 m, h. 4.9 m

Pit for burial chamber

0   50 m
0   150 ft

N

The Unfinished Pyramid at Zawiyet el-Aryan

Yet another puzzle associated with the passing of the 4th dynasty is the large unfinished pyramid at Zawiyet el-Aryan. It has been suggested that it belongs to a pharaoh who ruled between Khafre and Menkaure for such a short time he may have been overlooked in the king lists. Hieratic (shorthand hieroglyphic) inscriptions have been translated as Nebka, or Wehemka. Others see Baka, which was perhaps later remembered as Nebkare or Baufre, the Bicheris of Manetho's king list.

The measurements, in any case, compel us to date this unfinished scheme to the 4th dynasty. If finished, the pyramid would have been close in size to Khafre's. It has a large secondary precinct with walls of fieldstone and clay, like those around the Giza pyramids and of similar dimensions. Inside the pyramid a long, sloping passage leads down to a deep, square pit, like that of Djedefre (p. 120) and similar in size: 11.7 x 24 m (38 x 78 ft) and 21 m (69 ft) deep. At the bottom it was paved with gigantic blocks of limestone and granite. Clearly, this was a massive project, begun in the full confidence of a long reign. The granite sarcophagus took the form of a great oval tub, sunk into the pavement. The cover survived but the sarcophagus was empty.

The Mastabat el-Fara'un

Menkaure's successor, Shepseskaf, chose to be buried in South Saqqara, under a huge mastaba, 99.6 m (327 ft) long by 74.4 m (244 ft) broad, originally encased with fine limestone, except for a bottom course of red granite. With an outer slope of 70°, it may have risen in two steps and certainly took the form of a Buto shrine – a vaulted top between vertical ends. A corridor descends at 23° 30' for 20.95 m (69 ft) to a corridor-chamber followed by three portcullis slots and a passage to an antechamber. A short passage slopes down to the west to the burial chamber. Its ceiling, like Menkaure's, was sculpted into a false vault. Remains were found of a hard dark stone sarcophagus, decorated like Menkaure's (p. 135). From the southeast of the antechamber a narrow corridor leads to six niches, the equivalent of those in the tombs of Menkaure and Khentkawes, and the precursor of the three small magazines that would become standard. The mastaba was surrounded by a double enclosure defined by mudbrick walls. A small mortuary temple on the east had an offering hall and false door, flanked by five magazines. There were no statue niches though part of a statue of Shepseskaf was found in the temple. To the east lay a small inner court and a larger outer one. A long causeway led to a valley temple which has never been excavated.

Shepseskaf's giant mastaba measured 99.6 m (327 ft) by 74.4 m (244 ft) and had a slope of about 70°, reaching a height of about 18 m (59 ft).

The arched roof of Shepseskaf's granite burial chamber is carved into the undersides of the ceiling slabs.

The Pyramid of Userkaf

With Userkaf, probably a son of Khentkawes, Manetho begins a new dynasty, the 5th. It is interesting that Userkaf returned not just to Saqqara but also chose a site as close as possible to the complex of Djoser, building his pyramid at its exact northeast corner. Unas, the last king of the 5th dynasty, placed his at the opposite southwest corner. Userkaf also returned to the pyramid form.

Userkaf's reign was short – under 10 years, perhaps even as few as seven (c. 2465–2458 BC) – and his pyramid, 'Pure are the Places of Userkaf', was much smaller even than Menkaure's. It was originally encased in fine limestone, but this disguised a core masonry that was so haphazardly laid that when the outer casing was stripped the pyramid slumped into a large heap of rubble. The choice of core masonry in this case may have been as much related to the geology of the Saqqara formation – which consists of thin layers of limestone – as to any change in building practices.

A granite head of Userkaf from a colossal statue that must have stood in the temple court.

Inside the pyramid

All the elements of the pyramid's substructure were constructed in a deep open shaft sunk below ground level before the pyramid itself was begun. A passage descended to the construction trench, the base of which was 8 m (26 ft) below the base of the pyramid. From here a horizontal corridor ran for 18.5 m (61 ft), partially clad with granite and plugged with blocks of the same stone, fragments of which survive. In the middle of the horizontal corridor was a huge portcullis slab and beyond this opened a T-shaped magazine. The corridor ran to an anteroom exactly on the pyramid's vertical axis. From here another short corridor led west to the burial chamber. This was the basic pattern for a pyramid substructure that would persist through the Old Kingdom.

The burial chamber was originally lined and paved with fine limestone. Its roof was pented, consisting of huge limestone beams leaning against each other. The sarcophagus, empty when archaeologists found it, was made of basalt.

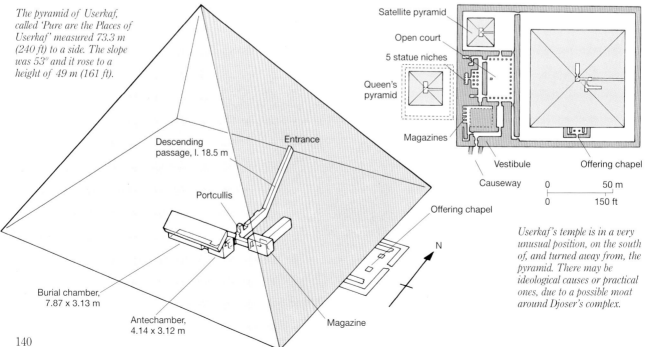

The pyramid of Userkaf, called 'Pure are the Places of Userkaf' measured 73.3 m (240 ft) to a side. The slope was 53° and it rose to a height of 49 m (161 ft).

Entrance

Descending passage, l. 18.5 m

Portcullis

Burial chamber, 7.87 x 3.13 m

Antechamber, 4.14 x 3.12 m

Magazine

N

Satellite pyramid

Open court

5 statue niches

Queen's pyramid

Magazines

Vestibule

Causeway

Offering chapel

Offering chapel

0   50 m
0   150 ft

Userkaf's temple is in a very unusual position, on the south of, and turned away from, the pyramid. There may be ideological causes or practical ones, due to a possible moat around Djoser's complex.

Some of the finest relief carving in Egyptian art decorated the 5th-dynasty pyramid temples. This fragment is from Userkaf's mortuary temple.

The pyramid complex

The position of Userkaf's mortuary temple is a significant departure from the plan of the standard pyramid complex. He separated his offering chapel, at the centre of the eastern base of his pyramid, from his mortuary temple, which he moved to the south side. Some have interpreted this change in terms of ideology. We know that the kings of the 5th dynasty became increasingly involved with the sun cult at Heliopolis, as hinted at by the legendary origins of the dynasty in the Westcar Papyrus. In addition to their pyramid complexes kings now began to build special solar temples of which Userkaf's at Abusir was the first (p. 150). By placing his mortuary temple on the south, Userkaf would ensure that the sun's rays would shine directly into it all year round. Others see this dramatic deviation from an established tradition as simple expediency, due to the fact that the ground was poor to the east.

Nabil Swelim has pointed to evidence of a large moat completely surrounding Djoser's enclosure on all sides, as deep as 25 m (82 ft), which could have been the quarry for the core stone of Djoser's complex. Userkaf's pyramid fitted between the enclosure wall and the eastern side of this depression – but the pyramid combined with the temple on its eastern side would not. If the 'moat' did exist, Userkaf's reason for moving his mortuary temple to the south may have been practical. Whatever the precise reason, it seems that it was important for Userkaf to place his pyramid in close proximity to the already ancient Djoser complex. And herein lies yet another possible reason for his peculiar layout. Dieter Arnold has pointed out the vacillation between the 'Djoser-type' pyramid complexes and 'Meidum-type' with eastern mortuary temples and causeways (p. 18). While switching back and forth between the two is more characteristic of the

Middle Kingdom pyramids, Userkaf returns to the 'Djoser-type' elements: a north–south rectangular enclosure and, by placing his temple on the south, an entrance at the far south end of the eastern side.

The mortuary temple seems to have had elements standard to every pyramid temple from the time of Khafre on, if in a different arrangement. The causeway entered the pyramid enclosure near the southern end of the east wall. A doorway led to a vestibule and then to a kind of entrance hall. That in turn led to an open court with a colonnade of monolithic granite pillars. A colossal head of Userkaf was found in the debris. South of the court was a small columned hall. Beyond, were the five statue niches – the statues of the king would have faced the pyramid in this position – a sanctuary and storage chambers. Not only was the temple moved to the south side, but, exceptionally, its elements are oriented towards the south rather than the pyramid, as in all other mortuary temples.

The offering chapel, of which only traces remain, consisted of a central room, containing a quartzite false door, with a narrow chamber on either side. Like the mortuary temple, the chapel had a floor of black basalt. The walls had a base of granite but were completed in Turah limestone, carved with very fine relief offering scenes. Userkaf's causeway has never been traced to the east and his valley temple remains to be discovered.

Userkaf also built a satellite pyramid, 21 m (69 ft) square, with a T-shaped substructure and a chamber with a pented roof as in the main pyramid. Yet a third pyramid, just south of and outside the enclosure wall, was apparently for a queen whose name is lost. It measures 26.25 m (86 ft) to a side and probably rose to a height of c. 17 m (56 ft). Its substructure was a smaller version of Userkaf's, without the magazines, and the pyramid had its own mortuary temple, decorated with reliefs.

In the 5th and 6th dynasties, pyramid chambers roofed by huge pented limestone beams were the rule, as seen here in the chamber of Userkaf's satellite pyramid.

The Pyramids of Abusir

Several places in Egypt are named Abusir. The Arabic word derives from the Greek name, Busiris, which in turn stems from the ancient Egyptian, *Per Wsir*, 'Place of Osiris' – the multiple Abusirs reflecting the myth of the murder of Osiris, whose body was cut into pieces and buried at different places. The pyramid field of Abusir is a northerly extension of the Saqqara necropolis. It lies on the desert slopes northwest of the Abusir lake that served as a natural harbour for the pyramid complexes. Just south of the lake are the great 1st-dynasty mastabas located on the high ridge (p. 78).

Userkaf initiated the royal cemetery at Abusir by building his sun temple slightly north of the plateau where his successors would create a pyramid cluster. As at Giza, three of the Abusir pyramids – of Sahure, Neferirkare and Raneferef – align on a northeast to southwest diagonal along their northwest corners. Miroslav Verner, director of the Czech mission at Abusir, suggests that the two diagonals converge at the site of Heliopolis,

where the quintessential icon of the pyramid, the sacred *ben-ben*, lay in an inner sanctuary of the sun temple. The Abusir diagonal was broken by Niuserre, who inserted his pyramid between Sahure's and Neferirkare's, his father. In addition to the four pyramids of kings, there are the smaller pyramids of Khentkawes, two, perhaps for queens (Lepsius XXIV and XXV), and an unfinished pyramid, possibly of Shepseskare.

The Pyramid of Sahure

When Ludwig Borchardt excavated Sahure's complex in 1902–8 he found a great wealth of relief carving. Walls of 4th-dynasty pyramid temples had also been decorated with reliefs, but here, with a vast reduction in the size of the pyramid, there is a proportionally greater emphasis on decoration.

The core of Sahure's pyramid was formed of roughly shaped blocks of limestone from quarries to the west of Abusir. It consisted of five or six steps, with the blocks loosely held together with mud mortar. In the north side a wide 'construction gap' allowed the builders to work on the inner structures while they raised the pyramid core all around; this gap was later filled with debris.

Inside the pyramid

Sahure's pyramid was entered by a passage opening on the north side, just east of centre, near the floor level of the court. A short, sloping section lined with red granite was blocked at the bottom by a granite portcullis. The passage next ascended slightly, now lined with limestone. A short, granite-lined, horizontal section led to the burial chamber, with a gabled roof of three tiers of enormous limestone beams. The substructure had been badly damaged and when Perring entered the burial chamber in the early 19th century he found only a single fragment of a basalt sarcophagus.

The pyramid complex

At the front of Sahure's valley temple, the waters of the Abusir lake lapped up to the main entrance, where there was a landing ramp. A canal or inlet led to a secondary entrance to the south, perhaps indicating that the palace lay in this direction. A wall here could belong to the pyramid town – 'The Soul of Sahure Comes Forth in Glory'.

The front ramp led to an elegant portico, the roof of which was decorated with carved and painted golden stars on a blue background and supported by eight granite columns with capitals in the shape of palm fronds. Here, as throughout Sahure's complex, was an interesting contrast of stones: the floor was black basalt; the dado was red granite; and the upper parts were fine limestone, decorated with painted reliefs featuring the king as a sphinx trampling on his defeated enemies.

The 5th-dynasty pyramid field at Abusir shows once again the concern for alignment as noted at Giza. Here the diagonal was interrupted by Niuserre. Just to the north, at Abu Ghurob, are the two remaining sun temples of six known from inscriptions to have been built by 5th-dynasty pharaohs.

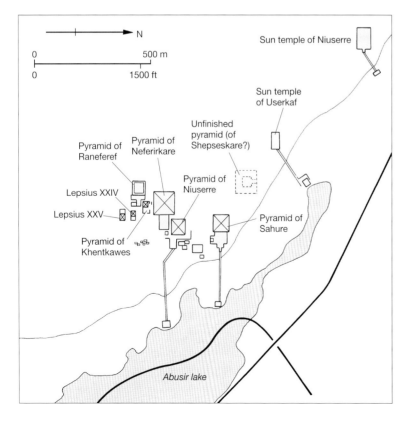

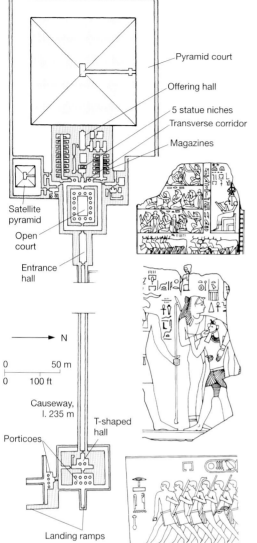

Pyramid court

Offering hall

5 statue niches

Transverse corridor

Magazines

Satellite pyramid

Open court

Entrance hall

N

0   50 m
0   100 ft

Causeway, l. 235 m

T-shaped hall

Porticoes

Landing ramps

Inside the valley temple a T-shaped hall gave direct access to the causeway, 235 m (450 cubits or 771 ft) long, leading straight to the entrance hall of the mortuary temple up on the plateau. For their entire length, the walls of the causeway were decorated with reliefs, including scenes of gods leading prisoners taken from Egypt's traditional enemies. Such scenes were meant to ward off any evil or disorder that might threaten the security of the inner temple. Sahure's are among the oldest known reliefs of this genre, which would be placed at temple entrances for the next 2,500 years.

The plan of the mortuary temple has been called the 'conceptual beginning' of all subsequent Old Kingdom examples. A granite-framed doorway led to a closed corridor around a pillared court. Reliefs on the north wall show the king fishing and fowling, while on the south he is hunting with his

At the south side of Sahure's mortuary temple was a sacred service entrance for deliveries to the temple magazines. Inside, the walls were decorated with scenes of Nile gods and offering bearers. This small portico also gave access to the satellite pyramid.

Sahure's pyramid 'The Rising of the Ba Spirit' stood 78.75 m (258 ft) square and 47 m (154 ft) high, with a slope of 50° 11' 40". His satellite pyramid was 15.7 m (30 cubits, or 51 ft 6 in) to a side, 11.55 m (38 ft) high, with a 56° slope. This artist's reconstruction is based on Borchardt's.

(Above) An estimated 10,000 sq. m (107,643 sq. ft) of fine relief carving covered the walls of Sahure's complex, a few fragments of which are redrawn here. In the mortuary temple the goddess Seshat records booty gained in war (top); in his valley temple goddesses suckle Sahure (centre) and troops greet his barque (bottom).

Satellite pyramid

Open court

Entrance hall

Causeway

Burial chamber, 12.6 x 3.15 m

Entrance passage, w. 1.27 m, h. 1.87 m

Portcullis

A statue of Sahure, builder of the first pyramid at Abusir.

courtiers. It is certainly not by coincidence that themes of capturing wild game are played out on the walls of the dark corridor surrounding the open court – a bright clearing tamed by the king, the guarantor of order. The colonnade of the court is supported by granite pillars with palm capitals, each with the insignia of Sahure. A white alabaster altar stood in the court. Reliefs on the walls show the king's victories over Asiatics and Libyans, including one scene showing the king about to execute a Libyan chief while his family beg for his life.

Beyond the court is a transverse corridor, separating the front from the inner temple. On the east wall are reliefs of sea voyages – one of the earliest examples of this subject on walls flanking a temple threshold. Small chambers to the west were decorated with processions of offering bearers, each personifying an estate. Side doors gave access to more magazines, where all the goods hunted, captured or cultivated were stored – if perhaps only symbolically. A small alabaster stairway directly on the temple's main axis led up to a chamber with five niches with an alabaster floor and a double-leaf door. Each would have held a statue of the king.

At the heart of the mortuary temple is the offering chapel with the false door, only fragments of which survived. The floor of this chamber was paved with white alabaster. Originally it contained a black granite statue and an offering basin with a drain of copper tubing. In the north wall a granite doorway led to five rooms, two of which also had limestone basins and copper drains, part of a complex drainage system that ran through the temple.

Sahure's satellite pyramid is in a similar position to Khufu's, at the pyramid's southeast corner. This would be its standard place until the end of the Old Kingdom. It was surrounded by its own small court entered by a portico with two round granite pillars inscribed with Sahure's titulary.

The Pyramid of Neferirkare

Neferirkare ascended the throne after his brother Sahure. Although he may have been advanced in age when, for unknown reasons, he rather than Sahure's son became pharaoh, Neferirkare attempted to build a pyramid that exceeded his brother's in size. Evidence suggests that it was planned as a step pyramid, rising in six tiers of well-laid, limestone retaining walls. However, on the south and west sides some of the loose masonry remains from what must have filled in the steps, suggesting that the step pyramid might have been transformed to a true pyramid. It is certain that at a later stage the builders began to enlarge the pyramid by adding a girdle of masonry and a casing of red granite. It seems the lowest course was laid, but not smoothed, and the pyramid was never finished.

Inside the pyramid

As with Sahure's pyramid, the substructure was very badly damaged. A descending corridor led from near the middle of the north side, roofed with great gabled limestone beams that discharged the weight to either side. The burial chamber was covered with three layers of such beams. No trace of the sarcophagus was found inside.

The pyramid complex

Neferirkare's mortuary temple appears to have been finished in haste. The inner temple with its five statue niches and offering hall were built in stone, but the court and entrance hall were completed in mudbrick, with wood columns in the form of bundles of lotus stalks and buds. Only the foundations of the causeway and valley temple had been built when work stopped. When Niuserre later took over the site of Neferirkare's temple for his own valley temple, the entrance to Neferirkare's complex was moved up to the mortuary temple. So, apparently, was the administration of the pyramid which normally would have focused in the town near the

Neferirkare's pyramid was called the 'Pyramid of the Ba of Neferirkare'. The length of the base was about 105 m (200 cubits, or 344 ft) and the faces of the steps incline by about 73°. Had the conversion to a true pyramid been completed, it would have risen to about 72 m (236 ft) at a slope of 54°.

(Opposite) Since Niuserre usurped Neferirkare's unfinished valley temple, the entrance, rudimentary pyramid town and administration moved up to the front of the mortuary temple.

Antechamber

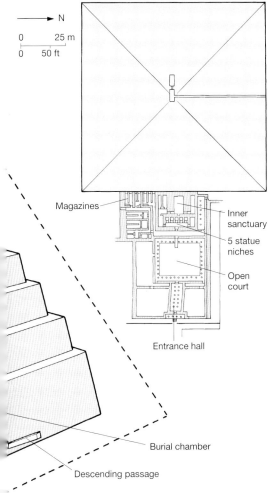

0 —— 25 m
0 —— 50 ft

N

Magazines

Inner
sanctuary

5 statue
niches

Open
court

Entrance hall

Burial chamber

Descending passage

valley floor. Thanks to this, one part of the administrative archives, the Abusir Papyri, was preserved. Nine or ten houses were built, probably for those in temple service (p. 234). Over time the wooden columns and roofs must have deteriorated and the inhabitants hid the columns in mudbrick walls that were part of new rooms.

Contrasting pyramid clusters: the slumped cores of the Abusir pyramids form a line in front of the giant pyramids of Giza in the background.

The Pyramid of the Queen Mother

On a limestone block from Neferirkare's pyramid found by Perring was a graffito mentioning 'the King's Wife Khentkawes'. She also appeared as Neferirkare's wife in a relief of the royal family on another limestone block from the site, along with his son, Raneferef. It was only in the 1970s, however, that the Czech expedition identified her as the owner of a small pyramid at Abusir.

The pyramid of Neferirkare, looking northwest across the mortuary temple of Queen Khentkawes's pyramid.

Queen Khentkawes, shown in a relief from the court of her mortuary temple. Like the Khentkawes at Giza (p. 138), she wears the uraeus of kingship and holds a papyrus sceptre, symbol of northern Egypt.

Khentkawes's pyramid is south of Neferirkare's pyramid and near its centre axis – the position occupied by the satellite pyramids of Sneferu's Bent Pyramid at Dahshur and Khafre's at Giza. This location hints at a link between the function of satellite pyramids, related to the king's *ka*, and the role of the queen mother, who transfers the royal *ka* from one generation to the next. A date inscribed on a block of the pyramid indicates that construction paused in Year 10 of an unnamed king. On another block, the word 'Mother' was added above 'King's Wife', perhaps when work resumed. Had a son of Khentkawes become king, enhancing her status?

When complete, Khentkawes's pyramid would have stood about 17 m (56 ft) high and 25 m (82 ft) square at the base, with a slope of 52°. The Czech team, under Miroslav Verner, retrieved the major elements of her mortuary temple, though the inner part was badly destroyed. She had five storage magazines and her own satellite pyramid. A potter's workshop occupied one corner.

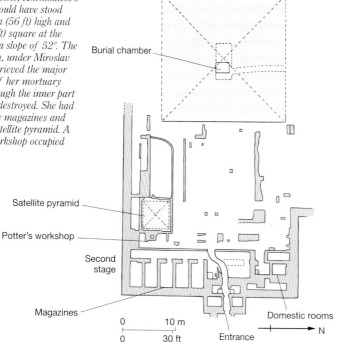

Burial chamber

Satellite pyramid

Potter's workshop

Second stage

Magazines

Domestic rooms

Entrance

0   10 m
0   30 ft

N

As with the superstructure, the substructure of the pyramid was badly ruined. The Czech team ascertained that the mortuary temple was built in two stages, and the entrance of the first included square limestone pillars painted red and inscribed with Khentkawes's name and titles. Similar pillars, gracing an open court, show the queen holding the papyrus *wadj* sceptre and wearing the royal uraeus on her brow, thought to be exclusive to kingship.

A granite false door was embedded in the west wall of the offering hall that backed on to the pyramid. Next to the hall, three deep recesses probably held statues of the queen. Carved and painted relief scenes covered the walls of the inner temple depicting processions of estates, agriculture and sacrifices. On one fragment she is given the same title as Khentkawes at Giza (p. 138). But the two are probably not the same person – this one was the mother of Raneferef and Niuserre. Verner has suggested that the title should be read as 'Mother of the King of Upper and Lower Egypt, [exercising office as] The King of Upper and Lower Egypt'.

The idea that Khentkawes II ruled as pharaoh in her own right is supported by the second stage of her mortuary temple. It was extended to the east and had the east–west axial alignment characteristic of kings' temples. Five storage chambers were added south of the entrance. Khentkawes also had her own satellite pyramid, for which stone was diverted from an enclosure wall of the pyramid. Khentkawes was worshipped at her small pyramid for 300 years, until the end of the 6th dynasty. Her temple yielded another collection of papyri, which, like those from Neferirkare's, provide a literary window on to the life of a pyramid complex

The Pyramid of Raneferef

The last pyramid on the Abusir diagonal was long known as the Unfinished Pyramid. In 1974 the Czech Expedition began to excavate it, suspecting it belonged to Raneferef, an ephemeral ruler whose mortuary temple was mentioned in the Abusir Papyri. Their research showed that the pyramid was indeed left unfinished, but was made functional for the cult of Raneferef. The site was less disturbed than others because there was no towering pyramid to attract robbers, and most of the temple had been finished in mudbrick rather than the limestone used by manufacturers of mortar. Thus the unfinished pyramid ironically provides much information about how pyramids of this period were built, and how they functioned as ritual centres.

Raneferef's builders levelled the site and laid out the square for the pyramid base with sides of 65 m (213 ft 3 in) – a respectable size, slightly smaller than Sahure's. In the middle of the square they dug a pit, in which the burial chamber would have been built while the core of the pyramid rose around it.

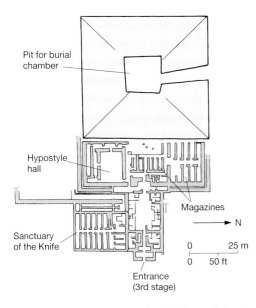

Pit for burial
chamber

Hypostyle
hall

Magazines

N

Sanctuary
of the Knife

Entrance
(3rd stage)

0   25 m
0   50 ft

An open trench, left to allow the builders to bring in the stone for the burial chamber, later contained the entrance passage. Although now missing, the substructure may have been finished when Raneferef died. Only one step of the core, however, had been completed, which was quickly faced with limestone at a slope of 78°, leaving the tomb in the form of a low mastaba. The top was finished off with a layer of clay into which desert stones were stuck. No wonder the pyramid is referred to as the 'Mound' in the fragments of papyrus found in its temple.

Here the Czech team had the opportunity to test the idea of Lepsius and Borchardt that the 5th-dynasty pyramids were built in steps in accretions around a tall, narrow central core, like those of the 3rd dynasty, albeit not with inward-leaning courses. If this was the case, under the capping layer, the accretions should have resembled the layers of an onion. Instead, the excavators discovered that the core consisted of an outer retaining wall of four or five well-laid courses of limestone blocks and an inner line of smaller blocks framing the trench of the burial chamber. Between these two walls was a fill of poor-quality limestone, mortar and sand.

The pyramid complex

Verner believes the first stage of Raneferef's mortuary temple was finished quickly, between the king's death and his burial – a period of perhaps 70 days. It was a small rectangular building, unusually oriented north–south, at the centre of the east side of pyramid platform. An entrance on the south led to a vestibule and three chambers, including the offering chapel with a red granite false door and an

The unfinished pyramid of Raneferef was begun with a base length of 65 m (213 ft 3 in). Its mortuary temple stretches out along it – the L-shape is due to an added third stage consisting of a columned courtyard and the 'Sanctuary of the Knife' – a slaughter house for sacrificial animals. Since the pyramid was never finished and the substructure is now completely missing, a reconstruction is not possible.

The Abusir Papyri

Three sets of pyramid archives have been found at Abusir, written in hieratic, a cursive form of hieroglyphics. Papyri associated with the pyramid of Neferirkare, found by local villagers earlier this century, have been studied and published by Paule Posener-Kriéger. The fragments, only a fraction of the original archive, date mostly from the reign of Djedkare-Isesi, who built his pyramid at South Saqqara but required a good administrative system to oversee the mortuary cults of family members buried at Abusir. Neferirkare's papyri can be divided into several main categories:

Schedules of priestly duties in the temple relating to daily and monthly ceremonies, as well as important festivals. They stipulate offerings, sacrifices and guard duties, as well as outlining the organization of the workforce (p. 233).
Inventories of the furnishing and equipment of the temple – knives, vessels, jewellery, boxes, etc.
Accounts of products and materials supplied to the temple, their use or storage, as well as financial transactions. These are key to our understanding of the economic function of pyramids. They record the goods flowing in from royal estates, and also from royal residences and other institutions. Neferirkare's sun temple, which has not been found, seems to have played a special role in this.
Architectural records form a small but interesting category. These relate to inspections of the masonry of the temple, checking for damage.
One fragment of this last category gave a clue to the existence of Raneferef's mortuary temple which was subsequently located by the Czech team. Another archive was discovered inside it, which is still being studied. It seems to contain similar categories as Neferirkare's archive, as well as a number of royal decrees. It also includes a mention of the Sanctuary of the Knife. Another archive, also still being studied, was found in the mortuary temple of Khentkawes.

Raneferef

Neferirkare

Khentkawes

A limestone statue of Raneferef, shown in the embrace of, and merging his identity with, the Horus falcon, god of kingship. The statue was found in his mortuary temple.

altar. Verner believes Shepseskare, who perhaps reigned for a short time after Raneferef, might have built this small chapel, because two mud sealings with his Horus name were found in the vicinity.

It is certain, in any case, that it was Niuserre who added the sprawling complex of mudbrick walls and chambers. This second stage enveloped the earlier stone chapel and spread to the east, extending the entire length of the pyramid. The entrance in the centre of the east side was marked by two limestone lotus-stalk columns. Immediately inside, a transverse corridor led to five large magazines. Two wooden cult boats were ritually buried in one, along with thousands of carnelian beads that may have adorned them. In the the northern part of the temple were 10 more magazines, arranged in two pairs of five. Here another cache of administrative papyri was found, as well as numerous objects including stone vessels and flint knives.

The southern part of the temple was taken up by one of Egypt's earliest known hypostyle halls. Four rows of five wooden columns supported the roof. Only the imprint of the columns remained on the limestone bases, but this showed that they took the form of sheaves of lotus buds. Among many fragments of statues found in the ruins of the court, the most beautiful shows Raneferef with the Horus falcon. Papyri inform us that the largest statue, in wood, was a special focus of cult activities. There were also small wooden statues of Egypt's traditional enemies – Asiatics, Libyans and Nubians – that were probably attached to the lower parts of the throne or dais on which the main statue stood.

One of the most remarkable features of Raneferef's complex was added at this stage– the 'Sanctuary of the Knife'. Its name was found in texts from the temple, as well as in inscriptions on vessels for animal fat. A wide entrance allowed workers to bring in animals to be ritually slaughtered in the court in the northwest corner of the building. Evidence from the papyri indicate that as many as 130 bulls could be slaughtered during a 10-day festival. The Sanctuary of the Knife was in operation for a short time before the third stage of the temple shut it down and it was used for storage.

A columned courtyard was added to the front of the temple in the third stage, giving the whole arrangement a T-shape. A new entrance was supported by two six-stemmed papyrus columns, while 24 wooden columns lined the court. Only the bases remain, but the imprint of the shaft on one indicates that they were palm columns.

The Pyramid of Niuserre

It was perhaps Shepseskare who made a start on another pyramid between Sahure's and the sun temple of Userkaf. It consists only of the base of the pyramid core and the beginning of the pit and trench for the substructure. It was never finished, and when Niuserre came to the throne he had to complete the pyramids of Neferirkare, his father, Khentkawes, his mother, and Raneferef, his brother. He did not finish the possible pyramid of Shepseskare, perhaps because that pharaoh was buried in a large mastaba that had been prepared before he assumed the throne for so short a time.

Niuserre reigned for more than 30 years but his pyramid is smaller than Neferirkare's and closer in size to Sahure's. He seems to have wanted to remain within this family of kings and inserted his pyramid in the space in the angle between Neferirkare's pyramid and Sahure's. Spatial limitations may therefore have determined the size of this pyramid. The pyramid core was built in steps and was originally sheathed in fine limestone as shown by some casing blocks found still in position.

Inside the pyramid

From the entrance at ground level in the middle of the north side a passage ran horizontally for the thickness of the casing and then sloped down to a chamber blocked by three granite portcullises. Beyond, the passage continued at a more gentle slope to the antechamber, deviating slightly to ensure that the threshold between the antechamber and the burial chamber was on the pyramid's vertical axis. The antechamber and burial chamber were clad in fine limestone and roofed with the standard three tiers of enormous limestone beams, each 10 m (33 ft) long and weighing 90 tons.

The pyramid complex

Niuserre took over the terrace and foundations that had been prepared for Neferirkare's causeway and valley temple. The valley temple was entered by a portico with two rows of four columns in the form of papyrus bundles. Inside, the pavement was black basalt, with walls of fine limestone with painted relief decoration above a dado of red

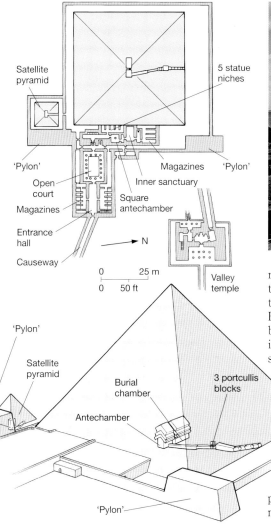

Satellite pyramid

5 statue niches

'Pylon'

Open court

Magazines

Inner sanctuary

'Pylon'

Magazines

Square antechamber

Entrance hall

N

Causeway

0   25 m
0   50 ft

'Pylon'

Satellite pyramid

Burial chamber

Antechamber

3 portcullis blocks

'Pylon'

Valley temple

red granite. Fragments of reliefs from the outer temple depict members of the court; in the inner temple, Niuserre enters the company of the gods. For the first time there is a small square antechamber, its roof supported by a single pillar, that leads in turn to the offering hall. Relief fragments depict scenes of homage. Another new element in this complex is a pair of massive blocks of masonry at the corners of the pyramid court. These appear to be the precursors of the great pylons at the front of later Egyptian temples. Niuserre's satellite pyramid within its own enclosure had the standard T-shaped substructure of passage and chamber. At the southern edge of the pyramid cluster are two badly destroyed possible pyramids, Lepsius XXIV and XXV, which may have belonged to queens of Niuserre.

Niuserre's pyramid was called 'The Places of Niuserre Endure' It measured 78.9 m (150 cubits, or 259 ft) square and 51.68 m (164 ft) high with a slope of 51° 50' 35". This view is looking north, across the corner of Neferirkare's mortuary temple. Niuserre built his mortuary temple in an L-shape in order to avoid older mastabas to the east, and to usurp his father's causeway. He also usurped the foundations of his father's valley temple to build his own.

granite. Limestone figures of fettered enemies may have stood near the exit to the causeway.

Niuserre's builders made great use of basalt, lining the bases of the walls of the entire length of the causeway with it. Above, the walls were decorated with reliefs, again showing the king as a sphinx or lion trampling his traditional enemies. The ceiling was a field of blue, studded with golden stars. Because it was intended for Neferirkare's pyramid, the causeway had to bend quite sharply to bring it to the entrance of Niuserre's mortuary temple. To avoid the older mastabas the temple had an unusual shape but kept the principal elements of previous ones, particularly Sahure's. The inner offering chapel is in its traditional place at the centre of the east side of the pyramid, lined up with the burial chamber. Five statue niches, complemented by five oblong magazines, flank the offering chapel with its red granite false door and offering slab.

Immediately north of the entrance to the five statue niches, a deep niche contained a huge lion of

Sun Temples of Abusir

Ancient documents, including the Abusir Papyri, inform us of six sun temples, one for each king of the 5th dynasty except Djedkare-Isesi and Unas. The name of Sahure's, 'Field of Re', was found on a

The Abusir pyramids, looking across the ruins of Userkaf's sun temple. The Swiss and German expedition were able to reconstruct the four major phases of the temple's construction.

Four phases of a sun temple:
1 a mound in a rectangular
enclosure; 2 Neferirkare sets
a granite obelisk on a pedestal
building, with two shrines in
front; 3 Niuserre rebuilds the
inner enclosure in limestone
and extends outer enclosure,
(re)builds valley temple;
4 inner enclosure cased in
mudbrick, new altar, stalls
and benches added.

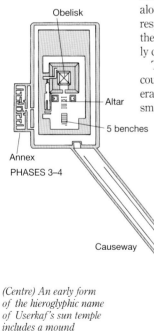

Symbolic mound

PHASE 1

Pedestal building

Obelisk

Statue
shrines

PHASE 2

Obelisk

Altar

5 benches

Annex

PHASES 3–4

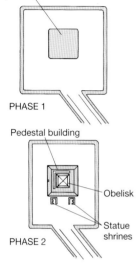

Causeway

(Centre) An early form
of the hieroglyphic name
of Userkaf's sun temple
includes a mound
surmounted by a mast.

(Right) A schist head of a
statue of Userkaf found in
his sun temple.

block of masonry in the mortuary temple of Niuserre. We know that Neferirkare's was called 'Place of Re's Pleasure'; Raneferef's was 'Re's Offering Table'; while Menkauhor's was named 'The Horizon of Re'. But archaeologists have found only two sun temples, those of Userkaf and Niuserre. In layout both resemble a pyramid complex – with a valley temple, causeway and upper temple.

Userkaf's 'Stronghold of Re'

Userkaf's is both the first sun temple to be built by a pharaoh in addition to a pyramid and the first royal edifice at Abusir. The only precedent is the 4th-dynasty Sphinx Temple at Giza (p. 128), which appears to have been dedicated to the sun and may have housed ritual activity similar to that carried out in the later sun temples.

Userkaf's sun temple was named *Nekhen-Re*, 'Stronghold of Re', after the ancient name of Hierakonpolis (p. 72). Herbert Ricke, who directed excavations of the site in 1955–7, ascertained that, in its earliest form, the upper temple may well have contained the principal elements of its namesake: a rectangular enclosure and a central mound. One of the early forms of the sun temple's hieroglyphic name shows a mast projecting from a mound, perhaps a symbolic perch for the sun god in falcon form.

As with so many pyramids, the temple underwent several major transformations – four in this case – following one upon another before the previous one had even been completed. This continuous construction process was not the work of Userkaf alone, however. Neferirkare and Niuserre were responsible for later stages on behalf of Userkaf, the progenitor of the dynasty who staked the family claim to Abusir as their eternal home.

The upper temple was so badly ruined that Ricke could retrieve only the major elements and considerable deductive skill was required to piece together small architectural fragments. Among these were

parts of a granite obelisk – a new form that Neferirkare erected in Phase 2 to match the obelisk he had built for his own sun temple, as seen in its hieroglyphic name. A pedestal building clad in quartzite and granite replaced the temple's central mound, with a winding corridor up to the roof and a sacristy. In Phase 3 the enclosure and the area around the obelisk were again completely rebuilt. It was probably Niuserre who added an inner enclosure wall and chambers of limestone that were not completely dressed before the next phase, 4, saw the exterior surfaces cased in plastered mudbrick.

A mudbrick altar at the east side of the pedestal building belonged to the last phase, although previous stages must also have had one. No signs of burning were found around the altar, which was surrounded by a curiously diminutive enclosure wall compared to the towering granite obelisk. Similar small partition walls describe two stall-like fields immediately east of the altar. The Palermo Stone mentions that in the reign of Userkaf two oxen and two geese were sacrificed daily in his sun temple, but the partitions hardly seem adequate for holding live animals.

More curious yet are five low benches made of mud and broken stone. Ricke thought they were places for setting out offerings – like the open-air altars in the sun temples of Akhenaten more than a millennium later – or low benches for priests. Here the correspondence between the five benches and the five phyles into which priests and labourers were organized (p. 224) is made more compelling by a small stela labelled *Wer* ('Great') phyle found completely hidden inside one bench. No additional stelae were discovered in the next two benches, and the last two were left unopened.

Several features of this sun temple would have made the movement and slaughter of sacrificial animals less of a problem than in the pyramid temples, with their narrow doorways and sharp turns.

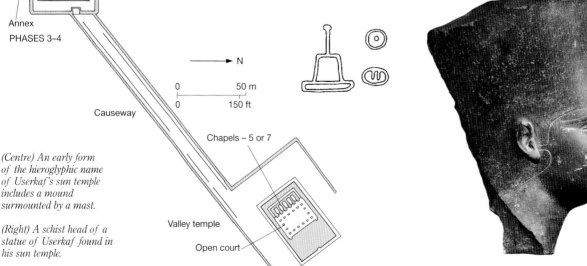

N

0   50 m
0   150 ft

Chapels – 5 or 7

Valley temple

Open court

The causeway was divided into three lanes along its length by low, thin mudbrick walls. Two narrow pathways ran on either side of a central roadway which would have been wide enough for driving reluctant oxen up to their fate on the hill. Ricke believed that the side paths may have aimed at two statue shrines, if these had already been set up in front of the obelisk in Phase 2.

At its lower end, the causeway entered a walled enclosure around the sides and back of the valley temple. Now, we might consider that the messy business of slaughtering and butchering animals might be more easily carried out in installations attached to the valley temples, after which priests would have ritually offered the meat in the upper temples. The slaughter hall named the Sanctuary of the Knife was built right in front of Raneferef's mortuary temple, but only because no valley temple was ever built for his pyramid. However, the broad court around the valley temple and the wide causeway of Userkaf's sun temple suggest that animals may have been led up it: the early, and possibly later, enclosure walls of the upper temple had rounded outer corners – a feature also found in 'Sanctuary of the Knife'.

The valley temple of Userkaf's sun temple had been extensively quarried for stone, but Ricke reconstructed its plan from fragments. It was considerably more than the glorified gateway represented by pyramid valley temples, or by the valley temple of Niuserre's sun temple, even though Niuserre may well have built this one also. The building is rectangular but not oriented to the cardinal directions, pointing generally – but not exactly – in the direction of Heliopolis. Ronald Wells has suggested that causeway and valley temple were oriented to stars that would have ascended in the sky just before sunrise around 2400 BC, so that the temple was a kind of astronomical clock for sacrifices that took place at dawn.

The front section of the valley temple was lost but may have contained an entrance hall and magazines. An open court with a colonnade of 16 rectangular granite pillars is certain. The few surviving elements behind the court left Ricke unsure whether there had been seven niches in the rear, or only five. If five, it bears a strong resemblance to the five niches in mortuary temples of most Old Kingdom pyramids since Khafre. The five niches could also relate to the five benches in the upper temple and to the five phyles of priestly service. Five niches also echo the five chambers built over the central mound at the original Nekhen temple after which this complex was named and with which our survey of pyramids began.

Niuserre's 'Delight of Re'

In addition to his extensive rebuilding of Userkaf's sun temple, Niuserre built his own, named 'Delight of Re'. In their excavations of 1898 to 1901,

Heinrich Schaeffer and Ludwig Borchardt found evidence that, like Userkaf's sun temple, Niuserre's was also first constructed in mudbrick and then rebuilt in stone. Why was this so? The renewal of both temples might have commemorated Niuserre's celebration of the Sed festival. On the other hand, the transformations could reflect changing ideas about sun temples, analogous to developments seen in the earliest pyramids.

Like the valley temples of the 5th-dynasty pyramids, Niuserre's was little more than a monumental gateway forming the entrance to the causeway. It lay within an enclosure defined by a thick wall. Borchardt thought this was the enclosure wall of a surrounding town but he did not investigate the assumed settlement, so it remains conjectural.

The valley temple's layout was only partly retrieved because its remains were few and stood in knee-high ground water. A pillared portico of four palm columns formed an entrance through a pylon-like façade clad in white limestone. In addition to the main doorway on to the causeway, porticoes on either side gave access to narrow corridors.

The causeway ascended to an impressive terrace formed by extending a natural hillock to provide a platform on which the upper temple was built. In the first phase, mudbrick walls formed a grid of compartments filled with debris. Thick mudbrick retaining walls also formed the sides of the terrace. In the second phase a casing of yellow limestone blocks was added over the retaining walls.

The upper temple was set within a rectangular enclosure oriented to the cardinal directions. A T-shaped entrance hall had five granite-lined doorways. Those on the centre axis gave on to a broad rectangular court, dominated on the west by the obelisk, 36 m (118 ft) tall, built of limestone blocks. It stood on a pedestal in the form of a truncated pyramid, itself 20 m (65 ft 6 in) high, and built of limestone with red granite around the base. The

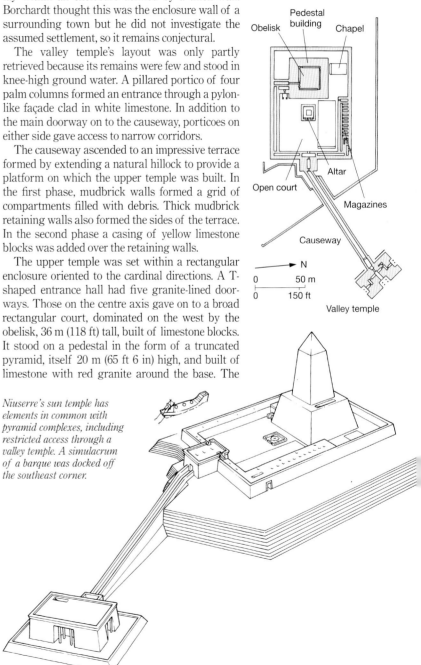

Niuserre's sun temple has elements in common with pyramid complexes, including restricted access through a valley temple. A simulacrum of a barque was docked off the southeast corner.

Niuserre – builder of a pyramid at Abusir and a sun temple at north Abusir.

combined height equalled or surpassed that of Niuserre's pyramid. In front of the obelisk and aligned with its centre axis stands an altar consisting of five slabs of white alabaster. The central element takes the form of a circle, 1.8 m (6 ft) in diameter, flanked by four slabs with the top carved in relief as the *Hetep* hieroglyph – a stylized conical bread loaf on a reed mat. This is the sign for 'offering', 'satisfied' or 'peace', commonly found at the base of false doors in Old Kingdom tombs. The whole arrangement can be read as 'May Re be satisfied'. There were no obvious signs of burning – perhaps burnt offerings were placed on another offering table fitted to a granite socket nearby.

Certain features were interpreted by Borchardt as belonging to a large 'slaughter court', including fragments of a limestone pavement that had been raised 15 cm (6 in) above the level of the surrounding court. Channels carved in the upper surface perhaps ran to a row of nine large alabaster basins that still survive. Each basin, about 1.18 m (3 ft 8 in) in diameter, had a series of small, circular shallow dips, between 24 and 26, carved around the rim. Borchardt thought that originally there were ten basins, and that the channels drained fluids – either the blood of sacrificed animals or the water used in cleaning up after the sacrifice – into them. However, Miroslav Verner doubts whether this was a place of slaughter at all. No tethering stones, flint knives or

An alabaster altar still stands in the court of Niuserre's sun temple. It can be read as a giant hieroglyph for 'May Re be satisfied' in the four cardinal directions.

bones were found, in contrast to such evidence in the abattoir next to the pyramid of Raneferef. Perhaps offerings were ritually purified by laying them on the alabaster altar. The channels and basins certainly suggest that liquids were involved. A similar but smaller installation was found north of the obelisk, with seven more basins, this time of limestone and containing three drainage holes each.

From the entrance hall a right turn led along a corridor to a set of magazines built against the north enclosure wall, probably for short-term storage of offerings. At the east end a stairway led to the roof. A left turn in the entrance hall led to corridors with a wealth of fine relief carvings. These include one of the earliest scenes of the Sed festival of the king's renewal. In a section that attached to the pedestal building the three seasons were depicted. Fragments of the harvest (*shemu*) and inundation (*akhet*) seasons were preserved, but the season of 'coming forth' (*peret*) was lost.

Just outside the enclosure of the upper temple a huge mudbrick model of a boat, 30 m (98 ft) long, was found. This colossal simulacrum of a ship perhaps signifies the mythic boat in which the sun god sailed across the ocean of the sky. It also hints that the sun temple, like the pyramid complexes, was seen as a symbolic port to the world of the gods.

Meaning and function

The two sun temples found comprise at least six building or rebuilding projects. This has led to the intriguing idea that the various phases of the two known monuments are in fact the six temples mentioned in texts – for instance that *Nekhen-Re* was rebuilt and renamed *Sekhet-Re*. But one argument against this is that in the tombs of officials of the sun temples more than one is mentioned, as though they were functioning at the same time. An inscribed block from Sahure's sun temple was found in the masonry of Niuserre's pyramid temple, so perhaps the missing sun temples were destroyed for their stone.

Suggestions as to the significance of the sun temples are numerous, for instance that they were mortuary complexes for the sun, or for the king in his identity as the sun before birth and after death. Another idea is that they were places where the communion between the sun and the king could be consummated, ensuring the welfare of the land.

The Abusir Papyri give us a glimpse of the functioning of Neferirkare's sun temple. On papyrus scraps and fragments we read of provisions delivered by canal twice daily from the sun temple to the pyramid. One ox a day was slaughtered and the meat sent over to the pyramid. Bread and beer were also delivered from the sun temple, suggesting that they may have been produced nearby – perhaps in the valley enclosure. The 5th-dynasty pharaohs seem to have built their sun temples to be a sacred filter for the goods that sustained their pyramids.

Not only are we missing four of the six sun temples found in texts, we are also missing a pyramid for Menkauhor, the king who ruled for eight years after Niuserre. Dahshur was a suspected location because Menkauhor's pyramid is mentioned in a 6th-dynasty decree relating to Sneferu's pyramid. But Stadelmann's excavations established that a small unfinished pyramid northeast of the North Pyramid cannot be Menkauhor's. However, Lepsius pyramid XXIX, the so-called 'Headless Pyramid' (p. 165) at Saqqara is a possibility.

The Pyramid of Djedkare-Isesi

Djedkare-Isesi ruled for 32 years or more. He moved 6 km (3¾ miles) from Abusir and built the first pyramid in South Saqqara, relatively new ground except for the mastaba of Shepseskaf. Djedkare's pyramid is now aptly named el-Shawaf, 'The Sentinel', for it stands on a high spur overlooking the village of Saqqara; its ancient name was 'Beautiful is Isesi'. It was badly damaged in antiquity and its excavator, Abdel Salam Hussein, died before publishing his work. As with Niuserre's, the core of the pyramid was built in steps. The entrance was at ground level, just east of the centre of the north side. Here for the first time, except for the offering place at the Bent Pyramid (p. 103), were traces of a small limestone entrance chapel.

Inside the pyramid

A granite-lined passage sloped down to an almost horizontal corridor-chamber lined with limestone, followed by three portcullis slots. Beyond was another passage, ending in an antechamber. Opening off the antechamber to the west was the oblong burial chamber. To the east were three magazines, a feature we have seen developing in the tombs of Menkaure, Shepseskaf and Userkaf. The burial chamber, constructed in an open shaft 9 m (29 ft 6 in) deep, was roofed with three layers of large gabled limestone 'rafters'.

Fragments of alabaster and a faience bead on a gold filament were found in the burial chamber. Scattered among the debris were enough fragments of the basalt sarcophagus to be able to reconstruct it. It was sunk into the floor, as was a niche for the canopic chest, originally concealed by a slab.

The pyramid complex

Although unexcavated, the course of the causeway can be discerned sloping in a straight line under the village of Saqqara. It joined the front of the mortuary temple between two massive masonry pylons. The symmetrical temple has yet to be completely cleared, but fragments of reliefs indicate it was as richly adorned as those at Abusir. A long vestibule led to a court surrounded by a colonnade of granite palm columns. Vestibule and court were paved in

The End of the 5th Dynasty

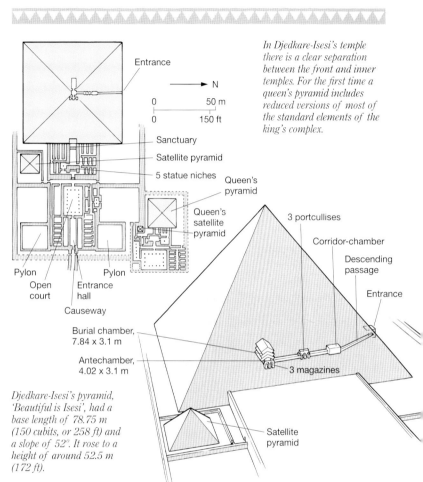

In Djedkare-Isesi's temple there is a clear separation between the front and inner temples. For the first time a queen's pyramid includes reduced versions of most of the standard elements of the king's complex.

Entrance

N

0   50 m
0   150 ft

Sanctuary
Satellite pyramid
5 statue niches
Queen's pyramid
Queen's satellite pyramid
Pylon
Open court
Entrance hall
Pylon
Causeway

3 portcullises
Corridor-chamber
Descending passage
Entrance

Burial chamber, 7.84 x 3.1 m
Antechamber, 4.02 x 3.1 m
3 magazines
Satellite pyramid

Djedkare-Isesi's pyramid, 'Beautiful is Isesi', had a base length of 78.75 m (150 cubits, or 258 ft) and a slope of 52°. It rose to a height of around 52.5 m (172 ft).

(Right) A gallery of brightly painted relief scenes would originally have lined Unas's causeway, 750 m (2,460 ft) long, lit by a slit in the great ceiling slabs.

Unas lay in the good earth, symbolized by his coffin, enclosed in a wood and reed-mat screen etched in the walls, the equivalent of the niched Archaic mastabas. He was the first pharaoh to have his burial chamber inscribed with Pyramid Texts.

alabaster. Magazines on either side of the vestibule were reached by passages at each end of the transverse corridor separating the front from the inner temple, which here was more of a separate building. A door and small stairway led to the standard chamber with five statue niches, followed by a square antechamber with a single column, whence another turn opened into the offering hall. On either side, the inner temple was filled with long narrow magazines. Between the mortuary temple and the enclosure wall of the pyramid complex were four large open courts. In one was the satellite pyramid, with a T-shaped substructure. Another court might have been for animal slaughter or purifications.

A queen's pyramid situated off the northeast corner of the mortuary temple has, for the first time, smaller-scale versions of many of the standard elements of a king's pyramid. These include: its own enclosure wall; an offering hall; magazines; a square antechamber with a single column; a room positioned where the five statue niches are normally found; and a colonnaded court. It even had its own small satellite pyramid.

In the valley below the pyramid, granite architraves and walls of limestone and mudbrick were retrieved, perhaps part of the pyramid town or even the palace. Excavations also recovered limestone statues of prisoners with their hands tied behind their backs, calves, part of a sphinx and a lion support – the realization in the round of themes in the reliefs on pyramid temple walls.

The Pyramid of Unas

Unas, the last king of the 5th dynasty, may have reigned over 30 years (*c.* 2356–2323 BC), but his pyramid is the smallest of all known Old Kingdom pyramids. It is located between the enclosures of Djoser's pyramid and Sekhemkhet's. Unas thus completed a historical and architectural symmetry – the pyramid of Userkaf, the first king of the 5th dynasty stands at the opposite, northeast corner. In selecting this place Unas also put his pyramid temple directly over the substructure of the 2nd-dynasty tomb assigned to Hetepsekhemwy.

The entrance, in the middle of the north side, opened not in the pyramid's face but at ground level in the pavement of the pyramid court. Traces remain of a small entrance chapel.

Inside the pyramid

From the entrance a passage slopes down to a corridor-chamber. This is followed by the usual horizontal passage, with three granite portcullis slabs. The passage then opened into the antechamber, directly under the pyramid's centre axis. To the east, a doorway opened to a room with three recesses. To the west lay the burial chamber, with its basalt sarcophagus still in place. Sunk in the floor to the left

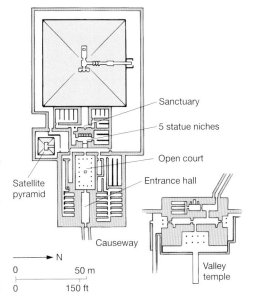

Sanctuary

5 statue niches

Open court

Satellite pyramid

Entrance hall

Causeway

Valley temple

N

0   50 m

0   150 ft

of the foot of the sarcophagus was the canopic chest. A few fragments of a skeleton found in the pyramid in 1881 are now in Cairo Museum.

Unas's chambers are the first since Djoser to be decorated. Around the sarcophagus the walls are lined with white alabaster incised and painted to represent a reed-mat and wood-frame enclosure. Unas thus lay inside his black coffin, representing the earth, within the divine reed-booth open to the sky, covered by the gabled ceiling with golden stars on a field of blue night sky. More significantly, the remaining walls of the burial chamber, antechamber and a section of the horizontal passage are covered with vertical columns of intricately carved hieroglyphs – the earliest example of the Pyramid Texts (p. 31). Each hieroglyph is painted blue, perhaps an allusion, like Djoser's blue-tiled chambers, to the watery aspects of the Underworld.

Unas's chambers contain only 283 of more than 700 known spells, some of which were already very

Antechamber,
3.75 x 3.08 m

3 magazines

Burial chamber,
7.3 x 3.08m

Corridor
chamber

Satellite
pyramid

3 portcullises   Entrance
chapel

*More than 1,000 years after
Unas, Khaemwaset, a son of
Ramesses II and high priest
of Memphis, had an
inscription carved to record
his restoration of Unas's
pyramid. Djoser's Step
Pyramid, visible behind, was
already falling into ruin when
Unas built his tomb.*

sure, suggesting it was falling into ruin. In the roof
of the causeway a slit was left open, allowing a
shaft of light to illuminate a gallery of brightly
painted reliefs. Only fragments were found, but
these hint at the astonishing array of scenes
that once covered the walls: ships transporting granite palm columns for
the temple (p. 202); craftsmen working gold
and copper; estate
labourers gathering
figs and honey, and
harvesting grain; and
lines of offering bearers. Other
scenes included bearded Asiatics and
battles with enemies, and wild animals,
such as lions, leopards and hyenas.

Two boat graves, each 45 m (148 ft) long, lay side
by side immediately south of the causeway at its
uppermost bend. From here the causeway led
straight to the granite temple doorway that Teti,
Unas's successor, completed and inscribed with his
name to commemorate the act. In plan, the mortuary temple follows Djedkare's, marking the transition to the standard arrangement of 6th-dynasty
pyramid temples. This consists of an entrance hall;
colonnaded court; transverse corridor separating
the front from the inner temple; statue chamber
with five niches; square antechamber with its single pillar; offering hall with a granite false door;
and the satellite pyramid. There are variations: for
instance, Unas's pylons were not as massive as
those of Djedkare; the palm columns of the court
were thinner and taller and the single column in the
antechamber is quartzite – from the Gebel Ahmar
('Red Mountain') near Heliopolis – a hard stone particularly associated with the sun.

Unas's pyramid had already fallen into ruin by
the New Kingdom. Khaemwaset, son of Ramesses
II and High Priest at Memphis, left an inscription
on its south side referring to his restoration work,
thus causing the name of Unas to live again.

*Granite columns with palm-
frond capitals graced Unas's
temples. This pair flank the
southern entrance to his
valley temple.*

ancient by his time. The wise men of the court
must have seen what was happening to the monuments and cult of former kings. By etching in stone
the sacred utterances and spells deep within the
pyramid, Unas would enjoy their effect continually
without having to depend for ever on the services of
an unreliable priesthood.

The pyramid complex

In choosing the site for his pyramid Unas took
advantage of two natural features. A long wadi
east of the pyramid provided a good route for his
causeway and opened on to a lake which formed a
harbour for his valley temple, with a sophisticated
arrangement of ramps, quays and a slipway.

The causeway must have been one of the most
impressive of any pyramid: at 750 m (2,460 ft) long
it was equal to Khufu's. Though the wadi provided
a natural route, gaps had to plugged with embankments. These contained blocks from Djoser's enclo-

Pyramids of the 6th Dynasty

(Right) Teti's pyramid with the ruins of his mortuary temple in the foreground and Djoser's Step Pyramid behind.

Teti is listed as the first king of the 6th dynasty, though there is no evidence of a break in succession from Unas. Teti's queen, Iput, was the mother of Pepi I and probably a daughter of Unas. Certain of Teti's high officials, whose mastaba tombs are immediately north of his pyramid, had also served under Unas. One, named Kagemni, must have seen the building of three pyramid complexes.

The Pyramid of Teti

Teti chose a spot in North Saqqara, at the southern end of the 1st-dynasty mastabas and northeast of Userkaf's pyramid. He may have been anxious to include his pyramid in the diagonal formed by Userkaf, Djoser, Unas and Sekhemkhet, but it presents a puzzle as to the location of his valley temple and pyramid town, both of which are missing. Teti's pyramid stands above relatively high ground and an enormous embankment would have been needed to carry a causeway, also missing.

Teti's pyramid follows the prototype established in the late 5th dynasty and its dimensions are practically the same as those of Djedkare-Isesi, and of his successors Pepi I, Merenre and Pepi II. The core was built in steps and accretions made of small, locally quarried blocks and debris fill. Some blocks of the fine outer casing are preserved on the east side, but most of it was removed, causing the core to slump into the rounded mound seen today.

The entrance is at ground level on the centre axis of the pyramid and was simply covered with heavy flagstones, with a chapel built directly over it. Pivot sockets indicate that the chapel was closed by double-leaf doors. The side walls had painted reliefs depicting offering bearers and the roof was a massive limestone slab decorated with stars. In the back wall was a large false door of black basalt.

Inside the pyramid

Teti's substructure is similar to Unas's, on a slightly larger scale. A granite-lined passage slopes down to a corridor-chamber followed by a horizontal passage, with three portcullises. The antechamber lies under the centre of the pyramid. To the east is a room with three niches; the burial chamber opens to the west. The basalt sarcophagus is well preserved and is inscribed, for the first time, with a single band of Pyramid Texts. Robbers broke through

Teti's private apartment under his pyramid: looking from the three-niche chamber through the antechamber to the burial chamber and sarcophagus. The wooden beam is a modern support for the ceiling.

the lid and only a few fragments of the mummy survived. As with Unas's chambers, the walls of the burial chamber, antechamber and the last part of the horizontal passage were inscribed with Pyramid Texts, but here they are far more damaged.

The pyramid complex

Stone robbers also left little of the mortuary temple but its plan conforms to a standard scheme, following the essentials of Djedkare and Unas. One variation is the entrance, as the causeway may have been shifted south of the central axis in order to miss Lepsius pyramid XXIX (p. 165). If this belonged to Menkauhor, it would already have stood in Teti's time. A long, narrow corridor led to a doorway on the mortuary temple's central axis. This led in turn to a vestibule with a roof decorated with stars.

In his colonnaded court Teti returned to the square granite pillars of the 4th-dynasty and Userkaf. A rectangular alabaster altar in the centre retained traces of reliefs. Similar altars are known from emplacements or fragments in the mortuary temples of Sahure, Neferirkare, Niuserre and Unas. Magazines arrayed on both sides of the court and vestibule were entered via the transverse corridor. The small alabaster stairway to the statue chamber with its five niches is well preserved but not the walls of the niches. Each niche had a double-leaf doorway with a granite frame inscribed with the titles of the king. The offering hall, entered by a vestibule and square antechamber with a single pillar, had a vaulted ceiling. At the west end, against the pyramid, was a false door resting on a quartzite foundation block and framed with limestone reliefs.

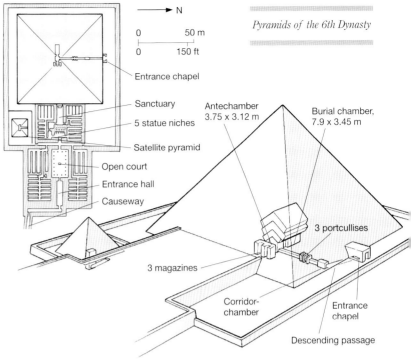

Entrance chapel

Sanctuary

5 statue niches

Satellite pyramid

Open court

Entrance hall

Causeway

Antechamber
3.75 x 3.12 m

Burial chamber,
7.9 x 3.45 m

3 portcullises

3 magazines

Corridor-
chamber

Entrance
chapel

Descending passage

The satellite pyramid was found in its standard place south of the inner temple and measured 15.7 m (30 cubits, 51 ft 6 in) square. In the court surrounding it were two basins of red quartzite on the eastern side and a third on the west; a small limestone basin was placed somewhere on the north.

Pyramids of Iput and Khuit

Two royal women of Teti's court were favoured with their own pyramids, in separate enclosures north of Teti's pyramid and behind the mastabas of court officials. Iput's pyramid was originally a mastaba, which her son, Pepi I, transformed into a pyramid. A. Labrousse ascertained the position of Khuit's pyramid, lost since the excavations of Loret in 1897–9 and Firth in 1922, but it was only excavated by Z. Hawass in 1997. It still stands for 7 m (23 ft) of its original 20-m (66-ft) height.

Loret could not find the entrance of Iput's, for the simple reason that it had none. The small pyramid, with sides 15.75 m (52 ft) long and a steep slope of 65°, was built over a vertical mastaba shaft and burial chamber. A small red granite false door on the north side was part of an 'entrance chapel' and a chapel on the east side had its own court, statue chamber with three niches, and offering hall with a limestone false door and a granite offering slab.

Iput's remains were found in a cedar coffin in a roughly dressed limestone sarcophagus. Although thieves had broken in, Iput's skeleton was intact, along with fragments of her necklace and a gold bracelet. Five crude canopic jars were also found. The room was filled with limestone chips to the level of the sarcophagus lid. On this were model

vessels of alabaster, pottery and copper, alabaster slabs inscribed with the names of sacred oils, and model gold-leaf covered copper tools. Although robbed, this burial assembly seems to have been far more meagre than that of Hetepheres at Giza.

The Pyramid of Pepi I

Teti may have exhausted the topographical opportunities for pyramid complexes in Central and North Saqqara. Pepi I returned to a spur of high desert in South Saqqara, defined by the broad Wadi Tafla on the south. His pyramid is now reduced to a low mound, about 12 m (39 ft) high, with a large

Teti's pyramid, 'The Places of Teti Endure', measured 78.5 m (258 ft) to a side and rose to 52.5 m (172 ft) high at an angle of 53° 7' 48". The enclosure measured 200 cubits (105 m) N–S by 243 cubits (127.57 m) E–W.

Audran Labrousse's computer model of Pepi I's pyramid complex. Except for the central court, all chambers and magazines were dark covered spaces.

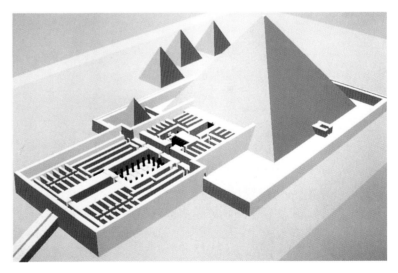

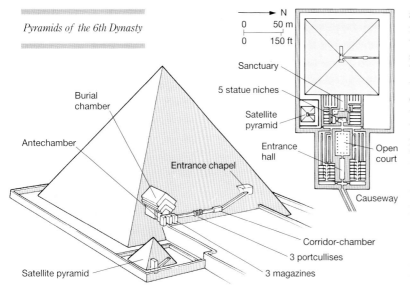

Burial chamber

Antechamber

Entrance chapel

Satellite pyramid

N

0   50 m
0   150 ft

Sanctuary

5 statue niches

Satellite pyramid

Entrance hall

Open court

Causeway

Corridor-chamber

3 portcullises

3 magazines

Pepi I's pyramid, 'The Perfection of Pepi is Established' followed the highly standardized pattern of the 6th dynasty. Though now badly destroyed it is estimated to have been 78.75 m (258 ft) to a side and 52.5 m (172 ft) high, with an angle of slope of 53° 7' 48".

crater in the centre dug by stone robbers. It was in this pyramid and Merenre's that the Brugsch brothers discovered Pyramid Texts in 1881. The pyramid and its mortuary temple have been systematically cleared and studied by the French Archaeological Saqqara Mission (MFAS), beginning in 1951 and directed by Jean Leclant since 1966.

Inside the pyramid

Pepi I's substructure is similar to Teti's, with the difference that the Pyramid Texts have expanded to cover more of the walls. Vertical columns of hieroglyphs were painted green, the colour of freshness, growth and renewal. In the course of restoration work, the French made a rare find in pyramid

archaeology. The pink granite canopic chest, with its lid, was still set into the floor niche in front of the sarcophagus. A complete packet of viscera, presumably Pepi I's, lay close by – the tightly wrapped bundle retaining the shape of the alabaster jar which once held it (p. 22). On both the interior and exterior of the sarcophagus of hard, dark stone was a line of Pyramid Texts; around it the walls of the chamber were decorated with the motif of the reed-mat booth. As in the pyramids of Unas and Teti, the room to the east of the antechamber was left uninscribed.

The pyramid complex

Like all the Saqqara mortuary temples, Pepi I's had suffered grievously from lime makers, but three decades of study by the French have shown that it had all the essential components of previous temples. A number of limestone statues of prisoners, broken at the neck and waist, were found in the southwestern part of the temple where they had been brought to be thrown into lime furnaces. Each represented a kneeling man, his hands tied behind his back, belonging to Egypt's traditional enemies. Remains of similar statues were found at the pyramids of Djedkare-Isesi, Teti and Pepi II. Lauer suggested that they lined the two sides of the causeway to signify the conquered peoples of the north and south. Alternatively they may stood under scenes of the king's victories in the mortuary temple.

Pepi I's valley temple and pyramid town have never been excavated, nor has his causeway, except for a few metres in front of the mortuary temple. However, the line of the causeway revealed by contours may point to the valley temple under the alluvium in the bay. The name of the pyramid and its town, *Men-nefer Pepi*, 'The Perfection of Pepi is Established', extended in the Middle Kingdom to the settlement around the nearby Ptah temple, and was handed down in Greek as Memphis.

Pepi I's satellite pyramid was in a better state of preservation than the mortuary temple. Statue fragments, parts of stelae and offering tables found in the debris indicate that the cult of Pepi I continued into the Middle Kingdom, though the pyramid was falling into ruin by the New Kingdom. In 1993, on the south side of the main pyramid, the French found another inscription of Khaemwaset, in

The burial chamber of Pepi I after the impressive work by the French Mission, who found the black stone sarcophagus (below) and canopic chest, with one packet of the king's viscera (p. 22). Thousands of fragments of Pyramid Texts were restored like a gigantic jigsaw puzzle.

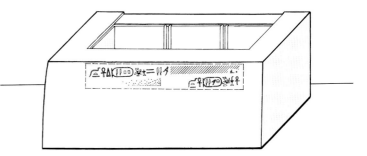

(Left) A copper statue of Pepi I and one of his sons, possibly Merenre, found in one of the five chambers on the temple mound at Hierakonpolis.

(Above) Two of the bound prisoner statues that may have lined the court of Pepi I's mortuary temple. As the king plants trees in orderly rows in the court (the columns) and clears a space of wild foliage (the court), so he ties the hands of 'wild' nomadic peoples on Egypt's margins. They had been deliberately broken at the neck and waist.

which he describes how he recalled for posterity the proprietor of a pyramid he had found abandoned. But the most dramatic finds of the last few years have been the queens' pyramids.

Queens' pyramids

An enormous accumulation of debris and sand covered an area south of Pepi I's pyramid. In 1988 the French team used electromagnetic sounding to look for boat-pits and queens' pyramids that they suspected might be buried here. Possible emplacements for three small pyramids were located and soon an apex stone and casing stones of a small pyramid emerged. Eventually three pyramids were cleared, all about 20 m (65 ft 6in) square, roughly aligned in an east–west row. Each had its own enclosure and small offering temple. They were ascribed to the 'Queen of the West', 'Queen of the East' and 'Queen of the Centre'.

On the fallen east jamb of the mortuary temple of the eastern queen was an image of the queen, with her name, Nebwenet, and her titles. The western queen's identity is preserved only

159

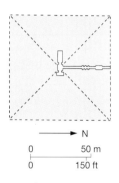

Queen Nebwenet – tall and slender in 6th-dynasty style – from her pyramid chapel.

Merenre's pyramid was badly destroyed and has yet to be fully cleared or surveyed. It may have been planned to follow the dimensions of his predecessors' pyramids.

(Right) The burial chamber with the sarcophagus and canopic chest.

as 'eldest daughter of the king' on a small obelisk in front of her pyramid. The name of the central queen, Inenek/Inti emerged when her visage, name and titles were found on jambs and small obelisks flanking the door to her temple.

The French team suspected yet a fourth queen's pyramid – a suspicion confirmed by the discovery of a stela inscribed with the name of Merytytyes, a royal wife and daughter. Recently a fifth queen's pyramid has been located. These women of Pepi's court would be deeply appreciative of the work of the French, who are fulfilling one of the highest hopes of literate ancient Egyptians by ensuring that their names live on after death.

The Pyramid of Merenre

Pepi I's eldest son and successor, Merenre, reigned only a short time. Although we are uncertain just how short, it was probably only nine years. Merenre probably planned his pyramid to the same standard dimensions (150 cubits square, 100 cubits tall, 53° 7' 48" slope) as his immediate predecessors, although an exact survey has yet to be done and so we do not have precise details or plans.

The pyramid is 450 m (1,476 ft) southwest of Pepi I's and the same distance directly west of Djedkare's. It is unusual for a pyramid to be located due west of an older one but perhaps Merenre wanted to use the Wadi Tafla as his harbour. He would have needed a causeway that spanned a drop of 27 m (86 ft) over a distance of only 300 m (984 ft). A linear feature may be the beginnings of an embankment.

Inside the pyramid

The substructure is very similar to Pepi I's, including the distribution of Pyramid Texts. The Brugsch brothers were the first archaeologists to enter, by crawling through a robbers' tunnel around the lowered granite portcullis slabs. Inside the burial chamber the huge limestone ceiling girders and

a gigantic slab between this room and the antechamber hung suspended after robbers had removed much of the lower supporting walls. But the black basalt sarcophagus was in good condition, its lid intact but pushed back. Amazingly, it still contained a mummy, apparently that of a young man, as the hair was braided into the side lock of youth. The great anatomist of Egyptian mummies, G. Eliot Smith, considered it an intrusive secondary burial, possibly of the 18th dynasty. Unfortunately the mummy, now in Cairo Museum, has not yet been properly studied. When the French team cleared the burial chamber they found the red granite canopic chest, with its lid, in front of one end of the sarcophagus.

The pyramid complex

On the pyramid's north side, the French found two corner stones of the entrance chapel in position, along with fragments of reliefs of deities walking towards the king to greet him as he entered their world. In the mortuary temple, the offering hall was paved with limestone. Traces of an offering table

vated by Gustave Jéquier (1926–36), however, it had been reduced to a low mound. The core comprised five steps, with retaining walls of small irregular stones set in tafla and Nile mud, the whole encased in heavy blocks of Turah limestone laid without mortar. The retaining walls are reminiscent of construction ramps at Giza. In effect, the descendants of the Giza masons built the pyramid core in the same way as the earlier ramps, with material far easier to mould and manipulate.

A unique feature of Pepi II's pyramid was an immense girdle, 6.5 m (21 ft) wide, added after the pyramid had been completed. It has been suggested that the builders wanted the pyramid to resemble the hieroglyph for 'pyramid', with a band across the base, or that they were worried about its structural security. In the standardized pyramid complexes of the 6th dynasty we see little of the successive rebuildings that characterize earlier ones. Considering Pepi's long reign, and if pyramid building was indeed part of a ritual cycle, the girdle perhaps celebrated one of his Sed festivals.

with a limestone trough at its side were found, and another small offering table against the north wall and an elliptical depression in the pavement. Only the base of the granite false door remained at the west end of the hall. Some of the relief decoration had only been outlined and not modelled. Work in the temple must have stopped when the king died.

A slab of limestone from a small chapel at Abydos is inscribed with one of the very rare contemporary texts about the building of a pyramid. The hieroglyphs convey to us the voice of Weni, whose career spanned the reigns of Teti, Pepi I and Merenre. Under Merenre, Weni became Governor of Upper Egypt, which gave him responsibility for bringing back stone for the pyramid, including the sarcophagus – trips he describes in great detail.

The Pyramid of Pepi II

Pepi II was the last Old Kingdom ruler of any substance. His pyramid was fittingly named 'Nefer-ka-Re [Pepi II] is Established and Living' since he lived 100 years according to Manetho and ruled 94 years – longer than any other pharaoh. He located his pyramid south of Merenre's and Djedkare-Isesi's across the Wadi Tafla, and only 120 m (394 ft) away from the mastaba of Shepseskaf. Despite such a long reign, Pepi II's pyramid was the standard size – 150 cubits (78.5 m/258 ft) square and 100 cubits (52.5 m/172 ft 4 in) high. By the time it was exca-

An alabaster statuette of Pepi II as a child, found near the five statue niches of his mortuary temple.

The pyramid complex of Pepi II is the culmination of Old Kingdom development, with three queens' pyramids, a classic mortuary temple and valley temple fronted by ramps and broad esplanade.

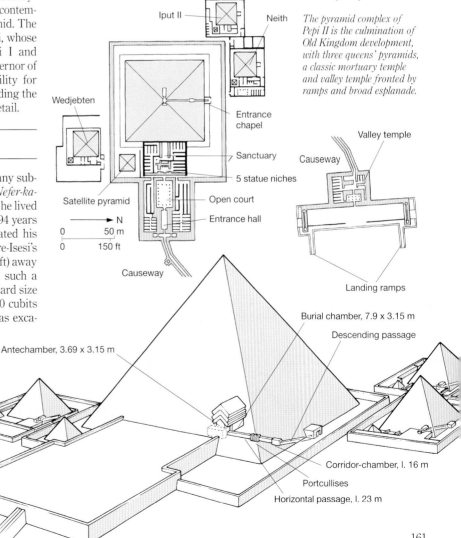

Iput II

Neith

Wedjebten

Entrance chapel

Sanctuary

5 statue niches

Open court

Entrance hall

Satellite pyramid

N

0   50 m
0   150 ft

Causeway

Valley temple

Causeway

Landing ramps

Burial chamber, 7.9 x 3.15 m

Descending passage

Antechamber, 3.69 x 3.15 m

Corridor-chamber, l. 16 m

Portcullises

Horizontal passage, l. 23 m

Pepi II's pyramid – 'Pepi is Established and Living' – was the standard size – 78.75 m (258 ft) square and 52.5 m (172 ft) high, with an angle of slope of 53° 7' 48", despite his 94-year reign.

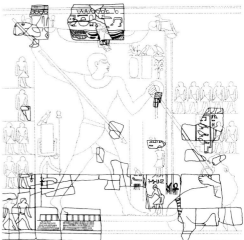

Inside the pyramid

From the entrance a passage sloped down to a corridor-chamber with a star-studded ceiling and
walls covered with Pyramid Texts. Here Jéquier
found fragments of alabaster and diorite vases,
perhaps for perfume, and a golden spatula. These
may have been used in a ritual performed at the
closing of the pyramid corridor. A further section
of the horizontal passage, lined with granite, was
blocked by three portcullises.

The inner chambers were covered with a gabled
ceiling decorated with stars. Single gigantic limestone blocks form the north and south walls of the
burial chamber. Around the black granite sarcophagus, inscribed with the kings titulary, the walls
were decorated in the niched pattern of the sacred
reed-mat booth. At the head and foot ends, the decoration featured false doors, painted green, topped
with a name plate of the king. Two low walls west
of the sarcophagus supported the lid until it was
pushed sideways to seal the king's mummy. Only
the niche of the canopic chest remained in the floor,
together with its granite lid.

The pyramid complex

If, as we suspect, there were pyramid towns below
the tombs of Djedkare, Merenre, Shepseskaf and
Pepi II, a substantial line of settlements must have
extended along the base of the escarpment by the
end of the Old Kingdom. Unfortunately it has never
been excavated.

Visitors could gain access to Pepi II's valley temple either from the desert or from the harbour via
ramps up to an esplanade and platform. A single
door, framed in red granite and inscribed with Pepi
II's name and titles, opened into a small hypostyle
hall with eight rectangular pillars. The walls were
decorated with reliefs of the gods receiving the
king, the suppression of enemies and a hunt in the
papyrus thickets. Other rooms were undecorated.

From the scattered fragments reconstructed by
Jéquier it seems Pepi II's artists copied much of his

decorative programme from Sahure's complex. The
lower part of Pepi's causeway showed the king,
transformed into a sphinx and griffin, trampling on
his enemies; the upper part had scenes of offering
bearers. The causeway changes direction twice to
take advantage of the most even slope.

At either corner of the east wall of the mortuary
temple was a kind of proto-pylon that temple
builders had been developing since Niuserre. A
door on the central axis of temple and pyramid led
to a vestibule where reliefs depicted the king's tri-
umph over human and animal forces of disorder –
the latter in the form of a hippopotamus, which the
king harpooned from a boat. Around the open court
was a colonnade of 18 rectangular quartzite pillars.
Each was decorated on the side facing into the
court with figures of the king and a god. Notwith-
standing the pillars and granite doorways, there
seems to have been a cheapening of materials and
decoration – the court was paved in limestone and
the walls of the open court were undecorated.

A doorway at the south end of the transverse
corridor opened to the court with the satellite pyramid which was 15.75 m (30 cubits, 52 ft) square and
had a slope, like most late Old Kingdom satellite
pyramids, of 63°. The T-shaped passage and small
chamber were left unsmoothed. The door at the
other end of the transverse corridor led to the main
pyramid court, where three basins sunk in the
pavement may have collected libation water.

Patches of relief from the east wall of the transverse corridor belonged to scenes of the king performing the ritual run of the Sed festival. Also
recovered was a scene from the Festival of Min. A
relief of the king about to execute a Libyan chief in
the presence of his family is a near-exact copy of a
scene in Sahure's mortuary temple. Reliefs on the
entrance to the inner temple depicted the king
being suckled by goddesses. The five statue niches
were framed in red granite; the middle one was
slightly larger and still held the limestone base of a
life-size royal statue – the only direct evidence we

have that these niches did indeed hold statues. Between the niches and the offering hall, as in other mortuary temples, is a masonry massif with an open core, perhaps a *serdab* for hidden statues.

The north doorway of the statue chamber led to five magazines, while that to the south gave access to a small vestibule and square antechamber on the route to the offering hall. In the vestibule the king was once more shown suppressing disorder, slaying enemies and hunting wild animals. The roof of the antechamber was supported by a single octagonal quartzite pillar. Here as many as 100 deities and 45 officials received the king. On the north wall the king sat enthroned, protected by the jackal-headed Anubis and by Nekhbet.

Nothing remained of the false door at the west end of the offering hall, which was covered by a vaulted roof. Fragments of reliefs reveal scenes of the king seated before a table laden with offerings. Behind him stands a small figure with the symbol of up-raised arms on his head – the king's *ka* (p. 22), here receiving *kau*, 'food sustenance'. Before the king were more than 100 dignitaries and residents of the pyramid town bringing ducks, geese, quail, pigeons, gazelle, goats and antelopes, cattle, fruit, wine, beer and bread. On the east wall were scenes of cattle being slaughtered. Pepi II's complex also featured prisoner statues as did Pepi I's, Teti's and Djedkare's, but much greater numbers have been found here. Each had been broken at the neck and waist before being cut into smaller pieces.

Queens' pyramids

Three queens of Pepi II had their own pyramid – with entrance chapel, temple and tiny satellite pyramid. Neith's was the finest and probably the oldest. Flanking the entrance to her enclosure were two small obelisks inscribed with her name and titles, indicating she was the daughter of Pepi I and wife of Pepi II. Reliefs on the walls of the court showed the queen and offerings. Her small temple had five magazines, a chamber with three niches, an offering hall with presentation scenes and a false door, missing before Jéquier's excavations.

The pyramid was 24 m (78 ft) square with a 61° slope. It was built around a three-step core encased in a limestone girdle like that around the king's pyramid. An entrance chapel contained scenes of offering bearers. In the south wall a granite false door closed the descending passage which sloped down to the burial chamber, blocked by a single portcullis. For the first time in a queen's pyramid the chamber and passage were inscribed with Pyramid Texts. As in the king's pyramid, a magazine to the east remained uninscribed. The flat ceiling of the burial chamber was carved with stars. Neith's empty red granite sarcophagus stands in the chamber, with her canopic chest of the same material before it. Around it the walls were decorated with the niched and false door pattern.

Neith's own satellite pyramid was 10 cubits (5.25 m, 18 ft) square, with a miniature passage blocked with stone. A rectangular chamber was filled with sherds of pottery vessels. Three alabaster vessels were perhaps used in the embalming of the queen's body, or they may have been for offerings for the queen's *ka*. Between Neith's satellite and main pyramid 16 wooden model ships were buried in a shallow grave – perhaps the queen's own funerary fleet.

Iput II's pyramid complex was built on to the southwest corner of Neith's. It had all the same elements, including a satellite pyramid, small obelisks at the enclosure entrance, vestibule and court, inner offering temple and magazines, here approached by a long corridor with several turns. A queen named Ankhes-en-Pepi was buried between the enclosures of Neith and Iput, without a pyramid of her own.

Near the southeast corner of Pepi's enclosure was the pyramid of Wedjebten, another daughter of Pepi I and wife of Pepi II. Like the other two, her tomb contained Pyramid Texts. A small vestibule and plain court led to a chapel with an alabaster offering table inscribed with her name. The walls of the chapel were decorated with reliefs of the queen before a goddess and scenes of slaughtering cattle. A fragment depicted the base of a throne, similar to a relief in Neith's chapel. Because of the glimpse it offers of the role of a pyramid in the economics of the Afterlife, the most remarkable feature of Wedjebten's pyramid is her secondary enclosure. Inside were chambers resembling houses and magazines. Inscriptions refer to a family line of priests. Each beneficiary had a chamber and small courtyard in which they set up proxy symbols of their real households and tombs. By being so honoured, they were allowed to share the endowment of her funerary estate, just as she had a share of Pepi II's.

A legal document etched in stone: the doorway to Wedjebten's secondary enclosure was inscribed as 'gate of the estate' of a family line of Wedjebten's priests.

N

0   20 m

0   50 ft

The secondary enclosure around Wedjebten's pyramid contained small houses and offering chambers of priests and their kin who shared in the queen's estate, as she shared in that of Pepi II.

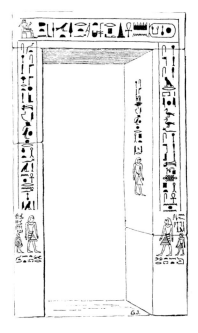

Pyramids of the First Intermediate Period

In spite of archaeological and documentary hints of instability, the abrupt end of the Old Kingdom pyramid sequence still surprises us. The Turin Papyrus ends the 6th dynasty with a Queen Nitokerti (Nitocris) – reminding us of Khentkawes at the end of the 4th (p. 138). But Nitokerti's rule followed a long period when an elderly Pepi II ruled over a deteriorating kingdom. Manetho lists the next dynasty, the 7th, as 70 kings in 70 days.

The Pyramid of Ibi

The 8th dynasty is listed as 27 kings in 146 years, but we know of only one ruler who attempted to build a pyramid. Begun on a low knoll near the causeway of Pepi II, this small pyramid is in marked contrast to the great pyramid complexes of the Old Kingdom. Here Jéquier found fragments of Pyramid Texts for a king named Hakare-Ibi. In the Turin Canon, Ibi is given only two years of rule. His pyramid is similar in dimensions and layout to the queens' pyramids of Pepi II – 31.5 m (60 cubits or 103 ft) square.

The pyramid's core of small stones took the form of a double girdle around the trench in which the inner chambers were built. Foundations for the outer casing were laid into a trench around the core, but it seems the builders never began to put the casing in place. In the north side of the pyramid a passage lined with Turah limestone sloped down to a horizontal corridor. The walls of the passage and burial chamber were inscribed with Pyramid Texts. A huge granite block in the west end of the burial chamber held the sarcophagus. On the east side of the pyramid, a small mudbrick chapel was built, approximately on its centre axis. An entrance on the north side of the chapel gave indirect access to an offering hall with a rectangular basin set in the floor in front of an emplacement for a stela or false door. A round alabaster platter and an obsidian mortar may have been used in rituals. The south side of the chapel was taken up by magazines opening off a central courtyard.

The Pyramid of Khui

In the absence of a unifying pharaoh local rulers took on the prerogatives of kingship during the First Intermediate Period, around the end of the 3rd millennium BC. One of these built a pyramid at Dara in Middle Egypt, near the western desert entrance to the Dakhla Oasis. Its excavator, Ahmed Kamal, believed it was a mastaba, but the mudbrick superstructure with rounded corners had sloping sides and a square ground plan with a base length of 130 m (426 ft 6 in) – nearly equal to the base of Djoser's Step Pyramid.

From the entrance an alternately sloping and horizontal passage runs to the door of a burial chamber, 8.8 m (29 ft) below the base level of the pyramid. The walls of the last part of the passage

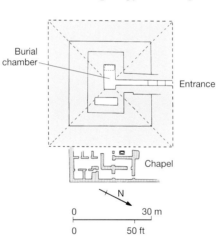

(Right) Plan of the small pyramid complex of Ibi. Its base length was 31.5 m (103 ft) and it was an estimated 21 m (69 ft) high. Today (below) it is in a very ruined state. Piles of mud and limestone chips remain from the core; the burial chamber, roofed now with modern concrete, is covered with Pyramid Texts.

(Below right) Plan of a pyramidal tomb of a local ruler, possibly Khui, at Dara in Middle Egypt. Today it stands just 4 m (13 ft) high.

Burial chamber

Entrance

Chapel

N

0   30 m

0   50 ft

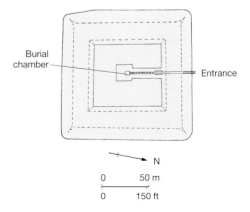

Burial chamber

Entrance

N

0   50 m

0   150 ft

were reinforced with pilasters, and both it and the burial chamber were lined with limestone robbed from tombs in a nearby cemetery, apparently of the 6th dynasty. A block found in a tomb south of the pyramid, and which may have come from the pyramid's own offering temple, had an offering scene with a cartouche with the name Khui.

Lepsius Pyramid XXIX

A cemetery near Teti's pyramid was in use through the First Intermediate Period. Among those buried there was an early 12th-dynasty priest of the pyramid, *Wadj Sut* ('The Fresh Places') of Merikare, a 9th- or 10th-dynasty ruler. It was suspected that the anonymous pyramid that Lepsius numbered XXIX (29) may have belonged to this king.

The pyramid – in Arabic the 'Pyramid Without a Top' (or 'Headless Pyramid') – is east of Teti's and was laid out with little regard to the cardinal directions. Maspero entered it in 1881 and Firth cleared the site in 1930 but did not produce a plan. Practically all that remains of the superstructure is the foundation, about 52 m (100 cubits or 170 ft) per side. The entrance is approximately in the middle of the north side. Two granite portcullises sealed the passage to the antechamber and burial chamber, indicating that a burial had taken place, and the broken lid of a fine sarcophagus was found. In spite of reasons to link the pyramid with Merikare, a study by Jocelyne Berlandini pointed to stronger associations with Menkauhor (p. 153), whose pyramid has not been located. Recently, however, Jaromir Málek has argued for Merikare as the owner. More investigation of this little-explored pyramid is needed to settle the question.

Terrace Tombs of the Intefs

For a second time rulers emerged from the Qena Bend. The founder of the line that would emerge as the 11th dynasty was simply a nomarch and chief priest of a local temple who was named Intef. Intef I declared himself King of Upper and Lower Egypt and he and his successors (Intef II and III) built their tombs at el-Tarif at Thebes, opposite what would later become the great Karnak complex. They are known as *saff* tombs from the Arabic for 'row', because of the rows of columns and doorways at their west end. An open trapezoidal court was cut into the sloping desert until sufficient depth was reached for a façade with columns hewn out of the rock. The king's burial was behind this colonnade. Side doors opened into chambers and shaft tombs of royal followers, with no substantial distinction, in plan at least, from the king's.

It was thought that the royal tomb was marked by a mudbrick pyramid in the court or above the façade. In the Abbott Papyrus, a report of a commission into the plundering of royal tombs written about a millennium after they were built (*c.* 1115 BC) it was said of the tomb of Intef II that its 'pyramid was crushed down upon it, its stela is set up in front of it, and the image of the king stands…with his hound, named Behka…'. In 1860 Mariette found this stela, with not one but five hounds, the uppermost named Behka. However, Dieter Arnold has established that it was found in an offering chapel east of Intef II's tomb. There is no evidence that the Intefs' tombs were surmounted by pyramids at all.

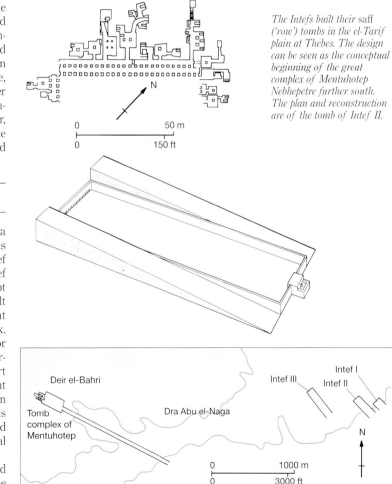

The Intefs built their saff *('row') tombs in the el-Tarif plain at Thebes. The design can be seen as the conceptual beginning of the great complex of Mentuhotep Nebhepetre further south. The plan and reconstruction are of the tomb of Intef II.*

0   50 m
0   150 ft

N

Deir el-Bahri

Tomb complex of Mentuhotep

Dra Abu el-Naga

Intef III

Intef I
Intef II

N

0   1000 m
0   3000 ft

Mentuhotep at Deir el-Bahri

Mentuhotep ('the god Montu is satisfied') Nebhepetre ('Lord of the Steering Oar of Re'), listed as Mentuhotep I or II, was the fourth king of the 11th dynasty. He came to the throne in around 2061 BC, reuniting the kingdom after the First Intermediate Period. His tomb complex was a gigantic *saff* tomb, much larger than those of the Intefs, in a deep bay in the cliffs on the west bank of Thebes called Deir el-Bahri. Excavations by Edouard Naville in 1903–7 and Herbert Winlock in 1920–31 were incorporated in a new study of the monument by Dieter Arnold. He clarified four distinct phases (A, B, C, D) in which Mentuhotep's builders created his complex.

Rather than clear a terrace in the desert as his predecessors had done for their *saff* tombs, Mentuhotep reserved the entire Deir el-Bahri bay. He defined his temple precinct with a wall built of natural field stones across its wide mouth. He may well have conceived and built the main part of his temple at about the time he changed his Horus name to 'Uniter of the Two Lands'.

At the base of the cliff a T-shaped terrace was partly built of masonry and partly carved into the rock. A ramp rose from the forecourt to this terrace. On the terrace, low walls bordered a platform on which an ambulatory was constructed of thick limestone walls decorated inside and out with painted relief carving. The corners of the exterior walls had torus moulding, and a cavetto cornice crowned the building – making the whole structure a stylized reed-mat 'divine booth'. The 'booth' enclosed a central edifice – a masonry-filled building, of which only the square base remained.

In the Abbott Papyrus this tomb, as well Intef II's (p. 165), is referred to with the word for 'pyramid' (*mer*). Further, the hieroglyphic determinative for the temple in later texts and graffiti is a pyramid. For these reasons the central edifice has been reconstructed as a solid limestone-clad massif which formed a podium for a pyramid. This reconstruction placed Mentuhotep's monument neatly into any iteration of Egyptian pyramids. But Dieter Arnold has now shown that there probably never was a pyramid above Intef's tomb and so by the late Ramessid period of the Abbott Papyrus *mer* may have been a general term for 'tomb'. Arnold also pointed out that the walls of Mentuhotep's edifice would not support the weight of a pyramid and no casing blocks with the angled face of a pyramid were found. This central icon of Mentuhotep's complex was, in Arnold's view, simply a solid building capped by a cornice. It perhaps symbolized the primeval mound and therefore carried some of the same meaning as a pyramid. More recently Stadelmann has reconstructed a rounded Osirian mound within the edifice – a tempting parallel to the mound inside the Archaic mastabas at Saqqara (p. 80), but completely hypothetical.

The royal tomb

From the ambulatory a doorway led to a cloistered court at the beginning of the leg of the T-shaped terrace. In the centre of the court and on the centre axis of the temple the king's tomb opens as a rectangular trench. Near its mouth is a socket for an altar or offering table. The trench becomes a tunnel, descending through the bedrock. Niches in the walls contained human figures from wooden models of bakeries, butcheries, granaries and ships, but none of the model architectural settings survive. From this point, the sides and vaulted ceiling of the tunnel are clad in sandstone. The cladding then suddenly ends, leaving the rough bedrock exposed.

The burial chamber is a marvellous structure, built in a cavern hewn 44.9 m (147 ft) below the level of the court and at the end of a tunnel 150 m (492 ft) long. It is a granite vault with a pent roof and side walls cut with a slight outward lean. Three-quarters of the floor space was taken up by an alabaster shrine with a top formed of a single gigantic granite slab. The shrine probably once

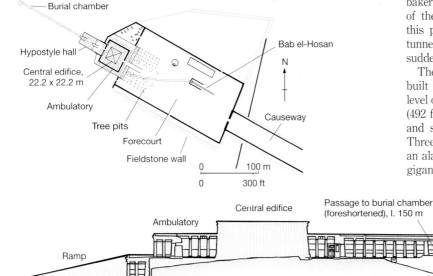

Burial chamber

Hypostyle hall

Central edifice,
22.2 x 22.2 m

Ambulatory

Tree pits

Forecourt

Fieldstone wall

Bab el-Hosan

N

Causeway

0   100 m
0   300 ft

Ramp

Ambulatory

Central edifice

Passage to burial chamber
(foreshortened), l. 150 m

Rock-cut niche
with statue of king

Burial chamber

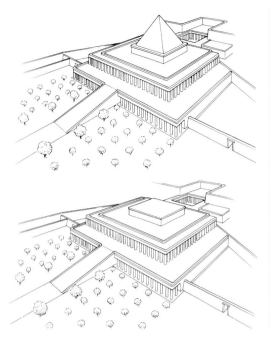

enclosed the king's mummy in its wooden coffin. Only a tiny space was left between the shrine and the walls of the chamber but the builders had managed to fill it with slabs of black diorite. The buried king was therefore enveloped by successive shells of costly stone, reminiscent of the fragments found around Djoser's chamber.

Behind the colonnaded court that covered the tomb entrance Mentuhotep built the first grand stone hypostyle hall in Egyptian architecture, with 80 octagonal columns. At the west end of the hall a statue of the king once stood in a niche hewn into the face of the cliff. Directly in front of it was an altar table at the top of a stairway ramp that ascended through the hypostyle hall. This statue was the central focus of the entire complex – every feature, natural and architectural, led to this point. Instead of emerging from his pyramid, Mentuhotep comes forth from the mountain. The peak called el-Qurn, rising slightly to the south, may have already been seen as a natural pyramid, and during the New Kingdom pharaohs were buried below it in the Valley of the Kings, behind Deir el-Bahri.

At the end of the third phase, the Mentuhotep temple must have resembled a step pyramid from the east, with three tiers formed by the façades of the lower terrace, the ambulatory and the central edifice. A Memphite element was the broad causeway running down to the valley. The valley temple must have disappeared when Ramesses IV levelled it for his mortuary temple.

One of the last elements added to the temple was a 'garden' of pits for trees and two rectangular flower beds. A series of standing sandstone statues of the king as Osiris stood facing the processional way in front of the tree pits. All 12 statues found

had been decapitated before they were buried in the pits. Also in the garden was a grove of 53 tamarisk trees and a large sycamore fig.

In the second phase of the complex a mysterious feature, the Bab el-Hosan, had been built in the forecourt. It took the form of an open trench, enclosed by mudbrick walls. The trench becomes a tunnel which leads to a chamber, in the centre of which a vertical shaft descends to another, unfinished chamber. Arnold sees this as the first royal tomb, which became a cenotaph by sealing a ritual burial inside it when the new tomb was prepared. After Phase C, the burial chamber of the Bab el-Hosan lay directly under the central edifice of the temple. Howard Carter excavated this feature and in the chamber under the temple he discovered a statue of the king, carefully wrapped in layers of fine linen like a mummy. In the centre of the room a shaft, perhaps a symbolic link to the Nile of the underworld, dropped to a rough grotto.

Meaning

Given Arnold's reconstruction of the central edifice as a solid building with the outline of the 'divine booth', the Mentuhotep temple does not, strictly speaking, belong to the series of royal pyramids. Some doubts remain, however, on the grounds of its description as a 'pyramid' in the Abbot Papyrus. Beautifully painted reliefs in the complex contain many of the same themes found in Old Kingdom pyramid temples: the king as a sphinx trampling enemies, fowling, fishing, hunting a hippopotamus, sowing, harvesting and reaping. The whole complex was a combination of royal tomb and temple to the deified king, and to Montu-Re and Amun-Re, the new state god.

(Above) The remains of Mentuhotep's complex. No name of the temple or of any of its parts has been found in the numerous texts and reliefs. But 12th-dynasty texts refer to the entire Deir el-Bahri bay as 'The Valley of Nebhepet-Re' and to the temple itself as Akh Sut Nebhepetre – 'Glorious are the Places of Nebhepetre.'

(Above, left) The central edifice of Mentuhotep's complex was reconstructed by Winlock as a solid massif forming the podium for a pyramid (top). This long-accepted view has been challenged by Dieter Arnold. In his view, the structure was simply a solid building capped by a cornice (below).

The Pyramids at Lisht

Another king began a large tomb that might have replicated the principal elements and scale of Mentuhotep's complex if it had been finished. It is situated in a bay on the other side of the Sheikh Abd al-Qurna hill, south of Deir el-Bahri. Whose tomb was this? Two kings also called Mentuhotep followed the first, taking the names Seankhkare and Nebtawire. The long-accepted attribution to the former made sense. He was the next ruler, graffiti of his priests were found nearby, and his short reign of about 12 years could explain why the complex was unfinished. Recently, however, Dorothea Arnold has argued that it was actually begun for the founder of the 12th dynasty, Amenemhet I, before he transferred his residence north, perhaps only in the last decade of his 30-year reign (1991–1962 BC). His new 'capital' was named *Iti-tawi*, 'Seizer of the Two Lands'.

The Pyramid of Amenemhet I

Iti-tawi's exact location is unknown, but if it was Amenemhet I's pyramid town it would have lain close to the desert edge near the modern village of Lisht, midway between Meidum and Dahshur. One attraction of the site may have been the growing economic importance of the Fayum. At Lisht, a canal called Bahr el-Libeini, thought to be an old Nile channel, swings west to run close to the escarpment at the foot of Amenemhet I's pyramid, perhaps providing a harbour.

Amenemhet I returned to the approximate size and form of the late Old Kingdom pyramid complex. The core of his pyramid was made of small rough blocks of local limestone with a loose fill of sand, debris and mudbrick. Perhaps the most remarkable feature is the fact that it included fragments of relief-decorated blocks from Old Kingdom monuments – many from pyramid causeways and temples, including Khufu's. Granite blocks from Khafre's complex went into the lining and blocking of Amenemhet I's descending passage. We can only conclude that they were picked up at Saqqara and Giza and brought to Lisht to be incorporated into the pyramid for their spiritual efficacy.

Inside the pyramid

The entrance to the pyramid was in the now-standard position, at ground-level in the centre of the north side. Above it was an entrance chapel with a red granite false door at the back. A passage, blocked with granite plugs, sloped to a shaft directly below the vertical axis of the pyramid. Ground water has prevented anyone entering the burial chamber in modern times.

The pyramid complex

Very little of Amenemhet I's mortuary temple was left standing for archaeologists. It was built on a terrace cut into the hill lower than the pyramid. Foundation deposits, in holes covered by limestone slabs, included an ox skull, paint grinders and model vases of pottery and alabaster. There were

Picking up the pieces to resurrect the pyramid age: Amenemhet I incorporated fragments of Old Kingdom tombs and pyramid complexes in his own pyramid.

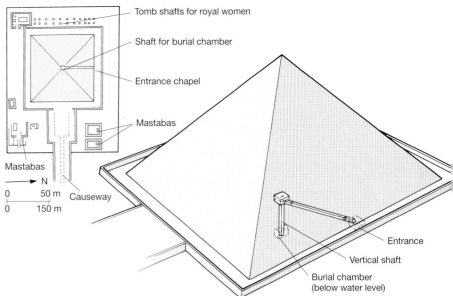

Tomb shafts for royal women

Shaft for burial chamber

Entrance chapel

Mastabas

Mastabas

N

0   50 m
0   150 m   Causeway

Entrance

Vertical shaft

Burial chamber
(below water level)

also bricks with plaques of copper, alabaster and faience inscribed 'The Places of the Appearance of Amenemhet', the name, perhaps, of the pyramid. Another name, 'The Perfection of Amenemhet is Exalted', found elsewhere, may refer to the pyramid temple. A limestone false door and a granite altar or offering table are all that survive of the temple equipment. The altar is carved with Nile gods and figures representing the nomes bringing offerings.

Among relief fragments found were some dating to the reign of Amenemhet but which were such faithful reproductions of Old Kingdom style that it was hard to tell copy from original. Some pieces of reliefs embedded in the foundations came from a pyramid temple of Amenemhet I that had been pulled down and they also included the name of his son and successor, Senwosret I. It is probable that father and son were co-regents from Year 20 of Amenemhet I. The reliefs may reflect the preparations for a Sed festival for the older king who was close to or in his 30th year of rule when he died. Senwosret I seems to have rebuilt the temple – relief blocks from the second temple with both names label Senwosret I as 'the king himself'. No evidence of a satellite pyramid has been found.

The causeway ran in a straight line on the axis of the pyramid and temple. Although it was unroofed, fragments of relief indicate it was decorated with processions of foreigners, estates, nobles and gods. The valley temple has not been excavated because it, too, lies below ground water.

Around the pyramid was an inner enclosure wall of limestone and an outer one of mudbrick. Privileged members of the king's family and court were buried in mastabas between the two. On the west side of the pyramid 22 tomb shafts in two rows were evidently for royal women. Fragments and small stone objects give us the names of some of

these women, including the king's daughter, Neferu, principal wife of Senwosret I, the king's mother, Nefret, and another wife, Nefrytatenen, mother of Senwosret I.

William C. Hayes has pointed out that there is a lack of grandeur and a certain degree of provincialism in the pyramid complex of Amenemhet I. Although he revived the general Memphite pattern, some elements are Theban in origin: the style of certain reliefs, the two terraces of pyramid and temple, the central shaft to the burial chamber and the open causeway. It was Senwosret I who moved the standard Memphite pyramid complex closer to its former level of sophistication before pyramid building reached a final stage of experimentation.

Amenemhet I (above left) re-established the pyramid complex as royal tomb, albeit with Theban elements – two terraces for pyramid and temple and an open causeway. Rows of tombs on the west were for royal women. The pyramid had a base length of 84 m (276 ft), a height of 55 m (180 ft), and a 54° slope.

This relief from the pyramid of Amenemhet I has Khufu's cartouche and probably came from his mortuary temple at Giza.

The Pyramid of Senwosret I

Senwosret I's pyramid is the first to have an internal skeleton of limestone walls forming compartments filled with roughly shaped stones. Nine subsidiary pyramids plus one satellite pyramid are more than in any other single pyramid complex. The pyramid's base length was 200 cubits (105 m/344 ft), and its intended slope was 49° 24', which gives an ideal height of 61.25 m (201 ft).

Senwosret I chose as his site a prominent hill about 2 km (1¼ miles) south of his father's pyramid. It may have had its own pyramid town named *Khenemsut*, 'The Places [of Senwosret] are United'. However, this could refer specifically to his pyramid. *Kha-Senwosret*, 'Senwosret Appears', written with the sign of a fortified enclosure, might be the name of the town. On foundation tablets the name of the pyramid was inscribed as *Senwosret Peteri Tawi*, 'Senwosret Beholds the Two Lands'.

Maspero ascertained that the pyramid belonged to Senwosret I in 1882 when he found objects with the king's name inside. Excavations by J.E. Gautier and G. Jéquier in 1894 were followed by work by the Metropolitan Museum of Art between 1906 and 1943. Arnold renewed study at the site from 1984 to 1987. More traces of pyramid-building have been found here than at any other pyramid. Quarries on the southeast, southwest and south of the pyramid furnished stone for its core. Ramps led from the quarries and harbour to the pyramid.

The base length of Senwosret I's pyramid – 200 cubits – surpasses all pyramids since Neferirkare,

and puts it in the class of the pyramids of Djedefre and Menkaure. Today, however, all that remains is a smallish hillock with its casing preserved up to eight courses in one spot. The pyramid's core is one of Senwosret I's innovations. A skeleton of eight walls radiates from the centre to the four corners and the middle of each side. The walls are built of huge, roughly shaped blocks which decrease in size towards the top. Each of the eight triangular sections is subdivided by three cross walls. The resulting 32 compartments were filled with slabs of stone set in steps. Backing stones rest on the steps, behind the pyramid's outer casing, which together form an exoskeleton. The framework and fill must have been built together as the pyramid rose.

Senwosret's masons used wooden cramps to join adjacent casing blocks, as shown by sockets cut for them and actual examples incised with Senwosret's name. A small step was cut in the foundation blocks and the lowest course of casing was laid directly above it, so that the baseline of the pyramid was formed by the court pavement. Rather than providing support, this arrangement weakened the casing: multiple patches are visible where it survives and east of the entrance a crack zig-zags down the pyramid. Arnold believes another source of instability was an open construction shaft under the pyramid. The builders' struggles are further demonstrated by the unevenness of the base – up to 13–15 cm (5–6 in) difference between the entrance and two of the corners.

The entrance to the pyramid opened in the pavement of the court in the middle of the north side. It has been completely destroyed but fragments of reliefs from the chapel that once stood over it were

Outer enclosure with 9 queens' pyramids

N

0   100 m
0   300 ft

Entrance chapel

Sanctuary

Entrance hall

Satellite pyramid

Causeway

(Below) The Entrance Cut and sloping construction passage used to bring in materials for the burial chamber were superseded by the final, higher granite-lined pyramid passage.

Satellite pyramid

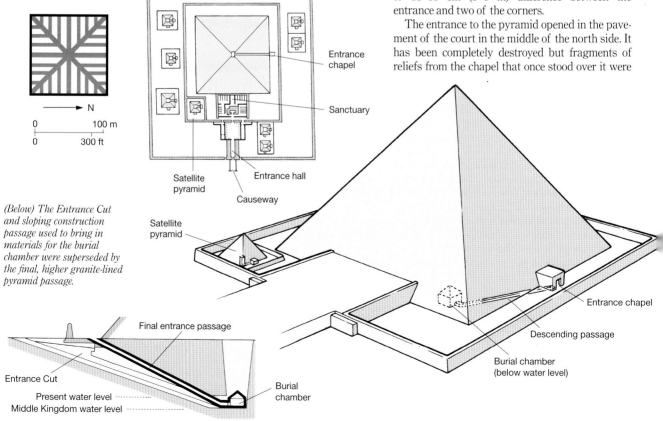

Final entrance passage

Entrance Cut

Present water level
Middle Kingdom water level

Burial chamber

Entrance chapel

Descending passage

Burial chamber (below water level)

found. The chapel fitted into a niche in the casing. Spouts in the shape of lions' heads allowed rain water to drain off the roof. The back wall of the chapel was mostly taken up by an alabaster false door, of which only fragments were found. Short wall panels to either side were decorated with gods. The entrance wall had scenes of butchering cattle and stacked offerings, while the side walls carried scenes of the king, with his *ka*, seated at an offering table, with lines of priests and offering bearers.

Inside the pyramid

Although the burial chamber of Senwosret I, like that of Amenemhet I, now lies below the water table and has never been entered by archaeologists, Arnold was able to make certain observations on the basis of careful analysis. Senwosret's builders began with a preliminary ramp or stairway north of the pyramid's north face, the Entrance Cut. Under the pyramid this ramp probably became a construction tunnel, though it has never been seen. At a higher level, and built later, was the sloping pyramid passage, too narrow to bring in anything except the king's body and burial goods.

The lower tunnel would have facilitated the excavation of a deep pit in which the burial chamber was built – as in the pyramids of Djoser, Djedefre and Zawiyet el-Aryan (Unfinished) and those of the 5th dynasty. From the slope of this tunnel and the pyramid passage, and from the rise in ground water, Arnold calculated that the burial chamber must lie 22 to 25 m (72 to 82 ft) below the surface.

When they began the sloping pyramid passage, the builders filled in the Entrance Cut apart from near the surface. Wood beams were laid in this section and buried in limestone chips and sealed with mud – the same materials as hauling tracks around the pyramid. This must have formed a slipway for the granite blocks – each weighing 8 tons – that lined the pyramid passage, except near the entrance where the lining is fine limestone. After the funeral, the passage was sealed with enormous granite plugs, weighing 20 tons, that fit the passage exactly. It is likely that the builders brought them in before they had completed the small and delicately decorated entrance chapel. The plugs slid down the passage, each hitting the next with a force that left fractures radiating through the blocks.

Arnold believes a large group of professional tomb robbers made their way to the burial chamber not long after the pyramid had been sealed. They dismantled the entrance chapel and, after repeated attempts, tunnelled their way around the granite blocking and lining of the passage. Maspero's workmen followed the robbers' tunnel to the point where it went round the second plug. Here they found the remains of the spoils from the king's burial that the plunderers had left behind: pieces of wooden boxes, alabaster containers, a gold dagger sheath and parts of four alabaster canopic vessels.

Rather than follow the robber's tunnel deeper into the pyramid, Maspero's workmen hammered away 30 m (98 ft) of granite plugging before – as would happen to later archaeologists, including Arnold in 1984 – they were halted by sand filling the passage and by water seeping through the masonry.

Arnold believes the sand may be fill left by Senwosret's workers to prevent the first granite plug from crashing into the horizontal passage to the burial chamber. A slight deviation of the passage is a clue that Senwosret followed the 5th-dynasty pattern of a burial chamber directly below the centre axis, perhaps entered from the antechamber to the east. If Senwosret's burial chamber is indeed under the vertical axis of his pyramid, it lies a frustrating 7 m (23 ft) from the archaeologists' stopping point.

Both Amenemhet I and Senwosret I showed a concern for placing chambers so deep that they were close to the level of the water table even when they were built. Amenemhet II, Senwosret II and Senwosret III would also use shafts and sloping passages to reach down close to the subterranean waters. This is one of several aspects that demonstrate a desire to connect with the realm of Osiris.

The pyramid complex

The valley temple has never been found, although it may lie under sand dunes and a Roman cemetery. The causeway was originally open, like those of Amenemhet I and Mentuhotep, flanked by limestone walls. A quarry inscription shows that it was built as late as Year 22 of Senwosret. In the next stage, a roof was added which required narrowing

The pyramid of Senwosret I is now only a low mound, just 23 m (75 ft) high. Here, the end of one wall of the internal framework skeleton is visible through the debris.

the passage by adding limestone blocks inside. Every 10 cubits there were niches, in which almost life-sized statues of the king were placed, wearing the red crown of Lower Egypt on the north and the white crown of Upper Egypt on the south. Eight complete statues were found, and some additional bases. It is not certain if the walls were decorated with relief scenes, but a painted dado was stippled red and black to imitate granite.

A doorway on the south side of the upper end of the causeway was connected to a small mudbrick building for priests or attendants. Mudbrick walls parallel to the stone walls of the causeway created a secondary lane on either side – a feature common to Middle Kingdom causeways. At the upper end, the outer lanes broadened into small courtyards with a gate leading into the pyramid's outer enclosure. Arnold's excavations in the northern court revealed that it had been used first as a site for cutting hard diorite, then for preparing gypsum. In its

Senwosret I in Osiride form, wearing the Crown of the South. This is one of a series of statues that lined the south side of the causeway. Those on the north side wore the Crown of the North.

A side panel from a throne of one of the statues found in a pit in the mortuary temple. Horus and Seth – here Lower (north) and Upper (south) Egypt – tie papyrus and lotus stems around a stylized windpipe, the hieroglyph for unity. The whole is topped by the cartouche of Senwosret I.

final phase, a small bath with a pottery pipe to drain it was installed. Here priests could ritually cleanse themselves before entering the outer enclosure to serve the cults of the queens' pyramids. Senwosret I surrounded his pyramid with two enclosures, defined by a outer wall of mudbrick and an inner enclosure wall of stone. The interior and exterior faces of the inner enclosure wall were decorated with 150 *serekh* panels.

Senwosret's mortuary temple was already badly destroyed when first excavated in 1894. It suffered further in later years, so that only a few blocks survive in place. Comparison with Old Kingdom examples reveals that it was very similar to mortuary temples from Teti to Pepi II. The front temple lay within the outer pyramid enclosure and the inner temple within the inner one. All the standard elements of the late Old Kingdom are present, though there is no evidence that alabaster, basalt or diorite were used and granite was used only sparingly.

In 1894 Gautier cleared a rectangular pit in an open area between the front temple and the enclosures of two subsidiary pyramids. It contained 10 complete limestone statues of Senwosret I seated on large, block-like thrones. These may have been set up under the colonnade of the temple court, but, as Arnold points out, they show no signs of weathering and the court lacks sockets for them. Perhaps the sculptors stopped work and the statues were buried after plans for the temple decoration were changed. The five niches in the statue hall – which Arnold reconstructed on the basis of Old Kingdom parallels though there were no traces – probably held standing statues.

Senwosret I built the last of the satellite pyramids and the only one known in a Middle Kingdom pyramid complex. It is more complicated than most, with two subterranean chambers and evidence of two or three phases of construction. In its first phase the pyramid was 15.75 m (30 cubits, 52 ft) square and the same height. The slope of 63° 26" 06' conforms to Old Kingdom satellite pyramids from Sahure on. In a later phase an enclosure wall was added to form a court entered by a doorway on the north. About the same time the pyramid was enlarged by the addition of a layer of casing and backing stones on the north and west, making a new base length and height of 18.38 m (35 cubits, 60 ft), bringing it closer to the standard Old Kingdom ratio to the main pyramid of 1:5.

The main shaft to the underground chambers lies under the southeast quadrant. At the bottom, two corridors led to chambers, both encased with limestone slabs. They are situated on the same axis but the northern one is slightly larger. Apparently the pyramid was built over the shaft before work was finished, so a new shaft was cut east of the centre of the pyramid's north side. Those cutting the new shaft seem to have had difficulty finding the chambers, only reaching them on their third

attempt. Robbers also found the chambers. Either they cleared them completely (except for some pieces of wood) or found them already empty, for nothing remained for the archaeologists.

The outer pyramid enclosure, defined by mud-brick walls, is a busy archaeological area. It contains priests' houses, granaries, low mudbrick walls, hauling tracks and slideways left over from building, numerous shallow pits for ritual burials of model dishes, ox bones and beads, and, in the western part, a mudbrick boat pit.

The pyramid cemetery extended well outside the royal enclosure. Here large and impressive mastaba tombs of high officials are found, such as those for the Vizier Mentuhotep with its own causeway, Imhotep, the High Priest of Heliopolis, named after his ancestor with the same title, and Senwosret-ankh, who had a copy of the Pyramid Texts in his burial chamber. Numerous small shaft tombs of those attached to these great households scatter about the large mastabas.

The nine subsidiary pyramids

Also within the outer enclosure are nine small pyramids, all about the same size except Pyramid 1 which seems to have been the first built. Each is situated in its own enclosure, except 8 and 9 which share one; each also had a chapel on the east and north. The angle of slope varied from 62° to 64°, the range of late Old Kingdom subsidiary pyramids. With the exception of Pyramid 1, the small pyramids seem to be paired: 3–4, 4–5, 6–7 and 8–9, suggesting a close relationship between two royal women. In their alignments and spacing they skilfully avoid the corners of the outer enclosure.

Rather than being planned as a set from the beginning, the series was built incrementally over a long time. Pyramid 9 may have been constructed as late as the reign of Amenemhet II or Senwosret II. It is curious, therefore, that, while the pyramids and their chapels were completed, including the relief decoration, the substructures seem never to have been finished. In fact it is not certain whether all received a burial. Although there are several shafts scattered around the base of each pyramid, none of those around 5, 6 and 9 led conclusively to a burial chamber associated with the pyramid.

The owners of only two of the pyramids have been identified. Pyramid 1 is assigned to Neferu, wife of Senwosret I, on the basis of three inscribed granite pieces. A shaft in the centre of the north side leads to a gently sloping corridor paved with limestone. This leads in turn to a chamber, lined with limestone, under the centre of the pyramid. In the floor is a receptacle for the sarcophagus, which was not found, and an unfinished niche was for the canopic chest. Neferu's chambers appear to have been neither completed nor used.

Pyramids 2 and 3 had two shafts each, one from the north to facilitate the construction of the sub-structure and a second to the east for access to the chambers after the first was sealed by the north chapel. Around Pyramid 2 were found many fragments of relief decoration from the east chapel and from a painted shrine that stood within it, as well as of 32-sided columns inscribed with the name of princess Itayket. Her burial chamber, sealed with mortared limestone slabs, was simply an extension of the entrance corridor. Although robbers had made a hole wide enough only to bring out small objects, no trace of sarcophagus, canopic chest or coffin were found. Pyramid 3 sat over a main burial chamber and a set of five burial niches. The main burial chamber, as under Pyramid 2, was formed by casing the end of the corridor with limestone slabs. It was blocked in three places by limestone slabs slid sideways on wooden skids in grooves cut into the passage. The chamber was almost filled by a beautiful quartzite sarcophagus and canopic chest. Pyramid 4 also contained a quartzite sarcophagus, but it was found parked in a crude side niche outside the limestone-cased burial chamber. There is no evidence it ever received a burial.

Red granite pyramidions may have crowned all nine pyramids – fragments were found close to Pyramids 3 and 5. Remains of an over life-sized granite female statue were found by Pyramid 6. Although Pyramids 8 and 9 form a pair, 9 was built with a core of mudbrick perhaps when, as Arnold suggests, all available building stone had run out.

Subsidiary Pyramids of Senwosret I

Pyramid	Enclosure	Base	Slope	Height	Shafts
1	100 x 75 c 52.5 x 39.37m	40 c 21m	62.5°	36 c 18.9 m	2
2	72 x 54 c 37.80 x 28.35 m	32 c 16.8 m	63.6°	16.8 m	2
3	50 x 50 c 26.25 x 26.25 m	32 c 16.8 m	63.25°	16.8 m	2
4	46 x 43 c 24.15 x 22.575 m	32 c 16.8 m	?	?	3
5	48 x 47 c 25.20 x 24.675 m	31 c 16.275 m	63.917°	31 m 16.275 m	?
6	49 x 56 c 25.725 x 29.4 m	30 c 15.75 m	?	?	?
7	49 x 49 c 25.725 x 25.725 m	30 c 15.75 m	?	?	?
8	47 x 86 c 24.675 x 45.15 m	30 c 15.75 m	?	?	1
9	Same as 8	30 c 15.75 m	?	?	? [c = cubits]

173

The Second Phase of Middle Kingdom Pyramids

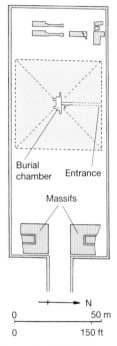

Amenemhet II's hybrid complex: a long rectangular precinct, as in the 3rd dynasty, orientated east–west as in the 4th, and with massive pylons, as in the 5th.

A pendant from a queen's tomb west of Amenemhet II's pyramid.

Amenemhet II began what Arnold sees as a second phase in the development of Middle Kingdom pyramids. Amenemhet I and Senwosret I, while incorporating innovative elements into their pyramids, were trying to revive the pyramid complex of the late Old Kingdom Memphite tradition. Amenemhet II gave this up and no consistent development is apparent in the pyramids that followed. Those who designed and built pyramids in the 12th dynasty seem to have been experimenting with new forms combined with old elements borrowed from earlier 11th- and 12th-dynasty complexes, the late Old Kingdom and even the 3rd dynasty.

New forms included long rectangular enclosures. Senwosret III's was oriented north–south, while Amenemhet II's was east–west. Amenemhet II situated his pyramid near the escarpment about halfway along the Dahshur plateau. From now on royal pyramids would alternate between Dahshur and the area around the mouth of the Fayum.

Amenemhet II's is one of the most poorly investigated and documented in the long sequence of pyramids. Jacques de Morgan excavated the site in 1894–5, but devoted much of his attention to the discovery of the jewellery and personal items of two princesses, Khnumet and Ita, whose burials he found among the row of tombs west of the pyramid within its enclosure wall.

Because of its proximity to the edge of the cultivation, the pyramid was quarried for the Turah limestone which formed the casing and the core skeleton of radiating walls, similar to the framework in Senwosret I's pyramid. Here, however, the cross compartments were filled with sand. When the pyramid was dismantled for its stone, the many limestone chips left behind prompted the modern name, 'White Pyramid'. Its ancient name was *Djefa Amenemhet*, 'Amenemhet is Provided'. Since no casing stones have been found we do not know the angle of the pyramid and as the base has never been adequately cleared its exact length is also unknown, though it is about 50 m (164 ft).

Inside the pyramid

The entrance is in the middle of the north side. A corridor slopes down to a short horizontal passage blocked by two portcullises, one of which slid vertically and the other sideways; beyond is the burial chamber. Four niches are connected to the chamber, one at either short end and two in the wall opposite the entrance corridor. These have been compared to the eastern niches of the Old Kingdom, thought to be for offerings or statues.

The sarcophagus, composed of sandstone slabs, was set into the floor against the west wall. Immediately in front of the entrance to the chamber a shaft drops a little less than 2 m (6 ft) to a passage leading north directly below the entrance corridor. A square hole sunk in the floor at the end of this passage may have been the receptacle for the canopic chest. The weight of the pyramid was diverted from the flat ceiling of the burial chamber by a hidden roof of six pairs of huge beams that lean against one another.

The pyramid complex

Amenemhet II returned to a broad, open causeway that sloped steeply down to the edge of the cultivation, but no one has searched for his valley temple. At the point where the causeway enters the pyramid enclosure on the middle of the east side, two massive structures recall the pylon-like thickenings in the same position in mortuary temples since Niuserre. The space between the massifs may be the entrance hall, but beyond that almost nothing is known about the layout of the temple.

Entrance passage and burial chamber of Amenemhet III's pyramid. The flat ceiling was protected by a roof of gabled beams. The hidden lower chamber was for the canopic chest.

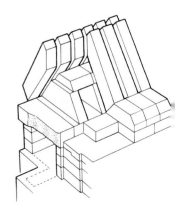

The Pyramid of Senwosret II

Senwosret II built his pyramid overlooking the opening of the Hawara Channel from the Nile Valley to the Fayum basin, near the modern village of Illahun. His choice reflects the growing importance of the Fayum in the Middle Kingdom. The pyramid was built around a stump of yellow limestone that was reserved in four steps when the perimeter was levelled. On this core, radial and cross walls were built of limestone to form a framework of compartments that were filled with mudbrick. Mudbrick was also used to build the upper part. The bottom course of the fine limestone casing was set into a foundation trench cut into the rock as a precaution against settling. As an additional measure, the base of the pyramid was surrounded with a cobble-filled trench to drain off rain water.

Inside the pyramid

Petrie spent months searching without success for the entrance to the pyramid, due to the fact that Senwosret II's pyramid marks a complete departure from the usual arrangement of an entrance on the north. Instead, the pyramid is entered by a narrow vertical shaft at the east end of its south side. The king's body and burial goods were probably carried down this shaft, but it was too narrow for the sarcophagus and blocks of the burial chamber, which may have been brought in by a wider shaft farther south, hidden beneath a sloping passage to the tomb of an unknown princess. This disguise, which required a radically new position for the pyramid's entrance, may be the architects' solution to the risk of the pyramid being robbed. That they regarded it as sufficient seems to be indicated by the fact that there was no blocking in the corridor.

At a depth of 16 m (52 ft 6 in) below the surface the construction shaft opens into a horizontal corridor which runs to a hall with a vaulted ceiling. From a niche at the east end of the hall a 'well', the bottom of which has never been reached, drops to

Mudbrick Pyramids

the water table. The corridor continues, rising at slight angle, with a chamber on the west. After an antechamber at a right-angle, a short additional section leads to the burial chamber, entirely clad in granite and with a gabled roof. This lies not under the centre of the pyramid but under its southeast quadrant. The red granite sarcophagus takes up

The pyramid of Senwosret II had a base length of 106 m (348 ft). With a slope of 42° 35' it rose to a height of 48. 6 m (159 ft).

Senwosret II's pyramid, the first of the giant mudbrick pyramids, was built over a reserved bedrock stump. Inside, all that remained of the king's burial goods was this uraeus. The cobra's body was of solid gold set with green faience, feldspar and carnelian, the head was carved from lapis lazuli with garnet eyes.

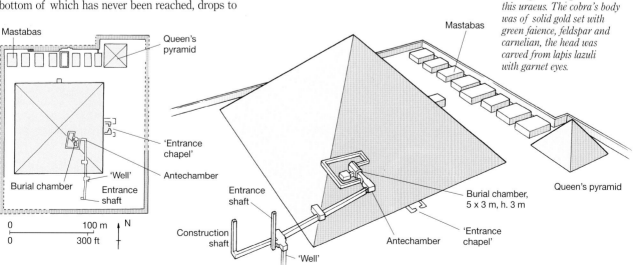

A diorite statue of the young Senwosret II, from Nag-el-Medamud.

the west end of the burial chamber. In front of it, an alabaster offering table was inscribed for Senwosret II. From the southeast corner of the chamber a short passage leads to a side room where Petrie found all that was left of the royal burial, lying in the dusty debris – a gold uraeus that once adorned the king's head band. Leg bones, presumably of the king, were also found.

A passage opens in the south wall of the corridor between the antechamber and burial chamber and then almost loops around the burial chamber, re-entering it in the northwest corner at the head of the sarcophagus. Stadelmann has pointed out that this last section allows a symbolic exit of the king's spirit to the north – it would then pass through the pyramid to emerge in the 'entrance' chapel built in the traditional spot at the centre of its north side. This arrangement reflects the old idea of the king's ascension to the circumpolar stars, but there may be an additional theme in the circuitous corridor. It created a subterranean 'island' – an important symbol of Osiris, whose worship was on the rise during the 12th dynasty at Abydos. The 'well' and the cobble-filled trench may also be reflections of the Osiris myth.

The pyramid complex

The inner enclosure wall had limestone casing that was decorated with niches, which, like Senwosret I's, is a nod to Djoser's complex and Archaic funerary enclosures. Rows of trees of unknown variety were planted parallel to the outer enclosure wall of mudbrick. The grove surrounding the 'mound' is another strong Osirian symbol. It would have been interesting to see if these new ideas found expression in the mortuary temple on the east side of the enclosure, but its ground plan is unknown. Numerous fragments attest to the use of granite with incised decoration. Senwosret retained a broad open causeway but we do not know how it attached to the enclosure or temple.

Within the north side of the outer enclosure, the builders began eight mastabas by isolating blocks of bedrock that they then built over with mudbrick – the same method as the pyramid. These were in addition to the tombs of princesses. At the north end of the row is a small pyramid, originally 27.6 m (90 ft 6 in) square and rising to a height of 18 m (59 ft). Although Petrie discovered foundation deposits, he never found a single passage or chamber beneath the pyramid, despite exploring it with tunnels and a deep vertical shaft. He did uncover the remains of a chapel at the north side. Part of a name on a vase, together with its position, are the only evidence that the pyramid belonged to a queen. If it is a satellite pyramid, it, and not Senwosret I's is the last satellite pyramid, though these are traditionally south of the mortuary temple.

Senwosret II's causeway has never been investigated. The location of the valley temple is known but its ground plan was destroyed. Immediately to the northwest of it lay the foundations of part of Senwosret II's pyramid town, named *Hetep Senwosret*, 'May Senwosret be at Peace'. The footprint of this town is one of the basic documents for the study of the history of Egyptian urbanism.

The Treasure of Illahun

In 1913 Guy Brunton and Petrie examined the plundered tomb of a princess named Sit-Hathor-Iunet. They found her red granite sarcophagus and canopic jars, but very little of her funerary furniture until they discovered a recess, plastered over,

In the tomb of Sit-Hathor-Iunet, daughter of Senwosret II and aunt of Amenemhet III, were found her canopic jars (left) and a pectoral (below left) with the cartouche of Senwosret II (the reverse side is shown here).

containing five boxes, two of which were of inlaid ebony. These contained the princess's necklaces, bracelets, anklets, scarab rings, mirror, razors and cosmetic containers. This 'Treasure of Illahun' also included a diadem formed of a band of gold adorned with a uraeus similar, though smaller, to that found in the king's pyramid. Her mirror was a disk of silver with a black obsidian handle in the form of an open papyrus, partly plated with electrum, with a face of Hathor. Two pectorals of chased gold inset with semiprecious stones revealed details of the life and death of the princess. One formed the hieroglyphic name of Senwosret II, her father, and the other was the name of Amenemhet III, her nephew.

The Pyramid of Senwosret III

Senwosret III returned to Dahshur to build his pyramid northeast of Sneferu's North Pyramid. It was built directly on the desert gravel with a core of mudbricks laid in stepped horizontal courses. The bricks are of different sizes, suggesting that standardized moulds were not used. Some still retained signs inscribed with a finger in the wet clay, apparently to monitor work. The bricks were laid without mortar – instead sand filled the seams. Turah limestone blocks joined with dovetail cramps formed the casing. The bottom course rested on a foundation, built in a trench, of roughly squared blocks on three courses of mudbrick. Behind the outer casing the builders laid backing stones on the mudbrick steps to tie casing and core together.

The pyramid of Senwosret III at Dahshur had a mudbrick core, covered with a casing of fine limestone – blocks of the casing were bonded with dovetail cramps (below, right). On its east side was chapel.

Labels: Magazine, Antechamber, King's burial chamber, Entrance, Queens' pyramids

(Below) Senwosret's enclosure was expanded to create a 'Djoser-type complex, with south temple and an entrance at the far south end of the east side.

The pyramid's side length is calculated as 105 m (345 ft). Casing blocks were found with an angle of 56° 18' 35", from which the original height was worked out as 78 m (256 ft).

Labels: N, 0 100 m, 0 300 ft, Boats, South Temple, Second enclosure, Weret's burial, King's burial, Entrance, 'Entrance chapel', East Temple

Inside the pyramid

Jacques de Morgan, the first archaeologist to enter the pyramid, tunnelled extensively into and under it before, in November 1895, he hit upon an ancient robber's tunnel that led him to the king's chambers. The real entrance lay outside the pyramid's base at the north end of west side. From here a passage slopes under the pyramid, then turns south to an antechamber. A small magazine opens to the east and the burial chamber lies to the west, an arrangement similar to that of late Old Kingdom pyramids. The burial chamber was built in granite but the walls were completely whitewashed with gypsum;

the granite sarcophagus filled its west end and a niche in the south wall was for the canopic chest. In the north wall a blocked opening is a corridor that communicated directly with the entrance passage. Above the vaulted granite roof of the burial chamber Arnold found a second 'stress relieving' gabled roof of five pairs of limestone beams, each weighing 30 tons. Above this was a third, mudbrick vault.

All that was found in this part of the pyramid were pottery vases and pieces of a bronze dagger with an ivory handle. There was nothing but dust in the sarcophagus. The lack of a canopic burial or other objects, and the absence of a blocking system, prompts the question whether Senwosret III was buried here. He built another tomb, perhaps his real burial place, at Abydos (p. 178).

The pyramid complex

As with so many other pyramid layouts, Senwosret III expanded his in at least two phases. In the first, his outer enclosure was nearly square and contained the inner enclosure wall, the pyramid with a small temple at the centre of its east side and an 'entrance chapel' at the centre of its north side and shaft tombs of royal women. In the second phase, the enclosure was extended both north and south.

(Below) A black granite statue of Senwosret III from Deir el-Bahri.

The king as double-plumed griffin trampling his enemies – order defeats chaos – on the pectoral of Merit, from her tomb under the north side of Senwosret III's pyramid enclosure.

zines and entrance chamber. The walls were decorated with panels containing the royal name and titles. These, like the interior decorations, were executed in very high relief. Based on comparisons with Old Kingdom chapels, fragments of scenes of deities moving towards the king must come from an antechamber in which lower registers showed rows of officials and the slaughter of cattle. An inner offering chamber seems to have had the standard repertoire: the king enthroned before an offering table, with rows of offering bearers, the offering list, cattle slaughter and gifts.

The south temple was also completely destroyed, probably in Ramessid times, though Arnold could read its outline in the preserved foundations. The fragments suggest two sections: a forecourt, with papyrus bundle columns, and rear sanctuaries. Fragments of lotus columns were also found. The reliefs depicted the king in the typical cloak worn for the Sed festival. Deities, such as the ram-headed gods Khnum and Herishef, played a prominent role. Arnold believes the south temple may be a precursor of New Kingdom mortuary temples at Thebes.

The southern extension enclosed a new temple. A causeway was also added in this phase.

No valley temple is known so far. The eastern mortuary temple is small in comparison to previous examples but it was so thoroughly destroyed that it is hardly possible even to reconstruct its plan. Arnold sees its size as evidence of the decline of the traditional mortuary cult, reduced to the offering hall with granite false door, storage maga-

Senwosret III's Abydos Tomb

In addition to a long and curving substructure, Senwosret III's Abydos complex included a small terrace on the cliff, a large T-shaped enclosure, a long desert road and a temple – all aligned on a northeast–southwest axis.

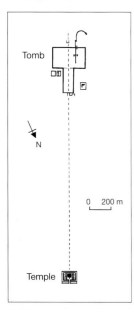

We should include Senwosret III's Abydos tomb in our survey because its layout has many similarities with a pyramid complex. That Senwosret should build another tomb, which some see as his cenotaph, at Abydos is consistent with a rising interest in the cult of Osiris in the Middle Kingdom. It was about this time that the tomb of the 1st-dynasty king, Djer, at Abydos (p. 75), was remodelled as a tomb of Osiris. Senwosret III's complex is immense. Stretched out over 900 m (2,953 ft), it consists of two main parts: an extensive subterranean tomb that opens within a T-shaped enclosure at the foot of the cliffs; and a mortuary temple at the edge of the desert.

The tomb opens via a long dromos in the north side of the court at the back of the enclosure. The builders used a variety of defences – dummy chambers, entrances hidden high in chamber walls, passages filled with blocks and shafts – against robbers. But endlessly persistent thieves got past all

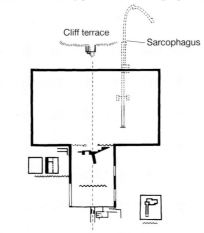

Cliff terrace

Sarcophagus

the ingenious devices, to reach the final chambers at the end of a curving passage. On tearing down much of the cladding here which could have hidden the royal burial they found nothing. But when they removed the quartzite facing of a previous chamber they found their royal quarry. Behind the cladding of the west wall lay the granite sarcophagus, fitted in a niche, while the canopic chest was built into the opposite corner of the chamber. The lid had been forced up and broken and the sarcophagus emptied.

A long road connected the great enclosure with a temple near the cultivation, which consisted of a limestone chapel flanked on either side by magazines and houses. The central building was fronted by a heavy mudbrick pylon and forecourt with fluted columns. As in many pyramid temples, an altar or offering table stood in the northwest part of the court. An elaborate system of channels facilitated the draining of purification water or other fluids. Relief fragments show that the decoration was similar to Old Kingdom offering halls, but a new element is the frequent reference to Osiris. Two large seated quartzite statues of the king graced the front of the chapel inscribed for Senwosret III, 'beloved of Osiris-Khenti-Amentiu, Lord of Abydos' and 'beloved of Wepwawet, Lord of the Necropolis'. Smaller calcite statues stood in the back hall.

There is evidence of 200 years of cult service to the memory of Senwosret III in this temple. The heart of the layout is the tomb, with one of the most complex defence systems of any royal sepulchre. Yet it was made to look like a cenotaph. Perhaps Senwosret and his planners thought that the best defence of all was to bury the royal mummy in the 'false tomb', the cenotaph in the tradition of Abydos, as opposed to the pyramid, which for generations had traditionally been the king's real tomb.

On the north of his pyramid was a subterranean gallery of graves for royal women, more complex than the four superstructures might suggest. A principal shaft gave access to a long vaulted corridor connecting four sets of chambers, each for a sarcophagus and canopic chest, plus one or two niches. Another gallery on a lower level communicated with 8 niches containing sarcophagi, two of which were inscribed – for princesses Ment and Senet-senebti. In a pit in the central corridor of the lower gallery de Morgan found a chest, once inlaid with the name Sit-Hathor, containing 333 pieces of her treasure. A gold pectoral spelled the name of Senwosret II and a scarab was inscribed with that of Senwosret III. The next day he found another treasure, belonging to Princess Merit, which contained many of the same elements as Sit-Hathor's but was even more extensive. It included a pectoral of Senwosret III and another of Amenemhet III.

On the south side of the king's pyramid were more tombs of royal women. In 1994 the shaft of 'mastaba' 9 was discovered. A tunnel leads to an antechamber, burial chamber and canopic chamber actually under the southwest corner of the king's pyramid. A granite sarcophagus fills the west end of the burial chamber, the floor of which was littered with pottery, wood, a few alabaster fragments and scattered bones. The name Weret, wife of Senwosret II and mother of Senwosret III, was found on a canopic jar and an inscribed board. It is interesting that the queen mother was buried under the southwest quadrant of her son's pyramid, given the emphasis on that direction throughout pyramid history. Outside this corner of Senwosret's enclosure was a mudbrick-vaulted building buried in the desert. Immediately to the east of this was a 'fleet' of at least six wooden boats, possibly more, each 6 m (20 ft) long. One or more wooden sleds were buried along with them.

In 1997, Dieter Arnold's investigations uncovered evidence that the seven superstructure bases north and south of the pyramid in its inner enclosure belonged in fact to small pyramids and not mastabas, as had previously been thought.

The Pyramid of Amenemhet III at Dahshur

Amenemhet III, son and successor of Senwosret III, ruled for 46 years. A builder's graffito from his pyramid casing dates to Year 2, suggesting that he began his pyramid as early as the first year of his reign when he was about 20 years old. Jacques de Morgan excavated the pyramid in 1894–5, and Dieter Arnold worked here in 1976–83. At only 33 m (108 ft) above sea level, it is one of the lowest pyramid locations. Perhaps Amenemhet III wanted to take advantage of Lake Dahshur, but his decision to build a pyramid here would be its undoing.

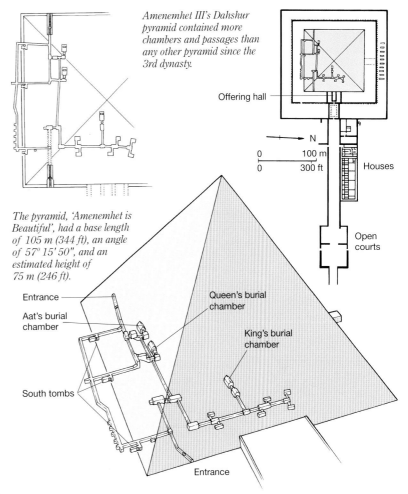

Amenemhet III's Dahshur pyramid contained more chambers and passages than any other pyramid since the 3rd dynasty.

Offering hall

N

0 — 100 m
0 — 300 ft

Houses

Open courts

The pyramid, 'Amenemhet is Beautiful', had a base length of 105 m (344 ft), an angle of 57° 15' 50", and an estimated height of 75 m (246 ft).

Entrance
Aat's burial chamber
Queen's burial chamber
King's burial chamber
South tombs
Entrance

In contrast to his father's north–south enclosure, with many elements reminiscent of Djoser's complex, Amenemhet III returned to the east–west layout of the post-3rd-dynasty pyramid complex. For his second pyramid, however, at Hawara, he preferred the Djoser-type of layout.

The pyramid's core was formed entirely of mudbrick without a framework of stone walls. The large mudbricks bear symbols impressed with a

A tower of mudbrick is the remnant of the core of Amenemhet III's pyramid at Dahshur after the outer casing of fine limestone had been robbed.

(Above left) An unusual archaizing statue probably showing Amenemhet III. On the pyramidion intended for his Dahshur pyramid (above, right) Amenemhet's eyes 'Behold the Perfection of Re'. Carved from black granite, it measures 1.87 m (c. 6 ft) per side and 1.31 m (4 ft 3 in) high. The composition represents Amenemhet III, resurrected from (and as) the mound of his pyramid, looking towards the sungod.

Amenemhet III's Dahshur sarcophagus was a reduced copy in granite of Djoser's enclosure wall, including a larger doorway bastion at the far south end of the east side. A pair of eyes at the opposite end are, magically, the king's, who gazes in the direction of the rising sun, image of rebirth.

finger in the wet clay. The outer mantle was formed of Turah limestone casing and backing blocks, both joined by dovetail joints or cramps.

Remarkably, the pyramidion was found in 1900 in debris along the eastern base. The edges of the underside are bevelled to allow it to be set into a socket of the casing block below. Near the base of all four sides is a band of hieroglyphs; on the side that would have faced east is an additional design. Due to its good condition, it has been questioned whether it was ever set in place. When Amenemhet III began a pyramid at Hawara, his Dahshur pyramid was not abandoned – was the pyramidion kept in the temple, like the *ben-ben* of Heliopolis?

Inside the pyramid

The pyramid has two entrances, opposite each other at the south end of the east and west sides. For the first time since the 3rd dynasty these take the form of stairways and lead to more chambers and passages than in or under any other pyramid since the 3rd dynasty. The eastern stairway ends in a small chamber with a vaulted roof. A niche high in the south wall was for the king's canopic chest. A short stairway in the north wall leads to a series of corridors, corridor-chambers and side chambers strung out underneath the entire east quadrant of the pyramid. In the burial chamber the sarcophagus lies at the west end, just east of the pyramid's central axis. The entire substructure is cased in white limestone.

Directly under the south baseline of the pyramid a chamber lined with Turah limestone is a *ka*-chapel, with six more small chapels beyond the pyramid's baseline. These form the counterpart of the burial chamber and the six chambers of the king and may have had the same significance as Djoser's South Tomb and later satellite pyramids. It seems the satellite pyramid has moved in and under the main pyramid – as do the queens tombs.

The western stairway entrance leads to two sets of passages and chambers for two queens under the southwest quadrant of the pyramid. The first to the west ends in a rectangular chamber with a niche for a canopic chest for a queen named Aat. Here the canopic niche is in the east wall and, as in the king's layout, it was above a stairway leading to the burial chamber. After a short passage and two antechambers is the burial chamber which contains Aat's sarcophagus. Although thieves had been inside long before archaeologists, they overlooked two maceheads, seven alabaster cases, in the form of ducks, an alabaster unguent jar and scattered pieces of jewellery. The canopic chest was broken but complete and one of the four canopic jars was present. Like the king, Aat had her own *ka*-chapel reached by a corridor leading south from her entrance corridor.

Arnold believes that Aat's burial complex was planned from the beginning of the pyramid. Before work was finished, plans were changed to include the burial of a second queen, east of Aat, with a layout similar to Aat's. Once again, robbers had entered but left some of the queen's possessions: an obsidian vase decorated with gold bands, three alabaster duck-shaped vessels, granite and alabaster maceheads and jewellery. She also had her own *ka*-chapel, located, like those of the king and Aat, exactly under the southern rim of the pyramid. Here Arnold found parts of her stone shrine, originally encased in gold and containing a *ka* statue – parts of a feminine wig remained. A canopic chest may indicate that in this period each *ka* burial had its own set of canopic vases. The bones of Aat and of the second queen show that they were aged 35 and 25 respectively.

Corridors connected the kings burial compartments with those of his two queens and probably facilitated bringing in construction materials. The plethora of turning corridors and chambers may mirror the winding ways of the Netherworld. But there is also a clear logical and spatial order to the principal elements. To the north lies the burial chamber containing the sarcophagus with a pair of eyes at the north end of the east side for the occupant to look out in the direction of sunrise and resurrection. The canopic chest lay to the south, on a higher level and overlooking the stairway down to the burial chamber. Farther south, and at the same level as the burial chamber, was the tomb of the *ka*.

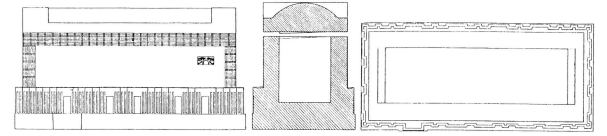

The substructure and most, if not all, of the superstructure of the pyramid, were finished by Amenemhet III's Year 15, though a considerable part of the queens' layouts had yet to be encased in limestone. It must have been about this time that the builders were alarmed by obvious structural stresses. The weight of the pyramid was pushing down the ceilings and walls so that they sank in some places up to 3 cm (2 in) below the pavements. When the settling of the pyramid caused door frames to buckle and pushed walls apart, fracturing them with long fissures, the workers quickly cased unfinished narrow rooms with mudbrick and roofed them with mudbrick vaults. They brought in cedar beams to roof and buttress broader chambers. While such measures prevented collapse, continuing to build in costly stone was out of the question. Like Sneferu, whose Bent Pyramid is due west, Amenemhet III began another pyramid.

What went wrong? Amenemhet III's planners founded the pyramid too close to the valley floor where the clay-like bedrock was further weakened by ground water. There were also too many rooms and corridors beneath the pyramid; and the builders placed too great a trust in their ceiling constructions which provided no real stress-relieving device above the king's chamber.

The pyramid complex

In spite of the fact that it would not be the royal grave, Amenemhet III's Dahshur pyramid had a temple, causeway and valley temple. His is the first 12th-dynasty valley temple to be located and partially cleared. It consisted simply of two broad open courts built on ascending terraces. The front and side walls of the first were thickened to form a pylon-like gateway. A short section of causeway led to the entrance and then continued from the back of the second court to the pyramid enclosure.

The mortuary temple was almost completely destroyed so that it is only an informed guess that it was reduced to a front court with papyrus-bundle columns and an offering hall. The existence of an 'entrance chapel' in the centre of the north side of the pyramid is not certain. Attached to the north side of the causeway is a rectangular block of rooms identified as priests' houses.

Aat may have been buried in Amenemhet III's Year 20, after which the pyramid was closed. The two entrance stairways, the king's chamber and antechambers, the queens' burial chambers, and the entrance corridors to the three *ka* chapels were filled to the ceiling with limestone blocks. Other chambers and corridors were filled with mudbrick. This may have been a precautionary measure against collapse, although corridors and chambers in the Hawara pyramid were similarly filled.

Fragments of Aat's false door and offering slab found in the buildings on the north of the causeway hint that the cults of the queens may have been carried out here, though it may previously have been a masons' workshop. The name of Amenemhet IV was found in the valley temple and it may have been during his reign that the pyramid was reopened to place sarcophagi in two chambers. Arnold wonders if these could have been for Amenemhet IV and the last regent of the 12th dynasty, Queen Sobekneferu. Two more burials bring the total to six royal family members laid to rest in the pyramid.

The guardianship of the pyramid was lax by the beginning of the 13th dynasty. Local inhabitants began to build granaries in the valley temple and the first breach of the pyramid happened about this time. There is evidence of restoration work perhaps 100 years later, when King Auibre Hor and his princess Nubheteptikhered were buried in two of the 10 shaft tombs in the north side of the outer enclosure. Were they descendants of the king's household, ruling, according to the Turin Canon, 12 kings after the end of the 12th dynasty?

The Pyramid of Amenemhet III at Hawara

Buried in the floor of the valley temple of Amenemhet III's Dahshur pyramid, the German excavators found an architect's model of a pyramid substructure (p. 227). While some details differ,

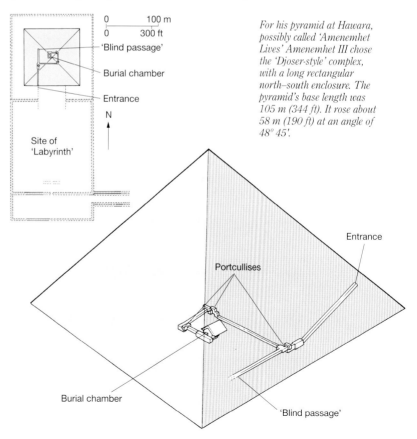

0   100 m
0   300 ft
'Blind passage'
Burial chamber
Entrance
N
Site of 'Labyrinth'

For his pyramid at Hawara, possibly called 'Amenemhet Lives' Amenemhet III chose the 'Djoser-style' complex, with a long rectangular north–south enclosure. The pyramid's base length was 105 m (344 ft). It rose about 58 m (190 ft) at an angle of 48° 45'.

Entrance
Portcullises
Burial chamber
'Blind passage'

Despite the fact that it now lacks its limestone mantle, the mudbrick core of Amenemhet III's pyramid at Hawara is still impressive. However, its vast temple, the legendary Labyrinth of Roman tourists, has been quarried down to a layer of stone chippings.

Amenemhet III ruled for 46 years, and, like his 4th-dynasty predecessor, Sneferu, built two large pyramids, albeit with mudbrick rather than stone cores.

there are similarities with Amenemhet III's second pyramid at Hawara. In his Year 15, Amenemhet III returned to the site of his grandfather's pyramid at the entrance to the Fayum, choosing a long spit of low desert. In design and location, this pyramid was a complete departure from that at Dahshur.

Richard Lepsius explored the Hawara pyramid in 1843. He mapped walls that he thought belonged to the large mortuary temple south of the pyramid, which he correctly identified as the site of the legendary Labyrinth. Petrie also explored the pyramid, reaching the burial chamber only after two seasons and great difficulty.

We are not certain of the name of Amenemhet III's Hawara pyramid. Rock inscriptions in the Wadi Hammamat speak of statues quarried for a building named 'Amenemhet-ankh, Who Always and Forever Lives in the House of the Fayumi, Sobek', possibly a name for the whole pyramid precinct; Sobek was the crocodile deity of the Fayum. The pyramid core was constructed entirely of mudbrick with an outer mantle of limestone. Like Sneferu, Amenemhet III built his second pyramid at a lower angle than his first, and probably for the same reason – as a precaution against the threat of collapse. The anxiety of his builders is reflected even more strongly in the plan of the substructure.

Inside the pyramid

The ground at Hawara was little better than that under the Dahshur pyramid, but the builders incorporated changes to protect the king's burial chamber from robbers and from the weight of the pyramid. There are far fewer tunnels and chambers and the main burial chamber was built near the base level of the pyramid.

The entrance, west of centre on the south side, is a stairway corridor sloping down to a level deeper than the burial chamber. At the bottom of the stairway is a small chamber from which a short passage leads to a dead end. Amenemhet III's builders then elaborated a device used in the Abydos tomb of Senwosret III: the route to the burial chamber con-

tinues as a short passage hidden in the ceiling. It was intended to be blocked by a massive slab of quartzite, weighing 20 tons, that could be slid sideways from a niche in the wall.

The ceiling passage leads to a second chamber, from which two passages depart. The first runs directly north. Petrie thought it was another blind passage and he had difficulty exploring it because it was filled with mud and water. The mud is probably disintegrated mudbrick that filled the passage. It is possible that the so-called blind passage might in fact lead to a south tomb, like that in the Dahshur pyramid. The second passage, once closed by a wooden door, makes a right-angled turn and runs directly east. At a point just under the southeast diagonal of the pyramid is a third chamber. After another right-angled turn the passage continues, hidden again in the ceiling and intended to be closed by another large quartzite slab. The third such arrangement is under the northeast corner, the only one actually closed by its quartzite blocking slab. From here a short passage leads to an antechamber. A channel in the centre of its south wall opens into the trench containing the burial chamber, slightly west of the pyramid's centre.

The burial chamber is a technical marvel and completely innovatory. It is beautifully carved from a single piece of hard sandstone or quartzite, in the form of a rectangular 'tub', measuring 7 x 2.5 x 1.83 m high (23 x 8 x 6 ft), set into an open trench. This was a considerable accomplishment since Petrie estimated it weighed 110 tons. Before roofing the chamber, the king's quartzite sarcophagus, its plinth decorated with niches, a second smaller sarcophagus and two canopic chests were placed in it. Although working under difficult conditions – the chamber was submerged in ground water – Petrie reported finding bits of bone inside the coffins.

In the antechamber Petrie found an alabaster offering table elaborately carved with depictions of food with hieroglyphic labels, and duck-shaped bowls. These objects bore the name of a princess Neferu-ptah. From Djoser to Amenemhet III, the male ruler, at the centre of a pyramid cemetery, was surrounded by royal women and it is the women's tombs that have given us some of the richest discoveries as well as the greatest puzzles of the pyramids – Neferu-ptah presents one of these. With a reduction in the number of chambers under the pyramid it may have been a logical development that Amenemhet III's favourite was buried with him in his burial chamber – two queens' tombs were incorporated within the substructure of his Dahshur pyramid. However, in 1956 another tomb for Neferu-ptah was found, southeast of Hawara, with a red granite sarcophagus inscribed with Neferu-ptah's name, along with other objects. In the waterlogged sarcophagus, were traces of two wooden coffins and fragments of linen bandages.

The mystery of Neferu-ptah is heightened by the fact that the pyramid burial chamber could be closed only once. Its roof was composed of three large quartzite slabs, one of which was propped up on smaller blocks to leave a space to introduce the king's (and queen's?) mummy and coffins. In order to close the burial vault, the Hawara builders installed the first known sand lowering device. Small pillars supporting the raised ceiling block rested in turn on sand filling shafts to either side of the vault. When the sand was removed by side galleries (that Petrie took for robbers' tunnels), the props descended and the ceiling slab with them, to close the vault. Not only would this quartzite vault not buckle as easily as the masonry chambers of the pyramid at Dahshur, but the builders also ensured that the weight of the pyramid would not press directly on it. The ceiling slabs extended beyond the sides of the vault to rest on a ledge cut in the sides of the bedrock trench. On top of the quartzite roof the builders set a row of triangular limestone blocks. These were then covered with a second roof of high gabled limestone beams set in pairs leaning against each other. Above this they built a third vaulted roof of mudbrick.

Pyramid complex as Labyrinth

The layouts of Amenemhet III's two pyramids are so different that we might wonder if there were ideological as well as practical reasons for having two. Measuring 385 x 158 m (1,263 x 518 ft) the Hawara enclosure, orientated north–south, was the largest of the Middle Kingdom pyramid enclosures. As with Djoser, the pyramid was in the north while the entrance was at the far south end of the east side where, as in Senwosret III's layout, an open causeway approached from the east. Between the entrance and the pyramid lay the 'mortuary temple' which here is something of a misnomer. This was apparently such an extraordinary architectural creation that it was seen by visitors in Classical times as a unique monument in a class of its own. They called it the Labyrinth, comparing it with the legendary Labyrinth of Minos at Knossos in Crete.

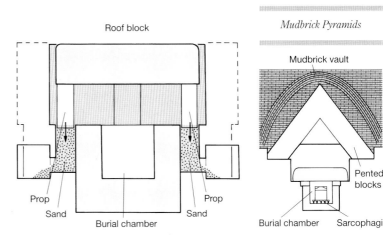

Roof block

Prop
Sand
Burial chamber
Prop
Sand

Mudbrick vault

Pented blocks

Burial chamber   Sarcophagi

The burial vault of Amenemhet III (above) was protected by triangular lintels, gabled beams and a mudbrick vault. The last great quartzite ceiling slab was lowered to close the vault (above, left) by an ingenious device. Sand which had supported props holding up the block was released via side tunnels, allowing the huge piece of stone slowly to descend to its resting place.

It is all the more frustrating, therefore, that the temple is almost completely lost to us. Quarried since Roman times, very little is left except a foundation bed of sand and limestone chips, which only hints at its vastness. This was not a labyrinth in the sense of nested passages and blind corridors. Its complexity instead arose from the replication of small courts and shrines, in an arrangement that Strabo called 'a palace composed of as many smaller palaces as were formerly nomes'.

All the Classical authors write of multiple courts but disagree on the number. Herodotus spoke of 12 main courts, and said the visitor was conducted 'from courtyards into rooms, rooms into galleries, galleries into more rooms, thence into more courtyards'. He mentioned lower rooms or crypts devoted to the sacred crocodile Sobek, noted also by Pliny the Elder. Close to the south side of the pyramid Petrie found remains of two great granite shrines, weighing 8 to 13 tons, each containing two figures of the king. These may have stood near their findspot at the back centre of the temple. Did they occupy a central place like the five statues in the Old Kingdom pyramid temples? Also close to the pyramid Petrie found the remains of a colossal granite statue of the king.

Other fragments must have belonged to statues that stood in the chapels and courts, including ones of the crocodile god, Sobek, as well as other deities like Hathor and an unusual palm goddess, statues of the king and offering bearers. Stadelmann sees these statues, probably assigned to their respective 'booths' and courtyards, as the translation into three dimensions of flat painted relief scenes that graced the walls of prior pyramid complexes. But the rows of chapels recall most strongly the Heb Sed court of Djoser, which was more abbreviated than the Labyrinth's fabled colonnaded courtyards. It seems fitting that Amenemhet III, who built the last major royal pyramid complex in Egypt, borrowed and elaborated the architectural expression of 'the palace composed of smaller palaces' from Djoser, the builder of the first great royal pyramid.

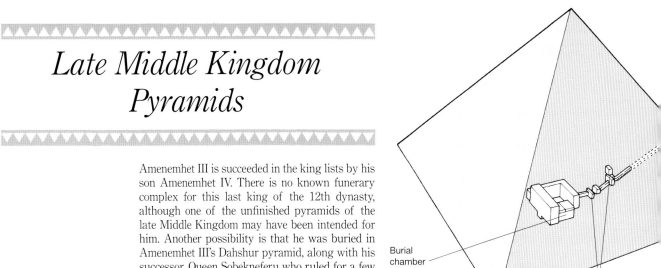

Amenemhet III is succeeded in the king lists by his son Amenemhet IV. There is no known funerary complex for this last king of the 12th dynasty, although one of the unfinished pyramids of the late Middle Kingdom may have been intended for him. Another possibility is that he was buried in Amenemhet III's Dahshur pyramid, along with his successor, Queen Sobekneferu who ruled for a few years in her own right. From the late 12th dynasty to the end of the 13th, while some 50 rulers are mentioned in texts over a period of about 143 years, only six to eight pyramids are known, not all of which were completed. Sites range from extreme South Saqqara in the north to Mazghuna, south of Dahshur. Once again, the lakes at the edge of the desert, particularly Lake Dahshur, may have had much to do with the choice of these locations.

The Pyramid of Central Dahshur

A poorly known pyramid south of Amenemhet II's may belong to this period. Fragments of limestone reliefs and the track of a causeway leading eastwards suggest some degree of completion. A fragment bearing the royal name Amenemhet could be derived from Amenemhet II's complex, or possibly belong to Amenemhet IV. The site was badly damaged by digging for a petroleum pipeline in 1975.

The Mazghuna Pyramids

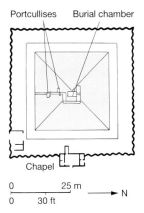

The southern Mazghuna pyramid had a wavy-wall enclosure and a fairly complicated substructure.

Amenemhet IV and Sobekneferu have been suggested as the owners of two unfinished pyramids at Mazghuna. However, the names of neither of these regents have been found at the sites.

The southern Mazghuna pyramid, about 4.8 km (3 miles) south of Sneferu's Bent Pyramid, was surrounded by a wavy-wall of the kind that we begin to see at earlier Middle Kingdom monuments. A broad entrance and vestibule were built into the far east end of the south side of the enclosure. Around the vestibule the ground was covered with a thick layer of limestone chips, suggesting that it was a work yard such as were found at the upper ends of the causeways of Senwosret I and Amenemhet III at Dahshur. A mudbrick chapel occupies the centre of the east side of enclosure consisting of a large central chamber, or court, and magazines to either side. An offering hall with a vaulted roof was attached to the southwest corner of the court.

The chapel indicates that a cult began, even though the pyramid superstructure was never finished. When excavated, the core consisted of one or two courses of brick, laid on edge on the desert gravel. No outer casing stones were found although a foundation trench indicated the intended pyramid baseline. The entrance opens in the centre of the south side to a stairway with shallow steps and side ramps sloping to a short horizontal passage.

At this point is the first of two great portcullis blocks. The lower part of the passage is blocked by a granite slab, so that when the plug was slid into place from its recess, it blocked the continuation of the passage at the higher level. From this higher opening another stairway ramp descends to the second portcullis. This is similar to the first except that the plug was left open. From here the route to the burial chamber was a series of corridors arranged in three turns around the burial chamber. A service chamber at the head of the burial chamber had a floor trench for introducing the burial down into the coffer. In this antechamber were found an alabaster vessel in the form of a trussed duck and three limestone lamps. A single block of red quartzite fills the chamber and is, in fact, an inner burial chamber like Amenemhet III's monolithic vault at Hawara. Receptacles for the coffin and the canopic chest were carved in the interior. Robbers made their way inside and left only a small alabaster kohl pot and a piece of glazed steatite.

The arrangement for closing the lid is another feature borrowed from the Hawara pyramid. Two large pieces of the lid rested on the rim of the vault, with a gap between. Slabs supported the missing lid piece and rested on sand-filled shafts. When the sand was removed through side tunnels, the props carried the middle part of the lid down.

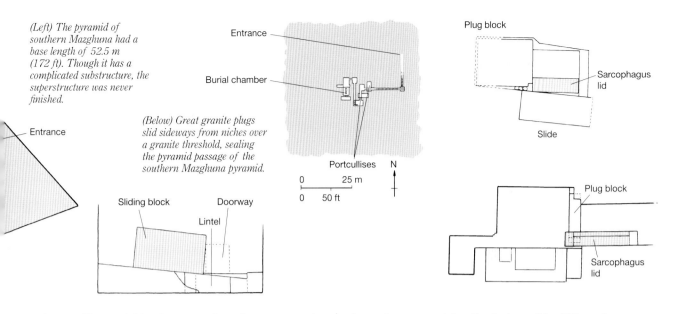

(Left) The pyramid of southern Mazghuna had a base length of 52.5 m (172 ft). Though it has a complicated substructure, the superstructure was never finished.

Entrance

(Below) Great granite plugs slid sideways from niches over a granite threshold, sealing the pyramid passage of the southern Mazghuna pyramid.

Entrance

Burial chamber

Portcullises

0   25 m

0   50 ft

N

Plug block

Sarcophagus lid

Slide

Sliding block

Lintel

Doorway

Plug block

Sarcophagus lid

A pyramid at north Mazghuna was planned on a larger scale than the southern one. The superstructure was never begun, and the system of closing the substructure – which resembles that of Ameny-Qemau but is more elaborate – was not used. The pyramid therefore may date well after the end of the 12th dynasty. Its position as the next pyramid south after Ameny-Qemau's may not be significant, since kings would shift back and forth between major pyramid sites.

The passage to the burial chamber here doubles back on itself in a U-shape before arriving at the chamber – a pattern also found in a Late Middle Kingdom pyramid at South Saqqara. A short stairway descends from the north on the east side of the pyramid. From a square chamber at the bottom, the passage turns a right-angle and continues as a stairway, sloping to the first portcullis chamber. A recess with a gigantic quartzite plug block, weighing 42 tons, opens to the north. This was meant to slide over a quartzite slab across the base of the passage and in front of a quartzite lintel at the top. Once in place, the assembly would have formed a wall of quartzite; the plug, however, was left open. The passage continued with right-angled turns, past a second portcullis similar to the first, although the block was smaller, and finally ends in an antechamber on the north of the burial chamber.

The burial chamber was filled by the sarcophagus vault, made from a quartzite monolith in which the coffin receptacle was fashioned in the north end and the canopic compartment in the south. Scarcely 2 cm (less than 1 in) of clearance was left between the sides of the vault and the burial chamber. To the north, the lid was still parked in a low chamber. This would have been slid over the top of the vault and locked in place by a slab pushed over from a side recess. All exposed quartzite was painted red, even the plug blocks. After carefully smoothing the

sarcophagus, the workers covered it with plaster which they also coloured red. On the painted surfaces they sometimes added series of vertical black strokes bounded by fine horizontal lines.

Outside the pyramid, mudbrick walls formed a causeway approaching from the east. This must have been the route for bringing in the massive plug blocks and burial vault, as well as other building materials. One block was found on the causeway where the builders may have left it when work was abruptly halted on this pyramid.

(Above) The northern Mazghuna pyramid was never finished, nor did it ever receive a burial – the lid of the sarcophagus was parked in its chamber and the blocking slab that would have been slid across to lock it in position was in its recess.

The Pyramid of Ameny-Qemau

One of the few 13th-dynasty pyramids to which we can attach a name is located close to the southeast rim of Lake Dahshur. Broken canopic jars from the pyramid bore the name Ameny-Qemau. His pyramid was originally about 50 m (164 ft) square. The burial chamber was shaped from a single block, like Amenemhet III's, with the receptacles for the sarcophagus and canopic chest formed together into the interior, like the north Mazghuna pyramid. The lid was slid on to the coffer from the entrance end of the chamber, after which it was locked in place by a sideways sliding portcullis slab.

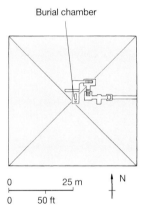

Burial chamber

0   25 m

0   50 ft

N

The pyramid of Ameny-Qemau, today barely visible in the surrounding landscape, originally had a base length of approximately 50 m (164 ft). Its substructure is now very badly damaged.

The Pyramid of Khendjer

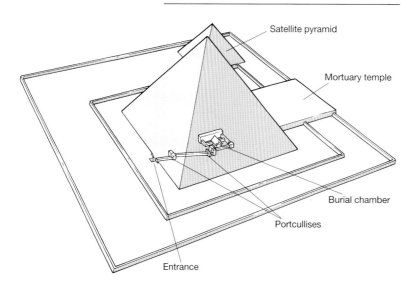

Satellite pyramid

Mortuary temple

Burial chamber

Portcullises

Entrance

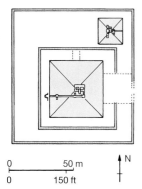

0 — 50 m
0 — 150 ft

N

The complex of Khendjer at South Saqqara is the only pyramid completed in the 13th dynasty. It had a base length of 52.5 m (172 ft) and rose to a height of 37.35 m (123 ft) at slope of 55°.

A black granite pyramidion, restored from numerous fragments, once brought Khendjer's pyramid to its point.

Khendjer was a pharaoh of the middle of the 13th dynasty whose Asiatic name may hint at Syrian or Palestinian ancestry. He sited his pyramid in far South Saqqara, between Pepi II's and Senwosret III's. This is the only known 13th-dynasty pyramid to have been completed. Originally it rose to a height of 37.35 m (123 ft) at a slope of 55° from a base 100 cubits (52.5 m/172 ft) square. Today its ruins rise just 1 m (3¼ ft). The core was mudbrick, with a mantle consisting of backing stones and a casing of limestone. Fragments of a black granite pyramidion were found on the east side.

Two enclosure walls surrounded the pyramid. The outer one contained, in the northeast corner, the only subsidiary pyramid known from the 13th dynasty. A mortuary temple on the east side spread across both inner and outer enclosures. All that remained of the temple were parts of the pavement and bits of reliefs and columns. A north chapel was built against the inner enclosure wall. In its north

wall was a yellow quartzite false door. Fragments of reliefs show standard scenes of offering bearers.

The inner enclosure wall was of limestone, patterned with niches and panels. This replaced an earlier wavy wall of mudbrick, which has prompted Stadelmann to suggest that the wave-form wall may be an abbreviated form of the niched wall, built as a provisional substitute under time constraints. A blocked, unfinished stairway in the southeast corner of the outer enclosure may indicate an earlier plan for the pyramid substructure, or the beginning of a south tomb for the royal *ka* that was never completed.

The pyramid entrance is towards the south end of the west side. A stairway ramp leads down to a portcullis chamber similar to those of the Mazghuna pyramids. The huge portcullis block in its recess was never slid across the passage. A second stairway of 39 steps continued on the same axis down to a doorway that had been closed with a double-leaf wooden door. A second portcullis, also left open, lay just beyond the wooden door.

Rather than indicating that the royal burial never took place, the open portcullises may suggest that, ultimately, these mighty closing devices were 'for show'. When the king was alive, he and his officials no doubt inspected work in progress. They would have been satisfied that such gigantic blocks of the hardest stone would protect the king's final resting place. However, once the pharaoh died it may have been relatively easy for a work crew to avoid the strenuous task of closing the plug blocks – particularly when other crews and even the palace had moved to another location.

Khendjer's second portcullis was installed at the corner of a trench in which the burial chamber was placed before the pyramid was built above it. The chamber was formed of a single huge quartzite block in which receptacles for the coffin and canopic chest were carved. Two quartzite beams formed the roof. Once the quartzite portcullis blocks and the sarcophagus chamber were in position, the builders roofed the corridors and built a gabled roof of limestone beams above the burial chamber. In addition they constructed a brick vault to relieve the weight of the superstructure.

The mechanism for closing the vault after the funeral was the same as in the Hawara and south Mazghuna pyramids. The props of the northern ceiling slab rested on sand-filled shafts. When the sand was drained through tunnels, the ceiling slab lowered on to the vault. It would have been necessary to scoop out the last of the sand, and workmen probably used short wooden supports to allow them to do this. The workers escaped through the tunnels, which they filled with masonry. Finally, they paved over the openings into the corridors.

The small subsidiary pyramid had a simpler corridor and closure system. A stairway ramp leads to a corridor through two portcullises to a central antechamber from which two burial chambers branch north and south. Both of these contained quartzite coffers. The lids were found propped on blocks, the coffers never closed. This small pyramid is generally considered as the burial place of a queen rather than as a satellite, or *ka*, pyramid of the king. However, while the last of the *ka* pyramids, which were always on the south or southeast of the main pyramid, was found in Senwosret I's complex at Lisht, it too had two chambers lined with masonry, on the north and on the south.

The Southern South Saqqara Pyramid

Southwest of Khendjer's pyramid lies the substructure for another unfinished pyramid. With a side length of about 150 cubits (78.75 m/258 ft) it was planned on a larger scale than Khendjer's. A wavy enclosure wall surrounds the site, but there is no evidence of cult buildings. A remarkable find here was two pyramidions before the entrance near the centre of the east side. Both are of black granite – one was polished smooth while the other was only roughly finished, with a truncated top. Two pyramidions in front of a pyramid for which the superstructure was hardly begun suggest that capstones could be brought to the site well in advance of the pyramid's completion – a note of caution against using Amenemhet III's pyramidion as evidence that his Dahshur pyramid reached its apex. One of the pyramidions may have been for a subsidiary pyramid. No inscription was found on them, or anywhere else on the site, to indicate the name of the king for whom this pyramid was begun.

This unfinished pyramid has a surprisingly elaborate substructure, similar to that of the north Mazghuna pyramid in the way the route to the burial chamber switches back on itself in a U-pattern. A long stairway ramp leads down to the first of three large side portcullises. There are the usual wider chambers at the turns, and a blind corridor runs parallel to a shorter stairway and chamber. These lead to a narrow passage, past the other two great portcullises to an antechamber and then to the main burial chamber. This chamber was again formed from a colossal quartzite block, here weighing 150 tons and with the sarcophagus and canopic compartments hewn into its interior. The chamber was intended to be closed by the system of sand-filled shafts. Like the portcullises, this closure system was never put into effect, the lid was left on its props.

An unusual feature is a second burial chamber to the north of the first, entered by a small stairway from the antechamber. This chamber had the same kind of closure system as in the pyramids of Ameny-Qemau and north Mazghuna – a horizontally sliding lid. A separate canopic compartment

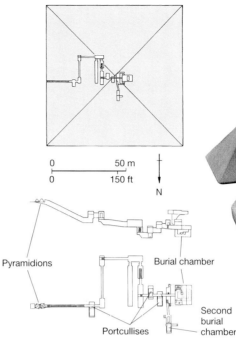

0   50 m
0   150 ft
N

Pyramidions

Burial chamber

Second burial chamber

Portcullises

The superstructure of southern South Saqqara pyramid was barely begun, but it was planned to have a base length of 78.75 m (258 ft) and had a well-built and elaborate substructure.

A pair of pyramidions was found at the entrance of the southern South Saqqara pyramid, although the pyramid's superstructure was hardly begun. Were they meant to be raised as the pyramid was being built, in order to solve the problem of transport to the top?

was provided in a niche off one corner of the chamber. This second burial chamber has been considered a queen's burial room or a 'decoy' to thwart robbers. However, if they got this far, robbers could hardly have missed the main chamber. Another possibility is that it is a *ka* tomb, but these are usually to the south of the main chamber.

Stadelmann points out that the workmanship of this tomb – the masonry of fine Turah limestone casing the corridors, painted in places to imitate granite, the unsurpassed construction of the burial chamber, and the elaborate closure system, to which we can add the large base length laid out for the superstructure, suggests that the pyramid was begun for a significant, or at least an ambitious, ruler. His plans for the Afterlife, however, did not come to fruition, at least not in this monument.

There may be at least two more pyramids of the 13th dynasty near Ameny-Qemau's in South Dahshur. These were first noted by Dieter Arnold and Rainer Stadelmann. They have yet to be explored and so beyond their probable Late Middle Kingdom date, little else is known about them.

The half-dozen attempts to build pyramids in the traditional zone of the Memphite cemeteries attest, on the one hand, to the confidence of kings early in their reigns and a persistent presence of skilled and experienced teams of royal quarrymen, masons and work crews who could, for example, hew and haul gigantic blocks. On the other hand, the same pyramids, of which only Khendjer's may have been completed, testify to short reigns, and, as Kemp pointed out, to the 'inability to promote the construction of a monumental court cemetery' by the ruling households.

New Kingdom Pyramids

Now covered in spoil heaps, the Dra Abu el-Naga plain was once crowned by a line of thin, pointed royal pyramids.

On the eve of the golden age of the New Kingdom, as they struggled to reunite Egypt, pharaohs of the 17th dynasty would build the last royal pyramid tombs in Egypt.

Pyramid tombs of the 17th dynasty

Opposite Karnak, already the temple of Amun in the late Second Intermediate Period, lies the Dra Abu el-Naga cemetery. Here a landing, personified later as *Khefet-hir-nebes*, 'Opposite her Lord', was the start of the road to the royal tombs. In later times it led to the wadi road to the Valley of the Kings. The 17th-dynasty pyramid tombs stretched from here to Mentuhotep's causeway to the south.

Until recently, our sources of information about this series of six or seven royal tombs were very limited. They are listed, along with those of the 11th dynasty, in the Abbott and Leopold-Amherst Papyri, reports of a commission appointed during the reign of Ramesses IX in the 20th dynasty to investigate allegations of tomb robbing (p. 165). Excavations, carried out under the authority, but unfortunately often in the absence of Mariette, were mostly unpublished. There was also some illicit digging by villagers from nearby Qurnah.

The pyramids at Dra Abu el-Naga were probably not much more than 20 cubits (10.5 m/34 ft) at the base. They must have appeared as a row of very thin, pointed pyramids. Simple plastering or white-wash replaced stone casing on these mudbrick pyramids, which have all but disappeared. They were apparently capped by pyramidions, as shown by that of Sekhemre-Wepmaat Intef V. It is damaged, but the four sides are inscribed with the name and titles of the king.

A small cult chapel, probably with a vaulted ceiling, was built in front of and sometimes against the small pyramids. The pyramid of the tomb of Nubkheperre Intef VI, which Mariette excavated in 1860, must have been on the higher ledge of rock above the terrace on which the chapel stood – although Mariette did not report finding remains of a pyramid. He did find two small obelisks inscribed with the royal name and titles, and similar ones may have flanked the fronts of all the chapels. The tomb robbery papyri also suggest that a stela was placed at the back of the chapel. A pit or stairway which led to the rock-cut burial chamber was sunk in the floor of the chapel or in an open front court.

This was the sum of our knowledge until 1991, when the first systematic archaeological investigation of the Dra Abu el-Naga cemetery was begun by Daniel Polz for the German Archaeological Institute in Cairo, later in collaboration with the University of California at Los Angeles. The royal tombs have not yet been located with certainty, but Polz has found three or four rock-cut tombs that are likely candidates. One of these, in addition to two large forecourts, has a mud mass that could be the remains of a pyramid. A passage leads to a hall with four pillars where a vertical shaft drops 10 m (33 ft). From the bottom a passage, already cleared in the 1920s, leads to an anthropoid recess sunk in the floor which once contained the wooden coffin.

It is interesting to compare these results with the descriptions of local villagers who found the tomb

of Intef VI in 1827, 33 years before Mariette. They might have seen the interior as it was left by the 20th-dynasty commission, 'in the course of being tunnelled into by thieves' but not yet robbed. The villagers are said to have found the mummy of the king in his coffin inside a sarcophagus cut from the natural rock, free-standing but attached at the bottom. With the king's body were two bows, six flint-tipped arrows, a diadem on the king's head and a gold-mounted scarab over his heart.

Polz is also revealing the context of these last royal pyramid tombs. In the plain at the northern part of Dra Abu el-Naga the expedition is clearing a cemetery of household tombs with great social diversification. He estimates that some 17,000 people were buried in this cemetery of Theban households, dominated by the pyramid tombs of the kings along the hillside.

In 1913 H.E. Winlock found a small pyramid, measuring only 8 m (26 ft 3 in) square, with a slope of 66°, in the area called Birabi at the north foot of Mentuhotep's causeway, which he thought might have belonged to the tomb of Kamose, the elder brother of Ahmose I.

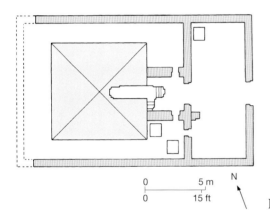

(Above) Could this be the pyramid of Kamose? This is what Winlock suggested when he found this small pyramid, only 8 m (26 ft 3 in) square, with a slope of 66° near the south end of Dra Abu el-Naga.

(Left) The pyramidion of Sekhemre-Wepmaat Intef V was found at Dra Abu el-Naga. It is inscribed with the king's name and has a slope of 60°.

Coffin Styles

The rishi *coffin of Intef VI, from Dra Abu el-Naga. It was made of wood and originally gilded. The name* rishi *comes from the Arabic for feather.*

In the 13th dynasty the inner coffin was a black varnished rectangular wooden box with painted decoration and a lightly vaulted lid with vertical ends. By the time of Intef V coffins were bulky wooden cases in the form of a wrapped mummy with a massive foot and the *nemes* headdress. The type is called *rishi*, the Arabic for feather, because of the painted, and later inlaid, decoration depicting the wings of a bird folded round the body. The human-headed bird transformed the coffin into the image of the *ba*, or soul. Tutankhamun's magnificent golden coffins are the most refined examples we know.

Four of the more primitive *rishi* coffins of the 17th dynasty were found buried in the debris of the lower Dra Abu el-Naga plain. These are reburials, perhaps by the same priests who transferred many of the later royal mummies from their tombs in the Valley of the Kings to hiding places for safekeeping, re-discovered in 1881. A 17th-dynasty *rishi* coffin found in the Deir el-Bahri cache contained the body of Seqenenre Tao II, father of Kamose and Ahmose. The massive proportions of these coffins convey the same mix of power and provincialism as was evident in the art of the earlier Theban revival of the 11th dynasty. Kamose and Intef VII had particularly crude coffins which were probably hurriedly borrowed from a non-royal – other royal coffins were covered with gold leaf.

The coffins correspond to Winlock's assessment that 'the kings who were buried in this cemetery were a far remove from the mighty and extravagantly wealthy Pharaohs of great periods'.

Royal tombs in the New Kingdom

Whenever the Egyptian kingdom expanded to the full extent of traditional territory – from the Delta to Elephantine – the royal tomb removed itself farther from the local cemetery. We have seen this at Umm el-Qa'ab in Abydos, where the 1st-dynasty royal tombs move away from the crowded predynastic cemetery. The giant pyramids of the early Old Kingdom achieve exclusivity by sheer size as well as location and by the axial layout of the temples and causeways.

When the New Kingdom was inaugurated by Ahmose I's defeat of the Hyksos, the royal tomb once again became removed. And now the artificial pyramid as the central icon of pharaoh's tomb was finally abandoned. Monarchs buried themselves in the communal royal cemetery of the Valley of the Kings. The peak called el-Qurn, whose patron goddess was Meretseger, 'Lover of Silence', served as a natural pyramid over the next 500 years for the kings of the 18th to the 20th dynasties.

Ahmose at Abydos

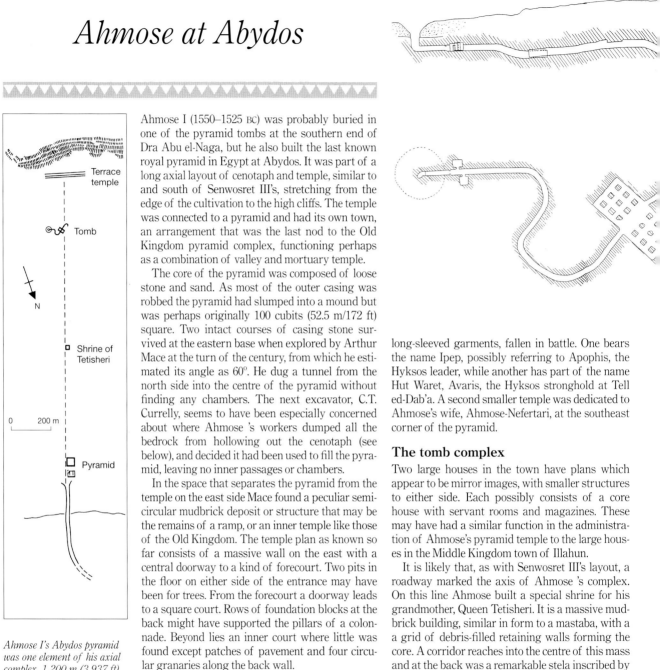

Ahmose I (1550–1525 BC) was probably buried in one of the pyramid tombs at the southern end of Dra Abu el-Naga, but he also built the last known royal pyramid in Egypt at Abydos. It was part of a long axial layout of cenotaph and temple, similar to and south of Senwosret III's, stretching from the edge of the cultivation to the high cliffs. The temple was connected to a pyramid and had its own town, an arrangement that was the last nod to the Old Kingdom pyramid complex, functioning perhaps as a combination of valley and mortuary temple.

The core of the pyramid was composed of loose stone and sand. As most of the outer casing was robbed the pyramid had slumped into a mound but was perhaps originally 100 cubits (52.5 m/172 ft) square. Two intact courses of casing stone survived at the eastern base when explored by Arthur Mace at the turn of the century, from which he estimated its angle as 60°. He dug a tunnel from the north side into the centre of the pyramid without finding any chambers. The next excavator, C.T. Currelly, seems to have been especially concerned about where Ahmose's workers dumped all the bedrock from hollowing out the cenotaph (see below), and decided it had been used to fill the pyramid, leaving no inner passages or chambers.

In the space that separates the pyramid from the temple on the east side Mace found a peculiar semi-circular mudbrick deposit or structure that may be the remains of a ramp, or an inner temple like those of the Old Kingdom. The temple plan as known so far consists of a massive wall on the east with a central doorway to a kind of forecourt. Two pits in the floor on either side of the entrance may have been for trees. From the forecourt a doorway leads to a square court. Rows of foundation blocks at the back might have supported the pillars of a colonnade. Beyond lies an inner court where little was found except patches of pavement and four circular granaries along the back wall.

Recent excavations under Stephen Harvey of the Pennsylvania and Yale University Expedition have recovered 2,000 fragments of painted relief that once adorned the temple, as well as pieces of torus mouldings, cornices, square pillars, memorial stelae and a star-studded ceiling. Some of the reliefs may have narrated Ahmose's campaign against the Hyksos. Tantalizing fragments show bridled horses, once harnessed to chariots, archers firing bows and Asiatics, with their characteristic beards and long-sleeved garments, fallen in battle. One bears the name Ipep, possibly referring to Apophis, the Hyksos leader, while another has part of the name Hut Waret, Avaris, the Hyksos stronghold at Tell ed-Dab'a. A second smaller temple was dedicated to Ahmose's wife, Ahmose-Nefertari, at the southeast corner of the pyramid.

The tomb complex

Two large houses in the town have plans which appear to be mirror images, with smaller structures to either side. Each possibly consists of a core house with servant rooms and magazines. These may have had a similar function in the administration of Ahmose's pyramid temple to the large houses in the Middle Kingdom town of Illahun.

It is likely that, as with Senwosret III's layout, a roadway marked the axis of Ahmose's complex. On this line Ahmose built a special shrine for his grandmother, Queen Tetisheri. It is a massive mudbrick building, similar in form to a mastaba, with a a grid of debris-filled retaining walls forming the core. A corridor reaches into the centre of this mass and at the back was a remarkable stela inscribed by Ahmose for his grandmother. In the lunate at the top the queen grandmother is shown twice. She is seated, wearing the vulture headdress of queens, while her grandson presents her with offerings. The hieroglyphic text quotes the king informing his wife, who is also his sister, of his plans for making a pyramid in the memory of their grandmother:

'I indeed have called to mind the mother of my mother, the mother of my father, the Great Royal Wife and Royal Mother, Tetisheri, the justified. Her grave chamber and

Ahmose I's Abydos pyramid was one element of his axial complex, 1,200 m (3,937 ft) long, orientated, like the cenotaph of Senwosret I and the Archaic royal tombs, both also at Abydos, from northeast to southwest.

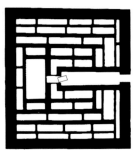

her cenotaph are at present upon the soil of the Theban and Thinnite Nomes, it is true, but I have told this to you because my Majesty has desired to build for her a pyramid and chapel in the Sacred Land (Abydos) near the monument of my Majesty.'

The king stipulates that the pyramid is to be endowed with a lake, land, livestock, plantations, priests and personnel. The 'pyramid' must refer to the mudbrick shrine where the stela was erected at the rear of the chapel, rather than the pyramid nearer the cultivation.

Further into the desert Ahmose had a cenotaph cut into the bedrock. Its curving subterranean route is again similar to the Abydos tomb of Senwosret III, but it is much more hurriedly and less skilfully executed. The entrance is a pit no larger than an ordinary person's tomb and an initial horizontal passage is so low that those who enter must crawl on hands and knees. Rooms on either side of the passage are crudely shaped and left unfinished. The corridor then begins to wind and turn, ending in a hall with nine pillars on either side making a total of 18. From here the way rapidly descends to end in a simple grotto.

So quickly and poorly was this cut, it seems to have been a only a token winding Osirian underworld. It lies across the great axial line through temple, pyramid and grandmother's shrine. We can see this as deliberately aligned to the Nile's orientation along the Abydos bay, or, if Ahmose's and Senwosret III's surveyors paid attention to the true cardinal directions, these long axes were laid out somewhat northeast–southwest, a significant orientation throughout pyramid history. A shrine to

the queen grandmother on this alignment fits the idea that it is the queen mother who ensures transmission of the royal *ka* from one king to the next.

The final element in Ahmose's great layout was a set of terraces built against the high cliffs to the southwest of the cenotaph. Caches of votive ceramic vessels, model stone vases and boats with oars were buried near the south end. The ascent up the terraces was from the south by a series of steps up through odd trapezoidal rooms. On a higher level a long corridor ran further south. At the end was a small chamber with a limestone dais, possibly the base for a statue of the king looking from the southwest, down the long line connecting his terraces, cenotaph, the shrine of his grandmother, his pyramid and his town and temple.

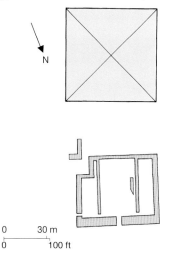

0   30 m
0   100 ft

'Private' Pyramids

After the pyramid was given up as the marker and symbol of the royal tomb it disappeared from funerary architecture for about two centuries. Towards the end of the 18th dynasty, necropolis workers and high officials began to build small pyramids above their so-called 'private' tombs. Although there was no concept of 'private' as opposed to royal in the modern sense, the pyramid was simply no longer the exclusive prerogative of the king. Archaeologists have also found remains of small New Kingdom pyramids at sites ranging from Nubia to Memphis. Their size was further reduced in proportion to the chapel than the 17th-dynasty royal tombs.

Workers' pyramids at Deir el-Medineh

The artists and craftsmen employed on the great royal tombs in the Valley of the Kings had their own cemetery above the workers' village of Deir el-Medineh, on the opposite side of the cliffs shielding the royal necropolis. On the terraced slope above their tombs perched small pyramids. The tombs consisted of a court enclosed by a stone or brick wall with an entrance from the east. In the dark shade of the colonnaded western side of the court was a chapel with a barrel-vaulted ceiling and painted wall scenes. It was presided over by the image of the tomb owner etched on a stela set in a recess in the back wall. Deep in the bedrock lay the burial chamber, its walls painted with scenes of the gods and the deceased in the Afterlife. The small

pyramids were built of mudbrick above the chapel and were hollow in order to relieve the weight on the roof. A niche in the east side of the pyramid contained a statue of the deceased, sometimes kneeling and holding a small stela. Many limestone capstones of such pyramids have been found, inscribed with figures of the tomb owner praising the sun god and seated before a table of offerings.

Return to Saqqara

At Saqqara, the 18th-dynasty tombs of high Memphite officials took the form of small temples with a pyramid of mudbrick sometimes built at the west end on the stone roofing slabs of the chapel. In the 19th dynasty tombs included stone pyramids built on the ground immediately west of the chapel.

In 1982, south of Unas's causeway, Geoffrey Martin discovered the pyramid of Princess Tia, a sister of Ramesses II, and her husband of the same name. Further east, Sayed Tewfik excavated more large Ramessid tombs with pyramids. The tomb of the two Tias consists of a paved forecourt with a small portico, a massive pylon gateway, a colonnaded court with a deep shaft in the centre descending to the burial chambers, an antechamber with two columns, and an offering hall. A small pyramid, made of solid rubble encased with limestone, was set slightly askew to the west side of the chapel. Its pyramidion was brought to Britain in 1722; drawings made before it was lost around 1792 preserve the scenes on its faces.

Lower Nubian pyramids

During the 18th to 20th dynasties small pyramid tombs were built at Aniba and Soleb in Lower Nubia. They were provincial imitations, with modifications, of those at Thebes. The pyramids were attached directly to chapels with vaulted roofs that were entered from small courtyards surrounded by high walls. From the centre of the court a shaft descended to the burial chamber. Rather than one element vastly exceeding the other in size, the combination of court and chapel were proportionate to the little pyramid. Here is perhaps the most abbreviated form in its long history of the essential elements of a pyramid complex: the pyramid as the central symbol of both grave mound and resurrection, the chapel as a place to commune with the dead and leave offerings, and the entrance to a grave chamber set within a hallowed space.

Saite pyramids

Another kind of pyramid tomb, with an internal dome or cupola, was built at Thebes and Abydos in the Saite Period (26th dynasty, c. 600 BC). For some time after Mariette found such tombs at Abydos in 1858, it was believed they dated to the Middle Kingdom. The discovery of similar tombs at Thebes by the Austrian Archaeological Institute ascertained their later date. The domed interiors of the small

A series of small pyramids once perched on the hillsides above the royal workmen's town of Deir el-Medineh. Below is a possible reconstruction of such a tomb and opposite is one that has been reconstructed at the site.

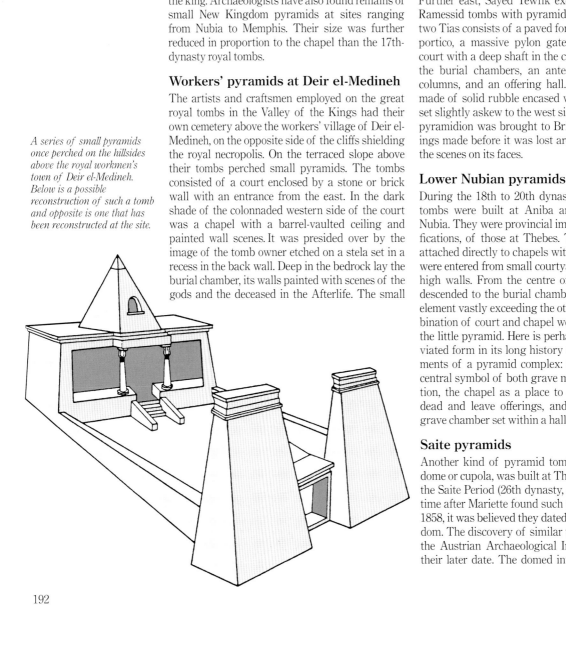

mudbrick pyramids are similar in structure to ancient Egyptian granaries and ovens, with a corbelled vault. Domed tombs are known as early as the Old Kingdom – in recent years Zahi Hawass has excavated a whole series of domed tombs in the cemeteries south of the Sphinx, but with exteriors dome- or beehive-shaped, rather than pyramidal.

The Abydos pyramids were built on a rectangular base or plinth. Attached to one side was a small rectangular chamber, entered at ground level by an arched doorway, and containing a stela of the deceased. A shaft in the floor led to a lower chamber with a small side passage to the burial chamber under the pyramid. A false floor separated the burial chamber from the cupola which was corbelled up in the body of the pyramid, resembling, in section, the corbelled chambers of Sneferu in his Meidum and Dahshur pyramids, although here the cupola is much larger in proportion to the pyramid.

(Left) Two of the four decorated faces of the pyramidion of the two Tias. The deceased worship Ra-Harakhte, Atum and Osiris. A small human-headed ba-bird standing behind each deity is labelled 'Osiris Tia'.

A reconstructed pyramid belonging to one of the tombs in the workers' cemetery at Deir el-Medineh, Thebes.

(Below) Section and plan of a pyramidal tomb at Abydos. The corbelled vault resembles ancient Egyptian granaries and ovens.

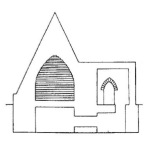

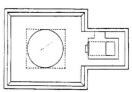

Pyramids of Late Antiquity

It is rather daunting to reach this point in a catalogue of Egyptian pyramids – already covering 1,000 years and over 90 royal pyramids, including subsidiary and satellite pyramids – only to realize that twice as many, about 180, were built in Nubia over the course of another 1,000 years. The Nubian sequence begins more than 800 years after the last royal pyramid was built in Egypt. Reviving the tradition of the royal pyramids was only one way in which Nubia was an upstream reservoir of ancient Egyptian culture well into late antiquity.

The first kingdom of Kush, as the land was known to the Egyptians, grew from a trading post established on Egypt's periphery as early as the Middle Kingdom. Its centre, the town of Kerma, lies just below the 3rd cataract. It was ruled by kings whom the Egyptians of the 12th dynasty apparently regarded a threat, judging by the series of fortresses built in Lower Nubia. In the final phase of the cemetery at Kerma, huge round tumuli were built over great underground circles subdivided by walls. The unmummified body of the king was placed on a gilded bed, surrounded by treasures and the bodies of servants, nobles and wives who went to their death as part of the royal funeral.

Nubia – a reservoir of royal pyramids long after they had ceased to be built in Egypt itself. Above the 3rd cataract the principle pyramid cemeteries are at el-Kurru, Gebel Barkal, Nuri and Meroe.

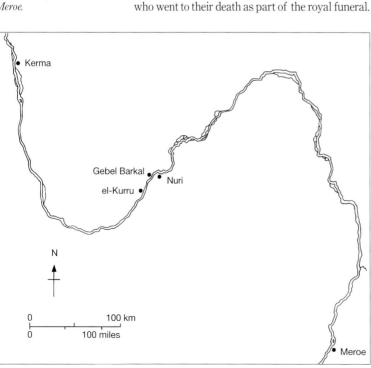

The 800-year hiatus

The emergent New Kingdom Egyptian state made Nubia a province of Egypt, ruled by the 'King's Son of Kush'. The southern limit of Egyptian control may have been Gebel ('mountain of') Barkal, where a Temple of Amun was built. When the New Kingdom declined into rival principalities, Egyptian control of Nubia was lost, probably already by 1070 BC. Historical and archaeological records are relatively silent about Nubia and Sudan for the following two centuries. Then a new Kushite kingdom emerged suddenly and with force on the stage of Upper Egypt.

As early as 770 BC a powerful ruler named Kashta hailing from Napata, at the foot of the Gebel Barkal, took control of Lower Nubia and Upper Egypt as far as Thebes where he had his sister installed as 'Divine Adoratice of Amun', a position that had become as politically significant as High Priest. The Thebans hailed Kashta as King of Upper and Lower Egypt. It was Kashta's successor Piye (formerly read Piankhi) who countered principalities in middle and northern Egypt. Piye led a campaign that he described in stelae set up in the temples at Karnak, Memphis and Gebel Barkal. Only the last survives. It is a remarkable document, part history and part literary recitation that casts Piye in the traditional role of Pharaoh, the restorer of order against the forces of chaos. There were now four rulers calling themselves 'Kings of Egypt'. And there was Tefnakhte, self-proclaimed Lord of the West. All are listed in the great stela submitting to Piye in person except Tefnakhte, who sent tribute and a token letter of surrender. Prior to the ceremony of submission, Piye set off to Heliopolis to worship the sun god and celebrate his coronation. The rites included an intimate moment with the sacred *ben-ben*.

'Mounting the stairs to the great window to view Re in the Pyramidion House. The king stood by himself alone. Breaking the seals of the bolts, opening the doors; viewing his father Re in the holy Pyramidion House; adorning the Morning Bark of Re and the Evening Bark of Atum.'

Piye returned to Napata as the founder of a century-long Nubian dynasty – the 25th – of kings of Upper and Lower Egypt. It seems fitting that Piye made his pilgrimage to the primal archetype of the Egyptian pyramid, the *ben-ben*, for he was the first king in 800 years to be buried in a pyramid.

The Pyramids of El-Kurru

Piye built his pyramid at el-Kurru, 13 km (8 miles) downstream from the Temple of Amun at Gebel Barkal. It is presumed that the residence of the Napatan kings lay nearby, although it has never been found. When Reisner directed excavations at el-Kurru in 1918–19, only one pyramid was still standing. Under low mounds of rubble he found

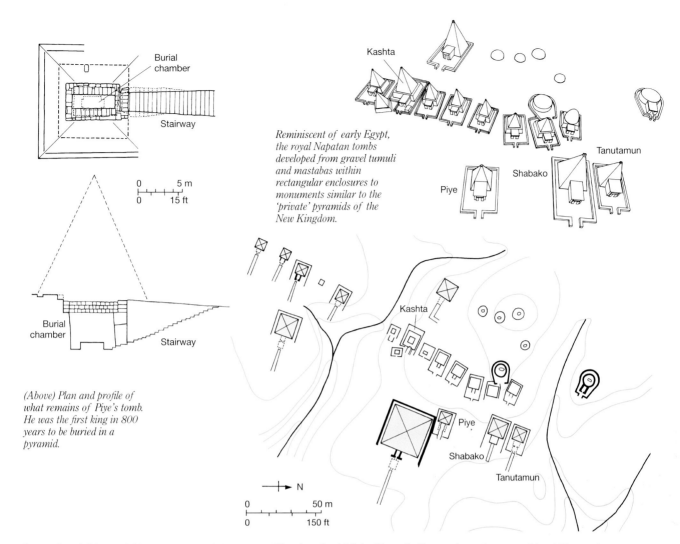

Burial chamber

Stairway

Burial chamber

Stairway

0   5 m
0   15 ft

(Above) Plan and profile of what remains of Piye's tomb. He was the first king in 800 years to be buried in a pyramid.

Reminiscent of early Egypt, the royal Napatan tombs developed from gravel tumuli and mastabas within rectangular enclosures to monuments similar to the 'private' pyramids of the New Kingdom.

Kashta

Tanutamun

Shabako

Piye

Kashta

N

Piye

Shabako

Tanutamun

0   50 m
0   150 ft

(Above) The royal cemetery at el-Kurru contained the tombs of Kashta, Piye's father, five earlier generations and Piye's successors – Shabako, Shabatko and Tanutamun. The cemetery also contained 14 queens' pyramids.

the tombs of Piye and his successors of the 25th dynasty, Shabako, Shabatko and Tanutamun. Pyramids once stood above these tombs, but they had been entirely removed.

It is commonly assumed that Piye was inspired by seeing the royal pyramids in Egypt, but his pyramid tomb bears a closer resemblance to the non-royal, 'private', New Kingdom pyramid tombs. Although the superstructure had been entirely removed when Reisner cleared it, the foundation trench indicates a pyramid with a base length of about 8 m (26 ft) and a slope of probably about 68°. A stairway of 19 steps opened to the east and led to the burial chamber cut into the bedrock as an open trench and covered with a corbelled masonry roof. Piye's body had been placed on a bed which rested in the middle of the chamber on a stone bench with its four corners cut away to receive the legs of the bed, so that the bed platform lay directly on the bench. While this was a native Nubian arrangement, Piye was probably embalmed in Egyptian style, since fragments of canopic jars were found, along with remains of shabti servant figures, a normal complement of contemporary Egyptian tombs.

The chapel, which had been built over the stairway after the funeral, was completely destroyed.

The pyramid of Piye's successor, Shabako, was similar in layout but the burial chamber was entirely subterranean, with a vaulted ceiling cut in the natural rock. The burial chamber was entered by a short tunnel from the bottom of the entrance stairway which began far enough east of the mortuary chapel to allow the pyramid to be entered after the chapel was built.

There were also 14 queens' pyramids at el-Kurru, 6 to 7 m (20 to 23 ft) square, compared to the 8 to 11 m (26 to 36 ft) of the king's pyramids. Northeast of the royal cemetery, Reisner found the graves of 24 horses and two dogs. Four of the horses belonged to Piye, four to Tanutamun; each group may have formed a chariot team. Ten horses belonged each to Shabako and Shabatko. The animals had been sacrificed, decapitated – the skulls were missing – and buried standing. The bodies were draped with beaded nets hung with cowrie shells and heavy bronze beads. They also had silver collars and gilded silver plume holders. Are these horses comparable to the boat burials of earlier pyramids?

The Pyramids of Nuri

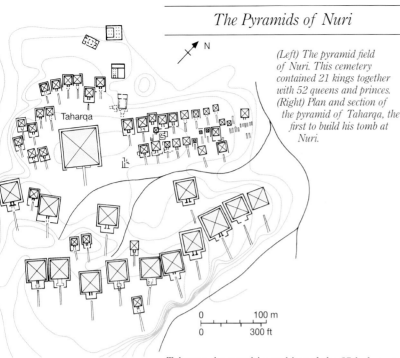

N

(Left) The pyramid field of Nuri. This cemetery contained 21 kings together with 52 queens and princes. (Right) Plan and section of the pyramid of Taharqa, the first to build his tomb at Nuri.

Taharqa

```
0         100 m
|----+----|
0         300 ft
```

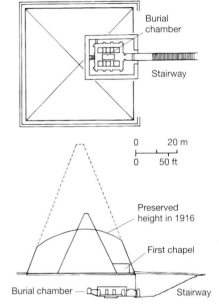

Burial chamber

Stairway

```
0     20 m
|--+--|
0     50 ft
```

Preserved height in 1916

First chapel

Burial chamber

Stairway

(Below) A shabti – 'answerer' – of Taharqa. His pyramid tomb contained 1,070 of these servant figurines (p. 59).

Taharqa, the penultimate king of the 25th dynasty (the Tirakah of II Kings 19:9) moved to Nuri, a site on the other side of the river from Gebel Barkal, for his pyramid. At 51.75 m (170 ft) square and 40 or 50 m (131 or 164 ft) high, Taharqa's was the largest pyramid ever built at Nuri. It is unique among the Nubian series in having two stages. The first pyramid was encased in smooth sandstone. Drawings and written reports of the early 19th century indicate that the truncated top of the inner pyramid could be seen projecting from the disintegrating core of the larger, outer pyramid. The outer pyramid was the first of a type with stepped courses and planed corners; its angle of slope was 69°. By the time Reisner worked at Nuri the inner pyramid had been much reduced in height. An enclosure wall formed a tight corridor around the pyramid. No traces of the chapel were found.

Taharqa's subterranean chambers are the most elaborate of any Kushite tomb. The entrance was by an eastern stairway trench, north of the pyramid's central axis, reflecting the alignment of the original smaller pyramid. Three steps led to a doorway, with a moulded frame and cavetto cornice, that opened to a tunnel, widened and heightened into an antechamber with a barrel-vaulted ceiling. Six massive pillars carved from the natural rock divide the burial chamber into two side aisles and a central nave, each with a barrel-vaulted ceiling.

A rectangular recess was cut into the floor to receive the sarcophagus, of which no traces survived. There were four rectangular niches in the north and south walls and two in the west wall. The entire chamber was surrounded by a moat-like corridor entered by steps leading down from in front of

the antechamber doorway. Another set of steps led to the corridor from the west end of the nave. The whole arrangement is similar to the Osireion, the subsurface temple and symbolic Osiris tomb built by Seti I at Abydos. Taharqa was buried in good Egyptian fashion.

During his reign Taharqa had increasingly come into conflict with the expansionist Assyrian empire. His successor, Tanutamun, having briefly received the submission of all the Delta leaders, was then forced back by the Assyrians to Napata. Napatan rule of Egypt ended when Psamtik I established himself as sole ruler of a united Egypt, but the kingdom lived on in Upper Nubia. With a marked silence about Egypt or other foreign powers in monumental texts, Tanutamun's successors ruled a territory that extended from the 1st cataract to the White Nile for another 350 years.

Tanutamun returned to el-Kurru to build his pyramid, but 21 kings and 53 queens and princes

(Above) A computer-generated diagram of King Aspelta's tomb of the 6th century BC. By this time pyramid substructures at Nuri had been increased by two or three chambers. Pyloned chapels were decorated with relief carving.

(Above centre and left) Pyramids at Nuri – these small pyramids have on the whole survived relatively well.

were buried at Nuri under pyramids of good masonry, using blocks of local red sandstone. The Nuri pyramids were generally much larger than those at el-Kurru, reaching heights of 20 to 30 m (66 to 98 ft). The chapels built against the eastern faces were decorated with reliefs, and a stela built into the pyramid masonry showed the king before the gods. The substructures, like the superstructures, were standard. Stairway trenches to the east of the chapels gave access to chambers, which Taharqa's successors increased to two or three rooms, sometimes inscribing the walls with the 'Negative Confession' from the Book of the Dead.

The Napatan royals were mummified in Egyptian fashion and accompanied in their tombs by multiple shabtis – Taharqa's alone contained 1,070. The royal mummies were adorned with gold jewellery, crooks and flails for the kings, green stone heart scarabs, gold chest pectorals and gold caps on fingers and toes. The bodies were laid in small wooden anthropoid coffins covered with gold leaf and inlaid with coloured stone. Outer coffins might be even more elaborate, covered with gold and stone inlays with the motif of falcon and vulture wings. The bodies of kings Anlami and Aspelta (568 BC) were placed in huge granite sarcophagi. Aspelta's, weighing 15.5 tons, and its lid, weighing 4 tons, were carved with Pyramid Texts, chapters from the Book of the Dead, and Egyptian deities.

The Pyramids of Meroe

The last king to be buried at Nuri died in about 308 BC. Thereafter the site of Meroe, between the 5th and 6th cataracts, rose to prominence, and kings began to build pyramids there. With the exception of three or four generations of pyramids near Gebel Barkal, Meroe remained the royal cemetery for 600 years, until AD 350. It had been the site of the royal residence before it became the location of the royal cemetery. The transfer from Napata may

The pyramids at Meroe were formed from stepped courses of good masonry blocks quarried from the local red sandstone.

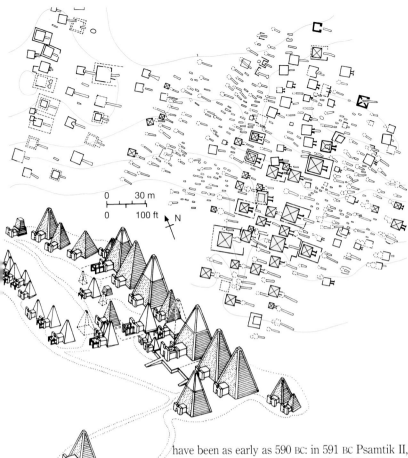

the whole cultural and political development started from Meroe'. The cemetery record shows Meroe to have been a 'place of consequence' as early as the reign of Piye. Lesser royalty and officials were buried there as early as the 7th century BC.

The heartland of Meroitic territory, the modern Butana, was known to Classical authors as the 'Island of Meroe'. Although bounded on three sides by rivers – the Nile, the Atbara and the Blue Nile – most traffic from Napata took the road along the Wadi Abu Dom that cuts across the great bend of the Nile from the 4th to 6th cataracts. This heartland was repeatedly a refuge for Napatan and Meroitic kings when they retreated from world powers who penetrated the Nile corridor. Meroe lay just beyond the reach of the Roman Empire, to which it was tied economically by trade.

The settlement of Meroe is about half a mile east of the river and its cemeteries lie in the desert further east. The first major king to build his tomb at Meroe was Arkamaniqo (the 'Ergamenes' of Diodorus), who ruled when Ptolemy II (285–247 BC) was king of Egypt. Arkamaniqo built his pyramid in the South Cemetery, in use since the time of Piye. Another king and a queen built pyramid tombs in the South Cemetery before the crowding caused by more than 200 individual graves prompted kings to move across a narrow valley to a curving ridge to begin the North Cemetery. There is a third cluster of pyramids at Meroe in the West Cemetery. These brick-faced and rubble pyramids of lesser royal family members are surrounded by a galaxy of graves, many richly furnished, of the important households of Meroe.

The North Cemetery is the source of the famous Ferlini Treasure, discovered in 1830 by the Italian explorer, Giuseppe Ferlini (in pyramid Beg. N.6, belonging to a queen, Amanishakhto, of the late 1st century BC). It consists of gold rings, necklaces and other ornaments that he reported he had taken from a 'secret chamber' at the top of one of the pyramids. This apparently prompted subsequent treasure seekers to lop off the tops of many others. But the valuables could only have come from a pyramid substructure, entered, as Reisner ascertained, by the standard eastern stairway descending to a blocked doorway in front of three adjoining chambers. Two of the chambers had square pillars carved from the natural rock, while the third, innermost, chamber was smaller. Ceilings were slightly vaulted in earlier chambers, and round vaulted in later ones which were much more roughly hewn.

At Meroe, the body was buried in the innermost chamber in a wooden anthropoid coffin placed on a raised masonry bier, sometimes carved with divine figures. Relief scenes in the chapels located against the east sides of the pyramids included depictions of mummies. This, and the remains of canopic equipment, suggest that the royal body was still mummified. Although all the royal tombs at Meroe

The pyramid field of Meroe was huge and crowded. It was in fact divided into the West Cemetery (plan above), the South Cemetery and the North Cemetery. The drawing above is based on F.W. Hinkel's reconstruction of the northern group.

have been as early as 590 BC: in 591 BC Psamtik II, the Egyptian pharaoh, had campaigned into Nubia. He seems to have defeated King Aspelta's troops and may have marched on Napata. But the reason for, and date of, the transfer are still unresolved.

Peter Shinnie, who excavated at Meroe, pointed out that it is not certain that the royal residence was in fact ever at Napata, since the settlement there has not been found. It is known, on the other hand, that Meroe was settled as early as the 8th century BC, so 'it may be that it pre-dated Napata, and that

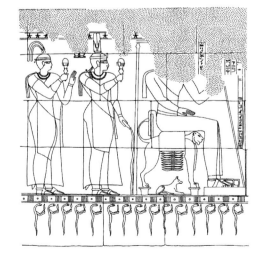

The pyramids at Meroe were decorated with reliefs, often showing the ruler seated on a throne in the shape of a lion, as here, from the pyramid of Arqamani (Beg. N.7).

had been plundered, Reisner's excavations found evidence that bodies had been adorned with gold and silver jewellery. Archaeologists retrieved bows, quivers of arrows, archers' thumb rings, horse trappings. wood boxes and furniture, bronze lamps, bronze and silver vessels, glass bottles and pottery. The chamber nearest the entrance contained wine amphorae and food storage jars. Accompanying kings and wealthy people to their graves were companions and servants who were apparently sacrificed at the time of the funeral. Animals, including yoked horses, oxen, camels and dogs, were also slaughtered and interred outside the entrances of the burial chambers.

The steep-sided pyramids of Meroe were built of sandstone, 10 to 30 m (33 to 98 ft) high. As at Nuri, the pyramids were stepped and built on a plinth, but now each triangular face was framed by smooth bands of raised masonry along the edges where the faces met. The pyramids at Gebel Barkal also have this feature. Where the upper parts of the pyramids are preserved, these lines are rounded, like the torus mouldings on the corners of Egyptian temples, for the upper fourth of the total pyramid height.

Towards the end of the Meroitic period, degeneration apparent in the substructure also appears in the pyramids, which return to a smooth face. Casing blocks become much smaller and they are laid on a poorly constructed core. The latest pyramids were built of rubble and brick and had a plastered surface. Meroe's decline, beginning in the 1st century AD, may have been due to changes in trade patterns and in its distant relationship with the Roman economy. The reason most commonly cited is that Meroe was overrun by its traditional tribal enemies. Aided by the camel, the Blemmyes disrupted old trade routes. Cattle-herding tribes, the Nubai and the Noba, from the savanna to the south and southwest of the Nile, may also have been major threats. Another power was growing just beyond the southern reach of Meroe – the civilization of Axum in the Ethiopian highlands.

The end of the pyramids

The re-emergence of the royal pyramid after a hiatus of 800 years is an interesting case of the transfer of an architectural idea from one region and culture to another. The Nubian pyramids are smaller, far more numerous, considerably more standardized and owned by more members of the royal household than those of Egypt's classic pyramid age. But we should consider the expenditure of the Napatan and Meroitic kingdoms on their pyramids in relation to population size, which may have been considerably smaller than Egypt's in the Old and Middle Kingdoms. Aspelta's colossal granite sarcophagus, for instance, may have been a much larger part of his gross national product than, say, Amenemhet III's quartzite burial vault.

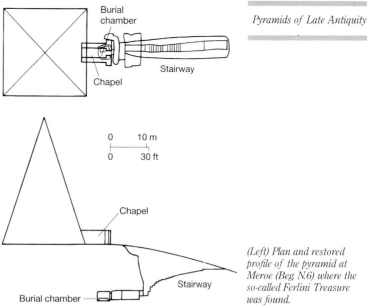

Burial chamber

Chapel

Stairway

0   10 m

0   30 ft

Chapel

Stairway

Burial chamber

(Left) Plan and restored profile of the pyramid at Meroe (Beg. N.6) where the so-called Ferlini Treasure was found.

(Above) An armlet from the pyramid of Queen Amanishakhto.

It is the very duration of a standard form that is most impressive about the Nubian pyramids. This standardization is more consistent and persistent than that of the late Old Kingdom pyramids, suggesting a conservatism of royal Nubian culture over a sweep of history equivalent to the span from Djoser to Ahmose I. The pyramid came to Nubia already evolved in its relative proportions, with substructure and chapel crystallized in the Egyptian New Kingdom.

Meroitic civilization was the last bearer of traditions and symbols dating back to most ancient Egypt. When the kingdom disintegrated around AD 350, the pyramid as the marker of a royal tomb finally became extinct.

Two of the pyramids of Meroe as restored by F.W. Hinkel.

H ow were the pyramids built? This is the question people most often ask when I tell them I work at the site of the Giza pyramids. It implies a single, simple answer – one which many theorists claim to offer. They have diagrams showing stones hauled up various types of ramp; levered up on the pyramid steps; or lifted with counterweights or hydraulic locks. But all too many enthusiastic ideas wilt in the Egyptian sun. Whatever we propose as the likeliest building methods must be rooted in bedrock reality at the pyramid sites.

Just as there was no absolutely standard pyramid, neither was there a standard method of pyramid building. The question 'how were they built?' implicitly refers on the whole to the most colossal and famous pyramids, such as those of Sneferu, Khufu and Khafre. But these are a tiny minority of the pyramids in Egypt. They are also the most varied – the products of the time of greatest experimentation in pyramid building. Nevertheless it was during these generations that the Egyptians honed masonry skills that became basic in the later pyramid age and beyond. And the Great Pyramid of Khufu itself marks an undeniable zenith in the history of pyramid building, when these skills were developed to an unsurpassable degree of exactitude.

To build a pyramid was to embark on a huge landscape project, especially in the case of the giant pyramids, and they must be looked at in their particular topographic context. Apart from the pyramid itself, one must identify other facets that together tell the entire story of the living pyramid including the evidence of the human elements of the workforce and personnel who maintained the pyramid.

Looking across the south side of Khufu's pyramid, to one of his queens' pyramids (GI-c).

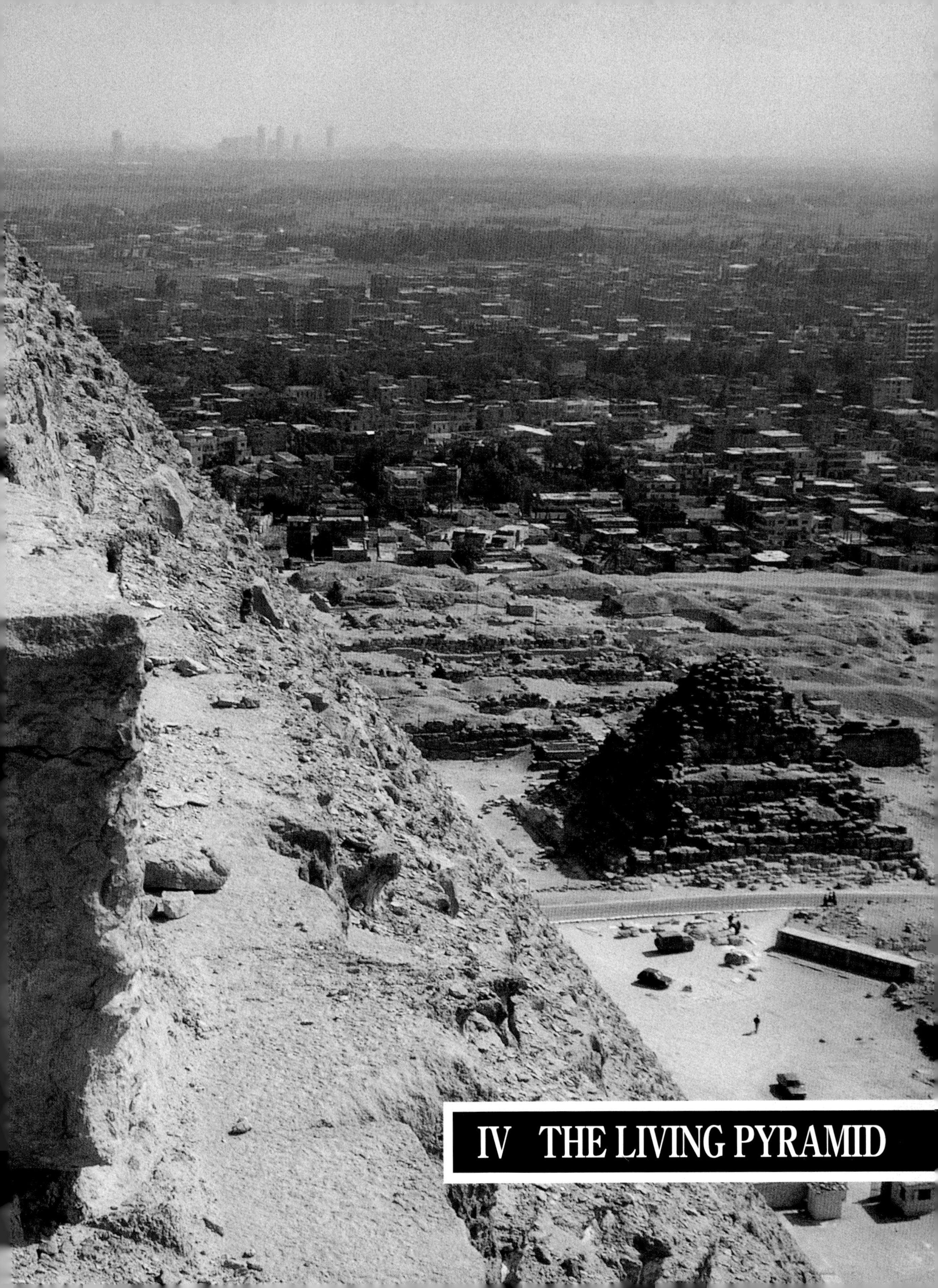

IV THE LIVING PYRAMID

Supply and Transport

Transporting granite palm columns by boat from Aswan for Unas's pyramid temples. This scene comes from a relief in Unas's causeway.

His majesty sent me to Yebu [Elephantine] to bring a granite false door, and its libation stone and granite lintels, and to bring granite portals and libation stones for the upper chamber of the pyramid 'Merenre-appears-in-splendour', my mistress.

Inscription of Weni

The pyramid site had to be constantly supplied with building material to ensure that the work rolled on at a regular pace and the pyramid complex was completed during the king's lifetime. Most of the stone for the three Giza pyramids was quarried from the plateau itself, downslope from the great northeast–southwest diagonal on which the pyramids are aligned (p. 106). But a massive amount of limestone was also imported from elsewhere. The fine, white homogeneous limestone used for the outer casing is of a quality not found locally. It was brought to Giza from the quarries to the east of the Nile – Mokattam, Maasara and, principally, Turah. Granite, the other major type of non-local stone in the pyramid complexes, was brought from Aswan. Gypsum and basalt were imported from the Fayum and copper from Sinai. Wood was required for levers, tracks and sledges; alabaster for statuary and temple pavements; gneiss for statuary; and dolerite and quartzite to make tools for pounding and polishing.

Bulk building material was not the only resource brought to the plateau. Considerable quantities of fuel were also needed for forging and servicing copper tools, slaking raw gypsum to make mortar, and for baking bread and brewing beer to provide the workers' rations. This fuel consisted of small trees and scrub which were systematically harvested from the Egyptian landscape. Food supplies included grain, fish, fowl, sheep and cattle – providing starch, calories and protein – which were probably brought in from provincial lands specifically set aside for the purpose of feeding the pyramid complex (p. 228).

Long-distance transportation

Supplies of fuel and food were carried on the small cargo ships which are frequently depicted in the relief decoration of Old Kingdom tombs. They are distinguished by a hooded matwork cabin at the stern and produce-laden decks. More problematic were the much heavier materials which had to be transported to the pyramid sites. The Unas causeway reliefs depict a barge carrying two of the large granite columns with palm-shaped capitals that were actually set up in Unas's pyramid temples. The inscription refers to 'the coming of these barges from Elephantine, laden with [granite] columns of 20 cubits'. Most likely this figure indicates the combined length of both: 20 cubits is equivalent to 10.46 m (34 ft), whereas Unas's columns range from 5.5–6.5 m (18–21 ft) in height.

This still represents a very considerable load. The columns are depicted resting end-to-end on sledges which are raised off the deck by a support framework of beams or girders. These supports probably relieved the weight on the deck, but they could also have had a role in loading and unloading – critical operations given that a 40-ton block of granite, like those in Khufu's pyramid, would capsize any boat if it rolled too far to one side. R. Engelbach proposed that Hatshepsut's great granite obelisks were loaded and unloaded from the large barges illustrated in her Deir el-Bahri temple by means of an earthen embankment, which would have been built up around the barge as high as the deck. Once the obelisk was loaded, the barge could have been dug out again. A possible means of unloading is that the transport barge was brought into a narrow canal and great cedar beams thrust beneath the load between the supports. With the ends of the beams resting on the canal banks, the barge could then have been weighted with ballast and slipped out from under the load.

The 6th-dynasty official Weni describes how he transported an alabaster offering table from Hatnub and granite from Aswan for the pharaoh Merenre's pyramid, which he refers to as 'my mistress'. His boasts about these achievements contrast with the silence of 4th-dynasty officials, though the latter had been responsible for transporting far greater quantities (and greater individual loads) of granite and alabaster.

From canal to pyramid site

Weni's account suggests that the peoples of Lower Nubia assembled boats locally from native wood. When ships were built of larger and costlier cedar from Lebanon, the pieces were stitched together with rope so that they could be taken apart and reassembled. Once these pieces became worn, pyramid builders reused them like railway sleepers in tracks for dragging heavy stones on sledges overland from the quarry to the canal or river and then again to the building site. Such hauling tracks were

found at Lisht near the 12th-dynasty pyramids of Amenemhet I and Senwosret I.

Hauling tracks had to be hard and solid – nothing stops a 2-ton stone block more quickly than hitting soft sand, as we soon discovered during the NOVA pyramid-building experiment (p. 208). The transport roads which survive at Lisht are up to 11 m (36 ft) across and consist of a fill of limestone chips and mortar with wooden beams inserted to provide a solid bedding. Over the beams a layer of limestone chips and white gypsum provided a solid surface. Above this, alluvial mud must have acted as a lubricant to ease the movement of the runners of the sledge over the track.

A number of tomb scenes depict statues of wood or stone being pulled on sledges, with one worker usually pouring liquid (probably water) under the front of the sledge's runners. The most famous of these is from the tomb of the 12th-dynasty nobleman Djehutihotep, at el-Bersheh, which shows 172 men pulling a statue. The Egyptians did also use cattle to drag stones or to assist humans in pulling. This is depicted in a number of scenes and was confirmed by the discovery of the carcasses of draft cattle in builders' debris at the 11th-dynasty Mentuhotep complex at Deir el-Bahri.

(Above left) Boat timbers were reused to form hauling tracks at Lisht, east of Senwosret I's pyramid.

(Above right) Twenty men easily pull a 2-ton block on a sledge along lubricated transport tracks for the NOVA pyramid-building experiment (p. 208).

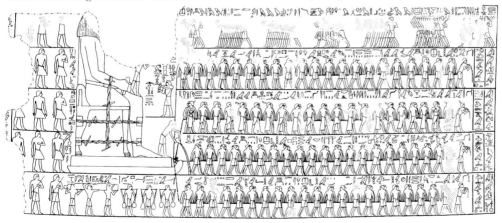

Hauling a nobleman's colossal statue: 172 men are shown pulling the estimated 58-ton statue of Djehutihotep in a relief from his tomb at el-Bersheh.

Transformation of the Giza plateau: around 9 million cu. m of stone were quarried and moved at Giza over three generations of the 4th dynasty. This is a reconstruction of the Giza plateau as it might have appeared near the end of Khufu's reign .

From the small knoll visible at the bottom, left of centre, Khufu's architect could have planned his necropolis. To his lower right was the mouth of the wadi where the harbour would be positioned, as shown here. To his left a bowl-shaped hollow could serve as a quarry for tafla clay and small stones used in enormous quantities to build ramps and secondary structures. The hypothesis of a segregated workmen's community here has not been supported by the last ten years of investigation. The high part of the Mokattam Formation in front was perfect for founding the pyramids. To the right and behind was an ideal area for settlement and the economic infrastructure of pyramid building.

The location of Khufu's valley temple was estimated from the contour lines of maps available in 1985, when this reconstruction was made. Since then our knowledge has grown dramatically – not least by the discovery of the location of the valley temple. We have also learned not only that the floodplain in the Old Kingdom was much lower than was believed, but that there is an extensive Old Kingdom settlement that may once have covered an area of 200 ha (494 acres). Its archaeological remains first came to light in 1989, when the American-British consortium, AMBRIC, began to install a sewage system for a suburb of modern Cairo which reaches up to the foot of the Giza plateau (p. 232).

KEY

1 *Great Pyramid of Khufu*
2 *ramps*
3 *housing for workers*
4 *supply tracks*
5 *harbour, canals*
6 *main quarry*
7 *Khufu's palace complex*

8 *causeway to valley temple*
9 *town*
10 *tombs of royal relatives and officials*
11 *future sites of pyramids of Menkaure and Khafre and of the Sphinx*

Quarries

Each pyramid ideally had a quarry close at hand that supplied the bulk of the stone for the pyramid core. The location of the quarry and the nature of the local stone must have been prime considerations for the pyramid builders. At Giza, the Khufu quarry is now a huge, horseshoe-shaped bite missing from the plateau, some 300 m (985 ft) south of the Great Pyramid. Its floor at its deepest is an extraordinary 30 m (98 ft) below the original surface. The calculated amount of stone removed – c. 2,760,000 cu. m (97.5 million cu. ft) – compares neatly with the total 2,650,000 cu. m (93.5 million cu. ft) in Khufu's pyramid.

Too neatly in fact. There should be more missing than this: modern masons and quarrymen estimate that between 30 and 50 per cent of stone was wasted in the extraction of the stone. However, the quarry extends an unknown distance to the south, beyond the line of Menkaure's causeway – traces of it were cleared here by Abdel Aziz Saleh for Cairo University in 1980. And much stone was taken from the Central Wadi, which served as a conduit for other materials such as Turah limestone and granite. We can be certain that most core stone was quarried locally. More specifically, this was probably the quarry which furnished the bulk of the core stone for Khufu's pyramid. Cut into the towering west face of the quarry is a series of 4th-dynasty tombs, three of them for children of Khafre – evidence that this quarry had fallen into disuse by or during Khafre's reign.

Limestone quarrying by channelling

Between the main Khufu quarry and the Sphinx lies a triangular area of rock honeycombed with tombs. Some are cut into and under rectangles of bedrock the size of small houses, separated by corridors wide enough for an entire tour group to walk through today. These rectangles are quarry blocks, left by 4th-dynasty quarrymen; the tombs were cut much later. The reason we can still wander through these silent stone corridors, once filled with the chink of stone hammers and the chanting of workers, is that the rock was not exploited as deeply as in the main quarry. And that is also why this area offers valuable evidence of ancient quarrying.

The vast quarry blocks would have been subdivided by narrower channels – just wide enough for one workman, who would cut his way through with a pick. In a few places, almost detached from the parent rock, blocks remain about the size of those forming the core walls of Khafre's temples. This and the Sphinx ditch were probably the quarries for those temples, which must have been the last element of Khafre's pyramid complex to be built.

Why start by carving such extraordinarily wide and deep channels, if the blocks they separate are only going to be subdivided further? The answer lies in the absence of iron tools in ancient Egypt. In modern quarries, channels are cut all around a block and then small slots are cut along its bottom bed and iron wedges hammered in until the block cracks from below. With only tools of stone, wood or copper at their disposal, the ancient quarrymen had to use large wooden levers to detach blocks, and needed considerably more room to manoeuvre.

In Menkaure's quarry, just southeast of his pyramid, great lever sockets are still visible. They follow one of the softer, thinner bands of the rock layers at Giza, facilitating the separation of blocks of the thicker, harder stone above. Some have suggested that these slots were not for levers but for wooden wedges, the stone cracking as the soaked wood expanded. However, there is some doubt that this would work and the most likely reconstruction is that once a block had been freed except for its base, rows of men would pry it up using levers.

How many quarrymen?

To build the Great Pyramid in 23 years (the minimum length for Khufu's reign), 322 cu. m (11,371 cu. ft) of stone had to be quarried daily. How many quarrymen would this require? Our NOVA pyramid-building experiment (p. 208) provided a useful comparison: 12 NOVA quarrymen produced 186 stones in 22 days' work, or 8.5 stones per day. But though they worked barefoot and without power tools, they had the advantage of a winch with an iron cable to pull the stones away from the quarry face. An additional 20-man team might have been needed for this task in Khufu's day. Even assuming that an extra 20 men (making a total of 32) were

Granite blocks were cut not with copper or bronze, but were separated from the bedrock by channels pounded out with hammer stones. Here the beginnings of such channels can be seen in a block of granite at Aswan.

required to match the daily rate of the NOVA quarrymen, 322 cu. m (11,371 cu. ft) per day could still have been quarried by 1,212 men (1 cu. m (35 cu. ft) being about the average size of a pyramid core block). That figure can be expanded further to compensate for other advantages of iron tools.

Other types of stone

The fine limestone for the outer pyramid casing was quarried at Turah and transported across the Nile Valley. The quarries now form galleries cut deep within the limestone escarpment. To follow the beds of highest quality stone, the ancient quarrymen tunnelled in and under the overburden of poorer material. Beginning with a 'lead' shelf cut along what would become the gallery ceiling, they then extracted the stone in terraces or banks. Merely to cover Khufu's pyramid, about 67,390 cu. m (2,379,842 cu. ft) of Turah limestone was needed.

Some 934 km (580 miles) to the south at Aswan were quarries which yielded the granite blocks that lined Khufu's burial chamber and plugged his pyramid passage, encased Khafre's pyramid temples and Menkaure's pyramid, and were used for columns of 5th- and 6th-dynasty pyramids, as well as for false doors, offering tables and pyramidions. As much as 45,000 cu. m (1.5 million cu. ft) of granite was quarried in the Aswan quarries in the Old Kingdom. Yet some claim that granite working had yet to be developed and that only natural boulders were used at this period. These would simply have been pried away along natural fractures, shaped and shipped north on great barges. However, the granite pieces forming roofing blocks of Khufu's burial chamber and relieving chambers were over

5.5 m (18 ft) long, as were many columns. It seems inconceivable that large enough boulders existed; more likely they were separated by channelling.

In the case of granite, however, the channels were worked with hand-held pounders of dolerite (p. 211), a hard stone like black granite. This technique is well attested for the New Kingdom and many hundreds of pounders have been found in the quarries at Aswan. There are also numerous channels pounded out by hand and unfinished blocks where a single man has worked away the surface. When I tried my hand at this it took five hours of pounding to produce a patch measuring *c.* 30 x 30 cm (12 x 12 in), worked down by *c.* 2 cm ($\frac{4}{5}$ in). To be 'sent to the granite' was surely to be condemned to the grimmest of the pyramid builders' tasks.

The larger the final block, the wider the channel for separating from the bedrock had to be. Monoliths for Khafre's temples were channelled out of a quarry southwest of the Sphinx.

NOVA quarrymen produced 186 blocks in 22 days by hand, but with the significant advantage of iron tools.

The NOVA Pyramid-Building Experiment

(Right) The critical first course of the NOVA pyramid is levelled, as the ramp covers the base. Our pyramid was just 9 m (29½ ft) to a side, dwarfed by the Great Pyramid in the background.

(Centre) We tested a suggested method of raising heavy blocks by levering. The framework of industrially planed timber was rather unwieldy and wood was in short supply in ancient Egypt.

(Below) Levering was required for the topmost stones, but now working space was restricted and in order to get purchase the levers were very long and high.

The question of how the ancient Egyptians built pyramids of such extraordinary size and precision has spawned many theories but less experimental archaeology. I teamed up with Roger Hopkins, a stonemason from Sudbury, Massachusetts, and a team of Egyptian masons, quarrymen and labourers, to build a small pyramid near the Giza plateau, in an experiment filmed for the NOVA television programme. Working in the shadow of the Great Pyramid, pressures of a film schedule allowed us only three weeks for quarrying and three for building, so we were forced to use tools and technology not available to the ancient Egyptians. Our masons used iron hammers, chisels and levers – their ancestors had only wood, stone and copper. And Roger brought in a front-end loader for shifting and setting the stones of lower courses so that we would have time to test different methods at the top, where restricted space created special difficulties.

Our aim was to test some of the current theories of armchair pyramid builders and try out ancient techniques as authentically as possible. We knew that to fully replicate pyramid building would require nothing less than replicating ancient Egyptian society. Although we failed to match the best efforts of the ancient builders, it was abundantly clear that their expertise was the result not of some mysterious technology or secret sophistication, but of generations of practice and experience.

Moving stones

We found that stones weighing as much as 2.5 tons could be moved by our NOVA workmen simply by tumbling. Just 4 or 5 men were able to lever up and flip over blocks of less than 1 ton. To shift heavier blocks, a rope was looped around the top and it was then pulled by up to 20 men, with a couple more on levers behind. This technique was ideal for shifting stones around the construction yard – but it is most unlikely that sufficient stones could have been tumbled up a ramp to build a whole pyramid within a king's lifetime. Faster methods were needed.

Wooden sledges on rollers offered a much quicker way of moving stones, even though, as we soon discovered, simply loading a block on to a wooden sledge is an operation requiring considerable skill. Next, on soft sand we built an artificial trackway of planed lumber, though ancient tracks were wider, with a surface of hardened gypsum or packed clay. Then we used rollers consisting of small, cylindrical pieces of wood. The lynchpin of the entire operation was the man who received the rollers from the back of the sledge and put them down in front, creating a continually rolling roadway. With 12 to 20 men pulling the load at a swift pace, his was a very skilled task. If he laid just one roller at an angle, both sledge and load immediately followed it off the track. A huge number of rollers would have been needed to move the stones up on to the pyramid. With neither abundant supplies of wood, nor the mechanical lathe this method must have had only restricted application.

Artificial slideways, as found at Lisht (p. 203) proved a much more efficient method. In our experiment we built two parallel retaining walls which were then filled with debris to create an inclined ramp. On top we built a roadbed with wooden crosspieces, following the approximate specifications of those at Lisht. We found that a 2-ton stone on a sledge could be pulled by 20 men or fewer. This success, in conjunction with evidence of tomb representations, remains of ancient embankments and trackways at Lisht, convinced us that this was the most likely means the Egyptians used to bring in the bulk of the core stones.

Raising stones

While it is widely agreed that ramps were used to raise blocks (p. 215), several theorists have pro-

posed that it was achieved by levering. Martin Isler proposed that there were temporary stairways in the middle of each pyramid face for levering up stones.

When we put levering to the test, unforeseen difficulties emerged. A set of levers is needed on two sides to lift a block: one side is raised and supported, then the other side is levered up to bring it level. As the stone is rocked upwards it is supported on a stack of wood. This required two deep notches in each side of a block, which are not found on pyramid core stones. Lever sockets are occasionally found in casing stones, but they are clearly for side adjustment. More critically, the wooden supports were precarious and unwieldy, in spite of our using planed lumber. Similar difficulties arose with the fulcrum, which had to rise with the load. It seemed to us, therefore, that some system involving a ramp or ramps was the most likely method used.

Many pyramid theorists resort to levering to explain how the capstone and the topmost courses were set, since by that level there was simply no longer room for ramps (p. 222). However, to climb the pyramids of Khufu and Khafre and look down their steep slopes and narrow steps is to realize that great bulk of the pyramid could not have been raised in this way.

Getting to the point: NOVA masons begin to trim the casing from the top downwards. We had just three weeks and 44 workmen to build our pyramid consisting of 186 stones and measuring 6 m (20ft) high. It would have fitted neatly on to the top of the Great Pyramid, in whose shadow we built it.

Tools, Techniques and Operations

Like all technology, ancient or modern, pyramid building was based on tools, techniques and operations. The Egyptian builders used their simple tools – such as plumb bobs, string, rope, wood, stone hammers, sledges, copper chisels and saws – in certain techniques – measuring, aligning, chiselling, levering, cutting and polishing and so on. The techniques were then combined into the operations, and operations into the technical ensembles that built pyramid complexes.

(Below) Ancient wooden tools: a square level with plumb bob (top); set square (left); and vertical plumb rod (right) in Cairo Museum.

Right angles, verticals and surfaces

The levelling of the pyramids, in all its finesse, was probably achieved with simple wooden instruments and plumb lines. The set square enabled right angles to be laid out or checked, while the plumb bob, suspended from a rod, was used for vertical adjustments. The square level – an A-shaped wooden frame with legs of equal length – was used for levelling surfaces. When its plumb bob (suspended from the corner where the two arms of the 'A' join) aligns with the mark at the centre of the crosspiece, the surface on which the two legs are standing is level.

It was long thought that the bases of pyramids were levelled by channelling water (p. 214). However, water-lifting technology in the Old Kingdom was limited to simple shoulder-poles with pots slung on either end. For levelling operations for a pyramid like Khufu's with a base area of 5.3 ha (13.1 acres), an impossibly large quantity would need to be carried up to the plateau – to say nothing of the problems of the water evaporating before a levelling trench could be filled to the requisite height.

Drilling and sawing very hard stone

How ancient builders cut through stone as hard as granite and basalt remains one of the truly perplexing questions of pyramid-age masonry. Drill holes in granite showing pronounced striations survive in many different 4th- and 5th-dynasty monuments. Whatever was used to cut it had to be at least as hard as the hardest of the minerals that granite is composed of – quartz.

It is most likely that a copper drill or saw was employed in conjunction with an abrasive slurry of water, gypsum and quartz sand. The copper blade simply acted as a guide while the quartz sand did the actual cutting. I have seen dried remains of this slurry, tinted green from the copper, in deep saw cuts in basalt blocks in Khufu's mortuary temple. Bronze – a harder alloy of copper with some tin – was probably not used in Egypt before the Middle Kingdom.

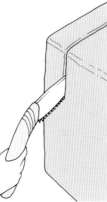

Ancient Egyptian masons drilled and sawed hard basalt (below right) and granite. Copper blades probably guided the gypsum and sand that did the actual cutting.

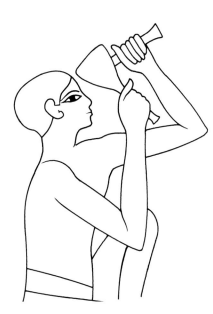

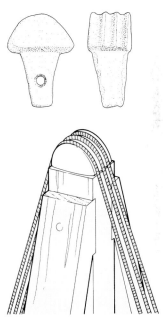

Smoothing the pyramid casing

The many acres of fine Turah limestone which cover the pyramids were dressed using chisels only *c.* 8 mm (⅓ in) wide. Wider blades of soft copper simply will not work on stone. But it is also consistent with what we know already of the Old Kingdom: massive projects were invariably undertaken in small increments repeated innumerable times.

Nick Fairplay, the English master carver working with my team, studied the evidence of ancient chisel working. Not only is he able to identify the striations left by the edge of an individual chisel, but also precisely at what point the corners of the chisel curled and forced the workman to stop and resharpen his tool. This had to be done far more often than by modern masons using steel tools. He estimates that a full-time tool sharpener was required for every 100 chiselmen working on the facing.

Pounding

Dolerite pounders were used in the laborious work of channelling out blocks from the granite quarries at Aswan. They were initially pear-shaped hammerstones, but through use they became increasingly rounded as the mason repeatedly turned them to exploit a new percussion edge when an old one wore away. Weighing *c.* 4–7 kg (*c.* 9–15 lb), they had to be held in two hands. Once fully rounded they were no longer as useful as pounders, but a number have been found beneath very heavy sarcophagi at Giza, suggesting that they were recycled as pivots and rollers – primitive ball-bearings.

The mystery tool

Examples of these have been found at Giza, apparently dating to the Old Kingdom. They are mushroom-shaped with one or two holes through the stem and three parallel grooves cut into the head. It has been suggested that they could have been bearing stones or proto-pulleys, with the stem inserted into a pole or scaffold and the grooves acting as guides for rope. There is no rimmed wheel, as in a true pulley, but the direction of pull could probably have been changed by running the ropes through the grooves.

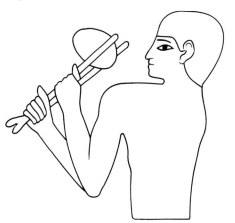

(Left) Dolerite pounding stones were grasped in two hands and used to shape granite. Smaller ones were sometimes hafted into wooden stick handles to tap out finer detail.

Survey and Alignment

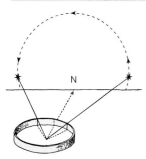

Finding true north by bisecting the angle of rising and setting of a star over a circular, level wall, as suggested by I.E.S. Edwards. The length of the north line achieved would be the radius of the circle.

Orienting the pyramids: by the stars...

Old Kingdom builders achieved amazing accuracy in orienting the sides of pyramids – the greatest deviation of any of the four sides of Khufu's pyramid, for example, is under 3' 26" of an arc, or less than $\frac{1}{15}$ of $1°$. I.E.S. Edwards argued that such precision could only have been achieved by observation of the stars. His method involved building a circular wall a few feet in diameter and tall enough to exclude all but the night sky from the view of a person standing inside. Acting as an artificial horizon, the wall had to be absolutely horizontal – Edwards suggested that this could have been achieved using water contained by mud banks. A person in the centre of the circle facing north would select a star and mark its rising and setting points at the top of the wall. These points would be extended to the foot of the wall using a plumb line and joined to the centre of the circle. North was the bisection of the angle of the lines at the centre.

Building the Base of Khufu's Pyramid

The building sequence of the northeast corner of Khufu's pyramid (*above* and diagrams): numbers indicate existing features or ones known from traces, or that exist at other places around the base of this pyramid and queen's pyramid GI-c. Features are shown at correct relative scale.

The builders first extended a reference line **(1)** oriented to true north. The next step was to lay out a square with precise right-angles. The massif of natural rock retained in Khufu's pyramid (**2** and *above*) prevented the builders from measuring the diagonals to check the accuracy of their square.

II The foundation platform

The extraordinarily accurate levelling of Khufu's pyramid was achieved on the surface of the foundation platform, not the bedrock. This platform **(10)** *was composed of Turah-quality limestone slabs with occasional backing stones of local limestone (stippled). The steps of the bedrock*

massif **(2)** *were incorporated into the platform as successive courses were built up.*

At the northeast corner of the platform was a very large slab **(11)**. *Its extraordinary size may indicate that this was the first corner to be established. The socket actually extends 0.9 m (3 ft)*

beyond the extrapolated lines of the platform **(12)**.

The setting line of the foundation platform **(9)** *would have been erased as large slabs were brought in. It would also have been covered by the extra stock of stone on the front face of the slabs. A line of rectangular holes* **(8)** *runs along the east and north sides of the pyramid. The holes could have held posts to which cord was pinned to form an outside reference line.*

The lines of the front face **(4, 9)** *and upper edge* **(13)** *of the platform would have been marked on each slab as it was laid by measuring in from the reference line. When slabs were dragged in, part of the line could have been removed and later restored.*

No post-hole **(14)** *marking the corner of the east and north reference lines has been found. If the perpendicular to the east reference line had been established by an intersecting arc, however, it would not have been needed.*

III The first course

IV Defining the pyramid base

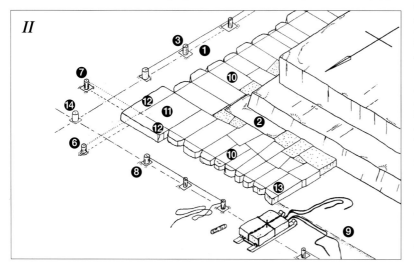

II

I Constructing a right-angle

The ancient surveyors could have achieved a right-angle in three ways:

a) with a set square

One leg of an A-shaped set-square is placed on the already established line and the perpendicular is taken from the other leg. The square is flipped and the operation repeated. The exact perpendicular takes into account the small angle of error between the two positions – exaggerated in the drawing. With legs 2.5 m (8 ft) long, this set-square is larger than any known from ancient Egypt. Even so, the perpendicular it provides is short considering the line was extended more than 230 m (754 ft).

b) with a 3-4-5 triangle

The 'Sacred' or Pythagorean triangle – three units on one side, four on the other and five on the hypotenuse – gives a right-angle. Such triangles seem to be present in the design of Old Kingdom mortuary temples, though the evidence is inconclusive. Here a unit of 7 cubits (1 royal cubit = 0.525 m x 7 = 3.675 m or c. 12 ft) is used because this is the average spacing between the series of holes along the sides of Khufu's pyramid (see below).

This method establishes a perpendicular line 14.7 m (48 ft) long (0.525 x 7 cubits x 4) – longer than that obtained using a set-square. Note that the triangle could not have been much larger without hitting the bedrock massif.

c) by intersecting arcs

The intersections of two arcs obtained by stretching and rotating cords of the same radius from two points on the same line also establishes a perpendicular. Some have doubted that this method was used because the elasticity of the cord would give inaccurate results, but it might explain several features of Khufu's pyramid.

In laying out the pyramid base it was necessary to fix the setting line for one side of the platform (4). The next step was to establish the corner (5). Exactly 10 cubits (5.25 m/17 ¼ ft) due north of the northeast corner of the foundation platform is a round hole (6). An arc from the corner point (5) touches another hole (7), due east of this and on the extension of the north line of the platform. This one is rectangular like those of the reference lines.

However, the perpendicular established by intersecting arcs with centres at points 5 and 6 falls neither along the north platform line (9) nor along the line of holes on the north side (8). But the ancient surveyors could have measured from any perpendicular to establish a reference or setting line.

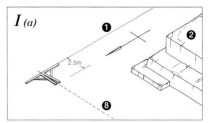

I (a)

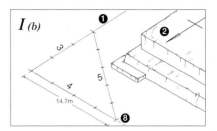

I (b)

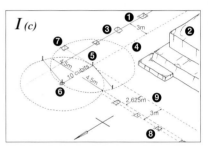

I (c)

The pyramid's first course rises slightly above the step cut into the bedrock massif (15). The setting line (16) for the foot of the casing is set back from the line marking the upper edge of the foundation platform (13). The extra stock and handling bosses (17) on the casing stones are modelled on examples on GI-c. Once again, sections of the reference line could have been taken out when a casing block was brought in, and then replaced.

Two blocks have been wedged up on rollers to cut their joint sides parallel before they are put into position and the pyramid slope marked on their fronts (p. 220).

The pyramid base would have been finally delineated only when the pyramid was complete and the extra stock cut from the casing blocks. A paved pyramid court extended 20 cubits (10.5 m or 34 ft) from the foundation platform on all sides, bounded by an enclosure wall (19).

Slabs of the same thickness as the foundation platform brought the pavement flush with the platform and completely hid its front face (18), leaving the foot of the casing (16) as the visual baseline of the pyramid. The slabs were custom-cut and set in an irregular mosaic.

Today the pavement is completely missing at the northeast corner of the pyramid and the diagram is therefore based on a patch preserved at the north side of the pyramid, and along the north side of Khufu's mortuary temple.

At this stage the holes for stakes along the reference lines, were no longer needed, so the masons closed them with small stones (20) before covering them with the court pavement.

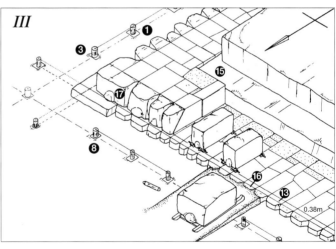

III

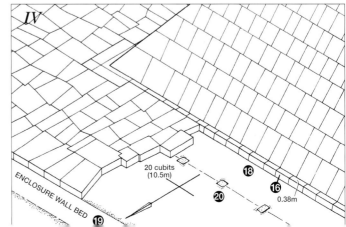

IV

(Above) The entrance to the descending passage of Khufu's first queen's pyramid. A notch is clearly visible in the lintel which may mark the axis of a satellite pyramid that was never built.

Finding north by the sun. A pole, or gnomon, is made vertical with the aid of plumb. True north is the bisection of the angle of the shadows cast by the pole before and after noon. A row of poles would give a series of north lines that could serve as a check on extending the reference line for the pyramid base.

...or by the sun?

Late, rather arcane texts that deal with the founding of temples mention 'the shadow' and 'the stride of Ra', the sun-god, hinting at a method using the sun. This could have been based on the fact that the sun rises and sets in equal but opposite angles to true north. In this method, a pole, or gnomon, is set up, using a plumb line to make it as vertical as possible, and its shadow is measured about 3 hours before noon. That length becomes the radius of a circle. As the sun rises the shadow shrinks back from the line and then lengthens in the afternoon. When it reaches the circle again it forms an angle with the morning's line. The bisection of the angle is true north.

The sun-and-shadow method may perhaps not be as accurate as that based on stellar observations and is certainly less consistent through the year, being more exact during the solstices. However, the next operation the ancient surveyors had to perform was extending the line to the length of a pyramid side without any deviation. For the NOVA pyramid experiment, Roger Hopkins used a gnomon 1.38 m (4½ ft) high to produce a line 1.45 m (4¾ ft) long. As his ancient predecessors might have done, Roger repeated the operation, producing a series of north lines, checking the orientation of the pyramid line as he went. Perhaps it is more realistic to envisage gnomons erected along the base of the pyramid than a series of circular walls and artificial canals.

Levelling the pyramid base

As with their orientation, the levelling of the pyramids was an extraordinarily precise feat. The base of Khufu's pyramid is level to within just 2.1 cm (*c.* 1 in). It has been argued that this was achieved using water: Edwards, for example, suggested that banks of Nile mud were constructed to form an enclosure which was flooded with water. A grid of trenches was then cut, the bottom of each at a uniform depth below the water. But the impracticality of working with chisels and stone hammers in water is clear. What might have been possible was to dig a network of channels, then flood this and mark the level of the water's surface on the sides. Once the water was drained off, the channels could be cut to a standard depth from those marks.

Such a theory might work for pyramids like Meidum and Dahshur which were built on desert surfaces and may have flatter bases. But in building the pyramids of Khufu and Khafre the ancient masons started on a sloping plateau *c.* 7–10 m (23–33 ft) higher than the eventual base and in each case left a massif of rock in the body of the pyramid. They only levelled (and then approximately) a strip around this massif and in the case of Khufu's pyramid it was the surface of the foundation platform that was precisely levelled, rather than the bedrock. For Khafre's pyramid the ancient builders cut down the northwest corner by 10 m (33 ft), but actually built up the opposite, southeast corner.

Any levelling technique using water must take into account the problem that water lifting and transport in the Old Kingdom was probably limited to pots slung from shoulder poles. Even if all this water had been carried up to the plateau, it would more than likely have evaporated or drained away before any measurements could be completed. Such practical hurdles make all theories using water unworkable.

The outside reference line

At roughly regular spacings parallel to the sides of both Khufu's and Khafre's pyramids are lines of holes. They form a double line of staggered pairs, each *c.* 30 cm (12 in) in diameter around Khafre's, the pairs spaced *c.* 10 cubits (5.25 m or 17 ¼ ft) apart. The spacings are not so accurate as to be incremental measurements of length. Rather, stakes in these holes perhaps carried a reference line, tied from one stake to another, for measuring perpendicularly to establish the final pyramid baseline. At the same time they could have been used as a levelling reference by all being marked or cut to the same height.

A section of cord and stakes could be taken out whenever a block had to be moved in, and then closed up again by replacing the stakes and extrapolating from the line still in place. Finally, the ancient builders would cut the stones to form the baseline of the pyramid.

Given the fact that the stones of a giant pyramid like Khufu's had to be raised as much as 146 m (479 ft) from the ground, if a ramp was indeed used it would have been a colossal structure in its own right. According to some ideas about its shape, it would in fact have required as much or more material than the pyramid itself.

Petrie failed to identify the quarry for Khufu's pyramid because it was filled with millions of cubic metres of limestone chips, gypsum, sand and tafla clay. This debris, partially cleared by Selim Hassan in the 1920s and 1930s, probably includes the remains of the construction ramp, pushed back into the quarry as the workers completed the pyramid. At Lisht ramps for the Middle Kingdom pyramids were made of mudbrick. But at Giza there is no substantial deposit of Nile alluvial mud. Whatever its precise configuration, the ramp must have been made of locally available materials. This artificial combination of gypsum, tafla and limestone chips is present in truly vast quantities on the plateau.

The configuration of the ramp

The question of what kind of ramp was used has produced a whole spectrum of possible answers: the straight-on or perpendicular ramp; the spiral ramp either built on the pyramid or sitting on the floor and leaning against it; the ramp which zig-zags up just one face (again, either built on the pyramid or leaning against it); and the internal ramp. It has also been suggested, for example by Uvo Hölscher, that ramps could have leaned against the face of each step of an inner step pyramid. But apart from failing to explain how the outer casing was then added, this also contradicts the evidence: the provincial pyramid at Sinki, South Abydos, and Sekhemkhet's pyramid, both unfinished step pyramids, have perpendicular rather than parallel ramps (p. 217). Finally there are theorists who argue that there were no ramps; rather that the stones were levered up to the requisite height for each course. As we have seen, the NOVA experiment suggests that levering was practical only for side movements, final adjustments and setting the stones of the very uppermost courses – not for raising the bulk of the core and casing stones (p. 208).

The straight-on ramp against one face of the pyramid has had strong advocates, and a variety of forms have been devised. One disagreement is whether it would have covered all, or just part of, one face. To cloak only part of the face meant it would have to be extraordinarily thin and tall in order to build the upper part of the pyramid. In order to maintain a functional slope – about one unit of rise in ten units of length – the straight-on ramp would have to be lengthened every time it was raised, inevitably slowing down the work on the pyramid itself and using up vast resources of manpower and materials. On the other hand, it left

Ramps

the four corners free for backsighting, still considered by some to have been important for maintaining control of the pyramid slope.

Alternatively, the ramp may have been spiral-shaped, winding up and around the pyramid. One form of this was suggested by Dows Dunham, following his work with George Reisner at Menkaure's pyramid at Giza. He suggested a total of four ramps, one running from each corner. Clinging to the pyramid, they would wind anti-clockwise up and around it as it grew, running on top of an embankment founded on the stepped, undressed courses of each face. This form of ramp would require far less material than the straight-on type, not needing to start so far out from the pyramid to achieve a functional slope. It would also leave the face relatively free for control of the rise and run of the pyramid itself. In this interpretation the undressed outer casing courses would have to be rather step-like to support the embankments. Evidence of unfinished casing stones on the north side of Menkaure's pyramid shows that there at least the unfinished faces, still with their handling bosses, were not step-like and probably could not have supported such a ramp.

A related theory suggests a zigzagging ramp going up one face of the pyramid. It has many of the same problems as the spiral ramp. I investigated a model of a spiral ramp which, rather than resting on the pyramid itself, is like an accretion (similar to the accretions of the early step pyramids) that actually leaned against each face of the

In building our NOVA pyramid (p. 208) we constructed an inclined ramp of retaining walls of tafla, limestone chips and gypsum. The ramp rose 1 m (3¼ ft) in a length of 14 m (46 ft) to reach the top of the first course of the pyramid at its northwest corner and then wrapped around three sides of the pyramid.

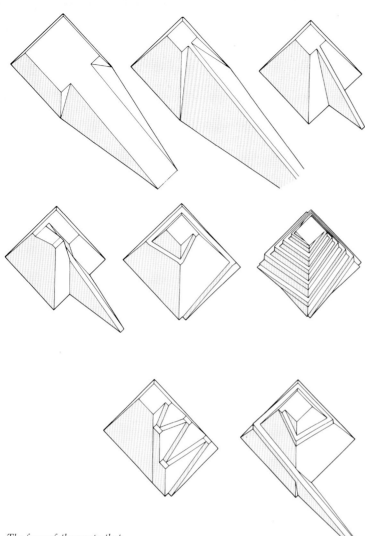

The form of the ramps that supplied materials to the workforce as the pyramid rose is a persistent puzzle and one that has given rise to a number of different ideas for configurations, from a zigzag ramp up one face of the pyramid to an internal ramp. In fact most of the other suggested variations can be broken down into one or a combination of two main types: a straight, sloping ramp up one face of the pyramid; or one or several ramps that begin near the base and wrap around the pyramid. It is possible that a combination of the two was used, with a straight sloping ramp up against one side and rising to about a third of the pyramid's height, which from this point wraps around the pyramid (third row, right).

pyramid. The entire ramp is like an envelope, built up at the same time as the pyramid and almost completely cloaking it, with a roadway on top. I arrived at this configuration by studying the topography of Khufu's pyramid – the ramp would start at the mouth of the quarry and run for 320 m (1,050 ft), the distance to the southwest corner of the pyramid, gaining a total rise of 37 m (121 ft) at a slope of about 6° 36'. A ramp of very similar dimensions is described in the Papyrus Anastasi of the late New Kingdom, when one scribe taunts another over whether he could build a ramp of such-and-such specifications. The next section of road bed would rise along the west side of the pyramid for a length of 250 m (820 ft) (slightly longer than the base of the pyramid) at the increased slope of 7° 18'. It then would run along the north side, and so on for 1¼ turns all the way up and around the pyramid. The angle of slope increases from 10–12°, to 14°, and finally for the last 40 m (131 ft), approaching the very top, it is as steep as 18° 39' – probably too steep – and the builders may also have been running out of room.

Other theorists disagree with this suggestion because it involves entirely cloaking the pyramid. They believe that the builders depended on having a clear view of masonry already completed in order to control the rise and run of the pyramid face. However, as we shall see, the Egyptians were already in effect cloaking the pyramid surface by leaving extra stock of stone on every casing stone that they set (p. 220). Sighting back to already laid masonry cannot have been a significant way of controlling the rising pyramid.

Stadelmann has suggested a ramp to one corner, which then leant against one side, much like the first part of the preceding model, for the middle part of the pyramid. For the lower part, many small straight-on ramps fed the pyramid. At 120 m (394 ft), a series of small ramps rested on the stepped faces that would be filled in after the pyramidion and corners had been delivered.

Finally we must include the internal ramp proposed by Dieter Arnold. This would not need to start so far away as the straight-on ramp because part of the rise is actually in the masonry of the pyramid itself. However, there is little evidence in support of such a configuration in the gigantic pyramids, although there are construction gaps in pyramids of the 5th dynasty for building the internal burial chambers.

The NOVA pyramid building project (p. 208) left me more sympathetic to the idea of ramps that clung to the pyramid face. Casing stones left projecting further than the others – whether an entire course or individual stones staggered across the face – could have served as a foundation for an embankment and roadway. Evidence that may support this configuration has very recently come to light: Zahi Hawass's excavations have revealed that the additional stock left on the undressed casing stones at the base of Khufu's queens' pyramids was a major protruding portion of the blocks.

Archaeological evidence

Knowing the position of Khufu's quarry helps us make deductions about the configuration of the ramp. It was unlikely to have been a straight-on ramp, running directly from quarry entrance to near the top of the pyramid, since it would have been impracticably steep to reach the higher courses. To maintain a workable slope it would have begun to overshoot the quarry by the time the pyramid rose to two-thirds of its final height. It is also unlikely that any ramp would have extended over the areas to the east or west of Khufu's pyramid, since we know that he was building cemeteries there early in his reign: hieroglyphic texts and graffiti reveal that the Western Cemetery for high officials was underway by year 5 of Khufu's reign, while the Eastern Cemetery of mastabas for his nearest relatives and queens had begun by year 12.

A few pyramid ramps have been discovered *in situ*, so most discussion on the subject is hypothetical. Ramps have been found at small, 3rd-dynasty pyramids. For example, a surviving ramp makes a perpendicular approach over the enclosure wall from quarries to the west of Sekhemkhet's pyramid at Saqqara, abandoned very early in construction. And at Sinki, South Abydos, Gunter Dreyer and Nabil Swelim discovered a frozen moment in the construction of a tiny pyramid with ramps still in place, perpendicular to its sides over the lower steps. And, as we have seen, evidence of the roadbeds that ran along the top of embankments and ramps survives at the sites of later pyramids, such as that of Senwosret I at Lisht.

At Meidum there is what appears to be a hauling track or possibly the remains of a ramp approaching from the southwest. This trackway seems to lead directly over the satellite pyramid and, if projected, reaches the higher courses of the pyramid's western side. Another so-called ramp approaches from the east, though this is more likely an earlier causeway than a construction ramp (p. 99). However, it does align with a recess in the face of the fifth and sixth steps of the second step pyramid, E2, which led Borchardt to reconstruct it as a very thin and startlingly high straight-on or sloping ramp up to the pyramid face at that point.

At the North Pyramid of Dahshur remains of two transport roads approach from southwesterly quarries. Composed of compact chips and marly sand, they come in very close to the pyramid, implying that the core stone was hauled right up to its base – and so lending support to the theory that the ramp clung to the pyramid. Two other tracks composed of white limestone chips approach from the east, marking the delivery, perhaps, of the casing stones.

East of Khufu's pyramid and south of the queens' pyramids and the mastabas in the Eastern Field, archaeologists from Cairo University excavated two parallel walls, formed, like so many other secondary walls at Giza, of small broken stone set in tafla clay. One of the walls is thicker and made of segments *c.* 10 cubits (5.25 m or 17 ft 3 in) long. Because the excavators cleared the debris between them they now describe a corridor, but we suspect that they were retaining walls – the debris fill being the body of a ramp or construction embankment. Similar structures have been found, for example an embankment which still leans against the incomplete southern wall of the mastaba field to the west of Khufu's pyramid. And George Reisner found construction embankments filling an unfinished room in Menkaure's mortuary temple.

Much of pyramid construction, including ramps and embankments, was simply the engineering of huge amounts of limestone chip, tafla and gypsum. One advantage of this material was that once structures were no longer needed, it easily disintegrated into its constituent parts when struck with a pick.

The Sinki pyramid at South Abydos, a small step pyramid with its ramp still in situ against one face.

On the basis of archaeological evidence, Borchardt reconstructed a very thin and high straight ramp at the pyramid of Meidum.

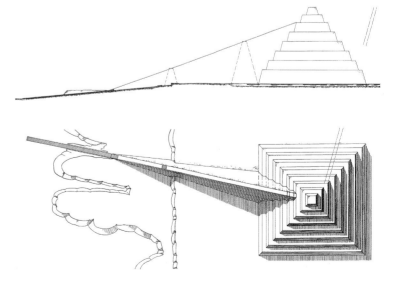

Rise and Run

The geometry of a pyramid is deceptively simple: a square base with its centre point raised to create four triangular faces; or, alternatively, a series of squares within squares, each decreasing in size and raised slightly to create the slope, or rise and run, in the face. When building a pyramid on a monumental scale absolute precision is crucial. If the four diagonal lines deviated, the builders would have to twist the top to make them meet – as can just be detected at the top of Khafre's pyramid.

A key question in pyramid construction is therefore how the ancient Egyptian masons controlled the diagonals and axes of the square as they built the pyramid upwards. They had to ensure that all

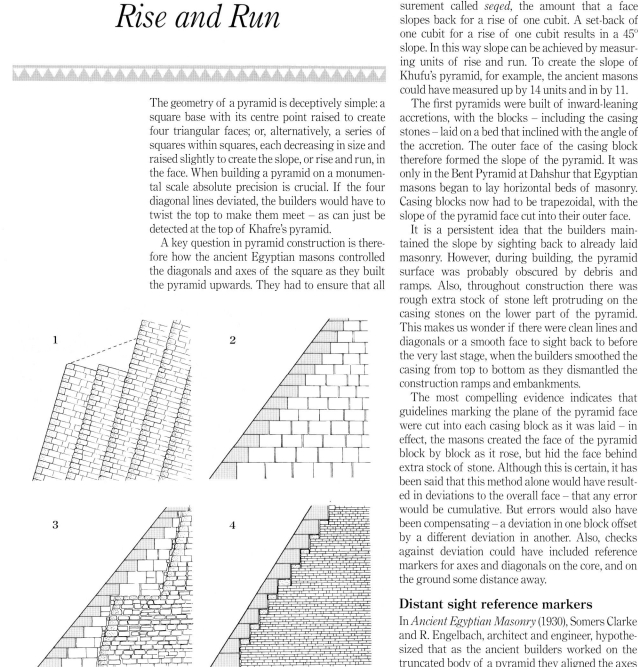

Not all pyramids were built in the same way, and methods varied greatly through time:
1 Pyramids of the 3rd-dynasty were built of inward-leaning accretion layers.
2 In the 4th-dynasty well-built horizontal layers with shaped casing stones were favoured.
3 Later pyramids had rough masonry cores. Between core and casing was a layer of backing stones. **4** From Senwosret III onwards pyramids had cores of mudbrick, with a fine casing.

met at the top at the central point – so that they literally did not miss the point.

Egyptian masons determined slopes with a measurement called *seqed*, the amount that a face slopes back for a rise of one cubit. A set-back of one cubit for a rise of one cubit results in a 45° slope. In this way slope can be achieved by measuring units of rise and run. To create the slope of Khufu's pyramid, for example, the ancient masons could have measured up by 14 units and in by 11.

The first pyramids were built of inward-leaning accretions, with the blocks – including the casing stones – laid on a bed that inclined with the angle of the accretion. The outer face of the casing block therefore formed the slope of the pyramid. It was only in the Bent Pyramid at Dahshur that Egyptian masons began to lay horizontal beds of masonry. Casing blocks now had to be trapezoidal, with the slope of the pyramid face cut into their outer face.

It is a persistent idea that the builders maintained the slope by sighting back to already laid masonry. However, during building, the pyramid surface was probably obscured by debris and ramps. Also, throughout construction there was rough extra stock of stone left protruding on the casing stones on the lower part of the pyramid. This makes us wonder if there were clean lines and diagonals or a smooth face to sight back to before the very last stage, when the builders smoothed the casing from top to bottom as they dismantled the construction ramps and embankments.

The most compelling evidence indicates that guidelines marking the plane of the pyramid face were cut into each casing block as it was laid – in effect, the masons created the face of the pyramid block by block as it rose, but hid the face behind extra stock of stone. Although this is certain, it has been said that this method alone would have resulted in deviations to the overall face – that any error would be cumulative. But errors would also have been compensating – a deviation in one block offset by a different deviation in another. Also, checks against deviation could have included reference markers for axes and diagonals on the core, and on the ground some distance away.

Distant sight reference markers

In *Ancient Egyptian Masonry* (1930), Somers Clarke and R. Engelbach, architect and engineer, hypothesized that as the ancient builders worked on the truncated body of a pyramid they aligned the axes and diagonals by eye using backsights on the ground some distance away. This possibility has never been properly investigated.

Over the years at Giza I have come across possible socket holes for marker posts. One, for example, now filled with ancient debris and covered with modern gravel, lies to the north of Khufu's pyramid and appears to align with its centre axis. There is a dashed series of notches carved in the rock floor a

(Left) The three queens' pyramids of Menkaure reveal details of their construction. Two of them were perhaps never completed.

short distance from, and aligned with, the southeast diagonal of Khafre's pyramid. Systematic mapping of such marks has hardly begun: the results may cast much light on ancient methods of controlling rise and run.

The inner step pyramid

As we have seen, Sneferu began his pyramid of Meidum as a seven-step pyramid and then enlarged it to eight steps (p. 97). At both stages, the steps were sheathed in white limestone with corners fine enough to serve as a reference for the casing of E3, the true pyramid, as some theorists believe they did. But while we can be certain that Meidum was originally a step pyramid, the same is probably not true of most large 4th-dynasty pyramids, beginning with the Bent Pyramid of Sneferu. However, the core could have been built as a stepped nucleus, slightly or completely ahead of the casing. Then there is the question of whether inner step pyramids were built, as at Meidum, of accretions. Some theorists, following Borchardt, believe that the so-called 'girdle stones' through which the Ascending Passage of the Great Pyramid was carved represent the accretions of an inner step pyramid. But the simple fact is that the masonry of the large 4th-dynasty pyramids is too complete for us to be certain either way.

Khufu's queens' pyramids, GI-a, GI-b and GI-c, certainly had each a stepped inner nucleus, not, however, formed of accretions. Thin walls of small limestone blocks at the denuded top and northwest corner of GI-a might be taken for accretions, but they are probably provisional walls for marking and building the steps of the nucleus. It is said these were four-step pyramids, but the fourth step is little more than a pile of roughly shaped stones on top of the third tier. The tiers are obscured by larger stones that filled in the steps. At the bottom, between remains of the casing and the core, is a packing of small blocks of soft, yellow limestone.

(Right) The southernmost of Khufu's queens' pyramids (GI-c), with the stepped inner core and finer limestone casing still visible. Small holes in the corners of the core masonry blocks align with the pyramid diagonals. Three tiers are visible, each made of rectangular blocks of masonry. Occasionally, vertical seams can be detected in these tiers, possibly reflecting the division of the workforce into competing gangs. Softer and smaller packing stones lie between the backing stones and the casing, while the upper part of the pyramid is a huge mass of loose, irregularly shaped limestone boulders.

Menkaure's subsidiary pyramids were also built with a stepped nucleus. The first, GIII-a, was begun as a satellite pyramid for the king and completed as a true pyramid. The other two are something of a puzzle. The fact that the outer masonry of the steps is so well finished leads some to conclude that GIII-b and GIII-c were intended to be left as step pyramids. Others believe these stepped cores were meant to have a mantle of packing and casing, creating true pyramids. This would have left little room for eastern chapels, so some believe that they were once encased as step pyramids, like Djoser's. Yet they show no residue of casing or packing, as does GIII-a. If stepped because they are unfinished true pyramids, it means that, here at least, the entire stepped nucleus was built before being filled out and encased.

That Menkaure's own pyramid was built in steps or tiers, each of mastaba-like parts, is hinted at by the patterns of core masonry showing in the great gash in its northern face.

Setting Casing Blocks and Pyramid Slope

These diagrams illustrate the first stages of setting corner casing blocks and the first blocks to either side. They all show the northwest corner of a pyramid, though the point of view alternates from looking southeast (straight on at the corner, I and III), to northeast (II and IV). Steps 1 to 16 are the same on either side of the corner block.

1 Corner block moved above its setting position on rollers. Only the underside is dressed.
2 Side joint faces of corner block dressed.
3 First normal blocks moved in on each side of corner block with undersides only dressed. Side joint faces dressed parallel with matching joint face of corner block. Exact join controlled by measuring with cord.

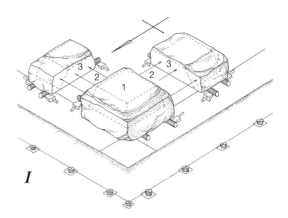

I

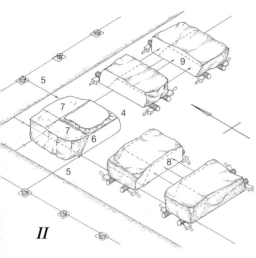

II

4 Corner block set down off rollers into its final position.
5 Measurement made from outside reference line (for first course at base only) to mark pyramid baseline on joint faces of corner block.
6 Slope (rise 14 units, run 11 units) marked on joint faces of corner block, using either a plumb line or set square made

with the correct angle, placed against the vertical smoothed face of block.

Extra stock on front of block bevelled away from slope line. Corners themselves (as opposed to joint faces of corner blocks) left unbevelled so as not to obliterate the extension of the pyramid face line.

7 Pyramid face line marked on top surface of corner block. Top surface dressed along outside of pyramid face lines.
8 Second normal block on each side moved in.
9 Side joint faces cut parallel with matching joint side of first normal block.

10 First normal block on either side moved up to join with corner block. Extra dressed stone on joint face protrudes above and in front of join with corner block.
11 Extra stock on front faces of first normal blocks bevelled away from slope line as marked and bevelled on joint faces of corner block.

12 Measurement made from outside reference line to mark pyramid baseline on opposite joint face of first normal blocks.
13 Slope (rise 14 units, run 11 units) marked on opposite joint faces of first normal blocks. Extra stock on front of block bevelled away from slope line.

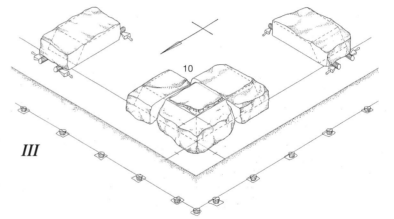

III

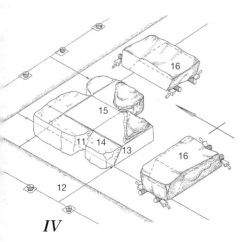

IV

14 Pyramid face line marked on top of block. Top surface dressed along outside of pyramid face lines.
15 Top surface of blocks finely dressed inside pyramid face lines to prepare bed for next course of casing stone.
16 Second normal blocks drawn up to repeat steps 10 to 15.

(Right) To mark the angle of the pyramid slope the builders could either measure in from a plumb line or use a wooden set square made at the required angle.

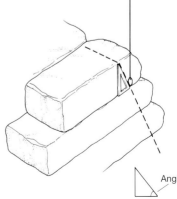

Angle of slope

Controls marked on the core masonry

The masonry of these step pyramids was clearly itself too roughly constructed to act as a reference for the outer slope. But it is possible that the stepped nucleus was built in advance of the outer casing so that guidelines and reference marks for laying in the casing could have been transferred up and on to its steps. On the southernmost pyramid of Khufu's queens, GI-c, we have found small holes (c. 5 cm (2 in) diameter) in the corners of the tiers of core masonry blocks that appear to align with the pyramid diagonals, though more mapping work is needed to verify this impression. These could have been for pegs that held the string to mark an inner reference square for measuring out to the pyramid facial lines in the casing. On the other hand, the string might have guided the less precise building of the stepped nucleus. This was the purpose of a provisional wall with red painted levelling lines and cubit notations at the northwest corner of GI-a.

At the back of the chasm on the north face of Menkaure's pyramid, created by Saladin's son Othman (p. 41), the stones of an inner tier still bear a red painted vertical line marking the pyramid centre axis. A host of other marks on the pyramids made by ancient masons, architects and surveyors, remains to be studied. There are crude notches in the core masonry on the centre axes above the entrances of the Bent Pyramid's satellite pyramid, queen's pyramid GI-a, the back side of the west wall of Menkaure's mortuary temple and the upper masonry block of Khentkawes's Giza tomb. Similar notches exist in core or backing stones at the corners of Khufu's and Khafre's pyramids, where they seem to be alignment markers for core masonry. Without further study, the discussion of the purpose of such marks must remain speculative, but we must look at the evidence that the ancient builders actually left in the stones as we hypothesize how the pyramids might have been built. Of course, as soon as the pyramids of Khufu and Khafre rose above the bedrock massif left in their cores, the builders could have controlled for squareness by measuring the diagonals.

Designing slope stone by stone

At any given point during construction, what the ancient builders were probably confronted with was a large masonry square, within which were chambers and passageways in the case of Khufu, packed around with core masonry and then the outer casing. The core may have risen somewhat in advance of the casing and packing stones.

While there may have been distant sight reference markers and controls marked on the core, the evidence indicates that the ancient masons designed the slope of the pyramid face into the individual casing stones as they were cut and custom fitted one to another. As the casing blocks were brought into their intended positions, only the bottom had been dressed. Once a casing block had been brought to its place next to its neighbouring stone, the still-exposed opposite and top join faces would be dressed smooth. But before these faces were obscured by other stones, they would be inscribed with a line marking the position of the sloping face – perhaps by measuring up and in set increments from a plumbed line or using a wooden set square of the correct angle. Then, crucially, the extra stone on the front face of the casing block was chamfered or bevelled as far as this line.

At the final stage in the construction process, when the ancient masons removed the ramps and dressed down the face of the pyramid, they knew precisely how much stone to shave away to achieve the smooth, flush plane of the pyramid face: they simply stopped at the point where the seams between adjacent stones closed up to a fine joint.

Evidence that this procedure was used can be seen in the granite lower courses of Menkaure's pyramid. These were left partially undressed, probably when building halted at the king's death, and so still carry the extra stock of stone that would have been cut away. Where stones have fallen away, the blocks still show the line marking the slope of the pyramid face on their side and top joint faces.

(Below) The granite lower courses of Menkaure's pyramid at Giza were left partially undressed and so the extra stock of stone was never cut away to achieve the pyramid's final smooth face. (Inset) I am pointing to the line and bevel that guided the trimming of the pyramid face from the extra stock left on the casing blocks.

Trouble at the Top

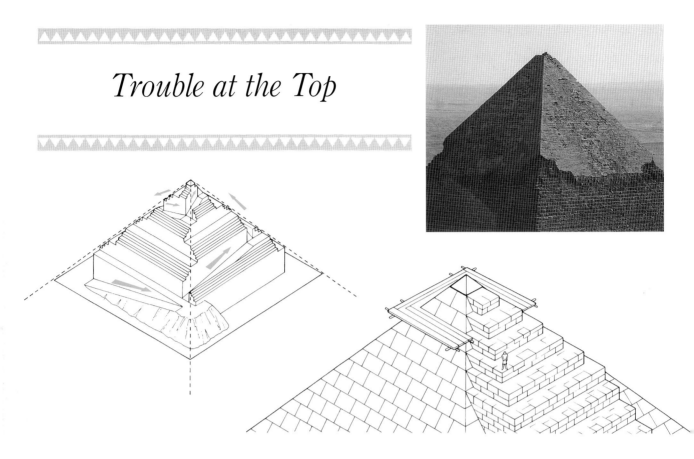

Surviving casing blocks at the top of Khafre's pyramid (top) are not quite flush – perhaps because they were cut before being put into place due to the problems of working in the restricted space at the top of the pyramid. There are different theories to explain how the topmost courses were laid in these difficult conditions. One suggestion (above left) is that there was a series of small ramps running around the very top; another consists of a wooden platform at the top of a large stone stairway (above right).

At the apex of Khafre's pyramid a slight twist is an indication that the highest courses posed particular problems for the ancient builders. Custom cutting of the casing blocks one to another may no longer have been possible by this height. The surviving casing blocks at the uppermost reaches of Khafre's pyramid not only grow steadily smaller and thinner, but they are no longer flush – the stone projects along the horizontal and vertical joins by millimetres. These features might be the result of settling caused by robbing of the casing lower down. It is also possible that these blocks were cut before being laid into place. On Khufu's pyramid – a feature not noted before – the quality of the core stone becomes gradually finer in the last several courses that are preserved before the top, until it almost matches that of the Turah limestone casing. This reflects the need for greater control as the pyramid neared its apex.

Clearly, we should be wary of assuming that what worked at the bottom was likewise successful nearer the top. The problems of raising and manoeuvring stones were most extreme at this level. There was simply no longer room for the kinds of ramps we have been discussing. Stadelmann hypothesizes that the bulk of the pyramid mass was built first by means of several straight-on ramps to all sides, later a single large straight-on ramp to one corner, and then by shorter, lean-to

ramps extended to the higher regions. But for the very last stage he proposes a series of step-like constructions supporting ramps running right to the top. Once the capstone or pyramidion was in place, the steps could be filled in or removed by the builders as they descended.

Many theorists fall back upon the technique of levering to explain how stones were raised to the very upper reaches of the pyramid. Dieter Arnold, for example, envisages the final stones being levered into place from a wooden platform reached by a stone stairway. At a height of 100 m (323 ft) above the base, 97 per cent of the pyramid was already in place; in other words, the upper 46.5 m (152 ft 6 in) represented only 3 per cent of the total volume of masonry. It is possible that despite all its attendant difficulties (p. 209), levering was the best option for completing this small remnant of the pyramid.

The diagonals and the pyramidion

As soon as building rose above any massif of bedrock in the pyramid core, the square of the outer casing could be controlled not only by reference to the course below but also by measuring the diagonals. Evidence from the satellite pyramid of Khufu, newly discovered by Zahi Hawass (p. 69), shows that this operation continued all the way up to the apex. This is one of only two Old Kingdom pyramids for which the pyramidion (capstone) survives (the other is the North Pyramid at Dahshur). And although the stone that fitted directly beneath it is missing, Hawass has identified the next one down, the third from the apex. By this height, the core had been capped and building was entirely in Turah casing stone. On the top of this third stone, dressed very finely with a bevel, are lines running from each corner to the centre – the builders were carefully controlling the square of each diminishing course by reference to the diagonals.

The joint between the pyramidion of Khufu's satellite pyramid and the next stone down was particularly subtle. It is not really a mortice and tenon join; rather the diagonals have been cut into the underside of the stone to create a convex surface with four triangular faces. The upper surface of the stone beneath would have been concave so that the two fitted together neatly and the stability of the pyramidion was assured.

The NOVA experience

The potential for 'trouble at the top' was amply demonstrated in our NOVA pyramid building experiment (p. 208). Levering became necessary for the last few courses, since conditions were too cramped to continue using the modern front-end loader which had accelerated work further down. There was little space to lever and the precariousness of the wooden supports caused some near disasters. Still, differences in masonry and technique between one early Old Kingdom pyramid and another tell us that ancient building methods were sometimes just as *ad hoc*. There was no standard manual for pyramid building in the early, experimental era of the giant pyramids.

Setting the NOVA pyramidion was a dramatic moment. First the workmen fashioned the stone itself and improvised a wooden support with four perpendicular crosspieces to carry it. Then came much nervous standing around and argument over how precisely to proceed. All of a sudden, with prayers, they acted in unison, hoisting it on to their shoulders and shouting encouragement, they set off up the spiral ramp nearly at a run – it was extremely heavy and it was clear that there could be no resting or turning back. It was a huge relief to get it in position without injury or disaster.

Zahi Hawass recently discovered a relief stone carving from the causeway of the 5th-dynasty pyramid of Sahure at Abusir which depicts dancing, singing and celebration following the setting of the capstone; perhaps the tension and relief that we experienced accompanied the setting of ancient capstones too.

There is little evidence of comparable stone-carrying in ancient Egypt, although wooden biers have been found. But it is quite likely that similarly improvised – methods were used to raise and position capstones. And of course even those of the giant pyramids need not have been much bigger

(Above and right) The capstone of Khufu's satellite pyramid as Zahi Hawass found it, lying upside down. Though it is badly weathered, the convex base where it joined the missing second casing stone underneath is still visible. The third stone down (right) was similarly cut to receive the second.

than ours, since the point can be cut off to make a capstone of any size. However, it is a much greater distance from the bottom to the top. Pyramidions found near the bases of Middle Kingdom pyramids (p. 186) may indicate that they were intended to rise with the pyramid as it was built. Once our pyramidion was in place, the NOVA workmen began the task of trimming down the pyramid face, freeing it from the extra stock of stone left on each block, just as their ancient counterparts must have done to the major lower parts of their completed pyramids.

(Right) Setting the capstone, or pyramidion, of a pyramid must have been a particularly difficult and dangerous operation, as we discovered in our own NOVA pyramid-building experiment.

The Workforce

How many workmen built the largest pyramids? Was it tens of thousands, or even more? Take, for example, the Great Pyramid of Khufu: with about 2,300,000 blocks not only is it a stupendous monument in terms of size and precision, but we must reckon with its having been built in 23 years or less, the length the Turin Papyrus gives for Khufu's reign (a longer reign is a possibility). Rainer Stadelmann has calculated that to complete the work, the ancient builders had to lay *c.* 340 blocks a day (a single block being approximately 1 cu. m (35 cu. ft)). Considering that daylight hours allowed at best a ten-hour working day, an astonishing 34 blocks must therefore have been laid per hour – one every two minutes.

Surely this must imply a workforce numbering into the tens of thousands, if not more? Herodotus (writing, admittedly, over 2,000 years after Khufu's pyramid was completed) claimed that the pyramid was built in 20 years by 100,000 men. It is possible – and more credible – that he meant this as an annual total, with teams of 25,000 working three-month stints, rather than the number at Giza at any one time. A figure in the range of 20,000–30,000 is generally accepted. This might seem remarkably few, but there are other facts to consider. There is a tremendous 'slop factor' in the pyramid core, with many irregularly-shaped stones and a fill of smaller stone fragments and debris – this in spite of the fact that Khufu's pyramid has probably the best-laid core masonry of any pyramid. Building would have been considerably speeded up by this lack of precision. And the bulk of the pyramid mass was

in place within 30 m (98 ft 6 in) of the base, so that the higher courses involved far fewer stones.

It is probable that skilled builders and craftsmen were in the permanent employment of the pharaoh. Although the exact numbers are speculative, we know that the mass of the workforce was made up of crews of peasant conscripts numbering probably 2,000 men. Each crew comprised two gangs of 1,000 with each gang divided into five groups called *zaa*, a word that in the Ptolemaic Period was translated as the Greek work for 'tribe' – *phyle* – of 200 men. The phyles themselves consisted of ten divisions of 20 men (or maybe twenty divisions of 10 men). The competing gangs had names compounded with that of the reigning king, such as 'Friends of Khufu' or 'Drunkards of Menkaure'. The five phyles of a gang always had the same set of names: the Great (or Starboard); the Asiatic (or Port); the Green (or Prow); the Little (or Stern); and the Last (or Good) Phyle.

It is possible to separate the general task of pyramid building into its constituent operations and roughly calculate how many men were needed for each. We have already done this for quarrying (p. 207); the other two major operations of building were hauling and cutting/setting the stones. Because the pyramid of Khufu seems the most problematic simply by being the biggest, it will continue to be the basis of our analysis, one of a variety of ways to estimate the workforce.

Stone haulers

Let us assume that the stone haulers could move 1 km (0.62 miles) per hour en route from the quarry to the pyramid. The return journey was done with an empty sledge and so was much faster. The distance from Khufu's quarry to the pyramid, a *c.* 6° slope, could probably therefore be covered in 19 minutes by 20 men pulling a 2.5-ton block. Certainly, this was well within the capacities of the NOVA team.

The French Egyptologist Henri Chevrier, experimenting with moving large stones during his work at the Karnak temple, found that 3 men could pull a 1-ton block (⅓ ton each) over a track lubricated with water to eliminate friction. Research into European megaliths has shown that one man can pull even more, as much as ½ ton. And during the building of the NOVA pyramid (p. 208), we found that 10–12 men could easily pull a 2-ton block mounted on a sledge up an inclined roadway. Further insights are provided by the famous scene from the tomb of Djehutihotep which depicts the moving of a large colossus over a lubricated surface (p. 203). That statue would have weighed *c.* 58 tons, given the scale and size indicated by the tomb scene and assuming it was alabaster – it was probably being pulled from the alabaster quarries near Hatnub. There are 172 men shown, each therefore pulling *c.* ⅓ ton. Modern trials confirm that this is possible on a fairly friction-free surface.

Despite the seemingly impossible statistics, the pyramids of ancient Egypt were very human monuments. Our own NOVA pyramid showed that teams of men could easily pull blocks of the required size.

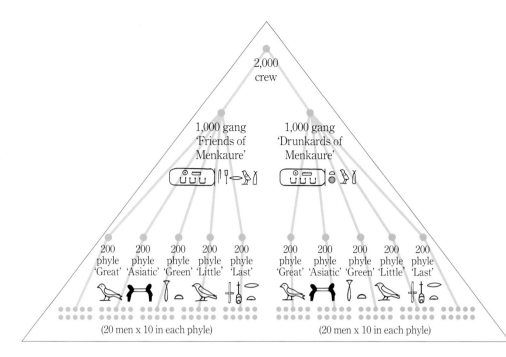

2,000
crew

1,000 gang
'Friends of
Menkaure'

1,000 gang
'Drunkards of
Menkaure'

200
phyle
'Great'

200
phyle
'Asiatic'

200
phyle
'Green'

200
phyle
'Little'

200
phyle
'Last'

200
phyle
'Great'

200
phyle
'Asiatic'

200
phyle
'Green'

200
phyle
'Little'

200
phyle
'Last'

(20 men x 10 in each phyle)

(20 men x 10 in each phyle)

By the same ratio ($\frac{1}{3}$ ton per hauler) a 2.5-ton block on a lubricated, level surface could be pulled by 7.5 men. If we assume that a division (20 men) moved 10 stones per day – allowing one hour to move the stone to the pyramid and return with an empty sledge – then 340 stones could be moved daily from quarry to pyramid by 34 divisions. There are points to note on both sides of this equation. More divisions could work simultaneously at the lower levels, when there may have been many ramps, and therefore a higher hauling rate. Far fewer could work nearer the top, where there was less space and ramp gradients were steeper. Also, the stones of Khufu's pyramid are not all 2.5 tons – this estimate of the average block size is frequently quoted but needs more study. Many stones, particularly near the apex, are smaller, while those of the core are by no means all neat, 2.5-ton cubes, and near the base many blocks exceed 2.5 tons.

Perhaps one hour per stone is too demanding a rate. If we halved it, so that each division moved only 5 stones per day, 68 divisions would then be needed to lay 340 stones per day. At 20 men to a division, that gives us a perhaps more realistic estimate of 1,360 stone haulers. The point is that it still seems eminently practicable.

Stone setters

What about the men cutting and setting the stones on the pyramid? As Petrie noted, there is simply not room for more than 8 handlers per average 2.5-ton block. If we assume 4 men on levers (in line with our experience on the NOVA pyramid) and 2 more to push and adjust, that gives 6 men. Add to that a further 2 masons to do the trimming – particularly necessary for the casing – and we reach a total of 8.

With an extra couple of handlers, we have 10 men per block. Like modern masons, the cutters probably worked inwards from the corners along the line of each pyramid face. But if we add two additional crews starting in the middle of each face and working outwards – the total number of setters on the casing would be 160. The casing stones would have been the most time-intensive because they were custom cut and bevelled as they were laid (p. 218). On Khufu's pyramid, supposing 34 stones were delivered per hour (an average for the whole pyramid) and that the stone setters could keep pace, with 10 men setting 1 stone per hour, 340 setters were working on the entire pyramid. Our estimates of the pace of work may be too tight. If we double the time for setting, arriving at a figure of *c.* 680 setters – it still means an average *c.* 1,000 or fewer workers would have been needed for the task of cutting and setting the stones of Khufu's pyramid.

Our calculations suggest that Khufu's pyramid could have been built by two crews of 2,000. Of course many others were required besides quarrymen and stone haulers and setters. A crew was probably necessary just for building ramps and construction embankments. Also needed were carpenters to make tools and sledges; metal-workers to make and sharpen cutting tools; potters to make pots for use in food preparation and for hauling up water to prepare mortar; workers to carry the water; as well as bakers; brewers – and no doubt others. It is possible that the numbers building and maintaining the infrastructure of Khufu's pyramid rose to 20,000, perhaps even 25,000. But while that implies a very large settlement, it also reinforces the point that the pyramids are human monuments, entirely achievable by the 4th-dynasty Egyptians.

Building a Middle Kingdom Pyramid

By focusing on the giant Old Kingdom pyramids in considering the question 'how were the pyramids built?' we overlook the very different methods used later. Middle Kingdom pyramids have produced a wealth of information, both about the unique design of each, and about masonry techniques that were standard to all pyramids.

Middle Kingdom innovations

When Amenemhet I began a pyramid at Lisht, no large royal pyramid had been built for 190 years, and so expertise may have been lost and experience forgotten. The core of his pyramid was composed of small rough blocks of limestone with a loose fill of sand, debris and mudbrick. Senwosret I's innovation was an internal framework of walls with stone slabs set in steps in the compartments between. Backing stones rested on the steps and were in turn covered by the casing. Amenemhet II's builders also used a masonry frame as did Senwosret II's, though the compartments of the latter were filled with mudbrick, which was also used for the upper pyramid core. Mudbrick was used for the cores of all subsequent Middle Kingdom pyramids.

Dieter Arnold's intensive study of Amenemhet III's Dahshur pyramid allowed him to estimate the size of the workforce needed to build a mudbrick pyramid. The total, rounded up to 5,000, is the same as Barry Kemp's estimate of the maximum yearly grain rations stored in the large houses of Senwosret II's pyramid town of Illahun (p. 231).

Middle Kingdom masons used dovetail cramps to join structurally important blocks to compensate for the lack of the extraordinarily fine joins characteristic of Old Kingdom casing blocks. Arnold estimates that 12,000 wooden cramps were used in Senwosret I's pyramid complex, each inscribed with the king's name. Numerous patches and cracks in the preserved casing of the pyramids of Senwosret I, Senwosret III and Amenemhet III are evidence of problems that seem to have plagued Middle Kingdom pyramid builders – settling and subsidence. At the pyramids of Senwosret I and Amenemhet III at Dahshur these problems were exacerbated by the fact that they were built over an open shaft or extensive chambers and passages in soft ground – 320 m (1,050 ft) of tunnels and 27 rooms under Amenemhet III's. The substructure of his Hawara pyramid – of which an architect's model was found in his Dahshur pyramid – was an attempt to remedy these weaknesses and set the pattern for later pyramids. (p. 181). Weaknesses in the foundations were another source of instability. The foot of Senwosret I's pyramid sloped directly to a 15-cm (6-in) step down, while Amenemhet's Dahshur foundation of three limestone courses was retained only by tafla clay and mudbrick.

Organizing the landscape

More transport roads, remains of ramps and stone-dressing stations have been found at Lisht than at any other pyramid site in Egypt. They tell the story of how this landscape was organized for building pyramids. Arnold was able to ascertain the locations of the quarries, landing quays and access wadis for Senwosret I's pyramid. He even identified

The Workforce for Amenemhet III's Dahshur Pyramid:

40 brick makers: 10 brick moulders with 3 assistants each could turn out 500 bricks daily: 10 x 500 x 350 working days/year x 15 years to build the pyramid = 26,250,000 bricks.

50 clay, straw, sherd carriers: for 5,000 bricks daily, with donkeys.

600 brick carriers: 1 man could have carried 4 bricks, 5 times a day to the pyramid = 300 carriers and 6,000 bricks a day. Fewer men were required if donkeys were used. For the ascent up the pyramid, 2 bricks per man, but 10 such shorter trips per day, requiring another 300 brick carriers.

30 sand carriers: the sand filling the joints between bricks (10 per cent of the pyramid) could have been provisioned by 30 men making 10 trips each day to the pyramid = 300 baskets.

250 stone cutters: Arnold estimated 122,000 blocks in the casing, around 3,000 smaller blocks lining chambers and corridors, and 130,000 blocks for the pyramid temple. 150 masons could have hewn raw blocks, plus 100 for the fine dressing.

1,500 stone transporters: 30 workers could have pulled one 2–3 ton block per day up the slope to the pyramid = 750 men hauling 25 blocks per day. The same number could have transported stone from the east bank quarry to the river.

200 sailors: 3 barges with combined crews of about 100 men could have transported 25 blocks a day; doubled for simultaneous coming and going.

600 stone lifters: the maximum for moving the stones up to the course under construction. Arnold favours the use of levers and stairway ramps.

1,500 auxiliary workers: carpenters, controllers, sculptors and painters, as well as bakers, brewers, potters, sandal makers, weavers and water carriers. Additional nautical crews to bring granite columns, architraves and sarcophagi from Aswan.

Total: 4,770

areas for storing and dressing stone by the massive quantities of limestone chips and granite dust. Local limestone for the core was quarried south of the pyramid. Granite was brought in and dressed on the north. Fine casing limestone was carried up the causeway. Along the routes from the quarries sections of slipways and roads are still preserved, formed of wood sleepers made of boat parts (p. 203). A large, debris-filled mudbrick ramp, flanked by mudbrick towers, sloped 8° up towards the pyramid from the southern quarries. Closer to the pyramid, Arnold identified the levelled remains of mudbrick ramps on the south and west sides. Their close proximity to the pyramid suggests rather steep ramps. The fact that they were of mudbrick and that they must have run nearly perpendicular to the pyramid are major differences from the postulated ramps used to raise stone at Giza.

The control notes

On the undressed parts of some paving, backing and casing stones are inscribed marks, perhaps the most intriguing evidence from the Middle Kingdom pyramids. Felix Arnold has distinguished two kinds of these 'control notes': for controllers and scribes. For the controller, a complete note recorded, in separate lines, the date of transport, the workmen in charge of the stone and the stage of transport. The route began in the quarry: 'brought from' or 'removal from' the quarry are common notes. The shipping of stones is mentioned, and we read of stone delivered at the *mereyt*, harbour or embankment. Stones are 'brought from the embankment' and delivered to 'storage enclosures'. They are also 'brought or 'dragged' to the pyramid or 'delivered to the ramp'. Cowherds are mentioned who may have driven oxen for pulling stone.

The second type of note takes the form of larger signs that sometimes overlap the more meticulous text. These are team marks, perhaps written and 'read' by the illiterate workmen, who rotated in and out of service for two to four months. Some are known hieroglyphs while others are invented signs such as pitchforks and crossed sticks. Felix Arnold believes the marks may have identified the workers' home towns, the made-up hieroglyphs representing smaller villages. The team marks may also stand for the subdivision of work gangs – *tjeset,* 'troops', of 10 men in the Middle Kingdom. In fact they may have been both place-names and troop divisions. Some teams are named after the householders to whose estates they were attached.

We often describe pyramid-building in terms of labour recruited in military fashion or the wage-labour of a large modern engineering project. Coupled with this is a popular notion of the pharaoh as totally autocratic. Both images obscure the way in which pharaoh's power was woven through the fabric of ancient Egyptian society, and the degree to which labour for large-scale, 'public' works was organized by towns, villages, estates and households in descending order. 'Forced' as opposed to 'voluntary' labour may be a modern distinction, not applicable to this flow of men from the provinces. Pyramid building was perhaps regarded as a ritual act embedded in social custom and tradition.

The towns mentioned in the control notes so far recovered are predominantly in one area of Middle Egypt; around the old capital, Memphis; Heliopolis and the Delta. This distribution is strikingly similar to the pattern of internal colonization of the Old Kingdom (p. 228). Was the raw labour for the Old Kingdom pyramids gathered from the newly colonized areas?

(Right) Map by Felix Arnold showing the geographical origin of the workmen mentioned in the control notes he studied. Lower Egyptians are often designated without specifying a particular town.

(Below) One of the control notes documented by Felix Arnold at the pyramid of Senwosret I at Lisht. The longer, more detailed note is for the controller and scribes, while the larger, somewhat clumsier marks are team marks – this one is of the 'Memphis team'.

Rainer Stadelmann discovered a draft plan of Amenemhet III's innovative Hawara pyramid substructure – in the form of a small limestone model buried in the floor of the valley temple of his Dahshur pyramid. The long approach corridors of the actual Hawara pyramid are here foreshortened, but one of the enormous, sideways sliding, blocking stones is shown in wood. The antechamber, burial chamber and the system for lowering the last ceiling block, as at Hawara, are all faithfully rendered. As a 'visual aid', it may have been particularly important to show the differences in level.

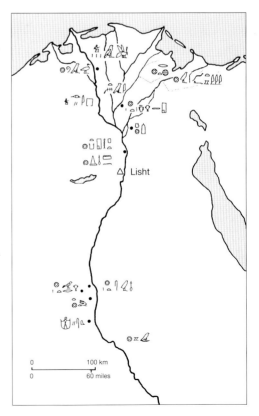

Pyramid as Landlord

Colonies, pyramids and the emergence of a centralized state

The puzzles of how the Egyptians built the pyramids are endlessly fascinating. Less obvious but more significant is the broader question of how the pyramids helped to build Egypt. The beginning of the pyramid age coincided with the emergence of a programme of internal colonization which saw the founding of new villages (*niut*) and estates (*hut*) throughout the Egyptian hinterlands. Such foundations contributed produce to pyramids, temples or élite tombs, creating a flow of resources from the periphery to the core of the state. In this way, pyramid building had a key role in forging Egypt as the world's first centralized nation state, unlike the city-state pattern that developed in Mesopotamia and North Syria.

Estates and ranches were being founded in the Delta as early as the 1st dynasty, but evidence increases at the time that the giant pyramids began

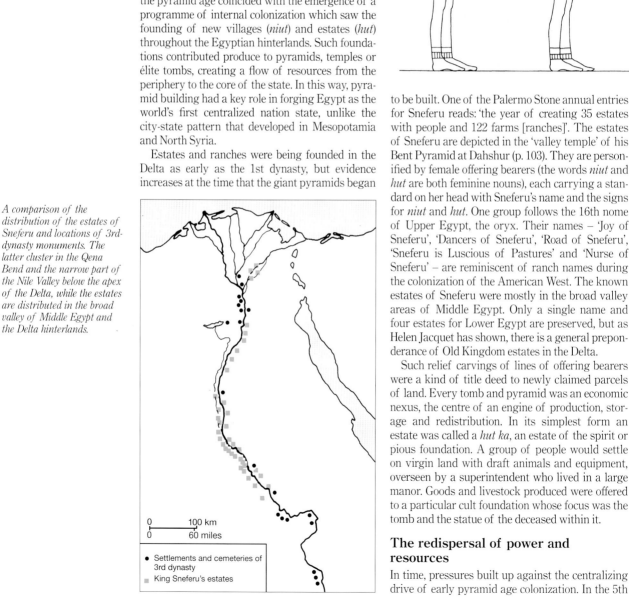

A comparison of the distribution of the estates of Sneferu and locations of 3rd-dynasty monuments. The latter cluster in the Qena Bend and the narrow part of the Nile Valley below the apex of the Delta, while the estates are distributed in the broad valley of Middle Egypt and the Delta hinterlands.

0   100 km
0   60 miles

• Settlements and cemeteries of 3rd dynasty
■ King Sneferu's estates

to be built. One of the Palermo Stone annual entries for Sneferu reads: 'the year of creating 35 estates with people and 122 farms [ranches]'. The estates of Sneferu are depicted in the 'valley temple' of his Bent Pyramid at Dahshur (p. 103). They are personified by female offering bearers (the words *niut* and *hut* are both feminine nouns), each carrying a standard on her head with Sneferu's name and the signs for *niut* and *hut*. One group follows the 16th nome of Upper Egypt, the oryx. Their names – 'Joy of Sneferu', 'Dancers of Sneferu', 'Road of Sneferu', 'Sneferu is Luscious of Pastures' and 'Nurse of Sneferu' – are reminiscent of ranch names during the colonization of the American West. The known estates of Sneferu were mostly in the broad valley areas of Middle Egypt. Only a single name and four estates for Lower Egypt are preserved, but as Helen Jacquet has shown, there is a general preponderance of Old Kingdom estates in the Delta.

Such relief carvings of lines of offering bearers were a kind of title deed to newly claimed parcels of land. Every tomb and pyramid was an economic nexus, the centre of an engine of production, storage and redistribution. In its simplest form an estate was called a *hut ka*, an estate of the spirit or pious foundation. A group of people would settle on virgin land with draft animals and equipment, overseen by a superintendent who lived in a large manor. Goods and livestock produced were offered to a particular cult foundation whose focus was the tomb and the statue of the deceased within it.

The redispersal of power and resources

In time, pressures built up against the centralizing drive of early pyramid age colonization. In the 5th

Personified estates (left) shown bearing offerings, from reliefs from Sneferu's valley temple, attached to his Bent Pyramid at Dahshur (above).

dynasty high officials and priests serving the memory of a king in his pyramid temple began to claim a share of the produce from its estates. The 5th-dynasty official Nenkhefetka, for example, lists 14 estates in his tomb at Saqqara, two of them named after king Userkaf (called 'Ladder of Userkaf' and 'Userkaf is Beautiful in Spirit') and three after Sahure ('Hathor Wishes that Sahure Lives', 'The Spirit Belongs to Sahure' and 'The Flood of Sahure'). It is no coincidence that Nenkhefetka's titles include priestly functions in the pyramids of Userkaf and Sahure .

Also in the 5th dynasty enormous tracts of land in the Delta were given to the sun god, Re, and the temple of Heliopolis. Later Old Kingdom pharaohs began providing endowments and tax exemptions to provincial temples. In Upper Egypt, the nome leaders were in charge of the temples. Their share of temple income, and their own local funerary estates, were locked into hereditary claims to the land that competed with distant cult foundations. They grew in power, building large tombs in their provinces, and becoming miniature ruling households in their own right, albeit still embedded in the fabric of the united kingdom.

By the late Old Kingdom the king's immediate family members increasingly assumed a more ceremonial function and high officials were beginning to be people other than senior members of the royal family. A true bureaucracy was emerging, with officials no longer so intimate with the royal household, but who did now take a share of the produce, goods and services offered to the pyramid temple. This created centrifugal forces that dispersed the centralized power of the early Old Kingdom throughout the colonies originally intended to feed it. This process was paralleled by the transition from the giant pyramids to the smaller standardized pyramids of the later Old Kingdom.

From internal colonization to empire

At the end of the Old Kingdom, with the collapse of the 6th dynasty, Egypt fragmented into local warring principalities. By the Middle Kingdom the land that the Old Kingdom pharaohs had taken over or newly settled for manorial estates must long have been tied up in hereditary rights and alienated from cult centres like Giza and Saqqara. What had once been an active economic engine had ground to a complete halt, its monuments dismantled, their stone dumped into constructions like Amenemhet I's pyramid at Lisht. Yet the inexorable processes of colonization and expansion were still under way. The Delta and broad areas of Middle Egypt continued to be areas of new settlement and land allocations, but these areas now featured sophisticated town centres in their own right. Middle Kingdom pharaohs turned their attentions to the Fayum, where the lake had receded leaving new land to exploit. Senwosret II and Amenemhet III built large pyramids at Illahun and Hawara along the gateway to the Fayum.

Egypt was now also looking outside its borders in a major way, beyond simple trade for coniferous products, wine and oil. Middle Kingdom pharaohs defended Egypt's frontiers with fortifications like Amenemhet's Wall of the Ruler at the northeastern Delta, and the string of forts near the 2nd Cataract. Eventually, after the collapse and resurrection of the kingdom in the Second Intermediate Period, Egypt expanded into empire. In the New Kingdom, garrisons were stationed throughout Palestine up to Syria and in Lower Nubia – Nubia was now simply a province of Egypt. The early Old Kingdom pyramids had not only helped to set Egypt on the course of becoming a fully consolidated kingdom and a true nation state; the processes they put in motion were finally to culminate in one of the world's first empires.

Pyramid Towns

Was all the produce and livestock from provincial estates literally brought to the pyramid necropolis? Or was only a token offering delivered here, while the major part was taken elsewhere? Inscriptions at Niuserre's sun temple list an annual inflow that included: 100,800 rations of bread, beer and cakes; 7,720 loaves of *pesen* bread; 1,002 oxen; and 1,000 geese. We might imagine even greater amounts for a pyramid like Khufu's. Somewhere, somehow, it all had to be stored, processed and redistributed. Where were the installations and apparatus for receiving such amounts of goods and materials?

The Giza necropolis as it might have appeared towards the end of the 4th dynasty, looking from southeast to northwest, with the three giant pyramid complexes complete. The flood plain is shown with modern contours.

We have examined the standard elements of the pyramid complex – the pyramid itself, the temples and the causeway – the elements designed for eternity. Each pyramid also had a pyramid town, usually at the foot of the plateau, where priests, officials and guards lived, plus all the personnel needed to support and supply them, while the pyramid functioned as a ritual centre. And was this separate from the sizeable, perhaps temporary, accommodation for the huge workforce that must have been required to build each pyramid?

Capital and 'great house'

In discussing pyramid towns we must consider the siting of the royal household and the role of Memphis, often referred to as the 'capital' of Egypt. In Old Kingdom Egypt, the closest approximation to a capital city in the modern sense was the residence of the king. While the king would have had provincial palaces, it is a long-accepted idea that a principal royal residence lay close to the pyramid complex while it was under construction.

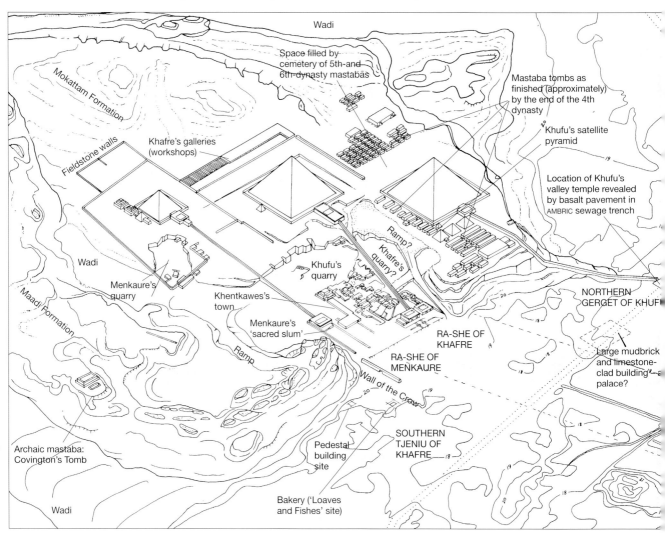

With pyramid and royal residence thus linked, the Egyptian 'capital' was fairly mobile within the pyramid zone along the Nile Valley. The same residence may have been used by successive kings who favoured the same necropolis, as at Giza and Abusir, but Menes's founding of a new town at Memphis was perhaps as much the rule as the exception. Akhenaten's famous but short-lived capital at Amarna may be the best-preserved example of a practice followed by the other pharaohs.

Inscriptions such as that found in the 5th-dynasty tomb of Nikanesut at Giza illuminate the organization of larger households. His included 2 overseers of the estates, 11 scribes, a director of the workforce, 2 directors of the dining hall, 2 overseers of linen, a seal bearer, 3 butchers, 2 bakers, a cook and 5 butlers. If the royal household – the 'great house' and greatest of households – moved to a site such as Giza or Abusir for three generations, then the butchers, the bakers, the sandal-makers and all the rest of the dependent workforce – to say nothing of other officials and everything

required by their households – must have moved with it in large numbers.

Indeed, the 5th-dynasty official Senedjemib mentions in his tomb that, as well as constructing a pyramid for Djedkare-Isesi, he also built him a new palace called 'Lotus Blossom of Isesi'. The numbers are difficult to read, but it seems to have measured around 1,220 x 440 cubits, or 640 x 231 m (2,100 x 758 ft). Even if this refers to the outer enclosure, it was still larger than the base of Khufu's pyramid and comparable to the enclosure of Djoser's Step Pyramid – not an inconsequential structure.

Tomb texts suggest that the people buried in the cemeteries around the pyramids were prominent residents of nearby pyramid towns. The names of these towns are often nearly identical to those of the pyramids. *Djed Sneferu* ('Sneferu Endures') was associated with Sneferu's Meidum pyramid, while his two Dahshur pyramids were accompanied by a double town, northern and southern *Kha Sneferu* ('Sneferu Appears'). At Giza, two settlement names are known, the northern *Gerget* ('Settlement') of Khufu, and the southern *Tjeniu* ('boundary mark', 'cultivation edge') of Khafre. The former may have been around Khufu's valley temple and the latter may have extended south of Khafre's valley temple and the large stone boundary wall, known now as the 'Wall of the Crow'.

Until the 5th dynasty, pyramid towns, with their population of craftsmen, farmers and necropolis guards, were administered by a second generation of princes. They and their progeny were in charge of the king's priesthood even after the royal court had moved on to another site. Later, the towns were governed by middle level and lower officials who enjoyed the income and tax-exemption that went with residence and service in a pyramid town.

Senwosret II's pyramid town at Illahun housed an estimated population of several thousand. In the western and southern parts there were 220 small houses, while the northeastern sector was occupied by just nine or ten substantial urban estates, probably inhabited by the senior officials of the king. Barry Kemp has compared these households to the wooden models discovered in the Middle Kingdom tomb of Meketre, Chancellor to Mentuhotep I (Nebhepetre). Among them is one of a large porticoed house with a pool in a grove of trees, as well as a bakery and a brewery, carpentry and weaving shops, and also a granary. Like the Meketre models, each large Illahun estate had a core house with a portico facing away from the street, and a garden court. Each also had a granary. Kemp has estimated that collectively these granaries could have stored enough grain to feed 5,000–9,000 people annually. It seems that the inhabitants of the small dwellings in the rest of the town must have worked for and in the large households in return for their sustenance and livelihood.

The 'Wall of the Crow', with a colossal gate which may have been the entrance to the Giza necropolis.

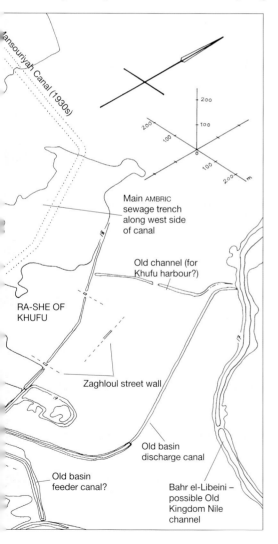

Mansouriyah Canal (1930s)

200

200
100
100
0
100
200 m

Main AMBRIC sewage trench along west side of canal

Old channel (for Khufu harbour?)

RA-SHE OF KHUFU

Zaghloul street wall

Old basin discharge canal

Old basin feeder canal?

Bahr el-Libeini – possible Old Kingdom Nile channel

have encompassed far more than the small housing near his temple. Where should we look for it?

The *ra-she*

The Abusir Papyri (p. 147) form our key documentary evidence for the life, society and economy of a living pyramid. Among other interesting institutions, they mention something called the *ra-she*, which seems to be a crucial component in the pyramid complex. It is written with the sign for a mouth and the alphabetical sign for a pool or basin, hence its literal meaning is something like 'mouth (entrance) of the basin'. The papyri reveal that it was a place of deliveries, storage and production.

Why was it called *ra-she*, 'entrance to the basin'? And where was it? Stadelmann's study of the use of the term *she* – such as *khentiu-she* (p. 234) and *she en per a'aa* (the *she* of the pharaoh) – led him to conclude that it signified a royal precinct. Inscriptions mention the planning, measuring and opening of *she*s with names like 'Thrones of the Gods', 'Libation of the Gods' and 'Nurse of the Gods', names that Stadelmann links to Archaic enclosures around royal tombs at Abydos and Saqqara. It is also possible that they were individual names of agricultural basins that held the annual inundation – like the named basins of Upper Egypt in the 19th century AD. If each pyramid complex was attached to its own basin, the *ra-she* would have been the interface between the world of the dead and that of the living, between pyramid precinct and flood basin, with the pyramid town and the *khentiu-she* organized on adjacent levees and high ground. The *ra-she* would then be the entrance to the valley ensemble, where the valley temple, harbour, canal and pyramid town were located. At Giza that would place a pyramid town on the stretch of low desert between the Nile Valley and the high pyramid plateau.

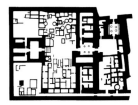

Menkaure's valley temple (centre) was overtaken by the residents of his pyramid town who invaded the front of the temple with their houses and granaries (top and bottom).

Sacred slums

Archaeological traces of other pyramid towns suggest small communities of mudbrick houses that become more crowded and shabby after the site of the royal necropolis moved on. Reisner excavated an agglomeration of small houses in front of Menkaure's valley temple. The tax-exempt pyramid town had expanded in a disorganized way, crowding up against and eventually invading the temple – small mud huts, storage bins and grain silos filled the temple's open court. Meanwhile the cult of the king was maintained, perhaps in the mortuary temple and certainly in a small, dark sanctuary at the rear of the valley temple.

This pattern – a small group of mudbrick houses next to a temple deteriorating into a kind of sacred slum after the royal house moved on – has been taken as the model for the Old Kingdom pyramid town. But Menkaure's facilities for the storage and processing of produce from his estates must

Lost City of the Pyramids?

In the late 1980s a project revealed extensive evidence of Old Kingdom settlement spreading out far beyond the Giza pyramid plateau underneath the modern city. Major works, by a consortium known as AMBRIC, to install sewers involved a network of trenches and borings in the valley floor east of the Sphinx and pyramids. The archaeology was directed by Zahi Hawass and monitored by Michael Jones. Remains encountered over a wide area included the foundation of Khufu's causeway and a basalt pavement that probably marks his valley temple.

In a deep trench along a modern canal a continuous layer of mudbrick buildings began about 50 m (165 ft) south of the possible location of the valley temple. Here, perhaps, lay *Gerget Khufu* ('settlement of Khufu'). Thousands of fragments of everyday pottery, bread moulds, cooking pots, jars, trays and bowls turned up, as well as animal bone, grinding stones and large quantities of charcoal and ash.

At a point about due east of the south side of Khufu's pyramid, the trench cut through massive mudbrick walls of a very large building – could this be a palace? Unfortunately the section provided by a sewage trench is less than ideal for archaeology, and it was quickly refilled, leaving many questions unanswered.

Later, in 1994, construction work turned up a huge limestone and basalt wall, 500 m (1,650 ft) east of Khufu's valley temple (seen in the photograph, *left*). Its orientation matches certain older drainage channels in the area and it may mark the border of the flood basin or harbour fronting Khufu's valley temple. The pyramid settlement attached to the giant pyramids of Giza was more than a small cluster of planned houses that later turned into a slum. The evidence points to a sort of proto-city – downtown Egypt during Giza's heyday – which continued to be inhabited by priests who maintained the cults of the Khufu, Khafre and Menkaure.

Providing and provided

Inside the mortuary temple daily services were conducted to the memory of a pharaoh and the deity he personified. Our understanding of temple ritual is fragmentary, but we do know that it centred on offerings presented before the royal statues and at the base of the false door. In essence, the entire temple is an elaboration of the place in the simplest tombs where food offerings could be presented to the *ka*, vital force of the deceased. The king was the '*ka* of the living' and the entire community shared a life force passed from creator god to king, from parent to child. The social reflection was a hierarchy of households, the 'greatest house' being that of the pharaoh. The funerary reflection was the concept *imakhu*, sometimes translated 'honoured'. Jaromir Málek has shown that it could mean 'provided for', and it signified receipt of a share of offerings from a tomb of a higher status household, by a *wedjeb*, or redistribution. A man named Netjerpuneseut recorded in his Giza tomb that he was 'possessor of provisioning' from six kings: Djedefre, Khafre, Menkaure, Shepseskaf, Userkaf and Sahure.

The evolving temple administration

Tomb texts indicate that temple organization in the early pyramid age was fairly simple. The pyramid

was administered by an *imy-ra*: 'overseer' (literally, 'one who is in the mouth'). There were *wabu*, purification priests, and *kheri-heb*, a lector priest who read the ritual. There were also the *hemu-netjer*, literally 'servants of the god', a title listed in the tombs of highly placed Egyptians, but which could also be held by simpler folk like craftsmen and farmers from the nearby pyramid town.

In the late 5th and 6th dynasties a more complex social and religious organization emerged contemporaneously with the dramatic reduction in pyramid size, the expansion of the mortuary temple and the development of the standard temple components. The Abusir Papyri from the temples of Neferirkare, Raneferef and Khentkawes are a textual window on the operation of a

Imy-ra (overseer)

Wabu (purification priest)   *Kheri-heb* (lector priest)

H e m u - n e t j e r

(Above) The organization of pyramid temple personnel in the early pyramid age.
(Below) A relief from the tomb of an important householder showing offering bearers bringing produce to the tomb from his estates.

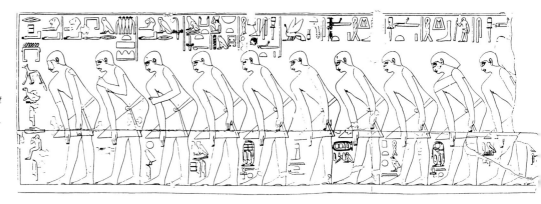

pyramid temple at about the time of these changes. In the Tables of Service the temple personnel are divided into two broad groups: the *hemu-netjer*, the older title, and the *khentiu-she*. While the literal meaning of the latter term is straightforward – 'those in front of the *she*' – its actual meaning, and the nature of these people, are more problematic.

In the New Kingdom *khentiu-she* seem to have been 'gardeners'. Translations of its Old Kingdom meaning range from 'settler' or 'tenant farmer' to 'palace attendant'. The problem again lies in the word *she*, which was used for ideas as diverse as 'cultivated land', 'lake', 'quarry', 'workshop'. The solution lies in the translation 'basin' and the awareness that the Nile Valley was organized into annually flooded basins (p. 12) that were virtual lakes, with trees and gardens on the banks. As we have seen, from ancient texts we know of institutions like the *ra-she* of the pyramid, and the '*she* of Pharaoh', perhaps the funerary precinct. However, if, as noted above, each pyramid complex was fronted by a large basin, which was part of a total ensemble of pyramid town, palace, harbour, canal entrance (*ra*) to the basin (*she*), the attachment of the *khentiu-she* to both the palace of the living king and the temple of the deified king makes sense.

The *khentiu-she* were residents of the pyramid town to which they may have been tied from birth. Many who hold this title compound their name with that of the king in whose temple they served. This made them members of the king's extended household, which included all classes – farmers, gardeners and, later, high officials. In the Abusir Papyri the younger *khentiu-she* were particularly occupied with the transportation of meat and other provisions into the temple, while elderly members did guard duty. Together they formed a human filter for the

transformation of all raw materials into sacred sustenance for the pyramid and its clientele. Although the title *khentiu-she* is only known from the reign of Djedkare-Isesi on, Paule Posener-Kriéger and Rainer Stadelmann believe that the institution goes back to the time of Sneferu. A decree of Pepi I protecting the *khentiu-she* of Sneferu's double pyramid town indicates that the town and its inhabitants must date back to the time when the pyramids were built.

The *hemu-netjer* seem to have been less tied to a specific pyramid. In the Abusir Papyri they appear to be of a higher status than the *khentiu-she*: they do not transport meat and provisions; they are listed first; they received their allocation of offerings in the inner sanctum of the offering hall; and their titles sometimes indicate middle to high rank. It seems, however, their status did not preclude them from performing what seem to us fairly menial tasks alongside people of lower rank. Thus we find a Judge and Scribe on guard duty over temple pottery with a dancer and a Coiffeur of the Palace.

However, we gain a clearer understanding of the pyramid temple if we realize the importance of a title like Coiffeur – one who actually touched the divine body of the god-king. Royal coiffeurs had a special importance in the intimate parts of the temple. The fact that those who touched the king's person and prepared his meals had significant roles in the innermost part of the pyramid temple fits with our understanding of the pyramid chambers as the eternal equivalent of the private rooms of the palace. When the king emerges from death each morning, his servants attend him before he strides forth as the statues in the front part of the temple.

The *khentiu-she* and *hemu-netjer* served together in phyles, the same organizational unit as the building crews and with the same names. Each phyle was divided into two sections, so that a half-phyle served one month in ten. The divisions were named with single hieroglyphs, denoting ideas like 'strength', 'life', 'dominion'. This rotating involvement in the temple cult allowed greater numbers to experience the elaborate symbolic programme and awe-inspiring effects of statuary and chiaroscuro of the pyramids than a permanent staff would.

Organization of service in Neferirkare's temple, both rotating and permanent, as revealed in papyri found in his mortuary temple.

ROTATING

Controller of Those Who Serve in a Phyle

Half-phyle

PERMANENT

Half-phyle

Inspector of Priests	Inspector of Priests	Lector priests
Assistant	Assistant	Purifiers
10 *Hemu-netjer*	10 *Hemu-netjer*	Scribes
10 *Khentiu-she*	10 *Khentiu-she*	Artisans, potters, pot-washers, handymen

'Parasite' phyles

Heriu-nesti (Those Who Sit in my Place)

TOTAL = *c*. 300 PEOPLE

Others served in the temple but did not appear to be part of the rotation, including the *wabu* – purification priests – the lector priests (possibly three at a time) and a group called *kheriu-nesti*, literally 'those who sit in my place', perhaps the heirs of the *hemu-netjer* and *khentiu-she*. There are also indications that the regular rotating personnel were supplemented by phyles attached to the mastaba tombs in the necropolis. Posener called these 'parasite phyles' since their role in the temple rotation probably gained them a share of its revenue.

At Neferirkare's temple the phyles were supervised by an Inspector of Priests and an assistant. Besides these any given shift would include about 20 *khentiu-she* and *hemu-netjer*, giving a total of around 220. Adding the lector priests, the non-rotating personnel, scribes, artisans and 'parasite phyles', the total reaches 300 to 350. Posener estimated about 70 to 100 people for the rotating service of Raneferef.

In death pharaoh's palace moved from the valley up to the pyramid – the primeval mound at the centre of the sun's rotation. The deceased king would awake each day, be coiffeured, dressed and prepared to meet (or be) the lord of heaven – so long as the daily ritual was conducted by those who serve.

Daily Service

What happened on an average day in a pyramid temple? Each day there were apparently identical morning and evening rites centred on a ritual meal. In the Pyramid Texts the king had five meals a day, three in the sky and two on earth. The earthly meals were the responsibility of those who served in the temple. This ritual meal required the opening of the mouth ceremony on the royal statues in the five niches at the interface between front and inner temples – standard since Khafre. Each statue represented a different aspect of the king. The Abusir Papyri reveal that the centre statue represented the king as Osiris, while the two at the ends portrayed him as king of Upper and Lower Egypt. We are not sure of the meaning of the other two.

Each shrine (*tjephet*, 'cavern') was opened in turn for a presentation of cloth and an unction of sacred oil, accompanied by a recitation of sacred formulae for each statue. The *khentiu-she* unveiled, cleaned, dressed and adorned the statues, while the *hemu-netjer* fumigated with incense. The offering ceremony

– the ritual meal – followed, but it is not clear if this took place before the statues in the court of the front temple, in the offering hall, or both. It consisted of libations and a wiping of the offering table. Purifications, censings, ritual meals and libations also made up the burial ritual. A further feast of each lunar month focused on the statue of the king as Osiris, lasting from the day of the moon's invisibility to the appearance of the first quarter. Elaborations on the ritual sequence were also enacted for feast days of deities like Sokar and Hathor.

At the end of the ceremony one of the *khentiu-she* and one of the *hemu-netjer* emptied the basin that had collected the libation water into an outlet under the east wall of the offering hall. Here we see the importance of the drainage systems such as are found in the mortuary temple of Sahure (p. 144). Basin, ewer, papyrus roll with ritual and other equipment were then carefully accounted for and put back into chests.

The Raneferef Papyri inform us that each phyle had its own set of sacerdotal equipment.

Then followed one of the most intriguing aspects of the daily ritual. A jar of natron water was half-emptied in quadruple salutations to the king. It was then carried away by a *khenti-she*. Each evening and morning one of the *hemu-netjer* and one of the *khentiu-she* took the jar and circumambulated the pyramid, sprinkling it with sacred natron water. The journey was called 'the way of the hem-netjer when he goes around the pyramid'. The pair departed from the south door of the inner temple and returned through the north door, making a clockwise tour that symbolized the circuit of the sun.

Pyramid and temple as the eternal palace with resemblances to the living palace. Here the dead king is attended by priests (hemu-netjer) and khentiu-she, *organized into phyles. Each phyle of 200 men was divided into sections of 100 men, who served for 1 month in 10 on a rotating basis.*

Court = visitation court or hall

Entrance hall = front foyer or vestibule

Antechamber = foyer

Offering hall = dining room

5 statue niches = formal reception dais in houses

Burial chamber = bed room and 'house of morning'

3 niches = magazines for food ? (or statues)

hemu-netjer 'servants of the god' – fumigate temple and statues of king with incense

khentiu-she 'those foremost of the royal precinct' – unveil, clean, dress and adorn temple statues of king

Loaves and Fishes

Seal impression from the pedestal building mentioning the wabet *(the kneeling man with a pot on his head and with water pouring over his outstretched arms).*

So far our reconstruction of the pyramid community has depended on the evidence of tomb scenes and inscriptions, the Abusir Papyri and analysis of the Giza landscape. It was not until 1988–89 that we actually began to excavate. This finally allowed us to test our theory that the workers' settlement and pyramid support structures were in the area of low desert at the south-southeast limit of the Giza plateau, just beyond the quarries, supply route and harbour. This region, designated Area A, lies south of a pharaonic wall, 200 m (656 ft) long (the *Heit el-Ghourab,* 'Wall of the Crow'), which may have been a boundary wall of or within the *ra-she* (p. 232). An imposing gateway topped by three large lintels was perhaps a sublime entrance to the entire necropolis. Our first excavations were northwest of a large soccer field on the outskirts of Nazlet el-Semman, where a tarmac surface had just been laid and floodlights installed. Pyramid-age deposits included pottery and walls exposed by villagers digging sand for the nearby stables.

Granaries or workshops?

In 1988–89 we excavated a rectangular building 9 x 6 m (30 x 20 ft) with stone rubble walls and a floor of desert clay. It had been so thoroughly cleaned out in ancient times that there was very little debris on the floors. On either side of a low central dividing wall was a row of rectangular pedestals *c.* 60 cm (24 in) high, separated by spaces of *c.* 20 cm (8 in). Too close together to be pillar bases, they were a mystery. Tomb scenes suggested they might have been supports for grain silos in a granary. The granary in ancient Egypt was designated by the term *shenuti*, actually meaning double granary. This, it seemed, might explain the two rows of pedestals.

Yet other clues emerged, particularly in a corridor connecting this building with another to the east, making us question our interpretation. The corridor was filled with garbage – ash, sherds and bone, as well as mud seal impressions – probably cleared from the pedestal building. Several impressions mention the *wabet* of Menkaure. *Wabet* means embalming workshop but it may have signified something more extensive, namely the entire royal unit that equipped the grave, including workshops and possibly storage for food offerings.

The evidence of these mud seal impressions, the small size of some of the storage compartments in the pedestal building and the fact that it was so thoroughly cleaned out in ancient times led us to suspect that something more precious than grain was stored in this building, perhaps that was part of the overall effort to equip the grave.

Feeding the workforce

In 1991 we again found ourselves playing the role of archaeological firemen. A machine, digging sand for a nearby building project with a backhoe, had gouged a huge trench in the desert about 200 m (656 ft) to the east of our 1989 excavation, revealing massive mudbrick walls and huge deposits of pottery, especially fragments of bread moulds. We cleared around this trench and excavated two rooms, where below a thin layer of disintegrated mudbrick we found black ash filling what were clearly two bakeries.

Unlike the pedestal building, these bakeries had not been cleaned out. Vats (or the holes where they had stood) were still embedded in the ash. These would have been for mixing dough or to hold water,

The bakery scene from the 5th-dynasty tomb of Ti at Saqqara is the most complete one known from ancient Egypt. The relief shows the stack-heating of bread moulds, the pouring of the dough, the opening of the moulds and the removal of the loaves.

flour and ferment. We also discovered a cache of large bell-shaped *bedja* pots used for baking bread. Old Kingdom tomb reliefs show these pots being stacked and heated over an open fire, perhaps to 'temper' their interiors with oil and grease to prevent sticking. Along the east wall of both bakery rooms were egg-carton-shaped baking pits, lying beneath a cake of ash. Pots placed in these pits would have been filled with dough, covered with more upside-down pots and finally surrounded by hot embers to bake the dough.

Bread and beer were the principal rations of ancient Egypt, sustaining any labour project. But did this pot-baked bread feed a workforce, or could it have been specially made for temple offerings or ceremonies? It is in fact much easier to make bread by simply slapping dough against a hot surface, like the Bedouin and other nomads do. The ancient Egyptians had only emmer wheat and barley; they had little or none of our far more glutenous *triticum aestivum* or bread wheat. This meant that despite leavening, loaves were very heavy indeed. Working with National Geographic and bread and yeast expert Ed Wood, we built a replica of this bakery and made bread with emmer and barley flour and locally cultured wild yeast. The resulting loaves were massively heavy units of starch and calories. Each would have sufficed to feed one person for days. Pot baking may have been the Old Kingdom answer to the need to mass-produce bread to feed large numbers of people.

Attached to the bakeries was a huge mudbrick building. A patch of its interior at the southeast corner had been exposed and we uncovered a cache of pottery dishes, including small bowls that were probably jar covers and cylindrical ceramic pieces used as bases to stand conical-bottomed vessels upright. There was also a series of low shelves (about ankle height) with partition walls only *c.* 20 cm (8 in) high. Extending well beyond our excava-

tion squares, these were made of alluvial mud, mudbrick and stone rubble, and had originally been paved with clean desert clay.

We initially speculated that these enigmatic shelves and troughs might have been used for laying out bread to be counted by scribes, an activity illustrated at the bottom of the relief scene from the tomb of Ti. However, a fine ashy deposit that contained fibrous organic material covered the floor. We had to drip a liquid consolidant on larger pieces to prevent them blowing away in the wind. By scraping back delicately we retrieved gills, fins and other parts of catfish and schal (*Synodontis*). Wilma Wetterstrom, our palaeobotanist, examined soil from the troughs under a microscope and found it full of tiny broken fish bone. Catfish breed soon after the inundation that turns the Nile Valley into a lake and spawning ground.

This part of our huge, orthogonally laid-out building was used, it seems, for processing fish. Fish decomposes quickly, especially without refrigeration. How was it stored? The systematic layout suggests large and organized – probably seasonal – harvests. The fish must have been dried, and perhaps smoked and salted. The troughs and benches, as well as being working platforms, may have served as a ventilation system as the fish were laid out on reed frames. We had, literally, found loaves and fishes – sources of starch, calories and protein that could have fed a workforce. The entire installation probably dates to the reign of Menkaure – the end of pyramid building at Giza. Since his pyramid complex was unfinished when Menkaure died, a pyramid workforce was being fed at the time our bakeries were in operation. So far we have only excavated the upper layers of the site. The deepest, and oldest, layers, exposed in the backhoe trench, reveal large burning pits, perhaps the remains of camp fires of a more loosely organized labour force.

(Above) In our reconstructed ancient Egyptian bakery, bread and yeast expert Ed Wood bakes the kind of bread that may have once sustained the pyramid builders, based on evidence from our excavations (left). We used the characteristic bedja *pots, some of the commonest and crudest pieces of Egyptian pottery and yet among the most interesting. They are shaped like large bells, with a bevelled rim and conical interior. The walls are very thick and full of chaff temper which burns out leaving a high porosity.*
These bread moulds comprise 40–50 per cent of Old Kingdom ceramic finds.

Delicate remains of a fish gill or fin, found in our excavations in the area of the bakeries.

The Royal Workshops

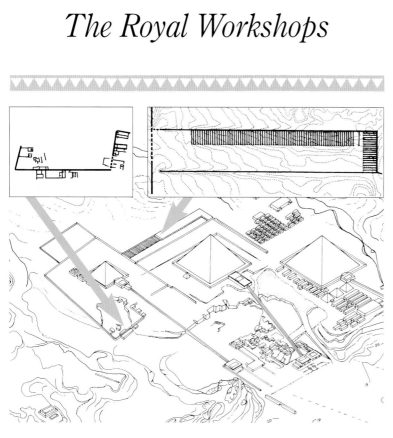

Industrial installations connected with the Giza pyramids. Each of Khafre's galleries (plan above right) were about 3 m (10 ft) wide – about the maximum width that can be roofed with palm log and plant material. Evidence of such roofing was found in impressions on mud. Thresholds were made of limestone paving which must have run the entire length of the galleries. The gallery walls were pointed with mud from the Nile Valley and had floors paved with a mix of tafla and alluvial mud. In Menkaure's enclosure (plan above left) evidence of working copper and alabaster was found, as well ovens, probably for baking bread, other ovens perhaps for pottery manufacture, possible reception halls, and storage pits for pots, foodstuffs and water.

Khafre's galleries

When we began excavating in 1988–89, our interest was not in finding more tombs, temples or statues, already the focus of two centuries of excavation at Giza. What we sought was evidence of the settlements and economic system that supported first pyramid building and then the functioning pyramid complexes. An obvious starting point was the immense rectangular enclosure along the western side of Khafre's pyramid. Perpendicular walls extend like the teeth of a comb from the west wall of this enclosure which is 450 m (1,476 ft) long, describing about 75 galleries, each 30 m (98 ft) long and 3 m (10 ft) wide. With another set leading from the north wall, there are nearly 100 galleries in all.

In 1881 Petrie excavated two of these galleries and, despite finding fragments of royal statuary, concluded that they were workmen's barracks. They have been labelled as such on most plans of Giza published since. But if people reside in an area for any length of time they generate considerable quantities of refuse, such as sherds and ash from hearth sweepings. There is little evidence of this here – in fact the area is surrounded by visible bedrock. Rather the galleries resemble the similar comb-like galleries associated with the temples of

the New Kingdom, particularly that of Aten at Tell el-Amarna. Barry Kemp identified its galleries as the temple bakeries on account of the millions of fragments of bread moulds found there. Earlier excavations there had also produced evidence of craft activity, including faience figures and inlay, a sculptor's trial piece and bronze rings and nails. These galleries clearly had a variety of functions; perhaps, despite being separated by a millennium or more, those attached to Khafre's pyramid housed similar – and similarly diverse – activities.

The galleries had been filled in by sand, so that only the spines of the walls were visible. Excavation showed that the entire structure had been meticulously cleaned out in ancient times. Occasionally, however, we found parts of tools, such as sandstone rubbers, made of consolidated sand in a gypsum matrix rather than sandstone proper, and used for abrading and polishing surfaces. Embedded in corners and the floor were fragments of malachite, feldspar, carnelian, copper and a piece of faience tile.

Finally, in the very last few days of the excavation, we reached shallow deposits that had not been cleaned out. In these we found pottery, a bead, bone and plant materials, collections of basalt chips, unworked pieces of granite and a flint core with flakes broken from it lying close by. Most exciting of all was a collection of tiny statue fragments, none longer than an index finger. They included a black-painted lion's paw; a lion sculpture, perhaps a gaming piece; and parts of human statues, probably royal figures. These included a finger-length figurine of the king striding forth, wearing the *shendyt* kilt and the crown of the south. His eyes, eyebrows and beard are painted black and while one leg was clearly broken off, the left arm had been sawn off at the shoulder in a smooth, straight cut. This was a sculptor's trial piece. To achieve the correct proportions and feel, the craftsman carved it and then shaved off those parts not to be included in the final sculpture.

That this was the refuse from a craft workshop was finally confirmed by the discovery of a fragment of a statuette of the king wearing the crown of the south, standing against a pillar from the top of which a short roof projects. The whole is painted red and stippled black to imitate granite. The piece represents a large statue in a temple court with the projecting roof of a colonnade, as found only in the courts in Khafre's mortuary temple and the Sphinx temple. This figurine, too small to be a working scale model, is a miniature conceptual piece. It was created in the process of deciding what was to be executed on a large scale and discarded when its head broke off from the back pillar.

The fact that the galleries had been so carefully emptied implied that some of the material worked there was precious. So too did the galleries' location, well away from the sites hypothesized as the major areas of settlement on the Giza plateau. However, two more substantial deposits contained a mix of cooking bowls, plant remains, animal bone and craft-related items. This is a caution against ascribing one simple function to these galleries. Many might be empty because they were never fully occupied or used. We might even wonder if they were to some extent symbolic – the above-ground equivalent of the extensive subterranean galleries along the west side of Djoser's Step Pyramid complex.

The alabaster workshops

Another set of workshops is known at Giza, this one lying south-southeast of Menkaure's pyramid. It forms part of the great secondary wall defining the huge precinct around this pyramid. Here, the wall does not describe a neat rectangle, but swings considerably south of due east to form a large 'elbow'. In the early 1970s a team from Cairo University under Dr Abdul Aziz Saleh excavated what seems to be a small industrial community, nestling in the crook of this 'elbow'.

This installation shows a far more laissez-faire arrangement than the Khafre galleries. It consists of a broad open courtyard and small house-like structures built against the sides of the thick precinct wall. In some of the buildings there is a small room containing a dais, probably the foundation of a bed. Sloping rows of pedestals surrounded by troughs may be supports for making reed baskets and containers. Two structures contain ovens which could be pottery kilns, and there are also 12 horseshoe-shaped hearths perhaps used in making and sharpening copper tools – a huge task

in pyramid building. Significantly, a large cache of alabaster boulders and fragments was discovered in the open court. This suggests that the installation in fact served Khafre's pyramid complex, for which immense quantities of alabaster were used. If so, that would explain the curious shape of Menkaure's precinct walls. Their 'elbow' enabled them to incorporate this installation, which then continued in operation after Khafre's reign. As Rainer Stadelmann has suggested, we may be looking at the *hemut-semit*, the desert or necropolis workshop referred to in workmen's graffiti on the granite blocks partially casing the walls of Menkaure's mortuary temple.

The 'hidden aspect' of pyramid building

Menkaure's workshop installation was founded on and buried by deep layers of construction debris – stone, gypsum and tafla. Pyramid building was in large part the manipulation of massive amounts of this material. Indeed, much of its infrastructure might be lost beneath it. When Khufu began building, most of the plateau was free for workmen's installations and settlements, but for Khafre and Menkaure this was no longer the case and any support structures that were in the way would have been razed and dumped elsewhere. This engineering of rubbish in-filling occurred on a vast scale. Barry Kemp has dubbed it the 'hidden aspect' of pyramid building.

In the early 1970s Karl Kromer excavated an area to the southeast of the industrial installation in the Menkaure enclosure, suspecting there might be a settlement there. But though he found settlement debris, it had all been dumped at this spot. There was also a ramp of construction debris leading up to the dump. This ramp, Kromer suggested, may have been created by the razing and dumping of a village or installation because they stood on the site of a new pyramid – probably Menkaure's since seal impressions bearing the names of Khufu and Khafre, but not Menkaure or Shepseskaf, were found.

Fragments of small limestone figurines, perhaps 'trial pieces' from galleries west of Khafre's pyramid.

(Below) The precinct walls and galleries west of Khafre's pyramid seen from the top of Menkaure's pyramid, looking north. (Left) One of the galleries attached to the north wall, after excavation.

Epilogue:
The Legacy of the Pyramids

The ancient Egyptians conceived and developed the pyramid in a programme of architectural simulation. They made mudbrick and then stone simulacra of wood and reed-mat shrines, following the 'false door principle', whereby a door or structure is efficacious in the Netherworld to the extent that it is a replica or simulacrum in this world. Thus the pyramid was a simulacrum of both the immaterial rays of the sun and the primeval mound – a giant version of the *ben-ben* symbol in the sun temple at Heliopolis.

Each pyramid was the central icon towering above a composition of simulacra, signs and symbols comprising an architectural narrative on the scale of acres. Today, Djoser's Step Pyramid complex is largely in ruins, its architectural elements in the process of being reconstructed by the work of J.-P. Lauer. When we comprehend Imhotep's original design, with its petrified shrines and statues of Djoser installed at each major stop for the king's virtual and perpetual movement through the dummy buildings, their doors frozen open forever, we can appreciate that the vast complex was conceived as a huge special effect. Here, and to a certain extent in the classic pyramid complex, we are inside a gigantic hieroglyphic text.

Simulation comes full circle from ancient Egypt to modern America, in the form of the Luxor Hotel/Casino Pyramid built by Circus-Circus Corporation in Las Vegas, one of the largest pyramids on the threshold of the 3rd millennium AD. In 1972 the architect Robert Venturi could point to Las Vegas as a compendium of 'architecture as grandiose cartoon', not altogether dissimilar in a formal sense from ancient Egyptian architecture as hieroglyph. Las Vegas today is a jumbled lexicon of icons borrowed from the recent and ancient past. And so a hotel/casino can mimic ancient Egypt, or, more accurately, the popular cinematic version of ancient Egypt – a bricolage of motifs taken indiscriminately from three thousand years of pharaonic style, witnessed by the very fact that the pyramid is named 'Luxor' after the religious capital at Thebes in a period when large royal pyramids were no longer built. This pyramid of gambling rises 30 storeys, 111.25 m (365 ft) high, at a low 39° angle.

Special effects and lasers create a story of an Egyptoid civilization. Meaningless 'crypto-Egypto' hieroglyphs decorate the colossal interior beams, and real Egyptian hieroglyphs are arranged so that they purposely say nothing – and so can offend no one. On the outside the black pyramid is ambivalent, a liminal zone to nowhere. Glass panels that were meant to reflect sunlight instead render the pristine form dark and sleek. But next to the pyramid, like a guard dog, is a colossal ten-storey Sphinx, twice the size of the Great Sphinx of Giza, frosted with bright pastel colours, serving as a carport. The eyes of the sphinx shoot laser beams that ricochet off an obelisk into dancing waters that project an image of King Tut. An attempt to render the idealized serenity and supreme confidence in the royal expression of the ancient Egyptian sphinx results here in a blank stare.

From Rome to the 20th century

Between ancient Egypt and Las Vegas, a trail of pyramids can be traced through time and across continents. Ancient Rome carried the pyramid from the close of antiquity to Renaissance Europe. The best-known, still standing, was built for Gaius Cestius in 12 BC, in the reign of Augustus. Measuring 36.58 m (120 ft) tall, it is built of brick-faced concrete covered with marble slabs, rising at a far more acute angle than the classic Old Kingdom pyramids and closer to later Egyptian and Nubian pyramids. Another, larger pyramid stood in the necropolis on the Vatican Hill, but was reduced to a small remnant by the 16th century, and there may have been more among the tombs that once lined the roads leading to Rome.

Following the fall of the Roman Empire, pyramids were kept in the collective consciousness by savants writing on Rome's antiquities, or artists recasting Egyptian motifs into very un-Egyptian combinations such as obelisks mounted on step pyramids, or obelisks mounted on balls. In the 17th and early 18th centuries ever more accurate travelogues became standard sources for designers. Small Cestius-type pyramids were built on pedestals and podiums in cemeteries and gardens. In the last quarter of the 18th century designs were drawn up for larger pyramidal monuments, sometimes on a scale rivalling the largest pyramids in Egypt. Mercifully, most were never executed.

Two opposite sources influenced 18th-century visions of pyramids. Giovanni Battista Piranesi (c. 1720–78) popularized Egyptian motifs in his extraordinarily ornate Rococo designs for café interiors, fireplaces and fantastical scenery. On the other hand, Johann Gottfried Herder (1744–1803) appreciated the purity and simplicity of Egyptian buildings, especially the pyramids.

French architects combined the sublimity of Piranesi's Egyptianizing with the simplicity of form that Herder emphasized in visions of huge monuments of simple mass and symmetry. Etienne-Louis Boullée (1728–99), a leader of this movement, designed monuments in the form of colossal sarcophagi, triumphal arches, domes and pyramids. He used the large surfaces of pyramids to achieve an awesome, mournful effect. One of his cenotaph designs was a gigantic truncated pyramid with a slope close to the Old Kingdom monuments. In another design, for a mortuary chapel, Boullée lowered the slope of a huge pyramid even more. He designed pyramids to convey the 'terror and desolation of death'.

In Europe and Scandinavia pyramids were built or designed for sepulchral temples, a dairy, crema-

A Roman pyramid: the tomb of Gaius Cestius, built in 12 BC.

toria, garden shrines and mausolea. Claude-Nicolas Ledoux (1735–1806), who immersed himself in Freemasonry and mystical ideas, designed a gun foundry for Chaux with pyramids as casings for the furnaces at the corners. His smoking pyramids appear to have been crossed with volcanoes.

Following Napoleon's Expedition to Egypt, greater archaeological correctness came to Egyptianized designs, with the publication of the *Description de l'Egypte*, and the earlier and more accessible volume by the artist, Vivant Denon, published in 1802. These sources were augmented by the work of artist-travellers such as David Roberts (1796-1864) and John Frederick Lewis (1805–76).

The 19th century saw a profusion of Egyptianized houses, gardens, parks, sphinxes, architraves, salons, pylons, bridges and pediments. In Germany commemorative pyramid monuments were built for princes. In England, Thomas Harrison (1744–1829) designed a monumental pyramid very similar to the Egyptian pyramids in its proportions. At Biddulph Grange in Staffordshire James Bateman (1811–97) and Maria Warburton created an Egyptian court and sphinxes in stone, but with pylon entrance and a great truncated pyramid all in clipped hedge.

(Opposite) Perhaps as far removed from the original pyramids as it is possible to imagine, the Luxor Hotel/Casino Pyramid in Las Vegas, guarded by a sphinx whose eyes shoot laser beams.

Pyramids have inspired artists and architects through the ages: Piranesi incorporated them into his designs for fireplaces (top); Ledoux designed a pyramid furnace for a foundry (centre); and Boullée created a plan for a pyramid cenotaph (bottom).

The Late 20th-Century Pyramid Revival

House Pyramids
Many people have turned to the pyramid form for their dwellings. Perhaps the best known house pyramid is that built by Jim Onan and plated with gold in Wadsworth, Lake County, Illinois. Burt Rutan, 'America's most innovative designer of airplanes, rocket ships, and other fast-moving objects' designed a three-story hexagonal pyramid. Al Pecor, a Wisconsin native, hypnotherapist and craftsman, built a white pyramid house in the Sonoran Desert of Arizona, south of Phoenix for his wife, Diane. The pyramid rises 13 m (45 ft); the interior rooms include much Egyptian paraphernalia. The guest room features a green carpet sarcophagus in which visitors lie and gaze at the stars through two huge triangular windows forming the pyramid peak.

Long Beach Pyramid
California State University at Long Beach built a $20-million Physical Education Pyramid, 56.62 m (178 ft) tall and 105.23 m (345 ft) square at the base.

In the late 20th century AD, a new revival has spawned more pyramids, not to house dead bodies or to commemorate the great, but for business and pleasure, housing bustling, living bodies.

Cleveland Pyramid
Cleveland is the home of the Rock and Roll Hall of Fame, a $92-million collection of pop music memorabilia and interactive computers housed in a five-storey glass pyramid on the North Coast Harbor.

Galveston Pyramid
The Rainforest Pyramid, located in Galveston, Texas is 38 m (125 feet) tall and is made of 1,700 pieces of glass set on to a steel frame. It houses the world's largest indoor rain forest. A pyramid shape was chosen because it offers optimal lighting conditions and it deflects hurricane-force winds.

Grand Rapids Pyramid
Steelcase Inc. built a $111-million Corporate Development Center and office building near Grand Rapids, Michigan in the form of a broad sleek steel pyramid that rises from the prairie at a low angle to seven levels.

Pyramids on the threshold of the 3rd millennium AD house a variety of functions for the living. (Top) The Galveston Pyramid houses an indoor rain forest. (Centre) The Long Beach Pyramid is a modern temple to physical fitness. (Right) The Grand Rapids Pyramid forms the corporate headquarters for a modern business. (Right) The new centrepiece of the Louvre Museum in Paris is a glass pyramid.

It was designed by Advanced Structures Inc. in Venice California for the architectural firm of Hugh & Donald Gibbs. This is a fractal pyramid, composed of many smaller pyramidal 'blocks' forming a 'multiple-layer space grid'. The pyramid contains 6,800 moveable seats for spectators, a health club and meeting rooms.

Louvre Pyramid

In the 1980s I.M. Pei created a sensation by designing a high-tech glass pyramid entrance in the court of the French bastion of culture, the Louvre. The base was composed of stone and exposed concrete, and the pyramid of custom-cast stainless-steel fittings and untinted glass. Because of its stark contrast with the older buildings, the glass pyramid created much controversy. The French Ministry of Culture and the Louvre director, Michel Laclotte, chose to complement the glass pyramid with another, this one inverted and subterranean, as part of Le Carrousel du Louvre, a complex of parking lots, fashion houses and restaurants between Pei's pyramid and the Arc de Triomphe. The inverted pyramid, providing light and visual focus, hangs like a chandelier down into the underground mall. The inverted pyramid was designed by Pei, Conn, Freed & Partners. The projected cost was $ 2.5 million.

Memphis Tennessee Pyramid

In the late 1980s Memphis embarked on the construction of 32-storey, $75-million pyramid sports arena along the banks of the Mississippi River. Called the Great American Pyramid. It houses a 20,000-seat arena for basketball and other events.

The San Francisco Pyramid

The headquarters of the Transamerica Corporation, San Francisco is so elongated and stylized that it barely squeaks into the 'pyramid' category. The 48-storey, 260-m (853-ft) tall building (including the spire) may be the only 'pyramid' that sways when shaken by earthquakes. While it is almost twice the height of the Great Pyramid of Khufu, the base is smaller. It was designed by William L. Pereira. Construction began in 1969 and was completed in 1972. The corporate advertising motto is 'the power of the pyramid working for you'.

Pyramids were common grave markers in 19th-century cemeteries, such as the pyramid mausoleum to 'Mad Jack' Fuller MP built in 1812 in the churchyard of St Thomas Beckett in Brightling, East Sussex, or the many pyramids (and obelisks) in Highgate Cemetery, designed by Stephen Geary in 1830 for the London Cemetery Company. In America, 19th-century Egyptian revivalists favoured obelisks, the greatest of which was the Washington National Monument designed by R. Mills in 1833.

The most bizarre idea for a pyramid, one that would have rivalled the Great Pyramid, was conceived by Thomas Willson in 1824 and published in 1842. In the spirit of Boullée, Willson proposed a 'pyramid to hold five million bodies', built of brick faced with granite, to cover an area of 7.3 ha (18 acres) near Primrose Hill, London. Surpassing St Paul's in height, the steep pyramid, topped by an obelisk, would contain 94 tiers of vaults.

In 1882 another Thomas Willson, perhaps the son of the above, designed a pyramid mausoleum for the assassinated US President Garfield. This would be topped by an obelisk, with an inner dome protecting the catacombs. The Egyptian Revival continued unabated into the early 20th century with small pyramids and obelisks serving as grave markers and commemorative monuments. Howard Carter's discovery of Tutankhamun's tomb in 1922 heralded a second Egyptian revival. Had the Nazis been successful, dark foreboding pyramids might have been built in the mid-20th century. Wilhelm Kreis and Albert Speer looked to the designs of Boullée and Ledoux for inspiration.

Form and function

The modern pyramids on the cusp of the 3rd millennium AD retain the form but invert the function of the giant Egyptian pyramids of the 3rd millennium BC. The ancient pyramids were massive, solid, 'dummy' hieroglyphic buildings, powerful symbols that focused society and cosmos. The modern pyramids are light skeletal structures whose purity of form nods to their ancient counterparts but which otherwise have no intrinsic metaphorical value. The ancient pyramids contained the most exclusive and inaccessible space – the burial chamber of the king, a place of death and arcane ritual. The interiors of the modern pyramids are designed to be optimally accessible to as many people as possible for work space and popular entertainment.

The pyramids of ancient Egypt enclosed physical death and celebrated spiritual rebirth. The modern pyramids celebrate physical recreation but do not explicitly intend to be spiritual. However, there is a lightness of being in most modern pyramids. Their purity of form – four points for the base, square on the earth, and a centre point drawn up towards heaven – conveys the uplifting of spirit that has inspired the human career.

(Above) Pyramid as tomb once more, in the monument of Maria Christina of Austria, 1798, designed by the sculptor Antonio Canova (1757–1822).

Visiting the Pyramids

Modern roads have a powerful effect on how we see the pyramids today. They channel visitors into pyramid sites along routes that often do not match the conduits of the ancient landscape. However, no matter how you approach them, the giant pyramids seldom fail to astound. If there is time for study, there is nothing better than comparing the drawings, maps and plans of the pyramids to ground truth. Equipment for the more exploratory traveller might include a book such as this, pen and paper to note observations and questions, a camera for visual notes, and, essential for the interiors, a good flashlight. For all visitors, a hat and supply of water are necessary, as for sites throughout Egypt.

It is beyond the limits of these pages to describe how to see all the major pyramids. Fortunately, several of the most significant are found in the accessible sites of Giza and Saqqara. Less frequented, but open to the public, or soon to be, are the sites of Dahshur, Abusir and Meidum. My remarks on visiting these pyramids are given in order of accessibility from Cairo.

Giza

Tickets to visit the Giza plateau are purchased at the base of the modern road leading past the Mena House Hotel at the end of the Pyramids Road. The interior of the Great Pyramid of Khufu and the Khufu Boat Museum need separate tickets. Tour leaders purchase tickets for the entire bus which then takes visitors up the paved road to the north side of Khufu. On foot, this approach is grand, as Khufu rises on the plateau, but the pathway affords a limited overall understanding of the whole Great Pyramid complex. Ancient visitors probably approached Giza from the north only rarely.

In the evening you can watch the Sound and Light show from seats east of the Sphinx and Khafre's valley temple. The script is decades old, but lasers have been added recently that project, for example, the interior passage and chamber system on to the Great Pyramid.

A reorganization of the Giza Plateau for tourism may soon be implemented.
I. The Great Pyramid of Khufu. The original access was from the east, via the valley temple and causeway, elements now lost under the modern town. Admire the exquisite stonework of the casing near the centre of the north base (the blocks to the west are restored), but also observe the 'slop factor' in the core. Where the core stones are preserved you can find chisel marks from the skilled hand of a mason who worked 4,600 years ago. On the east side you will find the patch of black basalt pavement of the mortuary temple's court, between two huge open boat pits. Three queens pyramids offer much evidence about building techniques.

The pyramid is entered by a tunnel blasted through the solid masonry. The visitor today joins the original passage system just past the junction between the Descending and Ascending Passages. From here it is a crouch and a climb up the very narrow Ascending Passage until the Grand Gallery. At the top of the Grand Gallery, after ducking through the Antechamber, one enters the King's Chamber.

The Boat Museum is well worth a visit. A truly sublime creation in organic material rather than stone, the boat is a powerful hint of the sophistication and grandeur of the society that built the pyramids.
II: The Sphinx and Khafre's complex. A second major approach to Giza is from the east. Originally it was by water (at least seasonally); today it is a paved road through the bustling suburb of Nazlet es-Semman. This route takes the visitor into the north doorway of Khafre's valley temple, through its well-preserved rooms and up the hallway leading to Khafre's causeway. Standing on the bedrock shoulder of the causeway, visitors look down into the Sphinx enclosure. This, too, may soon be reorganized.

The enterprising visitor might walk the length of Khafre's complex, for it is perhaps the most complete of any Old Kingdom pyramid. Near the pyramid, the mortuary temple is badly ruined compared to the valley temple, but the major features can be discerned. You may enter Khafre's pyramid on its north side with the general Giza ticket.
III. Menkaure's pyramid is approached by car or foot from the north, by turning off the modern road past the west side of Khafre's pyramid. This pyramid, too, can be entered with the general Giza admission ticket. Its vaulted burial chamber is small and elegant.

Outside, the granite casing is unfinished, and careful observation will reveal how the masons had already designed the sloping face of the pyramid into the blocks, so that it only remained to dress back the extra stone. If you walk around to the east side of the pyramid you can enter the mortuary temple. Looking down from the ruined entrance of this temple, the causeway is a simple band of dark mud and stone lining. The valley temple has disappeared beneath the sands since Reisner excavated it.

Saqqara

There is much to see at Saqqara – here I limit my remarks to pyramids. The modern visitor enters the necropolis from the east, before the ruins of Unas's valley temple, marked by two palm-form granite pillars that have been restored. Tickets are purchased at the booth on the right. Ascending on to the plateau, the low mound of Teti's pyramid is on the far right, while Userkaf's pyramid, looking like a pile of rock, is ahead, slightly to the right.
I. Djoser's Step Pyramid dominates modern tours of the Saqqara Plateau as it must have visits in ancient times. In the 3rd dynasty, the broad wadi leading up from the Abusir lake to the north may have been the main access.

The entrance to Djoser's enclosure was at the far south end of the east side. Here modern tours file through a doorway, barely 1 m wide, and down the colonnade entrance hall to emerge in the great south court with a perfect view of the Step Pyramid. Many tours turn right (east) to cross into the court of the Sed Festival booths, where Lauer has reconstructed the king's dais and a few of the stone models of the reed-mat shrines. From the court of the shrines to the north visitors pass the east side of the pyramid and the ruins, on the right, of the pavilions thought to represent northern and southern Egypt.

On the north side of the pyramid is the *serdab* box, tilted up towards the northern sky, and containing Djoser's statue (now a replica). The mortuary temple is on a higher terrace, mounted by stairs from the *serdab*. It is badly ruined, but restorations have made some of its plan recognizable.

Most visitors retrace their steps to pass by the deep pit of the south tomb, embedded in the southern enclosure wall. Here, a modern stair leads up on to the wall, past the cobra frieze. From here, the large tumulus along the western side of Djoser's enclosure looks like a massive bank of debris – extensive galleries, never thoroughly explored, lie below its entire length. From the top of the enclosure wall, on clear days, the southern view includes the mounds of the pyramids of South Saqqara, Shepseskaf's giant mastaba and, farther south, the pyramids of Sneferu and Amenemhet III at Dahshur.
II. Other Saqqara pyramids. As with the Giza pyramids, those at Saqqara are arrayed diagonally northeast–southwest. Farthest to the southwest, beyond Unas, lie the ruins of the unfinished pyramid of Sekhemkhet. The layout is not easily recognized close up, but the entrance trench and the niched white limestone wall along the north side of the first building phase can be seen. From the mounds of debris inside the enclosure, the huge low-lying enclosure called the Gisr el-Mudir is visible to the west.

Descending from Djoser's south wall, one comes to Unas's pyramid. The Pyramid Texts on the walls of its chambers are hailed as the world's oldest written religious literature. Unfortunately, the moisture from thousands of tourists has caused the blue hieroglyphs to fade, and for some time the pyramid has been closed to visitors. It is hard to see much of the plan of the mortuary temple, although the granite frame of the entrance door has been restored.

Walking down Unas's causeway, with low walls and pavement that still exist or have been restored, gives one the sense of what these structures were like. Part way down are two huge stone-lined boat pits.

For Pyramid Texts the visitor must now go to Teti's pyramid, to the northeast of Djoser's and Userkaf's, on the other end of the Saqqara diagonal. There is not much to see of the pyramid itself and the temple, like that of Unas, was practically levelled by lime manufacturers.

The pyramids of South Saqqara – Djedkare-Isesi, Pepi I, Merenre and Pepi II are harder to get to: either a drive along a desert track west of the main Saqqara Plateau or, to Pepi II and the Mastabat el-Fara'un of Shepseskaf, a road through the modern village of Saqqara, which skirts round the cultivation edge.

Dahshur

The site of Dahshur has recently been opened to the public. Tickets are purchased at the end of the road from Dahshur village, about 20 km south of Saqqara, just before ascending the plateau.

I. The North (Red) Pyramid can be entered with some physical exertion. Here a powerful flashlight is certainly useful. Climbing up the modern steps gives a sense of how the builders had to locate the entrance high up in order to make a long descending passage to a burial chamber close to ground level. A wooden scaffolding and stairway from high up in the second antechamber leads to the burial chamber. Pits in the floor were dug by those in search of treasure. Look up at the exquisite corbelling, which also crowns the antechambers.

Outside, a walk around the northeast corner of the pyramid brings you to the remains of the mortuary temple, as excavated and partially reconstructed by Rainer Stadelmann, with the reconstructed limestone capstone.

II. The Bent (Southern) Pyramid. A desert road leads from west of the North Pyramid to the Bent Pyramid, a good walk if not taken by car. The western entrance can be spotted as a small opening high up in the casing on its west side, but is not easily accessible. At the northeast corner, the path of the causeway is still visible as limestone chips. A walk down the causeway brings you to the ruins of the so-called valley temple, of which little is visible. A walk along the east side of the pyramid brings you to the remains of the small chapel, with the stumps of two stelae and the stone canopy that protects a *hetep* offering slab. Rounding the southeast corner of the Bent Pyramid, you come upon its small satellite pyramid. Ahmed Fakhry found remains of two more stelae on the east side. The entrance to the satellite pyramid is open, but the passage is sanded up and is not accessible.

The Middle Kingdom pyramids at Dahshur are far from the beaten tourist tracks. The pyramid complex of Senwosret III is now being excavated by Dieter Arnold, and is off limits.

Abusir

Abusir is soon to be organized for more easy access. The site is approached by a west turn off the road between Saqqara and Nazlet es-Semman near Giza, through the bustling town of Abusir, if coming from the south.

I. Sahure. Recently the area of Sahure's valley temple has been cleared. Sahure's causeway, of which the foundation is well preserved, delivers you to the mortuary temple's entrance hall and court. Two of the granite palm-capital columns have been re-erected and bases of other columns can be seen. The ambulatory is recognizable and parts of Sahure's titulary are visible on stone fragments. Nearer the pyramid, the inner temple is a jumble of stone, but various parts are quite well preserved.

The pyramid is a fallen heap resulting from the removal of the outer casing. A recent earthquake has left the entrance and burial chamber in a precarious state, and so the pyramid should not be entered. Stand back from the entrance to observe the 'construction gap',

defined by the better masonry of the retaining walls, in the lower part of the core. This was left open for building the chamber and passage, then filled with looser material.

II. Niuserre. To view the other Abusir pyramids, retrace your steps back to the southeast corner of Sahure's pyramid, and walk the diagonal expansion of the necropolis to the southwest. The next pyramid in space but not time is Niuserre's. You arrive near the ruins of a pylon that thickened the front eastern corner of the court. To the south is the pavement of the court, and the ruins of the inner part of Niuserre's mortuary temple. Niuserre bent his temple into an L-shape, and the leg of the 'L' brings you to the entrance hall, roughly outlined by large pieces of basalt dado. The causeway, diverted from Neferirkare's complex, is flanked by basalt pieces which lined the lower parts of the walls for its entire length.

III. Neferirkare. Proceeding southwest, you pass the southeast corner of Niuserre's pyramid, now a rounded mound, to look down across the low traces of Neferirkare's mortuary temple. Very little remains, although the major outlines can be seen. Look up at the southwest corner of Neferirkare's pyramid to see the masonry layers that prompted Egyptologists to think Neferirkare first intended a step pyramid.

IV. Khentkawes. Crossing the irregular ground at the south of Neferirkare's pyramid, you look down on Khentkawes's pyramid and temple. The pyramid is badly ruined – the pit of the burial chamber opens through the loose debris. Not much remains of the inner stone temple, although the bottom of a pillar, painted red and inscribed with the queen's figure and titles, remains standing. Only a small corner of the satellite pyramid remains standing within its mudbrick enclosure. Farther east, and better preserved, are the walls of five magazines. Beyond Khentkawes to the south, you see the partially excavated ruins of the 'pyramids' that Lepsius numbered XXIV and XXV.

V. Raneferef's pyramid, the last to the southwest, may be accessible once the site is opened to the public. Here is a good example of the very beginning of a 5th-dynasty pyramid – a low mastaba with a central pit and a construction gap on the north side. Only bits of pavement and walls remain of the inner stone temple, but the mudbrick walls of the rest still stand to a surprising height, retaining much of their gypsum-plastered surface.

VI. The Sun Temples are a good walk south over the sands from the Abusir pyramid cluster. You can take the high ground, which means walking up and down desert hillocks, or the low desert close to the cultivation. The ruins of Userkaf's sun temple come first, although if you are not looking for them you might not notice them. All that is left of the upper temple are scattered large stones from the obelisk pedestal, the terrace of the court and the spoil heaps of excavations. To the west, is a jumble of large stone pieces, including parts of a huge quartzite drain. Many of the limestone pieces have etched hieroglyphs of the workers' notations. Almost nothing can be seen of the valley temple.

Moving south you approach the better

preserved sun temple of Niuserre. Prominent on the hill are the core of the enclosure wall and of the obelisk pedestal. The ruins of the valley temple have been reclaimed by the desert sands. At the top the causeway core walls are preserved, which open out to a broad court with the remains of the obelisk pedestal. Straight across the court is the large alabaster altar. A piece of relief carving on a broken granite block near the northwest corner of the altar bears the name of the temple, 'Delight of Re', with the obelisk on its pedestal as the ideogram. North of the altar you will find large pieces of limestone pavement carved with low channels. These are thought to have been part of the terrace on which animals were slaughtered. They may have drained to the nine large alabaster basins lined up to the east. Three more alabaster basins, less elaborate and with three drainage holes each, are on the north side of the pedestal.

Meidum

Meidum is 50 km south of Saqqara, 70 km south of Cairo, and so you should plan a full day for a trip from Cairo and back. The site is best reached by the Upper Egyptian highway from Cairo. You turn off the main road to drive west through the village of Meidum, then out into the desert south of the pyramid.

The pyramid looks like a tower, complete in its own right – although we know that the shape is the result of rebuilding and robbing – rising from a prominent white mound of debris. As you follow the road west of the pyramid there is a government rest facility. On the north side of the pyramid is the antiquities authority outpost for tickets. When you arrive at the end of the paved road, Dr Ali el-Khouli's excavations at the northwest corner give a clear view of the masonry of E3 that filled out the step pyramid and created a true pyramid. You see the intact Turah-limestone casing, with blocks laid horizontally. Behind is the yellow limestone which is packing material between core and casing. Higher up you can see the limestone corners of E1 and E2 peeking through the masonry of large core blocks used to fill out E3.

The pyramid is entered by climbing up a short wooden stairway from the top of the debris, followed by a crawl through the long descending passage. As you climb the vertical shaft to the burial chamber, note the large cedar logs embedded in the masonry. The burial chamber is small and unfinished. Note the stump of a cedar log just above the entrance shaft, another higher up, and a complete one across the top – remnants of the system for lifting the sarcophagus into the chamber?

You may walk around to the east side of the pyramid on the debris, or along its base. This brings you to the small mortuary temple or chapel. From high up you can see the track of the causeway shooting towards the cultivation. From below, you see protruding above the chapel roof the tops of the stelae. Each should have been carved with the Horus falcon perched on Sneferu's *serekh*, but were left blank – part of the mystery of Meidum. The location of the satellite pyramid, at the far west end of the south side, is marked by pits in the debris.

Further Reading

Abbreviations

AA   *Agyptologische Abhandlungen*
ASAE   *Annales du Service des Antiquités de l'Égypte*
BÀBA   *Beiträge zur ägyptischen Bauforschung und Altertumskunde*
BdE   *Bibliothèque d'Étude*
BIFAO   *Bulletin de l'Institut française d'archéologie orientale*
BMFA   *Bulletin of the Museum of Fine Arts*
BSFE   *Bulletin de la Société française d'égyptologie*
CAJ   *Cambridge Archaeological Journal*
CdE   *Chronique d'Égypte*
CRAIBL   *Compte-Rendus de l'Académie des Inscriptions et Belles-Lettres*
CRIPEL   *Cahier de Recherches de l'Institut de Papyrologie et d'Égyptologie de Lille*
DE   *Discussions in Egyptology*
EG   *Egyptian Archaeology*
GLECS   *Groupe linguistique pour les études Chamio-sémitiques*
GM   *Göttinger Miszellen*
JARCE   *Journal of the American Research Center in Egypt*
JEA   *Journal of Egyptian Archaeology*
JNES   *Journal of Near Eastern Studies*
JSSEA   *The SSEA Journal*
KMT   *KMT. A Modern Journal of Ancient Egypt*
LÄ   *Lexikon der Ägyptologie*
MDAIK   *Mitteilungen des Deutschen Archäologischen Instituts, Abteilung Kairo*
MIFAO   *Memoires publiés par les membres de l'Institut française d'archéologie orientale du Caire*
NARCE   *American Research Center in Egypt Newsletter*
RdÉ   *Revue d'Égyptologie*
RecTrav   *Recueil de travaux relatifs à la philologie et à l'archéologie égyptienne et assyrienne*
SAOC   *Studies in Ancient Oriental Civilization*
SSEA   *Society for the Study of Egyptian Antiquities*
VA   *Varia Aegyptiaca*
ZÄS   *Zeitschrift für Ägyptishce Sprache und Altertumskunde. Leipzig/Berlin*

INTRODUCTION

Chronology

Dates used throughout the book follow the chronological table used from: Baines, J. and J. Málek, *Atlas of Ancient Egypt* (Oxford and New York, 1980), 36–7.

General chronology of ancient Egypt:

Clayton, P., *Chronicle of the Pharaohs: the Reign by Reign Record of the Rulers and Dynasties of Ancient Egypt* (London and New York, 1994)

Rainer Stadelmann's chronology of the 'Sneferu transition', with important implications for 'counting years' and regnal years, the reliability of the Turin Canon, and absolute length of the Old Kingdom, in:

Stadelmann, R., *MDAIK* 36 (1980), 437–49; *MDAIK* 38 (1982), 379–93; 39 (1983), 225–41; *MDAIK* 43 (1987), 229–40

Radiocarbon dates of pyramids:

Haas, H. et al., 'Radiocarbon chronology and the historical calendar in Egypt', in O. Aurenche, J. Evin, and F. Hours (eds), *Chronologies in the Near East*, BAR International Series (1987), 585–605

Pyramids and the Landscape

Butzer, K.W., *Early Hydraulic Civilization in Egypt: A Study in Cultural Ecology* (Chicago, 1976). Still the basic discussion on Egyptian geomorphology

Hayes, W.C., 'Most ancient Egypt', *JNES* 23, no. 2 (April 1964), 74–113. While the later chapters are outdated, chapter 1 of Hayes's uncompleted work, posthumously published, is still useful

Kees, H., *Ancient Egypt: A Cultural Topography* (London, 1961)

Said, R., *The Geology of Egypt* (Brookfield, VT, 1990)
—*The River Nile: Geology, Hydrology, and Utilization* (Oxford, 1993)

Said, R. and L. Martin, 'Cairo area geological excursion notes', in F.A. Reilly (ed.), *Guidebook to the Geology and Archaeology of Egypt* (1964), 107–21

Land and water management in ancient Egypt:

Baer, K., 'The low price of land in Egypt', *JARCE* 1 (1962), 25–45

Eyre, C. J., 'The water regime for orchards and plantations in Pharaonic Egypt', *JEA* 80 (1994) 57–80

Gardiner, A.H., *The Wilbour Papyrus, Vol. 2, Commentary* (Oxford, 1948)

Menu, B. (ed.), Les Problemes institutionels de l'eau en Egypte ancienne et dans l'Antiquité méditerranéene, BdE 110 (Cairo, 1992)

Schenkel, W., *Die Bewässerungsrevolution im alten Ägypten* (Mainz am Rhein, 1978)

Willcocks, W. and J.I. Craig, *Egyptian Irrigation*, 3rd ed., 2 vols (London, 1913)

The Pyramids, their Rise and Fall

Kemp, B.J., 'From Old Kingdom to Second Intermediate Period', in *Ancient Egypt, A Social History* (Cambridge, 1983), 71–182, see 86–92

Stadelmann, R., *Die grossen Pyramiden von Giza* (Graz, Austria, 1990). See 258–62

The Standard Pyramid Complex

Simple A-group burial tumuli

Smith, H., *Preliminary Reports of the Egypt Exploration Society's Nubian Survey* (Cairo, 1962). See 64–9

Djoser-type vs. Meidum-type

Arnold, D., 'Das Labyrinth und sein Vorbilder', *MDAIK* 35 (1979), 1–9
—*Der Pyramidenbezirk des Königs Amenemhet III in Dahschur, Band 1: Die Pyramide*, vol. 1 (Mainz, 1987)

I. TOMB AND TEMPLE

The *Ka*, the *Ba* and the Body Embalmed

Dismemberment and mummification:

Assmann, J., 'Death and initiation in the funerary religion of ancient Egypt', in J.P. Allen, et al. (eds), *Religion and Philosophy in Ancient Egypt* (New Haven, 1989), 135–59, see 137–9.

Hermann, A., 'Zergliedern und Zusammenfügen. Religiongeschichtliches zur Mumifizierung', *NUMEN* 3 (1956), 81–96

Spencer, A.J., *Death in Ancient Egypt* (Harmondsworth, 1982). See 'Beginnings of Mummification', 29–44

Wright, G.R.H., 'The Egyptian Sparagmos', *MDAIK* 35 (1979), 345–58

Zandee, J., *Death as an Enemy* (Leiden, 1960)

Ka, Ba and *Akh*:

Allen, J.P., 'Funerary texts and their meaning', in S. D'Auria, P. Lacovara and C.H. Roehrig (eds), *Mummies and Magic: The Funerary Arts of Ancient Egypt* (Boston, 1988), 38–49

Bell, L., *Mythology and Iconography of Divine Kingship in Ancient Egypt* (Chicago, 1994)

Kaplony, P., '*Ka*', *LÄ*, III.2, 275–82

Lloyd, A.B., 'Psychology and society in the ancient Egytian Cult of the Dead', in J.P. Allen et al. (eds), *Religion and Philosophy in Ancient Egypt* (New Haven, 1989), 117–34

Otto, E., '*Ach*', *LÄ* I.1 (1972), 49–51

Zabkar, L.V., *A Study of the Ba Concept in Ancient Egyptian Texts*, SAOC, vol. 34 (Chicago, 1968)

Burial Rituals and the Pyramid Complex

Altenmüller, H., 'Bestattung–Bestattungsritual', *LÄ* 1.5 (1973), 743–65

Edel, E., *Das Akazienhaus und seine Rolle in den Begrabnisriten des alten Ägyptens*, ed. MÄS 24 (Berlin, 1970)

Otto, E., *Das ägyptische Mundöffnungsritual*, ÄA 3 (1960)

Reisner, G.A., 'The scenes of funerary priests performing ceremonies', in *A History of the Giza Necropolis* (Cambridge, MA, 1942), 369–71

Roth, A.M., 'The social aspects of death', in S. D'Auria, P. Lacovara, and C.H. Roehrig (eds), *Mummies and Magic: The Funerary Arts of Ancient Egypt* (Boston, 1988), 52–9

Settgast, J., *Untersuchungen zur Altägyptischen Besttantungsdarstellungen*, ADAIK (Glückstadt, 1963)

Simpson, W.K. *The Mastabas of Qar and Idu*, G7101-7102 (Boston, 1976)

Wilson, J., 'Funeral services of the Egyptian Old Kingdom', *JEA* 3, no. 4 (1944), 201–18

Mortuary Temple – Meaning and Function:

Altenmüller, H., *Die Texte zum Begrabnisritual in den Pyramiden des alten Reiches*, ed. W. Helck and E. Otto, ÄA, 24 (Wiesbaden, 1972)

Arnold, D., 'Ritual und Pyramidentempel', *MDAIK* 33 (1977), 2–14

Bonnet, H., 'Ägyptische Baukunst und Pyramidenkult', *JNES* 12 (1953), 257–73

Brovarski, E., 'The Doors of Heaven', *Orientalia* 46, no. 1 (1977), 107–15

Drioton, E., 'Review of B. Grdseloff, 'Das Reinigungzelt'', *ASAE* 40 (1940), 1007–14.

Grdseloff, B., *Das ägyptische Reinigungzelt* (Cairo, 1941)
—'Nouvelles données concernaut la Tente de Purification', *ASAE* 51 (1951), 140

Ricke, H., *Bemerkungen zur ägyptischen Baukunst des Alten Reiches II*, BÀBA 5 (Cairo, 1950)

Schott, S., *Bemerkungen zum ägyptischen Pyramidenkult*, BÀBA 5 (Cairo, 1950)

Spiegel, J., *Das Auferstehungritual der Unas-pyramid*, ÄA, 23 (Wiesbaden, 1971)

Stadelmann, R., 'Totentempel I', *LÄ*, 694–9
—'Taltempel', *LÄ* VI.2 (1985), 189–94

This World and the Netherworld

Allen, J., *Genesis in Egypt: The Philosophy of Ancient Egyptian Creation Accounts*, W.K. Simpson (ed.), vol. 2 (New Haven, 1988)

Allen, J., 'The cosmology of the Pyramid Texts', in J.P. Allen, et al. (eds), *Religion and Philosophy in Ancient Egypt* (New Haven, 1989), 1–28

Gardiner, A.H., *The Attitude of the Ancient Egyptians to Death and the Dead* (Cambridge, 1935)

Hornung, E., *Ägyptischen Unterweltsbucher* (Zurich, 1972)
—*Das Amduat. Die Schrift des verborgenen Raumes*, AA 7, 13 (Wiesbaden, 1963–67)
—'Zu den Schlusszenen der Unterweltsbucher', *MDAIK* 37 (1981), 217–26

Lesko, L., *The Ancient Egyptian Book of Two Ways* (Berkeley, 1972)

Piankoff, A., *The Tomb of Ramses VI*, Bollingen Series, vol. 49.1 (New York, 1954)
—*The Mythological Papyri*, Bollingen Series, vol. 49.3 (New York, 1957)

Schott, S., 'Die Schrift der verborgenen Kammer in Konigsgrabern der 18. Dynastie', *Nachrichten der Akademie der Wissenschaften in Gottingen 1. Philologische-Historische Klasse* Nr. 4 (1958) pp. 315–72
—'Zum Weltbild der Jenseitsfuhrer des neun Reiches', *Nachrichten der Akademie der Wissenschaften in Göttingen I. Philologische-Historische Klasse* 11 (1965) pp. 185–97

Velde, H. T., 'Funerary mythology', in S. D'Auria, P. Lacovara, and C.H. Roehrig (eds), *Mummies and Magic: The Funerary Arts of Ancient Egypt* (Boston, 1988), 27–37

Letters to the Dead:

E. Wente (tran.) and E. Meltzer (ed.), *Letters from Ancient Egypt*, ed. B.O. Long (Atlanta, 1990). See 210–20.

Pyramid Texts

Allen, J., 'Reading a pyramid', in C. Berger, G. Clerc and N. Grimal (eds), *Hommages à Jean Leclant*, BdE 106/1 (Cairo, 1994), 5–28

Allen, T.G., *Occurrences of Pyramid Texts with Cross Indexes of these and Other Mortuary Texts*, SAOC, vol. 27 (Chicago, 1950)

Altenmuller, H., *Die Texte zum Begrabnisritual in den Pyramiden des alten Reiches*, W. Helck and E. Otto (eds), *ÄA* 24 (Wiesbaden, 1972)
—'Pyramidentexte', *LÄ* V.1, 14–20

Barta, W., *Die Bedeutung der Pyramidentexte für den verstorbenen König*, MÄS 39 (1981)

Faulkner, R.O., *The Ancient Egyptian Pyramid Texts. Translated into English*, 2 vols (Oxford, 1969)

Lacau, P., 'Suppressions et modifications de signes dans les textes funéraires', *ZÄS* 51 (1914), 1–64
—'Suppressions des noms divine dans les textes de la chambre funéraires', *ASAE* 26 (1926), 69–81

Osing, J., 'Zur Disposition der Pyramidentexte des Unas', *MDAIK* 42 (1986), 131–44

Piankoff, A., *The Pyramid of Unas* (Princeton, 1968)

Sethe, K., *Die altägyptischen Pyramidtexte*, 3 vols (Leipzig, 1908–22)
—*Übersetzung und Kommentar zu den altägyptischen Pyramidentexten*, 6 vols (Gluckstadt, 1935–62)

Per Duat – House of the Morning

Blackman, A.M., 'The House of the Morning', *JEA* 5.2 (1918), 148–65
—'Some notes on the ancient Egyptian practice of washing the dead', JEA 5.1 (1918), 117–24

Pyramid as Icon

Baines, J., '*Bnbn*: Mythological and Linguisitic Notes', *Orientalia* 39 (1970), 389–404

Bennett, J., 'Pyramid names', *JEA* 55 (1969), 174–6

Deaton, J.C., 'The Old Kingdom Evidence for the Function of the Pyramids', *VA* 4 (1988), 193–200

Dorman, P., 'The inscriptions of the model coffins of Wahnoferhotep and Bener', in *The Pyramid of Senwosret I, The South Cemeteries of Lisht 1* (New York, 1988), 147–9. Compares texts on model cofins to pyramidions

Kuhlmann, K.P., 'Die Pyramide als König? Verkannte elliptische Schreinweisen von Pyramidennames des Alten Reiches', *ASAE* 68 (1982), 223–35

Trench, J.A. and P. Fuscaldo, 'Observations on the pyramidions', *GM* 113 (1989), 81–90

II. EXPLORERS AND SCIENTISTS

Clayton, P., *The Rediscovery of Ancient Egypt* (London and New York, 1982)

David, R., *Discovering Ancient Egypt* (New York, 1993)

Fagan, B.M., *The Rape of the Nile* (New York, 1975)

Greener, L., *The Discovery of Egypt* (New York, 1966)

Goyon, G., *Les inscriptions et graffiti sur le Grande Pyramide* (Cairo, 1944)

Wilson, J., *Signs and Wonders upon Pharaoh* (Chicago, 1964)

Early Legends

Ancient Egyptians:

Leclant, J., Le prince archéologue', *Energies* 16 (1993), 39–41, for Khaemwaset

Lichtheim, M., *Ancient Egyptian Literature*, 3 vols (Berkeley, 1975)

Wildung, D., *Die Rolle ägyptischer Könige im Bewusstein ihrer Nachwelt. Teil I. Posthume Quellen über die Könige der ersten vier Dynastien*, Munchner Ägyptologische Studien 17 (Berlin, 1969)

Zivie, C., *Giza au deuxième millénnaire*, BdÉ LXX (Cairo, 1976)

—*Giza au premier millénnaire* (Boston, 1991)

Classical Authors:

Bissing, F.W. von, *Der Bericht des Diodor über die Pyramiden* (Berlin, 1901)

Herodotus, *The Histories*, trans. A. de Selincourt, revised by A.R. Burn (Harmondsworth, 1972)

Iverson, E., 'The Hieroglyphic Tradition', in J.R. Harris (ed.), *The Legacy of Ancient Egypt* (Oxford, 1991)

Jones, H.L. (trans.), *The Geography of Strabo*, vol. 8 (London, 1967)

Lloyd, A.B., *Herodotus, Book II, Commentary 99–182*, 3 vols (Leiden, 1988)

Waddell, W.G., 'An account of Egypt by Diodorus Siculus', *BFAC* I, parts 1 and 2 (1933)

Whiston, W. (trans.), *Josephus: Complete Works* (Grand Rapids, 1976)

Myths of the Copts and Arabs

Abd al-latif al-Baghdadi, *The Eastern Key: Kitab al-ifadah wal-itabar of Abd al-latif al-Baghdadi*, trans. K. Hafuth, J.A. Videan and I. Videan (London, 1965)

Burton, R.F., *The Book of the Thousand Nights and a Night*, 12 vols, vol. 5 (London, 1894–97)

Carra-de-Vaux, B., *L'Abrégé des Merveilles* (Paris, 1898)

Fodor, A., 'The origins of the Arabic legends of the Pyramids', *Acta Orientalia Academiae Scientiarum Hungaricae* 23, no. 3 (1970), 335–63

Graefe, E., *Das Pyramidenkapitel in al-Makrizi's 'Hitat'*, Semitistische Studien 5 (Leipzig, 1911)

Haarmann, U., 'Die Sphinx, synkretische Volks-religiosität im spätmittelalterlichen islamischen Ägypten', *Saeculum* 29, no. 3 (1970), 367–84

—'In quest of the spectacular: noble and learned visitors to the pyramids around 1200 AD', in W.B. Hallaq and D.P. Little (eds), *Islamic Studies Presented to Charles J. Adams* (Leiden, 1991)

—*Das Pyramidenbuch des Abu Ga 'Fa al-Idrisi (St.649-1251)*, Beiruter Texte und Studien Band 38 (Beirut, 1991)

The First Europeans

Greaves, J., *Pyramidographia, or, a Description of the Pyramids in Ægypt* (London, 1646)

Sievernich, G. and H. Budde, *Europa und der Orient: 800–1900* (Berlin, 1989)

Voyage en Egypte, Collection des Voyageurs Occidentaux en Egypte, vols 1–26 (Cairo, 1970–88)

From Travelogue to Catalogue:

Maillet, B. de, *Description de l'Égypte…* (Paris, 1735)

Norden, F.L., *Travels in Egypt and Nubia*, trans. P. Templeman (London, 1757)

—*The Antiquities, Natural History, Ruins and Other Curiosities of Egypt…* (London, 1780)

Pococke, R., *A Description of the East* (London, 1743)

—*The Travels of Richard Pococke…through Egypt, interspersed with remarks and observations by Captain Norden* (Philadelphia, 1803)

Napoleon's Wise Men

Denon, V., *Travels in Upper and Lower Egypt* (New York, 1803)

Gillispie, C.C. and M. Dewacheter (eds), *Monuments of Egypt: The Napoleonic Expedition* (Princeton, 1987)

Belzoni and Caviglia

Belzoni, G., *Narrative of the Operations and Recent Discoveries within the Pyramids, Temples, Tombs, and Excavations in Egypt and Nubia* (London, 1821)

Mayes, S., *The Great Belzoni* (New York, 1961)

Digging by Dynamite

Vyse, H., *Operations Carried on at the Pyramids of Gizeh…*, 3 vols (London, 1840)

Lepsius and Mariette

Lepsius, C.R., *Denkmäler aus Ägypten und Äthiopien*, 5 vols (Leipzig, 1897–1913)

Mariette, A., *Voyage dans la Haute Égypte* (Paris, 1893)

Petrie at the Pyramids

Drower, M.S., *Flinders Petrie: A Life in Archaeology*, 2nd ed. (London and Madison, 1995)

Petrie, W.M.F., *The Pyramids and Temples of Gizeh* (London, 1883)

—*Ten Years Digging in Egypt* (London, 1891)

—*Seventy Years in Archaeology* (London, 1931)

Smyth, C.P., *Our Inheritance in the Great Pyramid*, 4th ed. (London, 1880)

The Great Expeditions

Dawson, W.R., E. Uphill and M.L. Bierbrier, *Who Was Who in Egyptology*, 3rd ed. (London, 1995)

Dunham, D., *The Egyptian Department and its Excavations* (Boston, 1958)

James, T.G.H. (ed.), *Excavating in Egypt, The Egypt Exploration Society 1882–1982* (Chicago, 1982)

Jéquier, G., *Douze ans de fouilles dans la nécropole Memphite* (Neuchâtel, 1940)

Kaiser, W., *75 Jahre Deutsches Archäologisches Institut Kairo 1907–1982*, Sonderschrift 12 (Mainz, 1982)

Thomas, N., *The American Discovery of Ancient Egypt. Essays* (Los Angeles, 1996)

Recent Discoveries

Brief updates in: Giddy, L., 'Digging diary', *Egyptian Archaeology* and Ikram, S., 'Nile Currents', *KMT*

Professional summaries in: Leclant, J. and G. Clerc, 'Fouilles et travaux en Égypte et au Soudan', *Orientalia*

Recent pyramid exploration using new technologies:

Alvarez, L., 'One researcher's personal account', in *Adventures in Experimental Physics* (Princeton, 1972)

—'Search for hidden chambers in the pyramids', *Science* 167 (1970), 832–9

Berger, C. (ed.), *Saqqara*, Les Dossiers d'Archéologie 146–7 (Dijon, 1990)

Dolphin, L. et al., *Electromagnetic Sounder Experiments at the Pyramids of Giza* (Menlo Park, 1977)

——*Applications of Modern Sensing Techniques to Egyptology* (Menlo Park, 1977)

Dormion, P. and J.P. Goidin, *Khéops: Nouvelle Enquête* (Paris, 1987)

——*Les nouveaux mystères de la Grande Pyramide* (Paris, 1987)

Esmael, F. (ed.), *Proceedings of the First International Symposium on the Application of Modern Technology to Archaeological Explorations at the Giza Necropolis* (Cairo, 1988)

Verner, M., *Unearthing Ancient Egypt* (Prague, 1990)

Yoshimura, S., T. Nakagawa and S. Tnouchi, *Nondestructive Pyramid Investigation, by Electromagnetic Wave Method*, Studies in Egyptian Culture no. 6 (Tokyo, 1987)

———*Nondestructive Pyramid Investigation 2*, Studies in Egyptian Culture no. 8 (Tokyo, 1988)

III. THE WHOLE PYRAMID CATALOGUE
*Primary references are marked with asterisk

Surveys and Catalogues:

Borchardt, L., *Die Pyramiden, ihre Entstehung und Entwicklung* (Berlin, 1911)

Brinks, J., *Die Entwicklung der königlichen Grabanlagen des Alten Reiches*, HÄB 10 (Hildesheim, 1979)

Edwards, I.E.S., *The Pyramids of Egypt* (London, 1985)

Fakhry, A., *The Pyramids* (Chicago, 1969)

Firchow, O., *Studien zu den Pyramidenlagen der 12. Dynastie* (1942)

Grinsell, L., *Egyptian Pyramids* (Gloucester, 1947)

Hawass, Z., *The Pyramids of Ancient Egypt* (Pittsburg, 1990)

Jánosi, P., *Die Pyramidenanlagen der Königinnen…* (Vienna, 1996)

Kerisel, J., *La Pyramide à Travers les Ages* (Paris, 1991)

Labrousse, A., *L'Architecture des Pyramides à Textes. I. Saqqara Nord.*, L'Institut Française d'Archéologie Orientale. Mission Archéologique de Saqqara III (Cairo, 1996)

Lauer, J.-P., *Histoire Monumentale des Pyramides d'Egypte. I. Les Pyramides à Degrés (IIIe Dynastie)*, BdÉ XXXIX (1962)

—*Le Mystère des Pyramides* (Luçon, France, 1988)

Lepre, J.P., *The Egyptian Pyramids: A Comprehensive Illustrated Reference* (Jefferson, N.C., 1990)

Maragioglio, V. and C.A. Rinaldi, *L'Architettura delle Piramidi Menfite*, 8 vols (Turin and Rapallo, 1963–77)

Perring, J.S., *The Pyramids and Temples of Gizeh*, 3 vols (London, 1839–42)

Porter, B. and R.L.B. Moss, *Topographical Bibliography of Ancient Egyptian Hieroglyphic Texts, Reliefs, and Paintings*. 7 vols (Oxford, 1927–51). 2nd ed., J. Málek.

Stadelmann, R., 'Pyramiden', *LÄ* IV (1982), 1205–63

—*Die Ägyptischen Pyramiden: von Ziegelbau zum Weltwunder* (Mainz, 1985)

Swelim, N., 'Pyramid research from the Archaic to the Second Intermediate Period: lists, catalogues and objectives', *Hommages à Jean Leclant*, BdÉ 106/1 (1994), 337–49

Tadema-Sporry, B. and A.A.Tadema, *Piramide en Farae* (Haarlem, 1982)

Origins of the Pyramid: Hierakonpolis

Adams, B., *Ancient Nekhen*, Egyptian Studies Association Publication No. 3 (Whitstable, 1995)

Kemp, B.J., *Ancient Egypt, Anatomy of a Civilization* (London and New York, 1989), 74–7

O'Connor, D., 'The status of early Egyptian temples: an alternative theory', in R. Friedman and B. Adams (eds), *The Followers of Horus: Studies Dedicated to Michael Allen Hoffman 1944–1990*, ESA Pub. No. 2, Oxbow Monograph 20 (1992), 83–98

*Parker, R.A., J. Leclant, and J.-C. Goyon, *The Edifice of Taharqa by the Sacred Lake of Karnak* (Providence, 1979)

*Quibell, J.E., *Hierakonpolis Part I* (London, 1900)

*—and F.W. Green, *Hierakonpolis Part II* (London, 1902)

Williams, B., 'Narmer and the Coptos Colossi', *JARCE* 25 (1988), 35–59

Royal Tombs at Abydos

*The German Archaeological Institute has been reclearing the royal tombs at Umm el-Qaab; Werner Kaiser and Gunter Dreyer publish reports in *MDAIK*

Umm el-Qa'ab Cemetery:

*Amélineau, E., *Les nouvelles fouilles d'Abydos (1895–98)*, 3 vols (Paris, 1899–1905)

*Dreyer, G., 'Zur Rekonstruktion der Oberbauten der Königsgraber der I. Dynastie in Abydos', *MDAIK* 47 (1991), 93–104

*—'The royal tombs of Abydos', in *The Near East in Antiquity: German Contributions to the Archaeology of Jordan, Syria, Lebanon and Egypt, Vol. III* (Amman, 1992), 55–67

*—'Recent discoveries at Abydos Cemetery U', in E.C.M. van den Brink (ed.), *The Nile Delta in Transition, 4th–3rd Millennium BC* (Tel Aviv, 1992), 293–9

Kemp, B.J., 'Abydos and the royal tombs of the First Dynasty', *JEA* 52 (1966), 13–22

—'The Egyptian First Dynasty royal cemetery', *Antiquity* 41 (1967), 22–32

*Petrie, W.M.F., *The Royal Tombs of the First Dynasty, Part 1* (London, 1900)

*—*The Royal Tombs of the Earliest Dynasties, Part II* (London, 1901)

Valley Enclosures:

Helck, W., 'Die Herkunft des abydenischen Osirisrituals', *Archic Orientalni* 20, no. 72–85 (1952)

—'Zu den 'Talbezirken' in Abydos', *MDAIK* 28, no. 95–99 (1972)

Kaiser, W. and G. Dreyer, 'Umm el-Qaab, zweiter Vorbericht', *MDAIK* 38 (1982), 242–60

*O'Connor, D., 'New funerary enclosures (Talbezirke) of the Early Dynastic Period at Abydos', *JARCE* 26 (1989), 51–86

*—'Boat graves and pyramid origins', *Expedition* 33 (1991), 5–17

*—'The earliest royal boat graves', *EA* 6 (1995), 3–7

Archaic Mastabas at Saqqara

North Saqqara:

*Emery, W. B., *The Tomb of Hemaka* (Cairo, 1938)

*—*The Tomb of Hor-Aha* (Cairo, 1939)

*—*Great Tombs of the First Dynasty, 3 vols* (Cairo and London, 1949–58)

—*Archaic Egypt* (Harmondsworth, 1962)

Funerary Enclosures and 2nd-Dynasty Tombs, Saqqara:

Kaiser, W., 'Ein Kultbezirke des Königs Den in Sakkara', *MDAIK* 41 (1985), 47–60

*Makramallah, R., *Un cimetière archaïque de la classe moyenne du peuple à Saqqarah* (Cairo, 1940)

*Mathieson, I.J. and A. Tavares, 'Preliminary report of the National Museums of Scotland Saqqara Survey Project 1990–1', *JEA* 79 (1993), 28–31

——'Sensing the Past', *EG* 6 (1995), 26–7

Stadelmann, R., 'Die oberbauten der Königsgraber der 2. Dynastie in Sakkara', in *MelangesGamal Eddin Mokhtar II,* BdE 97/2 (Cairo, 1985), 295ff.

Swelim, N., 'Some remarks on the great rectangular monuments of middle Saqqara', *MDAIK* 47 (1991), 389–402

Transition to Pyramids:

Kaiser, W., 'Zu den königlichen Talbezirken in Abydos und zur Baugeschichte des Djoser-Grabmals', *MDAIK* 25 (1969), 1–22

Lauer, J.-P., 'Évolution de la tombe royale égyptienne jusq'à la pyramide à degrés', *MDAIK* 15 (1957), 148–65

Müller, H.W., 'Gedanken zur Enstehung, Interpretation und Rekonstruktion ältester ägyptische Monumentalarchitektur', in *Agypten Dauer und Wandel* (Mainz, 1985), 7–33

Stadelmann, R., 'Das Dreikammersystem der Königsgräber der Frühzeit und des Alten Reiches', *MDAIK* 47 (1991), 373–87

—'Origins and development of the funerary complex of Djoser', in P. der Manuelian (ed.), *Studies in Honor of William Kelly Simpson* (Boston, 1996), 787–800

Saqqara and Memphis:

Berger, C. (ed.), *Saqqara,* Les Dossiers d'Archéologie (Dijon, 1990)

Giddy, L., 'Memphis and Saqqara during the late Old Kingdom: some topographical considerations', in C. Berger, G. Clerc and N. Grimal (eds), *Hommages à Jean Leclant,* BdE 106/1 (Cairo, 1994), 189–200

*Jeffreys, D. and L. Giddy, 'Towards archaic Memphis', *EG* 2 (1992), 6–7

— and A. Tavares, 'The historic landscape of early dynastic Memphis', *MDAIK* 50 (1994), 143–73

Lauer, J.-P., *Les Pyramides de Sakkarah* (Cairo, 1972)

—*Saqqara, The Royal Cemetery of Memphis* (London and New York, 1976)

Djoser's Step Pyramid Complex

Altenmüller, H., 'Bemerkungen zur frühen und späten Bauphase des Djoserbezeirkes in Saqqara', *MDAIK* 28 (1972), 1–12

*Derry, D.E., 'Report on human remains from the great granite sarcophagus chamber in the pyramid of Zoser', *ASAE* 35 (1935), 28–30

*Firth, C.M., J.E. Quibell and J.-P. Lauer, *The Step Pyramid,* 2 vols (Cairo, 1935–6)

Friedman, F.D., 'The underground relief panels of King Djoser at the Step Pyramid complex', *JARCE* 32 (1995), 1–42

—'Notions of cosmos in the Step Pyramid complex', in P. der Manuelian (ed.), *Studies in Honor of William Kelly Simpson* (Boston, 1996), 337–51

*Hawass, Z., 'A fragmentary monument of Djoser from Saqqara', *JEA* 80 (1994), 45–56

Kaiser, W., 'Zur unterirdischen Anlage der Djoserpyramide', in I. Gamer-Wallert and W. Helck (eds), *Gegengabe. Festschrift für Emma Brunner-Traut* (Tübingen, 1992), 167–90

*Lauer, J.-P., *La Pyramide à Degrés, 3 vols* (Cairo, 1936–9)

*—*Études complémentaires sur les monuments du roi Zoser à Saqqarah* (Cairo, 1948)

*—'Sur certain modifications et extensions apportée au complexe funéraire de Djoser au cours de son règne', in John Baines, et al. (eds), *Pyramid Studies and Other Essays presented to I.E.S. Edwards* (London, 1988), 5–11

*Strouhal, E. et al., 'Re-investigation of the remains thought to be of King Djoser and those of an unidentified female from the Step Pyramid at Saqqara', *Anthropologie* 32, no. 3 (1994), 225–42

Swelim, N., 'The dry moat of the Netjerykhet Complex', in J. Baines, et al. (eds), *Pyramid Studies and Other Essays presented to I.E.S. Edwards* (London, 1988), 12–24

The Short Life of Step Pyramids

*Barsanti, A., 'Ouverture de la pyramide de Zaouiet el-Aryan', *ASAE* 2 (1901), 92–4

*Dreyer, G. and W. Kaiser, 'Zu den kleinen Stufenpyramiden Ober- und Mittleägyptens', *MDAIK* 36 (1980), 43–59

*Dreyer, G. and N. Swelim, 'Die kleine Stufenpyramide von Abydos-Sud (Sinki) · Grabungsbericht', *MDAIK* 38 (1982), 83–91

*Dunham, D., *Zawiyet el-Aryan: The Cemeteries Adjacent to the Layer Pyramid* (Boston, 1978)

*Goneim, M.Z., *The Buried Pyramid* (London, 1956)

*—*Horus Sekhem-khet, The Unfinished Step Pyramid at Saqqara* (Cairo, 1957)

*Kaiser, W., G. Dreyer, P. Grossman, W. Mayer and S. Seidelmayer, *Stadt und Tempel von Elephantine, Achter Grabungsberichte,* MDAIK 36 (1980), 276–80

Lauer, J.-P., 'À propos de la nouvelle pyramide à degrés de Saqqarah', *BIE* 36 (1955), 357–64

—'Les petites pyramides à degrés de la IIIᵉ dynastie', *Revue archéologique* (1962), 5–15

—'Nouvelles remarques sur les pyramides à degrés de la IIIᵉ dynastie', *Orientalia* (1966), 440–48

*—'Au complex funéraire de l'Horus Sekhem-khet. Recherches et travaux menés dans la nécropole de Saqqara au cours de al campagne 1966–1967', *CRAIBL* (1967), 496–508

*—'Recherche et découverte du tombeau sud de l'Horus Sekhem-khet dans son complexe funéraire à Saqqarah', *BIE* 48 & 49 (1969), 121–31

Lehner, M., 'Z500 and the Layer Pyramid of Zawiyet el-Aryan', in P. der Manuelian (ed.), *Studies in Honor of William Kelly Simpson* (Boston, 1996), 507–22

Lesko, L.H., 'Seila 1981', *JARCE* 25 (1988), 215–35

Maragioglio, V. and C.A. Rinaldi, *La Piramidi di Sekhemkeht, La Layer Pyramid di Zauiet el-Aryan e le minori piramidi attribute alla III dinastia,* L'Architecture delle Piramidi Menfite Parte II (Rapallo)

*Reisner, G.A. and C.S. Fisher, 'The work of the Harvard University-Museum of Fine Arts Egyptian Expedition', *BMFA* 9 (1911), 54–9

*Stiénon, J., 'El-Kolah. Mission de la Fondation Égyptologique Raine Élisabeth, 1949', *Chronique d'Égypte* 59 (1950), 43–5

Swelim, N., *The Brick Pyramid at Abu Roash, Numbered 1 by Lepsius* (Alexandria, 1987)

—*Some Problems on the History of the Third Dynasty,* Archaeological & Historical Studies (Alexandria, 1983)

*—*The Pyramid of Seila Locally Called "el-Qalah", season 1987* (March 1987), unpublished.

Meidum and Dahshur

Borchardt, L., *Die Entstehung der Pyramide an der Bau-geschichte der bei Meidum nachgewiesen* (Berlin, 1928)

Edwards, I.E.S., 'The collapse of the Meidum Pyramid', *JEA* 60 (1974), 251–2

*el-Khouli, A., *Meidum,* ed. G.T. Martin, Australian Centre for Egyptology: Reports 3 (Sydney, 1991)

Johnson, G.B., 'The Pyramid of Meidum', *KMT* 4, no. 2 (1993), 64–71, 81; *KMT* 5, no. 1 (1994), 72–82

Lauer, J.-P., 'Sur la pyramid de Meidoum et les deux pyramides du roi Snefrou à Dahshour', *Orientalia* 36 (1967), 239–54

—'À propos du prétendue désastre de la pyramide de Meidum', *CdE* 36 (1976), 239–54

Mendelssohn, K. *The Riddle of the Pyramids* (London and New York, 1974)

*Petrie, W. M. F., *Medum* (London, 1892)

*—, E. Mackay and G.A. Wainwright, *Meydum and Memphis,* vol. III (London, 1910)

*Robert, M.A., 'Sur quelque graffites grecs découverts au sommet de la pyramide de Meidoum', *ASAE* 3 (1902), 77–9

*—*Études complémentaires sur les monuments du roi Zoser à Saqqarah* (Cairo, 1948)

*Rowe, A., 'Excavations of the Eckley B. Cox, Jr. Expedition at Meydum, Egypt, 1929–30', *Museum Journal, Pennsylvania* (1931)

Wildung, D., 'Zur Deutung der Pyramide von Medum', *RdE* 21 (1969), 135–45

Dahshur General:

*Barsanti, M.A., 'Rapport sur la fouille de Dahchour', *ASAE* 3 (1902), 198–205

*Borchardt, L., 'Ein Königserlass aus Dahshur', *ZÄS* 42 (1905), 1–11

*Morgan, J. de, *Fouilles à Dahchour en 1894–95* (Vienna, 1903)

Varille, A., *À propos des pyramides de Snefru* (Cairo, 1947)

Bent Pyramid:

*Batrawi, A., 'A small mummy from the pyramid at Dahshur', *ASAE* 48 (1948), 585–90

*Dorner, J., 'Form und Ausmasse der Knickpyramide. Neue Beobachtungen und Messungen', *MDAIK* 42 (1986), 43–58

*Fakhry, A., *The Monuments of Snefru at Dahshur, Vol 1, The Bent Pyramid, Vol. II, The Valley Temple* (Cairo, 1959–61)

*Mustafa, H., 'The surveying of the Bent Pyramid at Dahshur', *ASAE* 52 (1954), 595–601

*Ricke, H., 'Baugeschichte Vorbericht über die Kultanlagen der südlichen Pyramide des Snofru in Dahschur', *ASAE* 52 (1954), 603–23

North Pyramid:

*Stadelmann, R., 'Snofru und die Pyramiden von Meidum und Dahshur', *MDAIK* 36 (1980), 437–49

*—'Die Pyramiden des Snofru in Dahschur. Zweiter Bericht über die Ausgrabungen an der nördlichen Stein pyramide', *MDAIK* 39 (1983), 228–9

*— and H. Sourouzian, 'Die Pyramiden des Snofru in Dahshur', *MDAIK* 38 (1982), 379–93; *MDAIK* 39 (1983), 228–9

*— et al., 'Pyramiden und nekropole des Snofru in Dahschur.', *MDAIK* 49 (1993), 259–94

Giza

The publications on Giza, the Sphinx and especially Khufu's pyramid are numerous, there is space here only for a selection. The major excavations of the mastaba cemeteries are those of Reisner, Junker and Hassan. The Museum of Fine Arts Boston continues to publish mastabas excavated by Reisner. Volumes by W.K. Simpson, K. Weeks, E. Brovarski, A. Roth and P. der Manuelian have appeared.

Bauval, R.G., 'A master-plan for the three pyramids of Giza based on the configuration of the three stars of the belt of Orion', *DE* 13 (1989), 7–18

Hamblin, D., 'Unlocking the secrets of the Giza Plateau', *Smithsonian Magazine* (April 1986), 78–93

*Hassan, S., *Excavations at Giza,* 10 vols (Oxford and Cairo, 1932–53)

Hawass, Z., 'The Funerary Establishments of Khufu, Khafra, and Menkaura During the Old Kingdom' (University of Pennsylvania, 1987)

Helck, W., 'Zur Entstehung des Westfriedhofs an der Cheops-Pyramide', *ZÄS* 81 (1956), 62–5

*Junker, H., *Giza: Grabungen auf dem Friedhof des Alten Reiches,* 12 vols (Vienna, 1929–55)

Lehner, M., 'A contextual approach to the Giza Pyramids', *Archiv für Orientforschung* 31 (1985), 136–58

—*The Pyramid Tomb of Queen Hetep-heres and the Satellite Pyramid of Khufu* (Mainz, 1985)

O'Connor, D., 'Political systems and archaeological data in Egypt', *World Archaeology* 6, no. 1 (1974), 15–37

*Petrie, W.M.F., *The Pyramids and Temples of Gizeh* (London, 1883)

—*Gizeh and Rifeh* (London, 1907)

*Reisner, G., *A History of the Giza Necropolis, Vol. 1* (Cambridge, MA, 1942)

*Reisner, G. and W. S. Smith, *A History of the Giza Necropolis, Vol. 2, The Tomb of Hetep-heres, the Mother of Cheops* (Cambridge, MA, 1955)

Stadelmann, R., *Die grossen Pyramiden von Giza* (Graz, 1990)

Khufu's Pyramid

Badawi, A., 'The stellar destiny of Pharaoh and the so-called air-shafts of Cheops' pyramid', *Mitteilungen des Instituts für Orient-forschung des deutschen Akademie der Wissenschaften zu Berlin* 10, no. 2/3 (1964), 189–206

Borchardt, L., *Gegen die Zahlenmystik an der grossen Pyramide bie Gise* (Berlin, 1922)

—*Einiges zur dritten Bauperiode der Grossen Pyramide* (Berlin, 1932)

Edwards, I.E.S., 'Do the Pyramid Texts suggest an explanation for the abandonment of the subterranean chamber of the Great Pyramid?', *Hommages à Jean Leclant*, BdÉ 106/1 (1994), 161–7

*Emery, K.O., 'Weathering of the Great Pyramid', *Journal of Sedimentary Petrology* 30 (1960), 140–3

Goyon, G., 'Le méchanisme de fermeture de la pyramide de Khéops', *Revue d'Archéologique* 2 (1936), 1–24

—'La chaussée monumentale et le temple de la valléede la pyramide de Khéops', *BIFAO* 67 (1969), 49–69

—'Les rangs d'asises de la Grande Pyramide', *BIFAO* 78 (1978), 405–13

*Hawass, Z., 'The discovery of the satellite pyramid of Khufu', in P. der Manuelian (ed.), *Studies in Honor of William Kelly Simpson* (Boston, 1996), 379–98

*Lauer, J-P., 'Le temple funéraire de Khéops à la grande pyramide de Guizeh', *ASAE* 46 (1947), 245–59

*—'Note complémentaire sur le temple funéraire de Khéops', *ASAE* 49 (1949), 111–23

—'Raison première et utilisation practique de la "Grande Galerie" dans la pyramide de Khéops', *BÁBA* 12 (1971), 133–41

*Messiha, H., 'The Valley Temple of Khufu', *ASAE* 65, no. 9–14 (1983)

Petrie, W.M.F. and J. Tarrell, 'The Great Pyramid Courses', *Ancient Egypt*, June, Part II (1925), 36–9

Thomas, E., 'Air channels in the Great Pyramid', *JEA* 39 (1953), 113ff.

Trimble, V., 'Astronomical investigation concerning the so-called air shafts of Cheops' pyramid', *Mitteilungen des deutschen Akademie Berlin* 10 (1964), 183–7

Khufu's Boats:

*Abubakr, A.M. and A.Y. Mustafa, 'The funerary boat of Khufu', in *Festschrift Ricke* (Wiesbaden, 1971), 1–16

Cerny, J.A., 'A note on a recently discovered boat of Cheops', *JEA* 41 (1955), 75–9

*El-Baz, F., 'Finding a pharaoh's bark', *National Geographic* 173, no. 4 (1988), 512–33

*Esmael, F. (ed.), *Proceedings of the First International Symposium On the Application of Modern Technology to Archaeological Explorations at the Giza Necropolis, Cairo, Dec. 14–17, 1987* (Cairo, 1988), 7–65

Firchow, O., 'Königsschiff und Sonnenbarke', *Wiener Zeitschrift fuur die kunde des Morgenlandes* 54 (1957), 34–42

Jenkins, N., *The Boat Beneath the Pyramid* (London and New York, 1980)

Lipke, P., *The Royal Ship of Cheops*, BAR International 225 (Oxford, 1984)

Nour, M. Z. et al., *The Cheops Boats, Part I* (Cairo, 1960)

Thomas, E., 'Solar Barks Prow to Prow', *JEA* 42 (1956), 65–79

Djedefre at Abu Roash

*Chassinat, E., *CRAIBL* (1901), 617–19

*Grimal, N., 'Travaux de l'Institut français d'archéologie orientale en 1994–1995 §2, Abou Rawash', *BIFAO* 95 (1995), 545–51; *BIFAO* 96 (1996)

*Marchand, S. and M. Baud, 'La ceramique miniature d'Abou Rawash', *BIFAO* 96 (1996), 255–88

Valloggia, M., 'Le complexe funéraire de Radjedef à Abou-Roasch: état de la question et perspectives de recherches', *BSFE* 130 (June) (1994), 12–13

Khafre's Pyramid

Edwards, I.E.S., 'The air-channels of Chephren's pyramid', in W.K. Simpson and W. Davis (eds), *Studies in Ancient Egypt, the Aegean, and the Sudan, Essays in Honor of Dows Dunham* (Boston, 1981), 55–7

*Hölscher, U., *Das Grabdenkmal des Königs Chephren* (Leipzig, 1912)

Lacovara, P. and M. Lehner, 'An enigmatic object explained', *JEA* 71 (1985), 169–74

The Great Sphinx

Anthes, R., 'Was veranlasste Chefren zum bau des Tempels vor der Sphinx?', *BÁBA* 12 (*Festschrift Ricke*, 1971)

*Birch, S., 'On excavations by Capt. Caviglia, in 1816, behind, and in the neighborhood of the Great Sphinx', *The Museum of Classical Antiquities* 2 (1852), 26–34

Borchardt, L., 'Uber das Alter des Sphinx bei Giseh', *Sitzungsberichte der Preussischen Akademie der Wissenschaften, Berlin* 35 (1897), 752–60

Esmael, F. A. (ed.), *Book of Proceedings: The First International Symposium on the Great Sphinx* (Cairo, 1992)

*Gauri, K. L., 'Deterioration of stone on the Great Sphinx', *NARCE* 114 (Spring) (1981), 35–47

*—'Geologic Study of the Sphinx', *NARCE* 127 (1984), 24–43

Hassan, S., *The Sphinx: Its History in the Light of Recent Excavations* (Cairo, 1949)

*Hawass, Z. and M. Lehner, 'The Passage Under the Sphinx', *Hommages à Jean Leclant*, BdÉ 106/1 (1994), 201–16

*—'The Sphinx: Who built it, and why?', *Archaeology* 47, no. 5 (Sept./Oct.) (1994), 30–47

*Lehner, M., *Archaeology of an Image: The Great Sphinx of Giza* (Ph.D., Yale University, 1991)

— 'Computer rebuilds the ancient sphinx', *National Geographic* 179, no. 4 (April) (1991), 32–9

—'Reconstructing the Sphinx', *CAJ* 2, no. 1 (1992), 3–26

*—, J.P. Allen, K.L. Gauri, 'The ARCE Sphinx Project: A Preliminary Report', *NARCE* 112 (1980), 3–33

*Mariette, A. and M. d. Rougé, 'Note sur le fouille executées par Mariette autour du grand Sphinx de Gizeh. Lettre de Mariette citées par M. de Rouge', *l'Athenaeum française* 3ᵉ anée, no. 28 (1854)

*Ricke, H., 'Der Harmachistempel des Chefren in Giseh', *BÁBA* 10 (1970), 1–43

Schott, S., 'Ägyptische quellen zum plan des Sphinxtempels', *BÁBA* 10 (1970), 49–79

Menkaure's Pyramid

*Hawass, Z. 'The discovery of a pair-statue near the pyramid of Menkaure at Giza', MDAIK 53 (1996), 1–4

Lacovara, P. and N. Reeves, 'The colossal statue of Mycerinus reconsidered', *RdE* 38 (1987), 111–15

*Reisner, G., *Mycerinus, The Temples of the Third Pyramid at Giza* (Cambridge, MA, 1931)

Wood, W., 'A reconstruction of the triads of King Mycerinus', *JEA* 60 (1974), 82–93

The Passing of a Dynasty

*Smith, W.S., 'Inscriptional evidence for the history of the Fourth Dynasty', *JNES* 11 (1952), 113–28

Zawiyet el-Aryan, Unfinished Pyramid:

*Barsanti, A., 'Fouilles de Zaouiet el-Aryan', *ASAE* 7 (1906), 257–86; *ASAE* 8 (1907), 201–10; *ASAE* 12 (1912), 57–63

Cerny, J., 'Name of the king of the Unfinished Pyramid at Zawiyet el-Aryan', *MDAIK* 16 (1958), 25–9

Dodson, A.M., 'On the date of the Unfinished Pyramid of Zawiyet el-Aryan', *DE* 3 (1985), 21–3

Lauer, J.-P., 'Sur l'age et l'attribution possible de l'excavation monumentale de Zaouiet el-Aryan', *RdE* 14 (1962), 21–36

Khentkawes at Giza:

*Hassan, S., 'Excavations at Giza IV (1932–33)' (Cairo, 1943), 1–62

Shepseskaf's Mastaba:

*Jéquier, G., *Le Mastaba Faraoun* (Cairo, 1928)

Userkaf's Pyramid

*El-Khouly, A., 'Excavations at the pyramid of Userkaf', *JSSEA* 15, no. 3 (1985), 86–93

*Lauer, J.-P., 'Le temple haut de la pyramide du roi Ouserkaf à Saqqarah', *ASAE* 53 (1955), 119–33

The Pyramids of Abusir

*Verner, M., 'Archaeological survey of Abusir', *ZÄS* 119 (1992), 116–24

*—*Forgotten Pharaohs, Lost Pyramids: Abusir* (Prague, 1994)

*—'Abusir Pyramids, "Lepsius no. XXIV and no. XXV"', in C. Berger, G. Clerc and N. Grimal (eds), *Hommages à Jean Leclant*, BdÉ 106/1 (Cairo, 1994), 371–8

Yoyotte, J., 'Les Bousiris les Abousir d'Egypt', *GLECS* 8 (1961), 57–60

Sahure's Pyramid:

*Borchardt, L., *Das Grabdenkmal des Königs Sahu-Re, I. Der Bau* (Leipzig 1910). II. Die Wandbilder (Leipzig 1913)

Neferirkare's Pyramid:

*Borchardt, L., *Das Grabdenkmal des Königs Nefer-ir-ke-Re* (Leipzig, 1909)

Queen Khentkawes's Pyramid:

*Verner, M., *The Pyramid Complex of the Royal Mother Khentkaus* (Prague, 1994)

Niuserre's Pyramid:

*Borchardt, L., *Das Grabdenkmal des König Ne-user-Re* (Leipzig, 1907)

Raneferef's Pyramid:

*Verner, M., 'Excavations at Abusir season 1982 – preliminary report – The pyramid temple of Raneferef ("1")', *ZÄS* 111 (1984), 70–8

*Verner, M., 'A slaughterhouse from the Old Kingdom', *MDAIK* 42 (1986), 181–89

Sun Temples:

*Bissing, F. W. v., *Das Re-Heiligtum des Königs Ne-user-Re. I. Der Bau* (Berlin 1905). II *Die kleine Festdarstellung* (Leipzig 1923). III. *Die grosse Festdarstellung* (Leipzig 1928), vol. 3

Edel, E. and S. Wenig, *Die Jahreszeitenreliefs aus dem Sonnenheiligtum dess Königs Ne-user-re* (Berlin, 1974)

Kaiser, W., 'Zu den Sonnenheiligtümern der 5. Dynastie', *MDAIK* 14 (1956), 69–81

*Ricke, H., *Das Sonnenheiligtum des Königs Userkaf, I. Der Bau* (Cairo 1965), BÁBA 8. II. *Die Funde*, BÁBA 11 (1969)

The End of the 5th Dynasty

Djedkare-Isesi's Pyramid:

Strouhal, E. and M.F. Gaballah, 'King Djedkare Isesi and his daughters', in W.V. Davies and R. Walker (eds), *Biological Anthropology and the Study of Ancient Egypt* (London, 1993), 104–18

Unas's Pyramid:

*Hassan, S., 'Excavations at Sakkara (1937–8)', *ASAE* 38 (1938), 519–20

*—'The causeway of Wnis at Sakkara', *ZÄS* 80 (1955), 136–44

*Labrousse, A., J.-P. Lauer and J. Leclant, *Le Temple haut du complexe funéraire du Roi Ounas* (Cairo, 1977)

*— and A.M. Moussa, *Le temple d'accueil du complexe funéraire du Roi Ounas*, BdÉ 111 (Cairo, 1996)

*Maspero, G., 'La pyramide du rois Ounas', *RecTrav* III (1882), 117–224; *RecTrav* IV (1883), 41–78

*Raslan, M.A.M., 'The causeway of Ounas Pyramid', *ASAE* 61 (1973), 151–69

6th-Dynasty Pyramids

Teti's Pyramid:

*Firth, C.M. and B. Gunn, *The Teti Pyramid Cemeteries*, 2 vols (Cairo, 1926)

*Firth, C.M., 'Excavations of the Department of Antiquities at Sakkara', *ASAE* 29 (1929), 64–70

*Labrousse, A., 'Les reines de Téti, Khouit et Ipout I, recherches architecturales', in C. Berger, G. Clerc and N. Grimal (eds), *Hommages a Jean Leclant*, BdÉ 106/1 (Cairo, 1994), 231–44

*Lauer, J.-P. and J. Leclant, *Le temple haut du complexe funéraire du roi Téti* (Cairo, 1972)

Málek, J., 'The "altar" in the pillared court of Teti's pyramid-temple at Saqqara', in *Pyramid Studies and Other Essays Presented to I.E.S. Edwards* (London, 1988), 23–34

*Maspero, G., 'La pyramide du roi Teti', *RecTrav* V (1884), 1–59

Stadelmann, R., 'König Teti und der Beginn der 6. Dynastie', in C. Berger, G. Clerc, and N. Grimal (eds), *Hommages a Jean Leclant*, BdÉ (Cairo, 1994), 327–36

Pepi I's Pyramid:

This is a selection from many articles. For full listing see J. Leclant's and G. Clerc's reports in *Orientalia* .

Labrousse, A. *Regards sur une Pyramide* (Paris, 1991)

*Lauer, J.-P., 'Les statues des prisonniers de complexe funéraire de Pepi Iᵉʳ', *BIE* 51 (1971), 37–45

*Leclant, J., 'Recherches à la pyramide de Pepi Iᵉʳ sur le site de Saqqarah', *Mémoires de l'Academie de Lyon, 3e série* 44 (1990), 145–6

*—'Noubounet – une nouvelle reine d'Égypte', in I. Gamer-Wallert and W. Helck (eds), *Festschrift für Emma Brunner-Traut* (1991), 211–19

*—Recherches aux pyramides des reines de Pepi Iᵉʳ à Saqqarah en Egypte', *Academie Royale de Belgique, Bulletin de la Classe des Lettres et des Sciences Morales et Politiques* 4 (1993), 69–84

*Maspero, G., 'La pyramide du roi Pepi Iᵉʳ', *RecTrav* VII (1885), 145–76; *RecTrav* VIII (1886), 87–120

Merenre's Pyramid:

*Maspero, G., 'La pyramide du roi Mirinri', *RecTrav* IX (1887), 177–91; *RecTrav* X (1888), 1–29; *RecTrav* XI (1889), 1–31

Wissa, M., 'Le sarcophage de Merenre et l'expedition a Ibhat (I)', in C. Berger, G. Clerc, and N. Grimal (eds), *Hommages à Jean Leclant*, BdÉ 106/1 (Cairo, 1994), 379–87

Pepi II's Pyramid:

*Jéquier, G., *La pyramide d'Oudjebten* (Cairo, 1928)

*—*Les pyramides des reines Neit et Apouit* (Cairo, 1933)

*—*Le monument funéraire de Pepi II* (Cairo, 1936–41)

*Maspero, G., 'La pyramide du roi Pepi II', *RecTrav* XII (1892), 53–93, 136–95; *RecTrav* XIV (1893), 125–52

First Intermediate Period Pyramids

Ibi's Pyramid, South Saqqara:
*Jéquier, G., *La Pyramide d'Aba* (Cairo, 1935)
Headless Pyramid, Saqqara:
Berlandini, J., 'La pyramide "ruinée" de Sakkara-nord et le roi Ikaouhor-Menkaouhor', *RÉ* 31 (1979), 3–28
Mâlek, J., 'King Merykare and his pyramid', in C. Berger, G. Clerc and N. Grimal (eds), *Hommages a Jean Leclant*, BdÉ (Cairo, 1994), 203–14
Dara Pyramid, Middle Egypt:
*Kamal, A., *ASAÉ* 12 (1912), 128ff
*Vercoutter, J., 'Dara: Mission française 1950–1951', *CdÉ* 27 (1952), 98–111
*Weill, R., *Dara: Campagnes de 1946–48* (Cairo, 1958)
Tombs of the Intefs, Thebes:
*Arnold, D., 'Bemerkungen zu den Königsgräbern der frühen 11. Dynastie von El-Tarif', *MDAIK* 23 (1968), 26–37
*—*Das Gran des Jni-iti.f Vol. I Die Architektur*, MDAIK (Mainz, 1971)
*—*Gräber des alten und mittleren Reiches in El-Tarif*, MDAIK (Mainz, 1976)

Mentuhotep at Deir el-Bahri

*Arnold, D., *Der Tempel des Königs Mentuhotep von Deir el-Bahari, Vol. I: Architektur und Deutung; Vol. II: Die Wandreleifs des Sanktuares*, MDAIK (Mainz, 1974–81)
*Arnold, D. from. Notes of H. Winlock, *The Temple of Mentuhotep at Deir el-Bahari*, Publications of the MMA 21 (New York, 1979)
*Carter, H., 'Report on the tomb of Menthuhotep I', *ASAÉ* 2 (1901), 201–5
*Naville, E., *The Eleventh Dynasty Temple at Deir el-Bahari, vols I–III* (London, 1906–1913)
*Winlock, H.E., *Excavations at Deir el-Bahari* (New York, 1942)
Unfinished Theban Tomb (south of Sheikh Abd al-Qurna):
*Mond, R., 'Report of work in the necropolis of Thebes during the Winter of 1903-1904', *ASAÉ* 6 (1905), 78–80
*Winlock, H. E., 'Excavations at Thebes', *BMMA* 16 (1921), 29–34

Pyramids at Lisht

Work at Lisht from 1906 until 1934 was published in a series of preliminary reports in the Bulletin of the Metropolitan Museum: vol. 2 (Apr. 1907) 61–3, (July 1907) 113–17, (Oct. 1907) 163–9; vol. 3 (May 1908), 83–4, (Sept. 1908) 170–3, (Oct. 1908) 184–8; vol. 4 (July 1909), 119–21; vol. 9 (Oct. 1914), 207–22; vol. 10 (Feb. 1915), 5–22; vol. 15 (July 1920), 3–10; vol. 16 (Nov. 1921), 5–19; vol. 17 (Dec. 1922), 4–18; vol 19 (Dec. 1924), 33–43; vol. 21 (Mar. 1926), 33–40; vol. 28 (Apr. 1933), (Nov. 1933) 3–22; and vol. 29 (Nov. 1934), 3–40
Amenemhet I's Pyramid:
Arnold, Dorothea, 'Amenemhat I and the early Twelfth Dynasty at Thebes', *Metropolitan Museum Journal* 26 (1991), 5–48
Senwosret I Pyramid:
*Arnold, D., *The Pyramid of Senwosret I*, The South Cemeteries at Lisht, Vol. I (New York, 1988)
*—*The Pyramid Complex of Senwosret I*, The South Cemeteries at Lisht, Vol. III (New York, 1992)
*Gautier, J.E. and G. Jéquier, *Memoire sur les Fouilles de Licht*, MIFAO 6 (Cairo, 1902)
*Goedicke, H., *Re-used Blocks from the Pyramid of Amenemhet I at Lisht* (New York, 1971)
*Hayes, W.C., 'The entrance chapel of the Pyramid of Sen-Wosret I', *BMMA* 29 (1934), 9–26

Amenemhet II's Pyramid

This pyramid has been only cursorily excavated and published; De Morgan focused more on the treasures:
*Morgan, J. De, *Fouilles a Dahchour*, Vol I. (Vienna, 1894–95), 28–37

Mudbrick Pyramids

Cron, R.L. and G.B. Johnson, 'De Morgan at Dahshur, excavations at the 12th Dynasty pyramids, 1894–95. Part One', *KMT* 6, no. 2 (1995), 34–43; *KMT* 6, no. 4 (1995–96), 48–66
Dodson, A.M. 'The tombs of the queens of the Middle Kingdom', *ZÄS* 115 (1988), 123–36
*Morgan, J. de, *Fouilles à Dahchour*, 2 vols (Vienna, 1894–95, 1903)
Senwosret II's Pyramid:
*Brunton, G., *Lahun I, The Treasure* (London, 1920)

*Petrie, W.M.F., *Illahun, Kahun and Gurob* (London, 1890)
*—*Kahun, Gurob and Hawara* (London, 1890)
*—, G. Brunton and M.A. Murray, *Lahun II* (London, 1923)
Senwosret III's Pyramid:
*Arnold, D. and A. Oppenheim, 'Reexcavating the Senwosret III pyramid complex at Dahshur', *KMT* 6, no. 2 (1995), 44–56
*Oppenheim, A., 'A first look at recently discovered royal jewelry from Dahshur', *KMT* 6 (1995), 10–11
*—'The jewelry of Queen Weret', *EG* 9 (1996), 26
Senwosret III at Abdyos:
*Ayrton, E.R., C.T. Currelly, and A.E.P. Weigall, *Abydos III* (London, 1904)
*Wegner, J., 'Old and new excavations at the Abydene complex of Senwosret III', *KMT* 6, no. 2 (1995), 59–71
Amenemhet III at Dahshur:
Arnold, D., 'Vom Pyramidenbezirk zum "Haus für Millionen Jahre"', *MDAIK* 34 (1978), 1–8
*—*Der Pyramidenbezirk des Konigs Amenemhet III. in Dahschur* (Mainz, 1987)
Amenemhet III at Hawara:
Arnold, D., 'Das Labyrinth und seine Vorbilder', *MDAIK* 35 (1979), 1–9
*Farag, N. and Z. Iskander, *The Discovery of Neferuptah* (Cairo, 1971)
*Petrie, W.M.F., *Hawara, Biahmu and Arsinoe* (London, 1889)
*—, G.A. Wainwright and E. Mackay, *The Labyrinth, Gerzeh and Mazghuneh* (London, 1912)

Late Middle Kingdom Pyramids

*Arnold, D. and R. Stadelmann, 'Dahschur: Grabungsberichte', *MDAIK* 31 (1975), 169–74
Dodson, A.M., 'The tombs of the kings of the Thirteenth Dynasty in the Memphite Necropolis', *ZÄS* 114 (1987), 36–45
—'From Dahshur to Dra Abu el-Naga: The decline & fall of the royal pyramid', *KMT* 5, no. 3 (1994), 25–39
*Jéquier, G., *Deux Pyramides du Moyen Empire* (Cairo, 1938)
*Maragioglio, V. and C.A. Rinaldi, 'Note sulla piramide di Ameny 'Aamu', *Orientalia* 37 (1968), 325–38
*Petrie, W.M.F., G.A. Wainwright and E. Mackay, *The Labyrinth, Gerzeh and Mazghuneh* (London, 1912)

New Kingdom Pyramids

Dynasty 17 – Dra Abu el-Naga:
Dodson, A.M., 'The tombs of the kings of the early Eighteenth Dynasty', *ZÄS* 115 (1988), 110–23
*Polz, D., in *MDAIK* 48 (1992), 109–30; *MDAIK* 49 (1993), 227–38; *MDAIK* 51 (1995), 207–25
*—'Excavations in Dra Abu el-Naga', *EG* 7 (1995), 6–8
Winlock, H., 'The tombs of the kings of the Seventeenth Dynasty at Thebes', *JEA* 10 (1924), 217–77
Ahmose at Abydos:
*Ayrton, E.R., C.T. Currelly and A.E.P. Weigall, *Abydos III* (London, 1904)
*Harvey, S., 'Monuments of Ahmose at Abydos', *EA* 4 (1994), 3–5
*Randall-MacIver, D. and A.C. Mace, *El-Amrah and Abydos* (London, 1902)

'Private' Pyramids

*Bruyère, B., *Fouilles de l'Institut française du Cairo. Deir el-Medineh*, MIFAO 16 (Cairo, 1929); MIFAO 17 (Cairo, 1930); MIFAO 18 (Cairo, 1933)
Curto, S., 'Per la storia della tomba privata a piramide', *MDAIK* 37 (1981), 107–13
Davis, N.M., 'Some representations of tombs from the Theban Necropolis', *JEA* 24 (1938), 25–40
*Eigner, D., *Die monumentalen Grabbauten der Spätzeit in der Thebanischen Nekropole* (Vienna, 1984)
*Garnot, J.S.F., 'Les fouilles de la nécropole de Soleb (1957–8)', *BIFAO* 58 (1959), 165–73
*Martin, G.T., *The Hidden Tombs of Memphis* (London and New York, 1991)
*Rammant-Peeters, A., *Les pyramidions égyptiens du nouvel empire*, Orientalia Lovaniensia Analecta XI (Leuven, 1983)
Raue, D., 'Zum memphitischen Pirvatgrab im Neuen Reich', *MDAIK* 51 (1995), 255–68
*Söderbergh, T.S., 'Teh-Khet, the cultural and sociopolitical structure of a Nubian princedom in Thutmoside times', in W.V. Davies (ed.), *Egypt and Africa: Nubia from Prehistory to Islam* (London, 1991)

Pyramids of Late Antiquity

Adams, W., *Nubia, Corridor to Africa* (London, 1977)

*Berger, C., 'Les couronnements des pyramides méroïtiques de Sedeinga', *Études Nubiennes* II (1994), 131–3
*Dunham, D., 'An Ethiopian royal sarcophagus', *BMFA* 43, no. 253 (1945), 53–7
*—*The Royal Cemeteries of Kush. Vol. I, El-Kurru; Vol. 2, Nuri; Vol. 3, Decorated Chapels of the Meroitic Pyramids at Meroe and Barkal; Vol. 4, Royal Tombs at Meroe and Barkal; Vol. 5, The West and South Cemeteries at Meroe*, vol. i (Boston, 1950–63)
—'From tumulus to pyramid–and back', *Archaeology* 6, no. 2 (1953), 87–94
*Hinkel, F.W., *The Archaeologial Map of the Sudan* (Berlin, 1977)
*—'Reconstruction work at the royal cemetery at Meroe', in *Nubische Studien* (1985), 99–108
*—'Reconstruction and restoration work on monuments in the Sudan, 1984–85', *Nyame Akuma* 28, April (1987), 44–5
—'Die Pyramiden von Meroe 140 Jahre nach der Bestandaufname durch die Königlich-Prussische Expedition unter K.R. Lepsius', in , *K.R. Lepsius (1810–1884), Akten der Tagung 1984 in Halle* (Berlin, 1988), 322–7
*—'Les pyramides de Méroë', in *La Nubie l'archéologie au Soudan,* Les Dossiers d'archeologie 196 (Dijon, 1994), 60–3
Hintze, F., 'Die Grössen der Meroitischen Pyramiden', in W.K. Simpson and W.M. Davis (eds), *Studies in Ancient Egypt, the Aegean, and the Sudan* (Boston, 1981), 91–8
Kendall, T., *Kush: Lost Kingdom of the Nile* (Brockton, 1982)
*Labrousse, A., 'Sedeinga, état des travaux', *Études Nubiennes* II (1994), 131–3
*Leclant, J., 'La nécropole de l'ouest à Sedeinga en Nubie Soudanaise', *CRIPEL* (Apr.–June 1970), 246–76
Markowitz, Y. and P. Lacovara, 'The Ferlini Treasure in archaeological perspective', *JARCE* 33 (1996), 1–10
Priese, K.H., *The Gold of Meroe* (New York, 1993)
*Reisner, G.A., 'Excavations at Napata, the capital of Ethiopia', *BMFA* 15, no. 89 (1917), 25–34
Shinnie, P.L., 'Meroe in the Sudan', in G.R. Willey (ed.), *Archaeological Researches in Retrospect* (Cambridge, MA, 1974), 237–3
Shinnie, P.L., *Meroe, a Civilization of the Sudan* (London and New York, 1967)

IV. THE LIVING PYRAMID

The life of a pyramid began with its construction and continued as long as its cult was serviced. Questions about how the pyramids were built and their role as temples cannot be understood outside their social, historical and economic contexts.

Art and Architecture:
Badawy, A., *A History of Egyptian Architecture*, vols I–III (Berkeley and Los Angeles, 1954–68)
Smith, W.S. and W.K. Simpson, *The Art and Architecture of Ancient Egypt* (Harmondsworth, 1958)
History, Society, Economy:
Aldred, C., *Egypt to the End of the Old Kingdom* (London and New York, 1965)
Goedicke, H. *Königliche Dokumente aus dem Alten Reich* (Wiesbaden, 1967)
—'Cult temple and "state" during the Old Kingdom in Egypt', in E. Lipinski (ed.), *State and Temple Economy in the Near East* (1979), 113–33
Grimal, N.C., *A History of Ancient Egypt* (Oxford, England, and Cambridge, MA, 1992)
Helck, W., *Untersuchungen zu den Beamtiteln des Agyptischen Alten Reiches* (Gluckstadt, 1954)
—'Wirtshaftliche Bemerkungen zum privaten Grabbesitz im Alten Reiches', *MDAIK* 14 (1956), 63–75
—*Wirtschaftgeschichte des alten Ägypten im 3. und 2. Jahrtausends vor Chr.* (Leiden, 1975)
Janssen, J., 'The early state in Egypt', in H.J.M. Classens and P. Skalnik (eds), *The Early State* (The Hague, 1975),
Kanawati, N., *The Egyptian Administration in the Old Kingdom* (Warminster, 1977)
—*Government Reforms in Old Kingdom Egypt* (Warminster, 1980)
Kaplony, P., 'Die wirtschaftliche Dedeutung des Totenkultes im Alten Ägypten', *Asiat. Stud.* 18–19 (1965), 290–307
Kemp, B.J., *Ancient Egypt: Anatomy of a Civilization* (London and New York, 1989)
—'Old Kingdom, Middle Kingdom and Second Inermediate

Period, c. 2686–1552 BC', in B.G. Trigger, et al. (eds), *Ancient Egypt: A Social History* (Cambridge, 1983), 71–182

Málek, J. and W. Forman, *In the Shadow of the Pyramids: Egypt During the Old Kingdom* (London, 1986)

Martin-Pardey, E., *Untersuchungen zur ägyptische Provinzialverwaltung bis zum Ende des Alten Reiches*, HÄB 1 (Hildesheim, 1976)

Müller-Wollermann, R., 'Warenaustausch im Ägypten des Alten Reiches', *Journal of the Economic and Social History of the Orient* 28 (1985), 121–68

Strudwick, N., *The Administration of Egypt in the Old Kingdom* (London, 1985)

Trigger, B., 'The mainlines of socioeconomic development in dynastic Egypt to the end of the Old Kingdom', in L. Kryzaak and M. Kobusiewicz (eds), *Origins and Early Development of Food-producing Cultures in North Eastern Africa* (Poznan, 1984),

Building a Pyramid

The best book by far on pyramid building, in the general context of ancient Egyptian masonry, is:

Arnold, D., *Building in Egypt. Pharaonic Stone Masonry* (New York and Oxford, 1991)

followed by: Clarke, S. and R. Engelbach, *Ancient Egyptian Masonry* (London, 1930)

This is only a selection from a vast literature:

Badawy, A., 'The periodic system of building a pyramid', *JEA* 63 (1977), 52–8

Dunham, D., ' Building an Egyptian Pyramid', *Archaeology* 9, no. 3 (1956), 159–65

Hodges, P. and E.B.J. Keable, *How the Pyramids Were Built* (Shaftesbury, 1989)

Lauer, J.-P., 'Comment furent construites les pyramides', *Historia* 86 (1954), 57–66

Mencken, A., *Designing and Building the Great Pyramid* (Baltimore, 1963)

Petrie, W.M.F., 'The Building of a Pyramid', in *Ancient Egypt* (1930), 33–9

Supply and Transport

Bietak, M., 'Zur Marine des Alten Reiches', in , *Pyramid Studies and Other Essays Presented to I.E.S. Edwards* (London, 1988), 35–40

Fischer, H.G., 'Two tantalizing biographical fragments of historical interest, 1. a speedy return from Elephantine', *JEA* 61 (1975), 33–5

Goyon, G., 'Les navires de transport de la chaussée monumentale d'Ounas', *BIFAO* 69 (1971), 11–41

—'Les portes des pyramides et le grande canal de Memphis', *RdE* 23 (1971), 137–53

Haldane, C., 'The Lisht timbers: a report on their significance', in D. Arnold (ed.), *The Pyramid Complex of Senwosret I* (New York, 1992), 102–12

—*Ancient Egyptian Hull Construction* (Texas A&M, 1993)

Landström, B., *Ships of the Pharaohs* (Garden City, 1970)

Sølver, C. V., 'Egyptian obelisk ships', *Mariner's Mirror* 33 (1947), 39–43

Organizing the Landscape:

Aigner, T., 'Zur Geologie und Geoarchäologie des Pyramidenplateaus von Giza, Ägypten', *Natur und Museum* 112 (1983), 377–88

Lehner, M., 'The Development of the Giza Necropolis: The Khufu Project', *MDAIK* 41 (1985)

Quarries

Engelbach, R., *The Aswan Obelisk* (Cairo, 1922)

Harrell, J.A. and T.M. Bown, 'An Old Kingdom basalt quarry at Widan el-Faras and the quarry road to Lake Moeris', *JARCE* 32 (1995), 71–92

Harrell, J.A. and V.M. Brown, *Topographical and Petrological Survey of Ancient Egyptian Quarries* (Toledo, 1995)

Klemm, D. and R., *Steine der Pharaonen* (Munich, 1981)

Röder, J., 'Steinbruchgeschichte des Rosengranits von Assuan', *Archäologischer Anzeiger* 3 (1965), 461–551

The NOVA Pyramid:

Lehner, M., 'The Pyramid', in *Secrets of Lost Empires* (London and New York, 1996), 46–93

Tools, Techniques and Operations

Gille, B., *The History of Techniques, Vol. 1: Techniques and Civilizations* (New York, 1978)

Lucas, A. and J.R. Harris, *Ancient Egyptian Materials and Industries* (London, 1962)

Moores, R.G., 'Evidence for the use of a stone-cutting drag saw by the Fourth Dynasty Egyptians', *JARCE* 28 (1991), 139–48

Petrie, W.M.F., *Tools and Weapons*, Egyptian Research Account 22 (London, 1917)

Ryan, D.P., 'Old rope', *KMT* 4, no. 2 (1993), 72–9

Teeter, E., 'Techniques and terminology of rope-making in ancient Egypt', *JEA* 73 (1987), 71–7

Zuber, A., 'Techniques du travail des pierres dures dans l'Ancienne Egypte', *Techniques et Civilizations* 29.5 , no. 5 (1956) pp. 161–78

Survey and Alignment

Borchardt, L., *Längen und Richtungen der vier Grundkanten der grossen Pyramide bie Gise* (Berlin, 1926)

Cole, J.H., *The Determination of the Exact Size and Orientation of the Great Pyramid of Giza (Survey of Egypt Paper No. 39)* (Cairo, 1925)

Dorner, J., 'Die Absteckung und astronomische Orientierung ägyptischer Pyramiden' (Innsbruck, 1981)

—'Studien über die Bauvermessung und astronomische Orientierung', *Archiv für Orientforschung* 32 (1985), 165–6

Goyon, G., 'Quelques observations effectuée autour de la pyramide de Khéops', *BIFAO* 47 (1969), 71–86

Isler, M., 'An ancient method of finding and extending direction', *JARCE* 26 (1989), 191–206

—'The gnomon in Egyptian antiquity', *JARCE* 28 (1991), 155–86

Lauer, J.-P., 'À propos de l'orientation des grandes pyramides', *Bulletin de l'Institut d'Égypte* (1960), 7–15

Lehner, M., 'Some observations on the layout of the pyramids of Khufu and Khafre', *JARCE* 20 (1983), 7–25

—'The Giza Plateau Mapping Project ', *NARCE* 131, no. (Fall 1985), 23–56; *NARCE 135* (Fall 1986), 29–54

Petrie, W.M.F., *Ancient Weights and Measures* (London, 1926)

Pochan, A., 'Observations relatives au revêtement des deux grandes pyramides de Giza', *Bulletin de l'Institut d'Égypte* 16 (1934), 214–20

Zába, Z., *L'orientation Astronomique dans l'ancienne Égypte, et la précession de l'axe du monde* (Prague, 1933)

Ramps

Arnold, D., 'Überlegungenzum Problem des Pyramidenbaues', *MDAIK* 37 (1981), 15–28

Dunham, D., 'Building an Egyptian pyramid', *Archaeology* 9, no. 3 (1956), 159–65

Fitchen, J., 'Building Cheops' pyramid', *Journal of the Society of Architectural Historians* 37 (1978), 3–12

Isler, M., 'Ancient Egyptian methods of raising weights', *JARCE* 13 (1976), 31–41

—'On pyramid building', *JARCE* 22 (1985), 129–42; *JARCE* 24 (1987), 95–112

Rise and Run

Arnold, D., 'Maneuvering casing blocks of pyramids', in John Baines, et al. (eds), *Pyramid Studies and Other Essays presented to I.E.S. Edwards* (London, 1988), 12–24

Isler, M., 'Concerning the concave faces on the Great Pyramid', *JARCE* 20, no. 27–32 (1983)

Lally, M., 'Engineering a pyramid', *JARCE* 26, no. 207–18 (1989)

Lauer, J.-P., 'Sur le choix de l'angle de pente dans les pyramides d'Égypte', *Bulletin de l'Institut d'Égypte* 37 (1956), 57–66

—*Observations sur les pyramides,* BdÉ 30. (Cairo, 1960)

Robins, G. and C.C.D. Shute, 'Determining the slope of pyramids', *GM* 57 (1982), 49–54

The Workforce

Drenkhahn, R., *Die Handwerker und ihre Tätigkeiten im alten Ägypten*, ÄA 31 (Wiesbaden, 1976)

Dreyer, G. and H. Jaritz, 'Die Arbeiterunterkünfte am Sadd al-Kafara', *Leichtweiss-Institut für Wasserbau der Technischen Universität Braunschweig, Mitteilungen* 81 (1983), 2–20

Eyre, C., 'Work and the organization of work during the Old Kingdom in Egypt', in M.A. Powell (ed.), *Labor in the Ancient Near East*, American Oriental Series 68 (New Haven, 1987)

Haeny, G., 'Die Steinbruch- und Baumarken', in H. Ricke (ed.), *Die Sonnenheiligtum des Königs Userkaf, Vol. 2*, BÄBA (Wiesbaden, 1969), 67–77

Hawass, Z., 'Tombs of the pyramid builders', *Archaeology* 50, no. 1 (1997), 39–43

Helck, W., 'Die Handwerker- und Priesterphylen des Alten Reiches in Ägypten', *WdO* 7 (1973), 1–7

Pfirsch, L. 'A propos des constructeurs de Téti, Pepi I, et Merenre', in C. Berger, G. Clerc and N. Grimal (eds),

Hommage à Jean Leclant, BdÉ 106/1 (Cairo, 1994), 293–8

Roth, A.M., *Egyptian Phyles in the Old Kingdom*, SAOC 48 (Chicago, 1991)

Rowe, A., 'Some facts concerning the Great Pyramids of el-Giza and their royal constructors', *Bulletin of the John Rylands Library* 44, no. 1 (1961), 100–18

Verner, M., 'Zu den Baugraffiti mit Datumsangaben aus dem alten Reich', in *Mélanges Mokhtar* (Cairo, 1985), 339–46

—*Abusir II. Baugraffiti der Ptahschepses-Mastaba* (Prague, 1992)

Wier, S.K., 'Insight from geometry and physics into the construction of Egyptian Old Kingdom pyramids', *CAJ* 6, no. 1 (1996), 150–63

Building a Middle Kingdom Pyramid

Arnold, D., *Der Pyramidenbezirk des Konigs Amenemhet III. in Dahschur* (Mainz, 1987), 73–91

Arnold, F., *The Control Notes and Team Marks*, The South Cemeteries of Lisht (New York, 1990)

Arnold, D., 'Construction methods and technical details', in D. Arnold (ed.), *The Pyramid Complex of Senwosret I* (New York, 1992), 92–101

Building a Late Old Kingdom Pyramid:

Labrousse, A., *L'Architecture des Pyramides à Textes. I. Saqqara Nord* (Cairo, 1996, see 109–21)

Pfirsch, L., 'Les batisseurs des pyramides de Saqqara' in C. Berger (ed.), *Saqqara, Les Dossiers d'Archéologie* 146–7 (Dijon, 1990), 32–5

Building a Meroitic Pyramid:

Hinkel, F. W., 'An ancient scheme to build a pyramid at Meroe', in P. van Moorsel (ed.), *New Discoveries in Nubia* (Leiden, 1982), 45–9

—'Das Schaduf als konstruktives Hilfsmittel beim Wiederaufbau der Pyramide Beg. N 19', *Meroitica* 7 (1984), 462–8

The Pyramid as Landlord

Helck, W., *Die altägyptischen Gaue*, Beihefte zum Tübinger Atlas des Vorderen Orients (Wiesbaden, 1974)

Jacquet-Gordon, H., *Les nomes des domains funéraires sous l'Ancien Empire égyptien*, BdÉ 34 (1962)

Kees, H., *Ancient Egypt: A Cultural Topography* (London, 1961), 185ff.

Málek, J. and W. Forman, *In the Shadow of the Pyramids: Egypt During the Old Kingdom* (London, 1986), 35; 68–9; 72–4

O'Connor, D., 'The geography of settlement in Egypt', in P.J. Ucko, R. Tringham, and G.W. Dimbleby (eds), *Man, Settlement, and Urbanism* (London, 1972), 681–98

—'A regional population in Egypt to circa 600 B.C.', in Brian Spooner (ed.), *Population Growth: Anthropological Implications* (Cambridge, MA, 1972), 78–100

Strudwick, N., *The Administration of Egypt in the Old Kingdom* (London, 1985), 337–46.

Pyramid Towns

Hawass, Z., 'The workmen's community at Giza', in M. Bietak (ed.), *Haus und Palast im alten Ägypten* (Vienna, 1996), 53–67

Helck, W., 'Bemerkungen zu den Pyramidenstädten im Alten Reich', *MDAIK* 15 (1957), 91–111

Jones, M., 'A new Old Kingdom settlement near Ausim: report of the archaeological discoveries made in the Barakat Drain Improvements Project', *MDAIK* 51 (1995), 85–98

Kemp, B.J., *Ancient Egypt: Anatomy of a Civilization* (London, 1989)

Stadelmann, R., 'La ville de pyramide à l'Ancien Empire', *RdE* 33 (1981), 67–77

—'Pyramidenstadt', *LÄ* V.1 (1983), 9–14

The term *she* as 'basin':

Berlandini, J., 'La pyramide "ruinée" de Sakkara-Nord et le roi Ikauohor-Menkaouhor', *RdE* 31 (1979), 3–28

Sauneron, S., 'L'inscription: Pétosiris, 48', *Kêmi: Revue de Philologie et d'Achéologie* 15 (1959), 34–5

Yoyotte, J., 'Le bassin de Djâroukha', *Kêmi: Revue de Philologie et d'Achéologie* 15 (1959), 23–33

Those Who Serve

Abusir Papyri:

Posener-Kriéger, P., *Les archives du temple funéraire de Néferirkarê-Kakai, les papyrus d'Abousir; traduction et commentaire*, 2pts., BdÉ 65 (1976)

—'Apects economique des nouveaux papyrus d'Abousir', in Sylvia Schoske (ed.), *Akten des Vierten Internationalen Ägyptologen Kongresses München 1985*, BSAK 4 (Hamburg, 1990), 167–76

—and J.-L. de Cénival, *Hieratic Papyri in the British Museum. Fifth Series: The Abu Sir Papyri*, vol. 65 (London, 1968)

Khentiu-she:

Roth, A., 'The distribution of the Old Kingdom title *hntj-s*', in Sylvia Schoske (ed.), *Akten des Vierten Internationalen Ägyptologen Kongresses München 1985 BSAK 4* (Hamburg, 1990), 177–85

— *A Cemetery of Palace Attendants*, P. der Manuelian and W.K. Simpson (eds) *Giza Mastabas* (Boston, 1995)

Stadelmann, R., 'Die HNTIW-S, der Königsbezirk S N PR' und die Namen der Grabanlagen der Frühzeit', *BIFAO* 81, no. 155–64 (1981)

Loaves and Fishes

Hawass, Z. and M. Lehner, 'Builders of the pyramids', *Archaeology* 50, no. 1 (1997), 31–8

Lehner, M., 'Giza', in William M. Sumner (ed.), *The Oriental Institute Annual Report* (Chicago, 1992), 19–22; (Chicago, 1993), 56–67; (Chicago, 1994), 26–30; (Chicago, 1996), 54–61

—'Exploring the Giza Plateau', *The Explorers Journal* 73, no. 4 (1995–96), 32–7

Roberts, D., 'Rediscovering Egypt's bread-baking technology', *National Geographic* 187, no. 1 (1995), 32–5

The Royal Workshops

Kemp, B.J., *Ancient Egypt: Anatomy of a Civilization* (London, 1989), see 128–36

Kromer, K., 'Siedlungsfunde aus dem Alten Reich in Giseh', *Denkschriften Österreichische Akademie der Wissenschaften, Philosophisch-historische Klasse* 136 (1978), 1–130

Petrie, W.M.F., *The Pyramids and Temples of Gizeh* (London, 1883), see pp.100–3

Saleh, A., 'Excavations around Mycerinus pyramid complex', *MDAIK* 30 (1974), 131–54

V. EPILOGUE

The Legacy of the Pyramids

Assmann, J., *Stein und Zeit: Mensch und Gesellschaft im alten Ägypten* (Munich)

Curl, J.S., *The Egyptian Revival* (London, 1982)

Lowenthal, D., *The Past is a Foreign Country* (Cambridge, 1985)

Illustration Credits

Abbreviations: a–above; b–below; c–centre; l–left; r–right

Alinari 42r

Robert Partridge: The Ancient Egypt Picture Library 28b, 175c

Helen Lowell: from The Ancient Egypt Picture Library 186b

Carl Andrews/© Aera 214a

Archivio Mondadori 160c

G.B. Belzoni *Narrative of the Operations and Recent Discoveries within the Pyramids* 1820 48l, 48r

L. Borchardt *Grabdenkmal des Königs S'a hu-re* 1910 60

Courtesy, Museum of Fine Arts, Boston 9r, 117a, 117br, 196b, Egyptian Photographic Archive 58bl, 59, 65, 95a, 232a

Egyptian Museum, Cairo 8r, 9l, 22a, 23, 73br, 126a, 130al, 141ar, 159l, 161al, 172al, 174bl, 176a, 178a, 180al, 182b, 191ar

DAI, Cairo 68, 75, 227a

Service de Antiquités de l'Egypte, Cairo 139b, 176c

Oriental Institute of Chicago, 55b, 99c

Peter Clayton 47b, 126–127b

Czech Institute of Egyptology, Prague, Photo Milan Zemina 6, 140–41a, 145a, 146a, 147ar, 148, 149b, 152b, 159a

Description de l'Egypte 1822 14br, 36–37, 46a, 46b

Aidan Dodson 34bl, 139a, 153b, 160b, 165a, 185b, 187cr, 188a, 188b

Foto G. Dreyer/DAI, Cairo 76al

Michael Duigan 169al, 169b, 176b, 199c

© 1987, The Royal Observatory, Edinburgh 57c

W.B. Emery *Excavations at Saqqara* 1949 79bl, 81bl, 81c

Kenneth Garrett 233

J. Greaves *Pyramidographia* 1646 44a, 44ac

Jim Henderson AMPA 82

Fotoarchiv Hirmer 8l, 150br, 172

Image Bank (Louis Tarpey) 2, (Guido Alberto Rossi) 86–91, 103a, 109a

George B. Johnson 14al, 14cl, 35a, 96ar, 96c, 105a, 156b, 156–157, 168, 177a, 179b

Kircher *Turris Babel* 1679 42l

Labrousse EDF 157b

E.W. Lane *The Thousand and One Nights* 1839 40a

J.P. Lauer 62b, 87br, 89ar, 94b, 159c,

Mark Lehner 13, 15, 41a, 41c, 41b, 50a, 51al, 51ar, 58al, 58ac, 64, 67, 69, 85a, 85bl, 90al, 98a, 99a, 100al, 100ar, 100b, 101a, 102a, 105b, 106b, 116a, 116c, 118b, 119ar, 121a, 121c, 122bl, 123al, 123ar, 124a, 128a, 130ac, 130ar, 131, 135cl, 135c, 135br, 138al, 141b, 143ar, 145b, 149ar, 154a, 155b, 162al, 164bl, 167ar, 171, 175a, 193a, 200–01, 203al, 203ar, 206b, 207a, 207b, 208a, 208c, 209, 210l, 210b, 211ac, 211br, 212a, 214c, 214b, 215, 217a, 219a, 219r, 221b, 222a, 223a, 223c, 223b, 224, 226–227, 229, 231, 232bl, 236ar, 237a, 237b, 239a, 239c, 239bl, 239br, 240, 242a, 242–43

K.R. Lepsius *Denkmäler aus Ägypten* 1849 54a, 55a

Copyright British Museum, London 20–1, 24, 25, 177b, 189r

Bruce Ludwig 221a

MAFS/IFAO 158b

G.T. Martin 54b

David J. Nelson, CSULB 242c

F. Norden *Travels in Egypt and Nubia* 1757 45r

© Bibliothèque Nationale de France, Paris 241b

Musée du Louvre, Paris, 120a

NOVA/WGBH, 111b, 114

Petrie Museum, University College, London 56

G.B. Piranesi *Diverse Manière* 1769 241c

R. Pococke *A Description of the East* 1743 45l

Greg Reeder 14ar

John G. Ross 6–7, 32, 33, 62ar, 70–1, 90r, 119c, 125br, 133, 136, 137a, 140al, 144a, 152a, 155a, 161ar

Peggy Sanders, Archaeological Graphic Services/AERA 106–7, 109c, 124l, 132b

G. Sandys *Relation of a Journey* 1615 43ar

Chris Scarre 94al, 182a

Margaret Sears 97bl

Albert Shoucair 63b

Alberto Siliotti 113ar

A.J. Spencer 103b

Steelcase Corporation 242b

Frank Teichmann 14b, 28–29, 112–13c, 154b

Musée de Versailles 47a

R.W.H. Vyse & J.S. Perring *Operations Carried on at the Pyramids* 1840 49l, 49r, 51b, 52, 53a, 132a

Courtesy The Egyptian Cultural Centre, Waseda University, Tokyo. Photo Y. Karino 67, 118–19

Derek Welsby 196–97, 197c, 197b, 199b

Drawings and Maps

D. Arnold *Die Pyramidenbezirk des Königs Amenemhet III* 1987 180a

L. Borchardt *Die Pyramiden* 1910 44b, 217

Ian Bott 2a

Garth Denning 119bl (after Landström), 166b

L. Epron, F. Daumas and H. Wild, *Le tombeau de Ti* 234a, 236b

Tom Jaggers, Jerde Partnership 131

G. Jequier 26–7a,

Stuart Haskayne 22b

Audran Labrousse 31, 157, 158b, 160a

Mark Lehner 72, 73, 74, 96b, 99, 126, 128–129, 204–05, 212, 213, 220, 230, 236al, 238c

Mark Lehner/Jerde Parnership 106–107, 109b, 110–115, 124bl, 130–131a, 132b

after Kurt Mendelssohn 19,

ML Design 10–11, 83, 101

W. Flinders Petrie *Pyramids and Temples of Gizeh* 1883 39, 57a

C. Piazzi Smyth *Our Inheritance in the Great Pyramid* 1864 56br, 56ar

G.A. Reisner *Models of Ships and Boats* 1913 119br

William Riseman. Courtesy, Museum of Fine Arts, Boston 197ar

Lucinda Rodd 198b

W.K. Simpson, *The Mastabas of Qar and Idu*, 1976 26–27a

R. Stadelmann *Die Ägyptischen Pyramiden* 1985 116,

George Taylor 62–63, 64–65, 76, 78, 79ar, 113al

M. Verner *Forgotten Pharaohs, Lost Pyramids. Abusir* 1994 138c

M.E. Weaver 125

Tracy Wellman 7, 13, 15, 26l, 27, 106, 107, 129a, 143c, 162, 177cr, 178, 183, 190, 191, 194, 195, 196, 198a, 199, 227, 232, 238a

Philip Winton 16–17, 18 (after A. Labrousse), 33, 75, 80, 81, 84, 85, 87, 88-9, 93, 94, 95, 96a, 97, 98, 100, 102, 104, 105, 108, 109a, 111, 112–13, 120, 122–23, 124, 134–35, 137, 138r, 139, 140, 142, 143al, 143b, 144, 145, 146, 147, 148, 149, 150, 151, 153, 154, 155, 157a, 159a, 160cl, 161, 163, 164, 165, 166a, 167, 169, 170, 174, 175, 177cl, 179, 181, 184, 185, 186, 187, 189 (after Aidan Dodson), 202, 203, 210, 211, 216, 218 (after Dieter Arnold), 222 (after R. Stadelmann (l) and Dieter Arnold (r)), 225, 228, 228–229, 235 (after A. Labrousse)

Sources of Quotations

p. 1 'Any gods…the crown' Pyramid Texts 1650, from J. Allen, *The Inflection of the Verb in the Pyramid Texts*, p. 351. **p. 18** 'Every…presented' G.A. Reisner, *The Development of the Egyptian Tomb*, p. 237. **p. 22** 'This Unas…in the sky' Pyramid Texts 245, 250–51, J. Allen, *pers. comm.* **p. 25** 'Horus takes…Great House' Pyramid Texts 268. **p. 28** 'I come forth…I stand up' Book of the Dead, Chapter 68, from L.V. Zakbar, *A Study of the Ba Concept in Ancient Egyptian Texts*, SAOC, vol. 34, pp. 149–50. **p. 28** 'Opened for me…twin peep-holes' Book of the Dead, Chapter 68, from T.G. Allen, *The Book of the Dead or Going forth by Day*, SAOC, 37, p.62. **p. 29** 'You are given…the tomb' Pyramid Texts 616 d–f, from J.Allen, 'The cosmology of the Pyramid Texts' in J.P. Allen et al. (eds) *Religion and Philosophy in Ancient Egypt*, p. 17. **p. 30** 'As for anyone…eats himself' Pyramid Texts 1278–79, from A. Labrousse, *Regards sur une Pyramide*, p. 149. **p. 34** 'Atum Scarab…in them' Pyramid Texts 600, from J. Allen, *Genesis in Egypt: the Philosophy of Ancient Egyptian Creation Accounts*, New Haven, Yale Egyptological Studies 2, ed. W.K. Simpson, 1988, pp. 13–14. **p. 34** 'Atum is…Tefnut', from J. Allen, *Genesis in Egypt: the Philosophy of Ancient Egyptian Creation Accounts*, New Haven, Yale Egyptological Studies 2, ed. W.K. Simpson, 1988, p. 13. **p. 38** '[Khaemwaset]…Lower Egypt' Inscription of Khaemwaset on Unas's pyamid, quoted in L. Greener, *The Discovery of Ancient Egypt*, p. 3. **p. 38** '[he] brought…own advantage' Herodotus, *Histories*, Book II, 124, trans. A. Lloyd. **p. 39** 'no crime…Great Pyramid' Herodotus, *Histories*, Book II, 126, trans. A. Lloyd. **p. 39** 'including the…an island' Herodotus, Histories, Book II, trans. A. Lloyd. **p. 39** 'for [the Egyptians]…wore them out' Josephus, *Antiquities of the Jews*, IX, 55, trans. W. Whiston, *Josephus: Complete Works*. **p. 40** 'Then Surid… "Pied Pyramid"', quoted in A. Fodor, 'The Origins of the Arabic Legends of the Pyramids', *Acta Orientalia Academiae Scientiarum Hungaricae*, XXIII:3, 340 (1970). **p. 42** 'And some…of Joseph' *Voiage and Travaille of Sir John Maundeville*, quoted in L. Greener, *The Discovery of Egypt*, 27–28. **p. 46** 'In approaching…to the mind' V. Denon, *Travels in Upper and Lower Egypt*, trans. F. Blagdon, 1802, pp. 148–49. **p. 48** 'I reached…ancient and modern' Belzoni, *Narrative of the Operations and Recent Discoveries*, pp. 270–71. **p. 50** 'Reis 7…Boring' H. Vyse, *Operations Carried on at the Pyramids of Gizeh*, I, p. 170. **p. 50** 'Towards the end…great effect' H. Vyse and J. Perring, *Operations Carried on at the Pyramids of Gizeh*, I, p. 167. **p. 51** 'was prepared…through it' H. Vyse, *Operations Carried on at the Pyramids of Gizeh*, I, p. 183; 'being unwilling…in it' pp. 274–5. **p. 54** 'From the Labyrinth…yet done' K.R. Lepsius, *Discoveries in Egypt*, pp. 78 and 81. **p. 55** 'The discovery…had spoken' G. Maspero, quoted by L. Cottrell, *The Mountains of Pharaoh*, p. 160. **p. 56** 'If pink…for inspection' W.M.F. Petrie, *Seventy Yearis in Archaeology* p. 21. **p. 58** 'A laborious…the Pyramid' Mark Twain, *The Innocents Abroad*, pp. 621–3. **p. 59** 'The excavator…it contains' G. Reisner, from his unpublished excavation manual, 'Archaeological Field Work in Egypt'. **p. 77** 'By Merneith…the pyramids' W.M.F Petrie, *Royal Tombs of the First Dynasty*, I, p. 4. **p. 191** 'I indeed…my Majesty' inscription of Ahmose, from H.Winlock, 'The tombs of the kings of the Seventeenth Dynasty at Thebes', *JEA* 10 (1923), p. 247. **p. 202** 'His majesty…my mistress' inscription of Weni, from M. Lichtheim, *Ancient Egyptian Literature, Vol. I: The Old and Middle Kingdoms*, p. 21–22.

Index

Page numbers in *italics* refer to illustrations

Acknowledgments

For his friendship, support and advice through the years I would like to thank Zahi Hawass, Director General of Giza and Saqqara for the Egyptian Supreme Council for Antiquities. I am also grateful for the help and co-operation of the entire staff of the Giza Pyramids and Saqqara Inspectorates of the Supreme Council of Antiquities, particularly Sabry Abd al Aziz, Director for Giza, and Mansour Radwan, Senior Inspector at Giza.

My work on the subject matter of this book would not have been possible without the support of David Koch, Bruce Ludwig, Jon Jerde, Matthew McCauley, Frank Blanning and James Allen. I thank them for serving as directors of Ancient Egypt Research Associates (AERA). James Allen has been a steadfast supporter and teacher, and I have benefited from his scholarship, comments and advice. I wish to thank Rainer Stadelmann for his inspiration, guidance and contribution to our knowledge about Egypt's pyramids. For sharing thoughts, results of their work and photographs, I am grateful to Jean Leclant, Audran Labrousse, Miroslav Verner, Dieter Arnold and Nabil Swelim. McGuire Gibson, David Schloen, John Swanson and Peter Lacovara provided many inspiring and insightful discussions.

I would also like to thank Aidan Dodson for reading the manuscript and offering comments and suggestions. I am grateful to William Kelly Simpson, for his teaching and guidance during my years at Yale University, and for introducing me to Thames and Hudson. I am grateful to Lawrence Stager and everyone at the Harvard Semitic Museum for their support during the time that I prepared this book. I thank William Sumner, Director of the Oriental Institute, for his patience and support. Tom Jaggers and John and Peggy Sanders were more than generous with the time and creativity they put into computer modelling and illustration. I am grateful for the survey work of Ulrich Kapp, for whose collaboration I thank the German Archaeological Institute in Cairo, and David Goodman, Senior Surveyor for the Giza Plateau Mapping Project (GPMP), who, for many years, has been my friend in the field and who designed our survey control system. I thank John Nolan and Wilma Wetterstrom for their collaboration in the fieldwork and back home. I am grateful for the support of The American Research Center in Egypt (ARCE), and its Directors, Terry Walz and Mark Easton. Particular thanks go to Amira Khattab, Assistant Director of ARCE, and Amir Hassan Abdel Hamid, who has acted as Project Manager for the GPMP. This is another book that owes its existence to the editorial, design and production team at Thames and Hudson.

This book would not have been possible without the love and support of Julia Cort and her extended family. I am deeply grateful for the understanding and support of my sons, Ramsi and Luke Lehner. In my own Archaic Period, my sojourn in Egypt would not have happened without the support of Hugh Lynn Cayce, the Edgar Cayce Foundation, Norrene and David Leary, Sam and Rufus Mosely, Arch and Ann Ogden, Ursula Martin and Joseph Jahoda. Extending from my own predynastic until now, this book stems ultimately from the encouragement and sense of quest engendered in me by my parents, Paul and Ethel Lehner, and my mother's fascination, from as far away as North Dakota, for the distant land of Egypt.